Saudi Arabia
and its
Royal Family

Saudi Arabia

AND ITS

Royal Family

WILLIAM POWELL

LYLE STUART INC.   *Secaucus, N.J.*

First Edition
Copyright © 1982 by William Powell
All rights reserved, including the right to reproduce
this book or any portion thereof in any form, except
by a newspaper or magazine reviewer who wishes to
quote brief passages in connection with a review.

Queries regarding rights and permissions should
be addressed to: Lyle Stuart Inc., 120 Enterprise Ave.,
Secaucus, N.J. 07094.

Published by Lyle Stuart Inc.
Published simultaneously in Canada by
Musson Book Company, a division of
General Publishing Co. Limited, Don Mills, Ontario.

Manufactured in the United States of America

Library of Congress Cataloging in Publication Data

Powell, William, 1949–
    Saudi Arabia and its royal family.

    Bibliography: p. 368
    Includes index.
    1. Saudi Arabia.   I. Title.
DS204.P68   953′.805   82-3249
ISBN 0-8184-0326-8   AACR2

Dedication

This book would not have been possible without the help and assistance of literally hundreds of Saudi students and friends. For obvious reasons, they cannot be named individually. I also wish to express my gratitude to the University of Riyadh for providing me with the opportunity to use its facilities for research. I am also indebted to numerous friends in the expatriate community in Saudi Arabia.

However, I owe my deepest thanks to my own family—who, more than any other Western family I have ever encountered, practice the ideals of the Saudi family—the greatest compliment I can pay them. I am especially grateful to my father, who assisted in the research for this book, and to my wife, Ochan, who spent hundreds and hundreds of hours editing, rewriting, and criticizing the text. It is to Ochan that this book is dedicated—with respect and love.

Contents

8 *Contents*

IV
AN ARABIAN TINDERBOX

Publisher's Note

As this book was being prepared for press, King Khalid ibn Abdulaziz al-Saud died suddenly of a heart attack at the age of sixty-nine. A swift transition of power had been planned by the House al-Saud, and within hours he was succeeded by sixty-year-old Crown Prince Fahd. Prince Abdullah, Fahd's half-brother, was named Crown Prince. Announcing Khalid's death to the nation on radio, Fahd said, "Our love for him compels us to continue his march, pursue his hopes, and complete his plans."

Preface

With the possible exception of acutely xenophobic Albania, Saudi Arabia is probably the world's most difficult country to write about. The difficulty is a simple one—the paucity of accurate, up-to-date information.

Despite cries of indignation to the contrary from the Saudi Ministry of Information, the lack of information about Saudi Arabia is not a product of mere carelessness, the apathy or indifference of foreign journalists, or the malice of Zionist agents spreading lies about the Arab world. The information gulf that exists is in large part a product of Saudi consciousness.

Someone once described Saudi Arabia as the only family-owned business that had succeeded in winning membership in the United Nations. The emphasis here should be placed squarely on the word "family." What comprises family business in Saudi Arabia is by definition private, and there is very little that goes on within the kingdom that is not in some way "family business."

Understanding the Saudi concept of family privacy is no easy task for the Westerner. Much of what an average American or European would take for granted as "the public record" does not exist as such in Saudi Arabia. The Ministry of Information is still extremely reluctant to release background biographical information on the ruling members of the royal family, and it was not until 1977 that an attempt was made to compile a "Who's Who" of important Saudis.

If "family privacy" produces this information gulf, the present Saudi government is not at all hesitant about utilizing it to what it considers its own best political advantage. Censorship within the kingdom of Saudi Arabia is among the strictest anywhere in the world. The Ministry of Information, a title more Orwellian than accurate, strains to keep the country a closed society, protecting it from Western values, insulating it from Christianity, defending it against communist propaganda, and preserving, at all costs, the Islamic status quo.

No tourist visas are issued for entry. Foreigners who do enter the kingdom come as employees of large multi-national corporations that form the backbone of the country's enormous development program, or as pilgrims on the annual *Hajj* or pilgrimage to Mecca. In either case, the government's secret police keeps an extraordinarily close watch on all foreigners in the country and, with virtually no hesitation whatsoever, will order wholesale deportations. Early in 1980, Prince Naif, the powerful Minister of the Interior, decided that there were too many foreign women in Riyadh, the kingdom's capital city. Following the political turbulence of the takeover of the Holy Haram in Mecca in late 1979, Prince Naif was concerned that the example set by Western (unveiled) women on the streets of the capital would further provoke political and religious turmoil. Naif followed his pronouncement with a strict series of new regulations on the employment and granting of residency permits for foreign women. These new regulations are said to have cost the jobs of more than a thousand foreign women.

Equally strict is the censorship of incoming and outgoing news. While some Western newspapers and magazines are on sale in Riyadh, Jeddah, and Dhahran, they are often so chopped apart that some articles are rendered entirely nonsensical. It is not at all uncommon to pick up a copy of *Time* or *Newsweek* and have it fall to pieces in one's hands: while removing the politically or religiously offensive pages, the censor in the Ministry of Information has also removed the staples that hold the magazine together.

To compensate for the lack of hard, factual information, there exists an elaborate grapevine of rumor and gossip. In fact, it would be no exaggeration to say that gossip mongering is the principal form of amusement in Saudi Arabia for foreigner and native alike. Rumors run the gauntlet from the mundane to the truly bizarre, and the degree of accuracy fluctuates within the same spectrum. (It should be noted here that the term "bizarre" is used in a relative sense, for much of what is commonplace on the Arabian peninsula may strike the Western reader as bizarre.)

In a rare article (*The Arab News*, February 23, 1980) that came perilously close to criticizing the Saudi government's handling of information, Jihad Khazen, the London-based columnist, bemoaned the current "dark age" of Arab culture and influence in the world. "Why," he asked, "aren't Arabs these days like before in the old days, frank and not full of hypocrisy?" No sooner was the question asked than the author provided the obvious answer—"because they would be thrown into jail or worse."

No constitutional or legal guarantees exist in Saudi Arabia for an individual's freedom of speech, and the kingdom's prisons have their share of political dissidents. This makes full acknowledgment of the many individuals who helped in the preparation of this book virtually impossible. Whenever possible acknowledgment by name is made in the text itself; however, not wishing to cause legal difficulties for my Saudi friends, there are numerous times when specific acknowledgment is avoided. Whatever accuracies and insights this book contains can be credited directly to the many government officials, members of the royal family, and other Saudis who have dared to speak candidly with me. In addition, credit must go to my students at the University of Riyadh, whose hospitality and generosity have guided me through my two-year Arabian odyssey.

Attempting to present an accurate picture of the Arabian peninsula is much like trying to capture in the frozen lens of a camera the ever-moving, ever-shifting sands of the Empty Quarter, whose shape and color flow and blend beneath the changing arc of the desert sun. Nevertheless, it is hoped that the present work will remove some past misconceptions about the Kingdom of Saudi Arabia and will afford the Western reader a greater understanding and appreciation of a nation on which we in the West so heavily rely.

William Powell
Riyadh, Saudi Arabia

Introduction

"This is the closest place
to Heaven on earth."

    —Muhammad Ali, on arriving in Riyadh, 1980

"This is the ugliest, most
unfriendly place on earth."

    —A Filipino driver in Jeddah, 1979.

Standing on the observation deck of the new water tower in Riyadh, you can view a panorama of the old and the new, the opulent and the squalid of Arabia. To the right, you can see Airport Street, the main avenue of the Saudi Arabian capital, with its stately line of date palms, its steel-and-glass ministry buildings, brand new stores selling the latest in French perfumes and the most recent creations of Pierre Cardin, supermarkets that boast both air conditioning and fresh meat, hotels with penthouse swimming pools, and car rental agencies that may soon accept credit cards.

To the left, you can see the old Riyadh: a mysterious and filthy vista of crenellated baked-mud houses, eroding palaces, and austere mosques. It is this old Riyadh that formed the core of the pre–oil-boom city. Here one can see the *suqs* teeming with prematurely old men and veiled women hawking everything from gold ingots and Persian carpets to electronic calculators and one-humped camels.

One can also see the poverty of the shantytowns that blossom overnight on virtually every square meter of temporarily vacant land in the city. One can see the Bedouin tents, the corrugated iron shacks, the wandering goats and sheep, the piles of discarded tires and automobile parts that have become the symbols of twentieth-century poverty.

But what one cannot see from one's vantage point atop the Riyadh water tower is the Arab psyche, the cohesion that holds, or tries to hold, the contradictions and paradoxes together.

Depending on who and what you read, you will discover that Saudis are the most polite, most hospitable, most generous, most philanthropic, most idealistic, most devout, most fatalistic, most cynical, most hypocritical, most corrupt, most racist, most barbaric people on the face of the earth. In short, you will learn that Saudis are like most people in most places, *except more so.*

It would seem that living in one of the largest and least populated deserts in the world has helped create an exaggerated character type, for there is little about the Saudi that is tame, domesticated, or even moderate. The Saudi is characterized by intensity and enthusiasm whether one is referring to his generosity, his chivalry, his questionable business ethics, his unqualified devotion to Islam, or his thirst for vengeance.

Admire a Saudi's gold watch and you will summarily own it. Admire his Mercedes and he will, with perhaps a slight reluctance, hand you the keys and announce, "It is in your hands." But at the same time, should you inadvertently offend the honor of a desert Bedouin, you can expect a swift dispatch from this life.

If there is an intensity and an enthusiasm in the Saudi that is rarely found elsewhere in the world, it is nothing in comparison to the size and intensity of the economic and political revolution that has swept Saudi Arabia from the farthest and most isolated reaches of the international backwater to the pinnacle of world power and influence in less than a decade.

Since 1973, Saudi Arabia has emerged as a superpower equal in influence and economic power to either the United States or the Soviet Union. This emergence has taken place with a suddenness that has stunned and stupefied the rest of the world.

Never before in human history has an economic and political revolution taken place on the scale of the one that is currently taking place on the Arabian peninsula.

Saudi Arabia has burst through the back door into the twentieth century. Less than fifty years ago, Bedouin tribesmen attacked the first ARAMCO (Arabian-American Oil Company) plane to land at Dammam and burned it to a charred hulk, believing it to be the devil incarnate. When King Abdulaziz, also known in the West as King ibn-Saud, first allowed a motorcar into Riyadh in the thirties, its headlights were smashed by an angry mob who believed it was trying to stare at their veiled women. As Peter Iseman pointed out in a recent article, the wheel was introduced into Saudi Arabia less than fifty years ago—attached to the axle of an automobile.[1]

Today, a very different picture greets the eyes of the foreign visitor: building cranes seem to reproduce themselves, bulldozers are everywhere, swimming pools dot private compounds, and video machines have become as common as lawnmowers in an American suburb.

The prime mover behind this dramatic change is, of course, oil. Saudi Arabia has, buried beneath its sands, an estimated one third of the free world's supply of oil.

The reliance of the Western industrialized world on this Arabian oil flow was emphasized during Deputy Energy Secretary John Sawhill's testimony before a Senate Committee on February 20, 1980. Among other things, Sawhill stated that of the 545 billion barrels of the world's total proven oil reserves, 370 billion barrels are located in the Arabian Gulf. A little arithmetic leads us to the startling conclusion that at least seventy percent of the world's proven oil reserves lie beneath the sands of the Gulf area.

However, huge oil discoveries are being made virtually monthly, so that some oilmen have speculated recently that the Arabian Gulf oil reserves may contain as much as 500 billion

---

[1]Peter Iseman, "The Arabian Ethos," *Harper's*, February 1978.

barrels. At current production rates this oil could last for approximately one hundred sixty years.

Deputy Secretary Sawhill went on to expose the empty rhetoric of "energy self-sufficiency." By 1985, Sawhill speculated, the United States, Western Europe, and Japan will be just as dependent on oil from the Arabian Gulf as they are now. In fact, in the case of the United States and Japan, the dependency will grow even larger. In 1979 the United States received thirty-one percent of its oil from the Arabian Gulf. By 1985, according to Sawhill, America will rely on the Arabian Gulf for thirty-five percent of its total supply.

While there has been much talk in the media about alternative energy sources, such as synthetic fuels, oil from shale, and solar and nuclear power, and even some die-hard speculation on massive new domestic oil discoveries, all of these combined will not be able to compensate for the millions upon millions of barrels of Arabian oil burned daily in the United States.

The facts are clear. Shale is too expensive at present to process. Synthetic fuel could only compensate for a minute fraction of imported petroleum. Solar conversion, on a massive scale, would take too long. Nuclear power is not only dangerous to one's physical health but also dangerous to the election prospects of any politician who advocates it.

Unfortunately, the major oil companies report that the likelihood of any further major oil discoveries within the United States is small. Thus the United States will remain reliant on the nations of the Arabian Gulf, particularly Saudi Arabia, for some time to come.

According to a U.S. geological survey, the proven reserves of the United States are only 35 billion barrels. The United States is consuming petroleum at a present rate of 8 billion barrels a year. At this rate, without foreign imports or the unlikely event of large new domestic discoveries, all U.S. oil could be entirely exhausted in just over four years.

Currently Europe receives approximately sixty-three percent of its oil from the Arabian Gulf, and Japan seventy-three percent. While the oil reserves of the North Sea will account for a decrease of about one percent in Western Europe's reliance on Arabian Gulf oil in the next five years, Sawhill sees Japanese dependence remaining approximately the same.

Were something or someone to cut the flow of oil from the Arabian Gulf, the result would be truly apocalyptic for the United States, Western Europe, Japan, and much of the developing world. In the U.S. alone (notwithstanding the 100 million barrels of the U.S. strategic reserve stored along the Gulf of Mexico, which would be exhausted in about ten days) a sustained cutoff of Arabian Gulf oil would mean that one out of every three truck, car, and bus engines would be stilled, one out of every three homes heated with oil would be cold in the winter, and one out of every three petroleum-reliant industries would have to close its doors.

Although the percentages are roughly accurate, the overall picture would be much more serious. In short, were there a sustained cutoff of Arabian Gulf oil, the United States would grind to a halt, not with a nuclear bang, but with the hollow sound of an empty gas tank.

Contrary to current speculation, in the event of an oil cutoff from the Arabian Gulf, the United States would *not* have to ration gasoline. There simply would be no gasoline available at any price for private use. In a worst-case scenario, all gasoline available would go to essential services such as the military, the police and fire departments, and the transport of foodstuffs. Most nonessential businesses and industries would close. Unemployment would skyrocket.

All major cities would, in all probability, have to be placed under martial law. Curfews would be enforced at gunpoint. Looting during the blackout hours would be commonplace. The very old and the very young would alternately freeze and starve—with the worst suffering borne by the ethnic and racial minorities in the inner cities.

Inflation would metamorphose from the annoyance it is today into a lethal epidemic. We would enter a wheelbarrow economy like that of Germany prior to Hitler's rise to power, where a wheelbarrow of virtually worthless currency would be required to purchase a loaf of bread. A bicycle in good repair, the only real means of private transportation, might sell for the same price as a new Mercedes does now.

And even this brief scenario is in all probability too gentle, since it does not take into consideration the effect of total economic and military collapse in Japan and Western Europe. Can we, after the painfully explicit examples of Hungary, Czechoslovakia, and, more recently, Afghanistan, expect the Soviet Union to sit idly by and watch these classic opportunities for "intervention" to pass them by unutilized? Can we really expect the victims of such chaos and suffering to refrain from looking for new or old scapegoats to persecute?

In short, a protracted stoppage of oil from the Arabian Gulf would result in chaos, confusion, and savagery the like of which the world has never witnessed.

How realistic are these Jeremiah-like speculations? What kind of events could lead to an oil embargo? What sort of internal problems in Saudi Arabia could lead to a shutdown of the oil fields? How likely is a crippling production cut of Arabian oil? Could American interference in the internal affairs of Saudi Arabia backfire the way it did in Iran?

In part, this book will attempt to explore and answer these questions.

Oil is not the only power the Saudis have within their grasp. They also have the largest cash surplus of any nation at any time in the history of mankind. The figures are so large that they befuddle the mind. Never before has a nation been confronted with the problem of earning more money than it is physically possible to spend, invest, or even waste.

In the spring of 1981, Saudi Arabia was producing approximately 10.5 million barrels of oil a day. At the then-current price of thirty-two dollars per barrel, this represents an earning of 336 million dollars per day. With a total population of between three and six million (no one is certain, since the Bedouins will not stand still long enough to be counted), this means that if the oil revenues were distributed equally, every man, woman, child, dog, and camel could be assured at least twenty thousand dollars a year.

With polygamy still a fact of Saudi Arabian life and a dozen children not uncommon, these figures seem to ensure the proverbial "good life" to many, many generations of Saudis. However, the Saudi vision of the good life may bear very little resemblance to the more materialistic images conjured up in the mortgage-ridden Western mind.

Take, for example, the present-day monarch of Saudi Arabia, King Khalid ibn-Abdulaziz al-Saud, even by the most conservative standards one of the world's richest men. King Khalid's conception of the good life—shared, incidentally, by a remarkable number of Saudis—is to retreat into the desert (accompanied, it is reported, by no less than five hundred portable solar-powered telephones), live in an enormous goat's-hair tent, sip sugary tea, chat with local tribal worthies, and occasionally hunt with his prize falcons.

However, this is not the rule but the exception. Oil wealth is not being distributed equally, and while the government is in the process of creating a welfare system, poverty is very real and very stark in the desert kingdom. Despite more than eight hundred multimillionaire Saudi princes, there are hundreds of thousands of Saudis who are illiterate, poor, subject to many diseases that are extinct in the West, and given a life expectancy of no more than forty years.

But the obvious inequality of revenue distribution that may escape the notice of the casual visitor to Saudi Arabia does nothing to diminish the hugeness of the amount of money that pours into Saudi Arabia daily, about one hundred seventy thousand dollars a minute. Based on current oil prices, Saudi Arabia is earning approximately ninety billion dollars a year. With revenues like this overflowing their coffers, the Saudis could make some rather remarkable, if theoretical, purchases. Earning ninety billion dollars per year, Saudi Arabia could buy:

All the companies on all the world's major stock markets in under thirteen years.
The New York Stock Exchange in six years.
The London Stock Exchange in seven months.
IBM in two months, twenty-four days.

Exxon in twenty-seven days.
The Bank of America in seven days, fifteen hours.
De Beers Consolidated Diamond Mines in four days, nine hours,
    and twenty-four minutes.

True, none of the above is currently for sale. What does one do
with 90 billion dollars a year plus the interest accruing from investments of practically 100 billion dollars? Even Saudi Arabia's
vast development program, which disbursed over 140 billion
dollars in the last five years, cannot spend the oil revenues as
fast as they are earned. In 1975 not one of the Saudi government
ministries was able to exhaust its budget, and this certainly was
not for lack of trying. Hardly a week goes by in Riyadh without a
high government official "resigning" amid a flurry of rumors
involving graft and corruption.

"Absorptive capacity" is the newly coined term to describe
the inability to spend what one earns. Saudi Arabia's absorptive
capacity is vast. The Saudi surplus cash usually ends up in
short-term deposits in the West. But the very nature of these
short-term deposits makes them highly liquidatable—liable to
be moved out of a country virtually on a moment's notice.

Estimates vary widely as to the total of Saudi cash surplus.
The exact figure and the location of these assets are some of the
most closely guarded secrets in the world of finance. Conservative guesses place the figure between 50 and 60 billion dollars
while others suggest it could be as high as 100 billion. It does
not take too much imagination to foresee the kind of economic
chaos that would result from a massive Saudi liquidation of assets in a given country. It may be illustrative here to remember
that President Carter found it necessary to freeze Iranian assets
in the United States when Iran threatened to liquidate an estimated 6 to 10 billion dollars in assets. In the case of Saudi
Arabia, we are talking of assets that are four, five, or six times
greater.

A massive Saudi liquidation in a developing nation with a relatively fragile economy would result in immediate disaster. The
country would literally be drained of capital. Banks would be
forced to close and lock their doors in a drama not unlike the

Panic of 1929. The economic ramifications of a large-scale Saudi liquidation of assets in a more industrialized nation would be no less severe. It would just take a little longer before the real human suffering became manifest.

It is a common belief that the influence of Saudi Arabia and its royal family ends with the regulation of oil prices. Nothing could be less true. In the past the Saudi royal family has used its vast oil fortune to hire foreign armies to fight wars for it, to purchase foreign policy changes in other countries, to pay for assassinations and attempted assassinations, to finance guerrillas in countries in Africa and Asia, and, in several reported instances, to purchase influence from an American president.

Even in the area of commodities, Saudis have managed to raise the world's eyebrows in astonishment. An article in the *Arab Oil and Economic Report* (November 1979) reported that Arabs (the majority Saudi) had purchased 45 million ounces of silver in a matter of weeks. The white metal was estimated to be worth over 675 million dollars and represented an amount equivalent to half of America's total silver reserve. The article went on to suggest that in a matter of months most of the world's free-market silver and gold could be owned by Arabs.

Somewhat ironically, the article ended by lamenting the poor image of Arabs in the Western press.

This poor media image is a constant source of irritation to the Saudis. From their vantage point, they see themselves as the innocents maligned, slandered, caricatured, and libeled by the Zionist agents in control of the Western European and American media. In some respects, the Saudis have perceived the situation correctly.

The Saudi image in the Western press has been as grossly inaccurate as it has been insulting to them. Either one is presented with camels, Bedouin tents, and desert sunsets à la Lawrence or Philby, or one is subjected to detailed accounts of some young sheikh's extravagances in London or Paris. While some Bedouins do continue to live in tents and some young sheikhs do spend hundreds of thousands of dollars a day in London, they can hardly be considered representative of Saudi Arabia as a whole.

At the end of a class one day at the University of Riyadh, a student of mine came up to me and asked, without hostility, why Saudis knew more about the United States than Americans knew about Saudi Arabia. "Americans think of us as riding camels to our oil wells. They don't think of us as real people."

I can't remember my reply, probably because it was inadequate and rather defensive in tone, but his comment set me to thinking. Americans do have rather limited sources of accurate information about Saudi Arabia, much of which is deliberately or unconsciously biased. The student's words bothered me also because I could think of few words in any language as potentially dangerous as the ones he had spoken: *"They don't think of us as real people."*

While one of the major concerns of this book is to explore how secure the West's oil umbilical cord really is and to examine closely the world's most powerful family—the House al-Saud—the book is also a long-overdue reply to a student whose name I have already forgotten, an attempt to understand the people, culture, and politics of the world's most recent superpower, Saudi Arabia.

I

The Journeys of Three Men

"If all the Saudis are such good
Muslims, why does the government
enforce the religion at gunpoint?"

—Finnish expatriate in Riyadh, 1979

"First and foremost, we are Muslims.
Oil means nothing to us. Wealth means
nothing. If we must return to the
desert to obey God's law, then we will
return and live in tents and drink camel's
milk as our fathers and grandfathers did.
Saudi Arabia is Islam, not oil."

—A Saudi student, Riyadh, 1980

There is an old Bedouin proverb that says, "When a man does not travel, his poetry fades, his animals die, and his women bring forth only girl babies. Travel, O my brother, travel is conquest!"

Travel has indeed meant survival for the nomadic Bedouins of central Arabia. And survival in the desert is a conquest that cannot be sneered at. Whether retreating from an enemy, advancing to attack, or simply searching for grazing land in the bed of a dry wadi, the Bedouins of the desert have been in motion for thousands of years.

The entire manner of existence, their intricate code of justice and honor, their values, and in fact their religion reflect this incessant mobility. Once when I was on a picnic near the village of Salbuk, I ran into an old Bedouin camped in the desert, one of the few who still refuse to be resettled in the cities. After being served tea and uttering the prescribed Islamic blessings upon each other, we began to compare customs in Arabia and the United States. After some time the old Bedouin, a twinkle in his eye and a cartridge belt strung across his chest, asked how long it was in New York before a host could kill his guest. When I showed some confusion, if not consternation, a friend explained that three days' hospitality in the desert was mandatory even to one's mortal enemy. But after the three days' sanctuary, a host could with a clear conscience, murder his guest. Our chat with the old Bedouin was, needless to say, cut short well before three days had passed.

In many respects, the history of central Arabia can be summed up as a series of travels or journeys, but there are of course some journeys that are historically more significant than others. The stories behind the three journeys that form the core of this part are mileposts on the historical journey of Arabia. The effects of these three journeys still determine the destinies of millions of Arabs from the Arabian peninsula.

1

The First Journey

Toward the close of the sixth century of the Christian era, a boy was born in the city of Mecca into the powerful merchant family of the city, of the tribe called Quraysh. However, the boy's parents were not part of the hierarchy of the tribe; in fact, they were quite impoverished. The boy was named Muhammed.

Mecca at this time was already a major trading center and caravan oasis. The more powerful members of the Quraysh family governed the city, which was a major shrine and site of an annual pilgrimage. The focus of the pilgrimage was the Kaaba, a jet-black stone—probably a meteorite—which was surrounded by three hundred and sixty idols representing lesser deities that were currently in vogue.

When Muhammed was about six years of age, his parents died. Historical records tell us very little about them, and we must guess at the amount of influence they had on the young boy's life. Muhammed was taken in by an uncle named Abn-Taleb. The relationship between the nephew and uncle seems to have been a good one. We are not told explicitly what the uncle did for a living, but it is reasonable to assume that he was a merchant plying his trade among the visitors and pilgrims who came to worship at the pagan shrines of Mecca.

Abn-Taleb probably acted as a responsible guardian for the young boy and trained him to be a merchant. But being a merchant in sixth-century Mecca involved much more than just opening a shop and selling merchandise. Among the many duties of a merchant was the acquisition of goods by traveling and trading. So it is very probable that Muhammed, from an early age, accompanied his uncle's caravans throughout what we now refer to as the Middle East.

Traveling on the Arabian peninsula had never been easy or safe, and raiding was not only commonplace but also an accepted means of survival among many of the Bedouin tribes. It is therefore very likely that among the other things Muhammed learned as a young boy, were some of the arts of desert warfare, skills he would use later in his life when he was exiled in Medina.

It was on one of his uncle's caravans to Syria that the adolescent Muhammed began his most important spiritual journey. He met a man named Bahira. Bahira was an ascetic Christian monk who took an immediate liking to the wild, uneducated, but obviously gifted young boy. Muhammed spent much time in the company of Bahira, who attempted to convert the boy to Christianity. In this Bahira failed, but his impact upon Muhammed has never been questioned. He convinced the boy of the truth of monotheism, something he would never forget.

Given Muhammed's importance in the history of the world, we know remarkably little about his early life. We do not even know what kind of an education he received, if any. For many years there has been a debate among the Islamic religious scholars as to whether or not the Prophet was literate. The argument follows that if Muhammed was illiterate, he could not possibly have composed the complicated poetry that makes up the Koran, thus proving the Koran to be a revelation from God. Historically, it is hard to imagine an impoverished orphan of this period becoming literate, but given Muhammed's obviously gifted intelligence, it is quite possible that he taught himself the rudiments of reading and writing.

In his early twenties Muhammed was employed as the manager of the caravans for a wealthy widow named Khadija. This was quite a responsible and lucrative position for a young man, since Arabian caravans were often composed of several hundreds or even thousands of camels and men. We must assume that Muhammed did his job well, because at about the age of twenty-four, Muhammed married Khadija, who was fifteen years his elder. For the next sixteen years, Muhammed lived the life of a wealthy merchant of Mecca.

Soon after he was forty, Muhammed fell into a prolonged and intense depression. Suddenly the social injustices of Mecca that he had witnessed every day of his life became unbearable to him. Equally unbearable was the sight of pilgrims worshiping the pagan idols that surrounded the Kaaba. It was then that Muhammed began withdrawing from the business of Mecca and started going to a cave in a nearby mountain to meditate and pray.

It was not long thereafter that Muhammed began to have visions. It is said that while he was praying in the cave one day, he felt a growing tightness in his chest. This constriction of the chest grew more and more intense until he believed he could no longer breathe. In panic, Muhammed gasped for breath and uttered a low guttural sound: *qur'an*. Transliterated this becomes "Koran"—the command to read or recite.

The Prophet's divine revelations continued for some time. It was disclosed to him that God had chosen him as a messenger to teach his people the true faith. The Message, transmitted by the Angel Gabriel to the Prophet Muhammed, forms the revealed Word of God, the Koran, the Holy Book of Islam.

Among the Hadeeth, the traditions associated with the Prophet, is the story of how Muhammed returned to his house in Mecca, after having had his first vision, deeply troubled.

According to the story, Muhammed sat with Khadija and talked with her about what had happened to him in the cave. Khadija's response was immediate. She had complete faith that her husband had indeed been chosen by God. But Muhammed was more skeptical. How, he argued, could he be sure that the visions were caused by God and not by a demon?

Khadija extracted a promise from her husband that when the visions started again, he would tell her. Within a few days, the Prophet announced to his wife that the visions were beginning. At this point Khadija did everything in her power to distract her husband from the revelations that were filling his mind. But none of her distractions worked, and the Prophet continued in his almost trancelike state.

In desperation, Khadija pulled up her skirt, exposing herself naked from the waist down. Instantly, Muhammed demanded to know what she was doing. In turn, she asked if the vision was still present. Perhaps a little sadly, Muhammed admitted that it was not. To which Khadija announced triumphantly that indeed the vision must be from God since a demon was never known to flee from a woman's nakedness.

While the story is probably apocryphal, the early teachings of the Prophet are not. The focus of these early teachings was that the people of Mecca should turn away from the worship of many gods and begin to worship the one God, Allah. Allah was already among the pantheon of pagan deities that surrounded the Kaaba, the god ascribed to having power over creation and preservation.

The perennial nemesis of God's various messengers seems to be the middle class, who have the most to lose financially by accepting or even tolerating the revealed Word. The merchant class of Mecca, in fact the Prophet's own Quraysh tribe, proved to be no exception to this rule. By threatening the polytheistic status quo, the Prophet Muhammed also threatened the profits of the merchants who relied on pilgrims as customers.

Despite the open antagonism of most of his own family, the Prophet was able to attract converts to this new religion. By far his most important convert was his cousin, Ali. This is the same cousin who would later marry the Prophet's daughter, Fatima, and become one of the successful leaders of the new Muslim faith.

The Prophet's new monotheistic message was gradually expanded to include the concept of brotherhood. Brotherhood, as the Prophet Muhammed used it, was not merely the passive acceptance of all men as brothers but rather a rigorously active program of egalitarianism. This new concept of equality was unsurprisingly popular among the poorer and slave classes, and the number of his converts grew.

As the number of Muslims grew larger and Muhammed's public condemnations of paganism grew more frequent and more persuasive, the fears of the merchants of Mecca increased. The early Muslims of Mecca soon found themselves ridiculed, mocked, threatened, and persecuted—ironically creating exactly the fertile medium needed for the young religion to grow stronger and flourish.

After some ten years of persecution, Muhammed's followers came to him and revealed to him a plot on the part of his own family to murder him. It is reported that Muhammed was reluctant to leave the city of his birth and that it took his cousin Ali and his other followers quite some time to convince the Prophet that he should escape from Mecca before it was too late. Muhammed had already been invited to come to the city of Medina to arbitrate in a dispute between rival warring families, and so it was in light of the impending plot on his life that the Prophet decided to accept this invitation.

The Prophet's journey from Mecca to Medina is unquestionably the most important journey in Islam. It is called the Hegira (literally, "flight") and took place in A.D. 622. The Hegira marked the beginning of the Islamic calendar and to all intents and purposes, the beginning of Islam.

Leaving Ali to impersonate him in his bed in Mecca, Muhammed and some two hundred followers marched and rode to Medina. The journey itself was relatively uneventful, and soon after his arrival in Medina Muhammed resolved the dispute between the two rival families and so earned himself a reputation for fairness and wisdom.

Medina during the time of the Prophet was much smaller than Mecca, and also poorer. It did, however, have a large Jewish community. Muhammed was almost immediately drawn to these Jews since they were, like his own followers, monotheists.

It was through the influence of the Jewish community in Medina that Muhammed learned and subsequently adopted many Jewish traditions and customs into his own religion. He set aside a Sabbath day as a day of public worship; he called upon all Muslims to face Jerusalem when they prayed; and he insisted on three obligatory daily prayers.

However, Muhammed's friendship with the Jewish community was short-lived. His lack of formal education, especially as far as the Old Testament was concerned, made him an object of condescension and mockery among the more educated Jews.

The Jews also refused categorically to accept that the Prophet's visions were divine in origin.

It is at this point that we see Muhammed and his followers attempting to separate themselves from anything that was remotely Judaic or Christian, and so we see Islam undergoing a purge of Jewish influences. (One can only speculate as to how the history of mankind might have been different had the Jews and Muslims of seventh-century Medina continued to live on cordial terms.)

Muhammed sought and found a pre-Judaic source for Islam in the Patriarch Abraham, who, with his son Ishmael, is said to have built the Kaaba (literally, "the house of God") in Mecca as the First Sanctuary. Muhammed continued his de-Hebraization of Islam by changing the Sabbath to Friday, by having the faithful called to prayer by the human voice of a muezzin rather than the ram's horn, and by proclaiming that from then on all Muslims should face Mecca when they prayed. He also proclaimed a month of fasting during the daylight hours (Ramadan) and the hajj, the annual pilgrimage to the Holy Kaaba in Mecca.

Conversions to the new faith were numerous, especially among the local Bedouin tribes that lived in the desert surrounding Medina. These Bedouins were by both inclination and occupation marauders who lived from raiding the richly laden caravans that traveled to and from the commercial center of Mecca. Muhammed did not discourage this marauding; on the contrary, he offered the Bedouins divine justification for their banditry, telling them that they were doing the Will of God. In addition to securing the loyalty of the local Bedouins, Muhammed received a share of their plunder. It was with this ill-gotten revenue that Muhammed financed the first decade of Islam.

During this period there were numerous small battles between the Muslims of Medina and the merchants of Mecca, who resented having their caravans robbed. Finally a truce of sorts was arrived at whereby the merchants' caravans were guaranteed a degree of security and the Muslims of Medina were granted the right to make the annual pilgrimage to Mecca.

To comprehend what happened next, one must understand a little about the Holy Haram of Mecca. The word *haram* in Arabic has no direct translation in English. When it is used to describe pork, it means simply "forbidden." However, when it is used to describe an area surrounding Mecca, its meaning has more in common with the word "taboo." The Holy Haram in Mecca is sacred land, forbidden to non-Muslims. It is a sacred space where all men and women stand equal before their God. It is the only public place in Arabia where women do not go veiled. Fighting of any kind is forbidden, as is the slaughter of any animal or the damaging of any tree or plant.

So strictly is the Holy Haram observed that many pilgrims shave their heads before going on hajj to prevent a single hair from falling from their heads while inside the Holy Haram. The violation of the sanctity of the Holy Haram is a crime against God, the most serious and most heinous in Islam.

In A.D. 630, during the pilgrimage to Mecca, a Muslim pilgrim was murdered while he was in *ihram*, the state of physical and spiritual purity a Muslim must enter before making the hajj. News of this crime against God spread quickly. While the murdered pilgrim was believed to be transported instantly to paradise, other surviving Muslims could not allow the crime to go unpunished. Muhammed mustered an army, composed primarily of his followers in Medina and local Bedouins, and launched an attack on the people of Mecca. The invasion was successful, and Mecca was quickly defeated.

Muhammed entered the city of his birth, the city from which he had fled ten years earlier, as a conqueror and a reformer, but foremost as the messenger of God on earth. He immediately went to the Kaaba and destroyed all of the idols, but left the black stone, the First Sanctuary of the Prophet Abraham, untouched.

Muhammed died two years later, in A.H. 10 (A.D. 632), and, in keeping with the custom of the day, was buried beneath the floor of the house of his favorite wife. At the time of his death, the Prophet had six wives, his favorite being a young girl named Ayesha, in whose arms he died. They were married in A.D. 625, when the Prophet was about fifty-five years old. It is probable that the marriage was never consummated: Ayesha was only nine years old. It is more likely that the Prophet looked upon Ayesha more as a daughter than a wife. Ayesha's father was Abu-Bakr, who had become a devout and powerful follower of the Prophet.

Within a matter of decades after his death, the religion that had begun with Muhammed's flight to Medina had spread throughout the known world—from what is now Pakistan to the Atlantic coast of Spain. No other religion, including Christianity, has spread so far so rapidly.

There were several reasons for the rapid spread of the Muslim faith. Probably the best known and most often cited reason in the West is that Muslims were forbidden by the Holy Koran to fight other Muslims, so they simply turned the razor edges of their swords against their as yet unbelieving neighbors. However, conversion by the sword is far from a full picture of what took place during that time and does not do justice to the very real appeal of Islam.

Like Christianity before it, Islam appealed initially to the poorer classes of society. It stressed equality, charity, honor, brotherhood among all believers, and justice. Islam provided the suffering, the downtrodden, and the illiterate with a simple, comprehensible faith and, equally importantly, with an orderly, coherent code of conduct.

It is an enormous error to view the rapid spread of Islam as simply a military conquest. Unfortunately, this is the way it is most often misunderstood in the West. Had this been the case, it is doubtful that Islam would have survived a century, let alone a millennium.

Conversion by the sword did occur, but it was the exception rather than the rule. Forced conversion is forbidden by the Koran and is entirely repugnant to most Muslims. Historically, Islam has been, in many respects, vastly more tolerant of other religions than has either Judaism or Christianity. It is a little-known fact that there was a thriving Jewish community in Saudi Arabia until the late 1940s, when it voluntarily emigrated to Palestine. Although Saudi Arabia now refuses to grant visas to Jews, this is not, at least in their eyes, a case of religious intolerance but rather a political reaction to the question of the rights of the Palestinian people.

The Prophet's successor was his pious father-in-law, Abu-Bakr, who immediately upon the death of Muhammed took over the leadership of the Muslim community. He became the Caliph. However, the Bedouin tribes of the area surrounding Mecca and Medina had felt a personal allegiance to the Prophet Muhammed and felt none towards Abu-Bakr. They dispersed in their individual directions and went back to their old pagan ways in the desert. In time, Abu-Bakr was forced to use military power to reunite the desert people under the banner of Islam.

Once united, the Bedouin tribes had no military equal. Trained in desert warfare and fired by the belief that they were performing God's Will, they burst into what is now Egypt, Syria, Jordan, Iraq, and Iran, conquering the local tribes and then inviting them to convert to Islam and join them in future raids.

Conversion was not the primary reason behind these raids; they were motivated out of the more mundane desire for loot. Many of the conquered refused to convert immediately, and in some cases it took over a century before the local people learned Arabic, became Muslims, and assumed the administration of the Islamic Empire.

Abu-Bakr died two years after becoming Caliph of Mecca, in A.D. 634. His successor, Umar, was also an expansionist. However, Caliph Umar's most important contribution to the growth of Islam was that he ordered his followers to record the Prophet's divine revelations in the form of a book that would later become known as the Holy Koran.

By A.D. 635 Caliph Umar had conquered Damascus and within a year had completely defeated the Byzantine army that had been sent against him. In the next five years, the Arabian army took complete control of Iraq, Jerusalem, and the Egyptian capital of Alexandria.

However, Caliph Umar's legacy to Islam was double-edged. While providing it with both a Holy Book and an empire, his death provided the occasion for rivalry that resulted in a schism that continues to this day. After Umar's death, the powerful Umayyid family of Mecca managed to manipulate one of their own, Othman, into the caliphate. Othman dutifully remembered who had been responsible for his position of power and correspondingly favored his own family. This evoked widespread resentment and jealousy, especially among the members of the Prophet's own family, the Quraysh. It was not long before Caliph Othman was murdered, but like most murders this did little to solve the interfamily problems; if anything, the murder of Caliph Othman exacerbated them.

After Othman was murdered in A.D. 656, the tensions between the Umayyid and Quraysh families grew even more pronounced. The dispute was no longer a simple family rivalry; it had grown into a full-blown theological and political tangle over the process by which the new caliph should be chosen.

On the one hand were those who believed the caliphate should be filled by one of the close associates of the Prophet, and on the other hand were those who believed that the position should be filled by a member of the Quraysh family elected by members of the tribe. Neither of the arguments was theologically sound of itself, and each was politically threatening to the opposition.

Out of this crisis emerged the Prophet's son-in-law, Ali, who had married Fatima and who was the closest surviving associate of Muhammed's. Ali was much too close to the Quraysh family for the likings of the powerful Umayyid family, and so his ascendency to the caliphate was blocked. Undaunted, Ali led the Arabian armies from one military victory to another, and once Iraq was securely in his hands, he announced that he was moving the caliphate from Medina to Kufa in Iraq.

The Umayyids promptly appointed a Syrian by the name of Muawiyah to be the caliph of Medina. So for a short time there were two caliphs. Muawiyah appointed his own son to be his successor and moved the caliphate from Medina to Damascus. Although little concrete historical evidence exists to prove complicity, it is often suggested that Muawiyah plotted, planned, and financed the assassination of Ali in Kufa. Despite the fact that we cannot be entirely sure who was responsible, Ali was indeed murdered.

When Muawiyah died, the supporters of the late Ali made a bid to make his son, Husayn, the new caliph. However, Husayn managed to get himself killed in battle in A.D. 680 and, though missing the caliphate, did achieve martyrdom.

The martyrdom of Husayn heralded a complete break between the followers of Ali, known even then as the Shiah, or Shiites, and those who claimed to follow the true path of the Prophet, known as the Sunni, or Sunnites. This momentous schism plunged most of the Arabian peninsula into the backwater of history for the next twelve hundred years.

The first half of the eighth century was filled with bloody warfare between the two branches of Islam, the Shiites centered in Persia and the Sunnites located in the Arabian peninsula. This warfare succeeded in fragmenting the tenuous tribal unity that had momentarily existed under the Prophet and Caliph Abu-Bakr. At the same time that Islam was spreading from the Atlantic to the Indian Oceans, the Arabian peninsula fell back into tribal feuding and pillage, and so it would remain for the next several hundred years.

During the sixteenth and seventeenth centuries both the Ottomans and the Europeans exerted an influence on the Arabian peninsula, but for the most part this influence was restricted to the coastal areas of the Red Sea and what is now the United Arab Emirates, Oman, and the two Yemens. Central Arabia continued to be one of the most isolated places in the world.

It was not until the eighteenth century that Arabs again attempted to unify the peninsula. During the first half of the century, there emerged an itinerant religious teacher by the name of Muhammed ibn-Abdul al-Wahhab, who began preaching that Islam had been corrupted from its original message. Soon, Wahhab had launched a crusade to purify Islam, to banish the superstition, idolatry, mysticism, and pageantry that had evolved since the time of the Prophet.

While Wahhab was unquestionably devout and remarkably courageous, he was, like most puritans both before and after him, vehemently intolerant of anything and everything that did not agree with his own particular conception of Islam. It was not long before the people of his own village grew weary of this holy but unpleasant man and expelled him. This was probably the luckiest thing that ever happened to Wahhab.

After a short time traveling, Wahhab found a new home in the village of Diriyah, just north of Riyadh, where he continued to preach his reforming sermons. In Diriyah his audiences were less hostile—some were openly enthusiastic. By 1744 Wahhab had managed to make a number of converts, including the tribal leader of Diriyah, a man named Muhammed ibn-Saud al-Saud, the ancestor of the present king of Saudi Arabia.

In Sheikh Muhammed ibn-Saud, Wahhab had found an ideal patron, and soon the crusade for the reform of Islam took on not only a more vocal but also a more militant aspect. Sheikh Muhammed ibn-Saud provided the warriors, and Wahhab provided the divine cause. The energy and enthusiasm of the sheikh and the holy man virtually ensured their success. Together they destroyed the revered shrines of the so-called holy men, cut down holy trees, and leveled monuments to the dead. Wahhabiism became the dynamic force behind both religious and political unification.

Depending on who is writing history, you will read that Wahhab was either the worst or the best thing that has ever happened to Arabia. His influence can still be felt in present-day Saudi Arabia.

Sheikh Muhammed died in 1773, but his son continued the military and religious crusade, and by the final decade of the eighteenth century, the House al-Saud had brought most of central Arabia under its direct control. Wahhabiism became widespread—even in the twin Holy Cities of Mecca and Medina.

But this was to be only a temporary situation. The sultan of Turkey, leader of the Ottoman Empire and Caliph of Islam, became quite naturally concerned about having the Holy Cities of Mecca and Medina in the hands of what he correctly saw as a group of fanatical zealots, and so he ordered his governor in Egypt, Ali Pasha, to launch an attack on the Wahhabis and reclaim Mecca and Medina.

It took Ali Pasha quite a few years to defeat the Wahhabis, who looked upon death in battle as a shortcut to paradise, but with vastly superior weaponry, including some of Napoleon's cannons, he was eventually successful. In 1818 his armies laid siege to the ancestral home of the al-Saud family at Diriyah, and by the end of the year there was nothing left but the ruins that still stand next to Wadi Hannifa today.

It would take the House al-Saud nearly another hundred years before it again made a bid for power, which brings us to the beginning of the second journey—the journey of a man and of Arabia into modern nationhood.

2

The Second Journey

The second journey begins with an invitation to dinner in Riyadh. The invitation itself was as odd as it was unexpected, and one can easily imagine the quizzical expression on the face of Abdul Rahman al-Saud as he listened to Governor Salim's messenger convey the invitation to dine at the fortress-palace, al-Masmak.

For years, the al-Sauds and the Rashids had been rivals for control of the central area of Arabia, that area known as the Nejd. This rivalry had most often exhibited itself at sword's length. But now, in the early summer of 1890, came an invitation from the Rashidi governor, Salim ibn-Sakhan, to feast with him. Wise counsel having been known to encourage longevity in Arabia, Abdul Rahman sought out the advice of his own family, only to discover that they too had received the same curious invitations. All the male members of the House al-Saud had been invited to the feast.

Abdul Rahman was far from being a fool, but equally far from being a coward. As emir (prince) of the family, he was posed with the difficult question of deciding whether the invitation was a genuine peace offer on the part of the Rashids or a treacherous plot to put an end to the al-Saud family. The few written records that survive from the period do not tell us how Abdul Rahman secured an informer within the governor's fortress. Perhaps he used what little money the al-Saud family possessed as a bribe, or perhaps he used the already well known al-Saud charm. Whatever the means Abdul Rahman used, the results were unequivocal.

Abdul Rahman quickly passed the word to his own family: the invitation was as fraudulent as the hospitality was pretended. It was indeed a plot to massacre the entire House al-Saud. Abdul Rahman called a secret meeting of the male members of his family.

It is important to remember that the relationship between host and guest is virtually sacred in Arabia. The host is bound by custom, tradition, and honor to protect and defend his guest for a strictly prescribed three-day period. Thus the Rashidi murder plans were doubly treacherous and dishonorable.

History records nothing of what was said at the al-Saud family meeting, but it is not too hard to reconstruct it. Had the al-Saud males simply refused the invitation, it would have given warning to the Rashids that the al-Sauds knew of their assassination plans and would have allowed the Rashids to seek them out and murder them individually. The al-Sauds obviously felt that their strength lay in acting together as a family and that they should employ their most valuable weapon: surprise. It was decided that they would attend the feast, secretly armed, and at a prearranged signal would rise as one man against their hosts. It is certain that Abdul Rahman, as emir of the family, approved this plan personally.

However, what is less certain are his own thoughts concerning his son, Abdulaziz. At ten, Abdulaziz was in most respects considered an adult male. Even so, Abdul Rahman must have had many fatherly reservations about taking the boy into the governor's fortress: while the boy was a man in the eyes of the tribe, he was far from a physical equal to an adult Rashid assassin. But to leave the boy at home would have been an act of cowardice and would certainly not have insured his safety.

It is probable that Abdul Rahman's decision to take his son to the supposed feast was based on the belief that were the al-Sauds successful, Abdulaziz would be safest at his own side. On the other hand, were the al-Sauds defeated, it would only be a matter of time before the Rashids came to his house and cut the boy's throat.

So Abdulaziz was informed of the al-Saud plan, told of the prearranged signal, and armed with a double-edged dagger.

An Arabian feast makes up in ceremony what it lacks in gastronomic variety. The ceremonies seem endless. First there is a lengthy exchange of blessings, followed by an incensing of all present with either frankincense or sandalwood. Traditionally, as soon as the guest of honor has arrived, thimble-sized cups of green (unroasted), unsweetened coffee are served. One cup is mandatory, while indulging in more than three is considered excessive and can act as a laxative. There is also an elaborate code of gestures by which the guest signals either that he desires more coffee or that he is satiated.

In addition, there are a number of strictly adhered-to taboos, but unquestionably the most rigidly followed is the prohibition of employing the left hand while eating or drinking. While this rule of etiquette may seem odd to the Western businessman dining at the Intercontinental Hotel in Riyadh, it would not seem at all odd to him were he transported back a mere twenty or so years. Toilet facilities are a very recent innovation in Arabia, and water in the desert was much too scarce to provide for regular washings. Therefore, for very sensible reasons of hygiene, the left hand was reserved for private functions and was never used for eating.

So it must have been with enormous astonishment that the governor's retainers watched Abdul Rahman lift his coffee cup to his mouth with his left hand. The cup never reached his lips. The al-Saud family were instantly on their feet, weapons drawn, slaughtering the dumbfounded household. The battle was fierce but brief. The governor's guards had been so surprised by the attack that they could mount little or no defense. Most died with their swords still in their silver sheaths.

The governor, Salim ibn-Sakhan, was captured alive. On the orders of Abdul Rahman, the governor was bound hand and foot and taken to a courtyard within the fortress. He was then unceremoniously thrown down a deep well. The entire spectacle was witnessed by ten-year-old Abdulaziz, who would in thirty years become known in the West by the name ibn-Saud.[1]

Rashidi vengeance was swift and merciless. Emir Muhammed ibn-Rashid led the army that besieged Riyadh. For several months the people of Riyadh remained loyal to the al-Saud family, for they had delivered them from the brutal tyranny of Salim ibn-Sakhan. However, the army of ibn-Rashid was ordered to victory regardless of the cost to the civilian population. The palm groves that surrounded the then-walled city of Riyadh were cut down. The wells that supplied the only drinking water were poisoned.

It was not long before Abdul Rahman perceived that the people of Riyadh were beginning to turn against the al-Saud family and blame them for their suffering. In keeping with the Bedouin idea that a retreat is always better than a defeat, Abdul Rahman hid his ten-year-old son Abdulaziz and his eleven-year-old daughter Nura in the saddlebags of a camel and secretly set out into the desert.

Riyadh fell to the Rashidi army only hours after Abdul Rahman and his family escaped. Emir Muhammed ibn-Rashid sent soldiers after the family with orders to murder them all, and had they been successful, the history of Arabia, and indeed the modern world, would have been very different. Muhammed ibn-Rashid appointed a new governor of Riyadh, a man by the name of Ajlan ibn-Muhammed. Ajlan, like his predecessor, had a cruel and merciless streak.

Meanwhile, Abdul Rahman and his family wandered in the desert, accepting the obligatory hospitality of Bedouin tribes. It was here, homeless and dispossessed of power, that Abdulaziz had most of his education. It was certainly not an education that would have gained him entrance to Harvard or Yale, but it was an ideal education for a boy who was destined to become

---

[1]It should be noted here that Saudi Arabia's first king's correct name was Abdulaziz al-Saud. The word *ibn* in Arabic means "son of." Abdulaziz was the son of Abdul Rahman and therefore was Abdulaziz ibn–Abdul Rahman al-Saud. When Western Arabists refer to Abdulaziz as "ibn-Saud" they are confusing *ibn* with *al*, the latter meaning "of the family of." For the purpose of this book, the first king of Saudi Arabia will be referred to as Abdulaziz, the name by which he is still known in Arabia.

the most important individual in Arabia since the Prophet himself. Here among the nomadic Bedouins, Abdulaziz learned
firsthand the value of charity and generosity. The Bedouins
must have liked this strong, argumentative, bright young man.
They must, even then, have come to admire the speed at which
he grasped concepts of desert warfare, the wisdom behind his
resolutions for tribal disputes, and his remarkable skills in hunt-
ing and riding.

At the same time as Abdulaziz was learning the art of living in
some of the world's most forbidding terrain, he was also learning the Koran. Abdul Rahman was a devout Wahhabi Muslim,
and his son became even more so. What would distinguish
Abdulaziz in later years from other, more frenzied zealots was
his belief that justice should, as often as possible, be tempered
with mercy and compassion. It was this conception of justice,
more than anything else he possessed, that allowed him to
unify the Arabian peninsula. Here was not just another petty ty-
rant who would use whatever savagery he cared to to secure his
own ends. Here was a true leader of men.

After a short stay in Qatar, Abdul Rahman found sanctuary
for his family in Kuwait, whose leader, Sheikh Mubarak, had had
his own political and military problems with the Rashid family.
It was in Kuwait that Abdulaziz came into manhood. By the age
of seventeen, he was an unheard-of six feet three inches tall, a
giant by Bedouin standards. It was also here in Kuwait that
Abdulaziz took his first wife and experienced the pleasures of
the flesh. Arab modesty and propriety prohibits a man from discussing his wives with other men, but it does not prevent him
from proclaiming his enjoyment of them in general. In his later
years, such announcements were common from Abdulaziz,
and on one occasion Henry St. John Philby records Abdulaziz as
stating that sex was his chief enjoyment in life.

This may seem a strange statement for a puritan to make.
However, it should be understood that Abdulaziz never viewed
simple enjoyment as a sin. While extremely devout, Abdulaziz
saw absolutely nothing wrong with enjoying women, good conversation, or warfare. In fact, one of his favorite quotations from

the Koran was: "Your women are a field unto you; so plough them as you wish." (II:223)

And it was from Kuwait that this young man embarked on one of the most significant journeys in Arabian history. The journey was the romantic whim of a young man. No one actually thought anything would come of it. Abdul Rahman counseled him against undertaking it, and even the leader of Kuwait, Sheikh Mubarak, advised strongly against going. But the idea had already begun to germinate in the young man's fertile imagination, and at the end of the summer of 1901 Abdulaziz and thirty men on camels set out for the desert.

Only three men knew what Abdulaziz had in mind—Sheikh Mubarak, Abdul Rahman, and Abdulaziz himself. Even his friends and cousins who accompanied him were not aware of the full extent of Abdulaziz's ambitious plans. His men believed that they were going out into the desert to enjoy the perennial sport of the Bedouins—raiding caravans. What they did not know was that Abdulaziz was planning to gather support from the local tribes and then mount a full attack on Riyadh.

Abdulaziz was unsuccessful in uniting the Bedouins of the desert. While he was unquestionably adept at raiding ibn-Rashid's caravans, ibn-Rashid was equally good at making life miserable for anyone suspected of harboring the raiders. Abdulaziz and his men spent several months on the edge of the Rub al Khali (the Empty Quarter) attempting to gain support from the tribesmen, and while at one point the number of his followers may have reached close to four hundred, he soon found himself back where he started with a paltry thirty.

This must have been a time of great anguish for Abdulaziz. He must have entertained, at least for a short time, the idea that he was defeated before he had even started. It was madness to launch an attack on a Rashidi stronghold like Riyadh with only a handful of men.

A more sensible and more commonplace man would have seen this immediately and would have returned to Kuwait to live out his defeated life in anonymity. But Abdulaziz was neither sensible nor commonplace, and he devised a daring plan that would prove his leadership once and for all—if it succeeded.

Abdulaziz did not attack Riyadh directly; rather, he chose to wait. There may have been several reasons for his decision to delay the attack. The first was that ibn-Rashid was doubtless aware that a member of the al-Saud family was responsible for the raids against his caravans and so would almost certainly have reinforced the garrison at Riyadh.

The second was that Ramadan was approaching. Ramadan is the strictly observed month of fasting during the daylight hours. While bonafide travelers are exempted from fasting as long as they make up the fast later, it is probable that a man as devout as Abdulaziz would not employ such an excuse to avoid a religious duty.

It must have been one of the longest months any man has ever fasted through. At first sight of the new moon, Abdulaziz ordered his thirty men into the saddle. And so begins the journey of Saudi Arabia.

Just outside Riyadh, at an oasis called Ain Heet, Abdulaziz ordered his men to dismount and make camp. Ain Heet can in many respects be considered the birthplace of modern Saudi Arabia.

One can still visit Ain Heet, located less than a kilometer off the road south from Riyadh to Al Kharj. At a distance it appears to be nothing more than a large semicircular indentation in the escarpment, but as one comes closer one sees that in reality there is a huge cave descending for more than a kilometer. At the bottom of the cavern is a large underground pool of fresh water filled with blind fish that have never seen sunlight.

It was at this underground pool that Abdulaziz and his men watered their camels the night before they attached Riyadh. Thirty years later, it was in this same cavern at Ain Heet that two American geologists, while studying the prospects of drilling for water, uncovered the geological clues that would lead to the discovery of the world's largest supply of petroleum and would make Saudi Arabia the world's newest superpower.

By the time his men had pitched their tents, it was dark. Beneath the faint silver light of the new moon, Abdulaziz chose six men to accompany him to Riyadh. He instructed the remainder to stay at Ain Heet for twenty-four hours; if they had not received word from him by then, they were to assume he was dead and return to Kuwait.

Abdulaziz and his six companions rode to the baked-mud walls of Riyadh. There, they tied their camels a short distance away and used palm trunks as ladders to scale the city walls. Later in his life, on the frequent occasions when he was asked to retell this story, Abdulaziz himself would express surprise at how easy it had been to enter the city. The walls were unguarded, and the raiders had no difficulty in gaining entrance.

Abdulaziz, who had grown up in Riyadh and knew well the maze of narrow mud alleys, led his men silently to the center of the town, an area called Dira. In the center of Dira was Al-Masmak. Al-Masmak was a supposedly impenetrable fortress built by the Rashids for their governor. The fortress had only one gate, in which there was a postern or smaller door. The postern was so small that it forced a man to enter head first, thereby allowing the guard inside a chance to behead him before he had actually gained entry.

Abdulaziz knew the fortress would be impossible to take before daylight, when Ajlan's men would open the main gate, so he led his companions across a narrow square to where Governor Ajlan had a fortified house in which he kept his women. But this house was also securely locked.

Next door to the governor's harem was the house of a cattle merchant named Juwaisir. Abdulaziz knocked on his door, and after a short while a woman's voice answered by demanding to know who was there. Abdulaziz replied by saying that he had been sent by Governor Ajlan to buy two cows. He demanded to see the cattle merchant.

"You should be ashamed of yourself, son of a woman accursed," snapped Juwaisir's eldest daughter. "Anyone who knocks on a woman's door at this time of night is whoring! Go away!"

"Silence!" ordered Abdulaziz. "In the morning, I will inform the governor of this treatment, and he will rip open your father's throat."

Abdulaziz's threat must have been in keeping with the known habits of the Rashidi governor, since upon hearing it, Juwaisir flung open his door. Abdulaziz immediately seized him by the neck and threatened him into silence. The eldest daughter recognized the son of the exiled Emir Abdul Rahman and cried out a greeting.

Abdulaziz had only one plan, to cross from the roof of Juwaisir's house to the roof of Governor Ajlan's harem, then break into the harem and kill Ajlan while he lay with his women. However, when Abdulaziz got to the roof, he found the gap between the roofs too wide to jump across. Instead, he and his six companions leapt to the roof of an adjacent house, in which they found a man and his wife asleep in bed. Threatening the terrified couple with instant death, the raiders tied and gagged them and locked them securely in the cellar. At this point, Abdulaziz sent one of his men back to Ain Heet to bring the remainder of the men into Riyadh.

Ajlan's harem was some ten feet higher than the surrounding houses; Abdulaziz's men were forced to climb on one another's shoulders in order to get to the roof. Once on the roof, they pried open the roof door and silently entered the harem. Their objective was to seize the members of the household one by one to prevent the spreading of an alarm. This proved to be a successful tactic. Ajlan's slaves and concubines, terrified at the sight of the armed raiders, quickly identified the bedroom of their master.

Abdulaziz paused before the bedroom door and ordered another man to bring a candle. A moment later, the two men burst into Governor Ajlan's bedroom. There were two mounds beneath the bedclothes, and Abdulaziz raised his rifle to his shoulder, preparing to kill the Rashidi governor. The man with the candle ripped back the bedclothes, exposing two women—Ajlan's wife and his sister.

Abdulaziz lowered his rifle and silenced the now hysterical women by announcing who he was.

"What do you want?" demanded Ajlan's wife.

"Your husband, woman without shame, you have taken a Rashid."

"I am not a shameless woman," Ajlan's wife replied. "I only took a Rashid husband when you left us. What is your business here?"

"I have come to kill your husband."

After this brief exchange, Ajlan's wife vacillated between fear for her own welfare and a bravado that she shared with her husband. In her arrogance, Ajlan's wife provided Abdulaziz with not only knowledge of the governor's whereabouts and the strength of the garrison in Riyadh, but also with a remarkably detailed outline of her husband's usual morning routine.

"How can you hope to kill my husband?" she asked scornfully. "He sleeps in Al-Masmak with eighty armed men. He will not come out until after dawn." She went on to explain that after her husband left the fortress, he would cross the square to his harem, discover the raiders, and slaughter them all.

With this invaluable information, Abdulaziz and his men locked her and her sister with the other women of the household in the cellar and proceeded to dig a hole through the dried mud of the outer wall, allowing the rest of his men, coming from the oasis at Ain Heet, into the house.

Abdulaziz resigned himself to the fact that any attack would be futile until Ajlan had actually left Al-Masmak, so he and his men settled back to spend the remainder of the night eating dates, drinking coffee, praying, and plotting how to lure Ajlan out of the fortress.

Finally, the smallest man was chosen to be dressed up as a woman and open the door for the governor when the time came. The rest retired to an upstairs room with a view of the fortress gate to wait for the dawn call to prayer.

Almost in a staccato, the mournful chant began, and Abdulaziz and his men quickly set about saying their own devotions. Shortly, the fortress gate was opened, and the governor's slaves began to bring out the governor's horses. Whether sudden inspiration or simply foolish impulse seized Abdulaziz, we shall never know. The next thing his men knew was that their leader had grabbed his rifle and was running down the stairs towards the street, ordering his men to provide him with covering fire from the upstairs window.

By the time Abdulaziz had emerged from the harem, Governor Ajlan himself had come into the street with about a dozen armed men. The fortress gate had been closed behind them. Abdulaziz wasted no time. Rifle in hand, he charged at the Rashidi governor, screaming that he was Abdulaziz, son of Abdul Rahman, of the House al-Saud.

We shall never know why twelve armed soldiers should have panicked at the sight of one man charging, but nevertheless they did. The soldiers accompanying Ajlan fled back to the fortress gate and managed to scramble through the tiny postern door.

As in the climax of a Hollywood swashbuckler, Governor Ajlan stood his ground, drew his sword, and prepared to meet his nemesis. Ajlan lunged, but his sword flashed harmlessly over Abdulaziz's head. Abdulaziz threw his arm in front of his face and fired his rifle single-handed. Ajlan's sword fell to the ground and his wounded arm hung limply at his side. Ajlan had received a flesh wound in his right arm, but it was not enough to stop the Rashidi governor from dashing toward the tiny postern door.

Abdulaziz grabbed hold of the governor's leg and struggled with the desperate man. Ajlan gathered all his strength and kicked the Saudi leader in the abdomen. Winded and dizzied, Abdulaziz released his grip on the governor who again lunged for the postern door.

Had Ajlan made it through the postern door, the entire history of the Arabian peninsula might have been drastically altered. Unquestionably, Ajlan would have ordered his marksmen to the fortress battlements, where they would have had little difficulty in killing Abdulaziz in the street below.

However, a cousin of Abdulaziz's, Abdullah ibn-Jiluwi, hurled a spear at the retreating governor. The spear missed its target and lodged in the frame of the postern door (where its iron head can still be seen to this day). Seeing that his spear had missed, Abdullah ibn-Jiluwi threw himself at the postern door and just before the governor's men managed to slam it shut, he managed to wriggle through.

Perhaps the defenders of Al-Masmak thought that Abdullah ibn-Jiluwi was one of their own, or perhaps they were simply too confused by the sudden attack to act. Either way, they failed to decapitate him as he came through the postern door—a failure that would prove fatal to them and launch the Arabian peninsula into the modern age.

Abdullah ibn-Jiluwi immediately set about attacking the wounded governor and knocked Ajlan to the ground. He then seized Ajlan by the front of his *ghutra* (headdress), jerked the governor's head back, and severed his jugular vein. Others of Abdulaziz's followers wriggled through the postern door and managed to throw open the main gate. The remainder of Abdulaziz's men swarmed in, rifles barking and swords flashing in the light of early dawn.

There followed a bloody room-to-room fight for control of Al-Masmak. Outnumbered more than two to one, Abdulaziz's men fought savagely through the narrow corridors, hallways, towers, and courtyards of the fort. They succeeded in killing more than forty of the eighty soldiers garrisoned there. Some were shot, others died by the sword, still others were thrown from the battlements. Thirty-five of Ajlan's men surrendered and were locked in their own dungeon.

By the time the muezzin of the Eid Mosque began to climb the minaret to call the faithful to the noon prayer, Abdulaziz had already sent his men into the streets of Riyadh to proclaim that God's Will had been done and that the House al-Saud had returned to rule Riyadh.

This would seem to be the end of Abdulaziz's journey. He had, in a daring surprise attack, recaptured his birthright, the ancestral home of his family. However, like other historically significant journeys, the apparent end was but another beginning.

While glamorous, Abdulaziz's victory at Riyadh gained him little more than a reputation as a brave but irresponsible young man. Riyadh, by itself, was no military prize, a middle-sized town of baked-mud houses smack in the middle of an arid desert. It wasn't even as if Abdulaziz had won a decisive victory. He had taken the town by surprise, but he couldn't hold on to

Riyadh by using the same tactic. The question in everyone's mind was how long would it take ibn-Rashid to send his armies against Riyadh again.

Arabia, at this point, was not composed of states. It would not be until after the end of World War I, when the Europeans, particularly the British, would invent the concept of "mandates," that nationalism would raise its ugly head. At the turn of the century, Arabia knew no artificial cartographic boundaries.

While the British had some influence in Kuwait and Aden and the Ottomans were supplying the Rashids in Hail with arms, there was almost no outside influence in the interior desert—the terrain was apparently too hard for the teeth of colonialism.

The interior of Arabia was populated by drifting Bedouin tribes whose loyalties were as changeable as their settlements. The Bedouin was a master of the art of survival. He had to be. And if survival meant frequent shifts in loyalty, then the Bedouin, without any thought of shame or disgrace, would simply realign himself with someone whose chances of success seemed better.

As a boy, Abdulaziz had grown up with the Bedouins and knew only too well the difficult problem that faced him. The way to hold on to Riyadh was to unite the Bedouin tribes behind him. But how?

Unlike the popular conception of him in the West, the Bedouin of the Arabian desert is not a barbarian, nor is he a savage. He is a fiercely individualistic character, with extremely strong ties to his family, but one who recognizes no authority higher than the sheikh (which literally means "old man") of his tribe.

However, the Bedouins were not lawless. A strictly observed code of honor and behavior has existed in Arabia since the time of the Prophet. Some of this code comes from Islamic law; some predates it. Certain aspects of the code may appear crude or savage to the "civilized" Western mind, but the code of the desert was understood and accepted, and, most important, it made actions and reactions relatively predictable, which is, after all, the purpose of a "code."

Abdulaziz understood the code of the Bedouins, but he also understood that unity was contrary to their nature. They were people who rarely spoke about freedom because they were too busy exercising it. Abdulaziz understood that in order to unite the Bedouins, he would have to offer incentives. Material gain was part of the incentive he had in mind, but by itself this was not enough to influence the antimaterialistic Bedouins.

A greater incentive for the Bedouins was the thrill and excitement of a successful raid. At this point there were few forms of public entertainment on the Arabian peninsula other than raiding and storytelling, and most of the storytelling was about past raids and deeds of heroism.

Raiding had been raised above the level of mere banditry by the strictly observed code of Bedouin honor. Raiding had come to have a series of understood rules and regulations much like a sport, and a Bedouin would no more violate these rules than a proper English gentleman would clout an opponent with his cricket bat.

When a Bedouin tribe perceived it was either outnumbered or getting the worst of a battle, it would not hesitate to run away. This retreat would be accompanied by none of the disgrace that it would have elsewhere. It would be seen as merely common-sense adherence to the rules of Bedouin warfare.

The attackers would not take advantage of a retreat in order to butcher meaninglessly. The goal of a Bedouin raid was excitement and loot (this loot might include the women of an opponent's tribe, which rather strains the "sport" analogy), and when those were provided, slaughter became not only unnecessary but also undesirable.

Abdulaziz was, himself, the very image of the Bedouin hero—a self-confident, cunning, courageous leader whose reputation in battle preceded him from oasis campfire to oasis campfire. The story of his audacious attack on Riyadh spread across the desert as fast as a camel could gallop. With each retelling, the character of Abdulaziz grew larger and larger until a version of the story was almost certainly told in which the al-Saud leader defeated Riyadh single-handed.

But more important than the loot, the excitement of raiding, or his own reputation was the religious doctrine Abdulaziz provided the Bedouins. Wahhabiism embraced in large part a fatalistic doctrine that must have given the Bedouins an ordered, if not comforting, cosmology. The entire future was in the hands of an all-knowing, all-seeing, all-understanding Godhead. A warrior who fell in battle, doing the Will of Allah, gained immediate entrance to paradise.

Wahhabiism presented the Bedouins with a divine justification for raiding and looting and a common cause that fired them with ardor and zeal. Here, although unnamed as such, was the legendary *jihad*, the holy war to purge the corrupt and godless from the fold of the faithful.

It was not long before Abdulaziz and his men were riding forth from Riyadh, recruiting Bedouin warriors from the local tribes of the Nejd and raiding the caravans of ibn-Rashid.

It was seven months before ibn-Rashid moved his armies against Abdulaziz. The reason for this delay was that at the time of the fall of Riyadh, ibn-Rashid and his armies were three hundred miles away, on the border of Kuwait, attempting to oust Sheikh Mubarak from power. Then summer came to the peninsula, when only fools and Ottomans attempted to move armies across the blazing one-hundred-twenty-degree heat of the desert. As history records, fools and Ottomans lived short lives on the peninsula.

When ibn-Rashid finally did attack, it was not at Riyadh but at a small oasis-village some sixty kilometers southwest of Riyadh called Dilam. The battle that took place was entirely atypical and clearly illustrates the military cunning of the twenty-two-year-old Wahhabi leader.

Traditionally, Bedouin armies would assemble their horses and camels several hundred meters apart in the desert. Any safe area along the sidelines of the battle would be set aside for the women and children of the warring tribes, who would act as a cheering squad, alternately shouting encouragement to their own men, beating camel-skin drums, and roaring threats of doom at the enemy. At a given signal, the two armies would charge at each other, each warrior shouting his individual battle cry, which might have been his family name, the name of his father, or the name of a favorite sister.

The charging wave of horse and camel riders would fire their rifles until they had become too intermingled with the enemy to risk rifle fire. None of the Bedouins wore uniforms or any other form of identification, so that in the confusion of battle it was just as likely to shoot one's own father as it was the enemy. Once the warring tribes had actually met, swords and daggers were employed in close combat. One can easily imagine the din and confusion of such combat—the clouds of thick dust mingling with gunpowder smoke, the bloodthirsty battle cries of the warriors, the taunting cheers of the women, accompanied as often as not with a steady, frenzied, deafening drumbeat.

However, the picture of the battle between Abdulaziz and ibn-Rashid at Dilam is very different. Ibn-Rashid's armies vastly outnumbered those of Abdulaziz; the Wahhabi leader chose not to ride out into the desert and face his enemy but to keep his men behind the village walls. He issued the strange order "to spare no ammunition in destroying the godless Rashids." The order was strange in that the only thing scarcer than water in the desert was ammunition.

Ibn-Rashid's armies approached four times. Each time they were driven back by the abundant and wasteful rifle fire of Abdulaziz's men. However, they did not charge a fifth time; in accepted Bedouin tradition, they retreated. Ibn-Rashid, perceiving himself to be outmatched, ordered his armies back to Kuwait to renew their attacks on Sheikh Mubarak.

Had ibn-Rashid ordered his armies to attack a fifth time, he would have had no trouble in defeating and slaughtering Abdulaziz's men. They were virtually out of ammunition. While in retrospect the sympathetic might attribute Abdulaziz's military success to craft and cunning and the more objective to a desperate gamble, Abdulaziz would have unquestionably called it *maktoob* (literally, "it is written"; that is, the Will of God).

It would be another decade before Abdulaziz would finally defeat ibn-Rashid—a decade of battles, cunning, duplicity, and organization. And it was organization that filled the young Wahhabi leader's thoughts at this crucial time. The Bedouins of the central Nejd had never been organized except for brief periods of time. Abdulaziz set about this formidable task in several ways. First he made raiding under the al-Saud banner appear profitable and divinely inspired. Second, but no less important, he began his career as a husband. Actually, by the time he attacked Riyadh, he already had two wives, the first of whom had died. However, now faced with the problem of unifying the Bedouins, Abdulaziz threw himself into marriage with an enthusiasm that he matched only in battle.

The Koran is very strict about the number of wives a man may take. He may take up to four wives as long as he treats them absolutely equally. As a devout Muslim, Abdulaziz was bound by this law and never broke it. However, divorce for men in Arabia is a simple process of announcing to one's wife "I divorce you" and repeating it three times. Divorce also carries none of the stigma that it does in the West.

Abdulaziz married and divorced women with a frequency that might shock the Pope but certainly shocked no one in Arabia, including the women he divorced. Some of his marriages were ephemeral, lasting but a single night; others lasted many years and produced many children.

It should be stated that the wives he divorced were treated equally well. They were provided houses and allowances and had the prestige of having been married to the future king of Arabia. Many went on to marry other men; others, who had born him children, were given palaces in Riyadh.

Many years later, in 1930, while Abdulaziz was talking with Henry St. John Philby, the peculiar Englishman who became his lifelong friend, he announced that he had had one hundred thirty-five virgins and about a hundred other women. Abdulaziz went on to say that he had decided to limit himself in the future to two new wives a year.[2] If the figures are accurate and if Abdulaziz kept to his resolution, his lifetime total of wives would be close to three hundred.

---

[2]For a more complete and very readable biography of Abdulaziz al-Saud, see *The Desert King* by David Howarth.

While a Wahhabi puritan, he never allowed his puritanism to interfere with his pleasures. Whenever he left Riyadh to visit local tribal sheikhs, he divorced one of his four wives in order to leave room for the daughters or sisters of his hosts. Over a meal of *kabsa* (boiled mutton and rice), squatting on Oriental carpets within the black Bedouin goat-hair tents, an agreement would be settled upon, and Abdulaziz would withdraw to his tent to await his new bride. If the new bride pleased him she might accompany him back to Riyadh; if not, she was returned to her father or brother loaded with gifts and presents.

What may strike the Western reader as strange is that the faces of many of his wives were unknown to Abdulaziz. It was common practice in Arabia for a bride to wait a respectable period of time before unveiling herself before her husband. A woman's naked face was and still remains an extremely private sight, reserved for one's immediate family and one's husband. Since many of Abdulaziz's marriages lasted no more than a single night, it is probable that many of his wives came to his bed and left the following morning without ever removing their veils.

The next twenty years in the life of Abdulaziz were spent securing the territory that had traditionally been ruled by his family, extending his influence over the Bedouins, and fighting with the Rashid family.

Like most successful conquerors, Abdulaziz understood that an army without a cause was as impotent as an army without weapons. He correspondingly gave his armies the greatest cause that man has ever fought and died for—the Will of God. It was a situation in which it was impossible for the Wahhabi warrior to lose. They were blessed while they lived, for they were spreading the purified faith; and if they were to die, they would be instantly transported to paradise. Thus the Wahhabi warriors were not only fearless in battle, but they were also openly and actively searching for martyrdom.

Rebellions did occur from time to time, and for the first three decades of the twentieth century these uprisings were a constant source of concern to the House al-Saud. It is interesting to note how Abdulaziz handled these tribes in revolt.

If the rebellion were minor—a local sheikh who refused to pay tribute to Abdulaziz—the Wahhabi leader would invite the sheikh to a *majlis* (meeting or conversation) where gifts would be presented and charm employed. Most everyone who came to meet Abdulaziz, Bedouin and Westerner alike, agreed that Abdulaziz was a remarkably charming man. In part, this charm came from his almost total candor.

Even in duplicity, Abdulaziz was candid, and it was this straightforwardness that earned him the respect and friendship of Sir Percy Cox, the British political agent in Kuwait, various American oilmen, and, in later years, Winston Churchill and Franklin D. Roosevelt.

If the rebellion were more serious, Abdulaziz would order prompt military action, having his army surround a town or village and then lay siege to it. When the village finally surrendered, as they all did, Abdulaziz would have the leaders of the revolt paraded before him. The accepted punishment for treason was decapitation, so it was with enormous surprise that these doomed men heard Abdulaziz forgiving them, presenting them with gifts, and inviting them to Riyadh as his guests. On more than one occasion, an overwhelmed traitor had, upon hearing Abdulaziz's merciful announcement, fallen on his knees and declared his renewed loyalty to the House al-Saud.

The Wahhabi leader had great patience with the capriciousness of the Bedouins of central Arabia. He understood that they had no tradition of loyalty to anything larger than their own families. He also understood that much of whatever loyalty they felt would be directed toward him personally rather than at any European concept of nationalism. Thus he was patient and magnanimous, cunning and shrewd in battle, but merciful in victory.

There is only one recorded incidence of Abdulaziz's taking coldblooded revenge. In 1910 a major uprising occurred in the south of the Nejd on the border of the Rub al Khali. These same sheikhs had already revolted against Abdulaziz and had already been pardoned once. The second uprising prompted swift action by the Wahhabi leader. He massed his army and marched south, driving the rebels into a walled town.

The walls of the town were too thick to be breached by the type of weapons the Wahhabis had at their disposal, so Abdulaziz announced that he had mined the fortress within the town and could blow it up at will. His threat had no substance to it, but the possibility was enough to make the rebels surrender. Abdulaziz then took the rebel leaders to Riyadh, where they enjoyed his hospitality before returning to their respective homes.

However, it was not long before these same rebels, the *Araif*[3] (some of their leaders were blood cousins of Abdulaziz), announced the formation of a rival government. Again Abdulaziz was forced to mass his army and march south. Again he had little difficulty in defeating the rebels and capturing the leadership of the *Araif*. Some of the leaders did manage to escape to Oman and some to the Hejaz (the western coast of the peninsula), where they received sanctuary from the Hashemite sherif of Mecca.

This was the third time these sheikhs had rebelled against Abdulaziz's authority. Twice they had flaunted the mercy and hospitality of the Wahhabi leader. Abdulaziz had a dozen of the rebel leaders paraded in public wearing neck manacles. Shortly thereafter, the rebels were beheaded in their own marketplace in full view of their families and friends. It is reported that Abdulaziz pardoned his cousin, but only after the cousin had watched the heads of his fellow rebels fall and the double-edged scimitar had been readied over his own neck.

The pardoned cousin, whose name was Saud, was moved to Riyadh and housed at Abdulaziz's expense. In the years to come Saud would meet Nura, Abdulaziz's sister—the same sister who had shared a camel saddlebag with her brother as they escaped from the Rashids in Riyadh. Saud would fall in love with Nura and petition Abdulaziz to allow him to marry her. Abdulaziz granted him permission, and thus the wayward Saud eventually became the king's brother-in-law.

By 1912 Abdulaziz's cunning combination of military might and mercy had succeeded in bringing peace and stability to the

---

[3]*Araif* is an Arabic word which is most often applied to camels that have been retaken after having been stolen.

central Arabian desert. It was at this time that Abdulaziz launched his most spectacular—and most controversial—plan, the founding of the Ikhwan.

In years to come, the very mention of the word "Ikhwan" would bring fear into the eyes of Arabs from the Red Sea to the deserts of Iraq. A rumor that the Ikhwan were in the saddle would cause whole villages to erupt into panicked flight. Literally, *ikhwan* means "brotherhood," but few fraternal organizations were like this one.

A sympathetic historian has called the founding of the Ikhwan Abdulaziz's attempt at organizing an army of national defense. Less sympathetically, but more realistically, the Ikhwan were bloodthirsty, fanatical murderers who killed, plundered, and, on occasion, raped in the name of God. They were characterized by a lunatic zeal and a complete lack of mercy.

In their later years, the Ikhwan had become so psychotically frenzied that even the traditional Bedouin code of honor meant nothing to them.

This was not, of course, what Abdulaziz envisioned in 1912. He saw the Ikhwan as the warriors of God and country. He formed various settlements in the desert where young Bedouin men were fed a steady diet of Wahhabi puritanism and practical training in the arts of desert warfare. In a remarkably short time, Abdulaziz had what he wanted: a crack fighting force equal to any on the peninsula.

At this time, there were only three other bona fide armies in Arabia. In the north, in their ancestral home at Hail, the Rashid family had their army garrisoned. In the west, in that coastal area along the Red Sea called the Hejaz, the sherif of Mecca had his British-supported armies. In the east were the armies of the Ottoman Empire.

Quite wisely, Abdulaziz allowed the desert to defeat the Ottomans. Unaccustomed to the terrain and untrained in desert survival, the Turks soon found themselves in retreat from sunstroke, thirst, and cholera.

It is likely that the Ikhwan could have conquered all of the Arabian peninsula in a very short time if it had not been for the advent of World War I. In reality, the Great War meant very little in the Arabian desert, which no European power had thought worthy of colonizing. However, Abdulaziz had made several British friends, among them Sir Percy Cox and a rather adventurous young man named William Shakespear.

The Wahhabi leader came to trust these men and made the mistake of believing he could trust the government they represented as well. It was a natural mistake for a man who was the government of central Arabia, whose word was the word of the government, a man completely ignorant of the spineless bureaucrats who pushed pencils in Delhi and Whitehall.

Until he died, Abdulaziz would never come to understand the Western politician. When a promise made to him personally by Franklin Roosevelt was blithely broken by his successor, Harry Truman, Abdulaziz quite naturally, and not without justification, felt betrayed.

During World War I, the British were actively supporting any Arab force that was willing to fight against the Ottomans. Whitehall decided that if the peninsula was going to be united against Turkey, it would be under the rule of the Hashemite sherif of Mecca, a vainglorious man named Hussein.

In retrospect, it is relatively easy to criticize the judgment of Whitehall. However, one must remember that Whitehall had a great many things on its mind during the turbulent years of the war, and in all probability the least important was the fate of an arid wasteland called Arabia.

Nevertheless, the British did support the sherif of Mecca with arms and money and sent him a young man from the Arab Bureau in Iraq named T. E. Lawrence, whose military genius was unquestionable but whose conclusions on Arabian politics were more often than not erroneous.

On the other hand, the Rashid family was supported by the Ottomans, and the British openly encouraged Abdulaziz to attack their ancestral home at Hail. Abdulaziz would have probably chosen to attack the sherif of Mecca, whom he considered to have desecrated the Holy Cities of Mecca and Medina, had it not been for strong British opposition to such a plan.

The Ikhwan spent the duration of World War I consolidating their power, suppressing the occasional rebellion, and promoting the spread of Wahhabiism. However, even during the years of the Great War, it was already obvious to some clear-headed individuals that the Ikhwan were out of control.

By the end of the war, relations between Abdulaziz and the sherif of Mecca had deteriorated over possession of a certain tract of land that bordered on both the Hejaz and the Nejd. Letters claiming possession of the land were exchanged, followed by letters warning of military action.

The British remained convinced that the ruling power in Arabia was the pompous sherif of Mecca and correspondingly sided with him against Abdulaziz. Early in 1919 the sherif of Mecca sent seven thousand soldiers, under the command of his son, Emir Abdullah (later the king of Transjordan) into the disputed area. The sherif's army had no trouble in taking the town of Turabah and declaring themselves in control of the area.

However, during the night of March 25, 1919, the Ikhwan arrived outside the walls of Turabah. They surrounded the town and attacked without warning. Few battles in Arabia have been more fierce or more bloody. The Ikhwan, fired with religious zeal, were ruthless.

When dawn came, more than six thousand corpses covered the battlefield. Amir Abdullah had escaped with a handful of his men and was in full retreat towards Mecca. Soon after dawn, Abdulaziz arrived at Turabah. It is reported that the future king of Arabia wept openly at the sight of the carnage and ordered his men not to march on Taif, a strategic mountain town which currently serves as the summer seat of government. The only thing that was unexpected at the massacre in Turabah was that the Ikhwan obeyed Abdulaziz and did not continue their march of terror. For the moment, at least, Taif was spared.

Soon after this, trouble broke out on the border of Kuwait. The border had never been carefully defined, and both Abdulaziz and Sheikh Mubarak made claims, like the opening price of a merchant in an Arabian *suq*, that were vast exaggerations of anything that could be politically or historically justified. Thus the Ikhwan came to see action in northeast Arabia against the forces of Mubarak. Again the British sided with Abdulaziz's enemy.

This time there was no massacre. Fortunately for the people of Kuwait, Sheikh Mubarak died, and his son, Sheikh Ahmad al-Jaber, who had certainly heard of the carnage at Turabah, negotiated a peace settlement with Abdulaziz. Out of this peace treaty came the creation of the Neutral Zone, still a cartographic reality today, which became famous during the 1960s when massive oil reserves were discovered there.

Even as 1920 approached, Abdulaziz did not wish to alienate the British completely, and so he turned his anger away from the sherif of Mecca and directed it at his old archenemy, the House al-Rashid.

The House al-Rashid had never been a close family. In fact, fratricide was the rule rather than the exception in the Rashidi capital of Hail. In the entire hundred years of the nineteenth century, only two male Rashids were purported to have died of natural causes. The other fifteen or so had murdered each other in seemingly endless disputes over power.

True to the family tradition that Rashidi blood was more plentiful, if not thicker, than water in the northern desert, ibn-Rashid (the son of the ibn-Rashid who attacked Abdulaziz at Dilam in 1903) was murdered by a cousin during the first month of 1920.

While target shooting in the desert, ibn-Rashid made the fatal error of turning his back on his companion, who seized the opportunity and fired point-blank into the older man's head. The ambitious cousin was promptly hacked into pieces by the late ruler's still-loyal slaves. However, this murder left the position of Rashidi leadership in the hands of an eighteen-year-old weakling who inspired confidence in no one. Thus the House al-Rashid was divided against itself.

Abdulaziz was already leading the Ikhwan north toward Hail when he heard the news of this internal disorder. It was almost too good to be true. The eighteen-year-old ruler had barricaded himself in his fortress and had ordered the arrest of the one member of the Rashid family capable of mounting an effective defense, Emir (Prince) Muhammed ibn-Talal al-Rashid. The closer the Ikhwan came to Hail, the greater the consternation grew within the Rashidi capital until finally, judging that his chances of survival were better at the hands of Abdulaziz than at the hands of his own family, the eighteen-year-old Rashidi ruler disguised himself as a woman, made a nocturnal escape from Hail, and threw himself upon the mercy of the Wahhabi leader.

Emir Muhammed ibn-Talal al-Rashid was immediately freed from jail and attempted to organize a last-minute defense of the city. An indecisive battle followed, and the Rashid army was forced to withdraw within the city walls of Hail. Again Abdulaziz was faced with the problem of breaching thick baked-mud walls without the aid of artillery.

This time Abdulaziz did not threaten to blow up the city. Instead he employed a few well-placed gold coins, tempting a Rashidi captain conveniently to forget to lock the gate he was supposed to be guarding. Hail fell through treachery, and the Ikhwan took control of all of the city except the Rashid palace within a matter of hours.

The siege of the Rashid palace lasted several days. Emir Muhammed ibn-Talal was not a fool, nor was he a coward. He must have realized that the Rashid family was doomed, but still he held on to a slender thread of hope that with luck the Rashids would survive.

On the fifth day of the siege of the palace, Abdulaziz sent word to Emir Muhammed that if the Rashids surrendered they would be pardoned. It is a credit to Abdulaziz's own reputation that he was believed and that his offer was accepted.

We have an eyewitness account to the surrender of the Rashid family after more than a decade of war with the al-Sauds.[4] Abdulaziz assembled his army and in full view of the Ikhwan addressed Emir Muhammed: "I wish to assure you that you are as my sons and that you will live in Riyadh just as I and my sons live, no more, no less. Your clothes, food, and horses will be like mine, if not better. There will be nothing in my pal-

---

[4]Amin Rihani, *Nejd and Its Dependencies*, London, n.d., p. 294.

ace or in the country that, if you want it, you cannot have. If any one of you has any doubt about what I say, let him speak."

There was dead silence, and Abdulaziz continued: "By God, O Rashids, the harm that touches you moves my heart before my tongue to help you. And as for you, Muhammed ibn-Talal al-Rashid, consider yourself from now on as a member of my household; whatever I possess of means to defend you [will be yours] if the need arises—not only [for] you, but [for] all the Rashid family." At this point Abdulaziz extended his hand to the defeated Rashid leader, who took it without hesitation. Muhammed ibn-Talal al-Rashid then ceremoniously kissed Abdulaziz on the bridge of his nose and then on the forehead, exhibiting before both his own people and the Ikhwan his loyalty to the House al-Saud.

Abdulaziz defeated the people of Hail both with his military might and with his generosity. He used the food that was destined for the Ikhwan to feed the hungry of Hail. He took the favorite widow of the murdered Rashid ruler, ibn-Rashid, as a wife and adopted all the Rashid children as his own (this may be the single largest adoption in history, since there were said to be about a thousand Rashid children in all).

Thus the Rashids ceased to be serious rivals to the leadership of Arabia.

Although the Rashids were never able to resurrect their former power, Hail, the old Rashidi capital, has again become a center of controversy in recent times. For in this city a boy named Abdullah was born to an illiterate Bedouin woman named Bint-Asi al-Shureimi. The father was none other than Abdulaziz himself. The boy has grown into a man and today represents a significant threat to the future of Saudi Arabia and the Western industrialized world. Abdullah is the second deputy prime minister, commander of the National Guard, and only two steps removed from the crown. (More about the enigmatic Prince Abdullah later.)

The defeat of the House al-Rashid meant that Abdulaziz could finally turn his attention toward Mecca and the despised sherif. Perhaps at this point it would be more correct to address Abdulaziz as "Sultan," since that was the formal title bestowed

on him by the Ulema (religious authorities) after the defeat of
Hail. It was not the first title the Wahhabi leader had had. He was
born an emir (prince), and during the war the British, the great
white traders dazzling the natives with rhinestones, made him
a knight in order to prevent him from attacking the Hashemite
sherif of Mecca. But titles meant little to the Wahhabi leader, and
until the moment he died even the lowest Bedouin had the
right to address their king by his first name.

In contrast, the sherif of Mecca loved titles. In fact, it was his
craving after titles that brought about his defeat. Like other fool-
ishly ambitious men before and after him, the sherif fed on
dreams without substance. His moment of glory had already
passed, and in actuality little of the glory belonged to him but
rather to T. E. Lawrence. Nevertheless, Hussein, sherif of Mecca,
had a grand dream of lording over an Arab empire that would
stretch from Cairo to Baghdad. His two sons, reluctantly supported by the British, were already ruling in Transjordan and
Iraq.

The sherif of Mecca had already infuriated Abdulaziz by proclaiming himself King of Arabia in October 1917. However, annoyance turned to fury when, in the early part of 1924, Kemal
Atatürk, the postwar ruler of Turkey, abolished the Ottoman
caliphate, and the sherif of Mecca promptly proclaimed himself
the new caliph as well.

For hundreds of years the caliphs, the religious leaders of the
entire Islamic world, had been the sultans of Turkey. The caliph
was the successor of the Prophet Muhammed and the spiritual
leader of all Muslims.

It would be overly simplistic to draw an analogy between the
caliphate and the papacy. While both enjoyed substantial political power, the religious influence of the caliph was, at best, questionable. However, it was traditionally the right of the caliph
alone to declare *jihad*, the holy war to which every Muslim
everywhere in the world must respond.

As the Ottoman Empire declined, so did the influence of the
caliphate. More and more the office had become concerned
with nationalistic issues rather than with providing any core of

unity for the Islamic world. So when, in 1924, the sherif of Mecca declared himself the new caliph, the vast majority of the Muslim world simply refused to support him. They saw his proclamation for what it was, a bid to extend his political power beyond the borders of the Hejaz.

Mecca, under the rule of the sherif, had become as corrupt as it had been before the coming of the Prophet. The main occupation of the residents of the city was bilking the thousands of pilgrims who made the annual hajj.

Prostitutes walked the streets. Thieves and confidence men made those same streets dangerous after dark. Even outside the city itself, there was no safety for the devout pilgrim. Local Bedouin tribes, who had previously been paid not to raid pilgrim caravans on their way to Mecca, were once again raiding and robbing.

With the Ulema in a rage over the sherif's proclaiming himself caliph and the Ikhwan as restless as ever, Abdulaziz had little choice but to order his armies into the saddle. But this order was not given without some misgivings.

The Ikhwan, at this point, are said to have numbered more than twenty-five thousand and could be totally mobilized within ninety-six hours.

The size of the Ikhwan provided its own problems. The larger it grew, the more difficult it was for a single man to exercise authority over it. Local sheikhs from once powerful tribes were beginning to use the Ikhwan for their own ends. Abdullah ibn-Jiluwi, the cousin of Abdulaziz who had killed Governor Ajlan some twenty-two years before and who was now governor of the eastern province of Al Hasa, made a special trip to Riyadh to warn Abdulaziz about the growing danger of the Ikhwan. We do not know what Abdulaziz's response was, but he still needed the Ikhwan and gambled that as long as he could keep them in battle and victorious, they would stay loyal to him.

The Ikhwan rode west, growing in strength and number and confidence with every village they passed until finally they camped on the outskirts of Taif. Taif was, and is to this day, the summer resort for the wealthy of Jeddah and Mecca. During the summer, both Jeddah and Mecca become unpleasantly humid and hot, but Taif, located in the mountains, has a relatively mild climate, and its large villas and palaces are surrounded by lush gardens.

Abdulaziz had sent the Ikhwan ahead of him under the command of a psychotic individual named ibn-Humaid. Ibn-Humaid was impatient. Abdulaziz was still two weeks' camel journey behind the Ikhwan, so ibn-Humaid ordered his men to attack the city.

The sherif's soldiers deserted Taif, the sherif's son, Ali, leading the retreat. What followed was an Ikhwan-style conquest—in other words, a massacre. The Ikhwan broke into houses and threatened the inhabitants until they handed over their money. They beheaded old men and boys and were amused by the women, whose lack of faith in paradise caused them to scream at the sight of their fathers and sons being murdered. The imams of Taif were murdered while they prayed in their own mosque.

The Ikhwan then spent the remainder of the night slaughtering most of the males in the city and stealing everything that could possibly be moved. In all, some four hundred people were reported to have been butchered in that night.

Two days later, the few remaining survivors managed to escape from Taif and made their way to Mecca, taking with them stories of the massacre. Panic erupted in Mecca and Jeddah. Suddenly all the fears about the Ikhwan were confirmed. Terrified people thronged the road out of Mecca. Thousands of people from Jeddah bought passage of ships going to Egypt.

When Abdulaziz heard about the massacre in Taif, he was furious. Immediately, the Wahhabi leader sent messengers racing across the desert on camels to order ibn-Humaid to halt the killing and looting and to forbid the Ikhwan from entering the Holy City of Mecca.

There was no need for the Ikhwan to march on Mecca. The Holy City had already fallen—not by armed invasion but through sheer terror. Among those unceremoniously fleeing Mecca was the sherif himself, who filled several jerrycans with gold sovereigns, drove to Jeddah, and then set sail to Aqaba in the north. From there the British granted him exile in Cyprus.

Four Ikhwan appeared at the gates of Mecca the day following the sherif's departure. They were dressed in *ihram*, the prescribed costume for a pilgrim—two seamless pieces of coarse white cloth, one draped about the waist, the other slung across the chest. The four Ikhwan made no attempt to enter the city but, on the instructions of Abdulaziz, proclaimed the safety and security of all those "who surrendered to God and Abdulaziz." The people who remained in Mecca, deserted by their ruler and fully aware of the fate of the people of Taif, threw open their gates and welcomed the Ikhwan as the purifiers of Islam. This time there was no carnage.

The Ikhwan, however, did set about purifying the Holy City. They destroyed tombs, ornamental mosques, and the shrines that had grown up over the years. They also destroyed all representations of the human form and confiscated and burned all musical instruments. These are forbidden in fundamentalist Islam, and the Ikhwan's iconoclasm was therefore admirable in the eyes of the puritans.

Two weeks later, on October 13, 1924, Abdulaziz himself, dressed in *ihram*, rode into Mecca, as much a humble pilgrim making hajj as the conquerer and unifier of Arabia.

The fall of Jeddah on the Red Sea took just over a year. This was not because the Ikhwan had become any less bloodthirsty or that any fight remained in the sherif's army. The fall of Jeddah took over a year because Abdulaziz was reluctant to attack it, since it housed many foreign diplomats, and the Wahhabi leader was fully aware that after unifying the peninsula he would need outside assistance in ruling his virtually penniless desert kingdom.

The siege of Jeddah dragged on through late November 1925. With supply routes to the city cut by the Ikhwan, the people of Jeddah were reduced to near starvation. Begging for water became common in the city.

One foreign diplomat commented that the one good thing about the long siege was that it had cleaned the streets of camel dung. The diplomat was unaware that the undigested corn in the camel dung formed a large part of the diet of the city's poor during this period.

By December, Ali, the son of the sherif of Mecca, had agreed to surrender the city on two conditions: first, that the bloodthirsty Ikhwan not be allowed to enter it, and second, that he and his family be given safe passage out of Arabia. Abdulaziz granted both conditions, and within a matter of days Abdulaziz rode into Jeddah, as ruler of a kingdom that stretched from the Arabian Gulf to the beaches of the Red Sea.

In January 1926 the religious leaders of Mecca, Medina, and Jeddah met. They proclaimed Abdulaziz ibn–Abdul Rahman al-Saud king of the Hejaz. It was the first time in more than one hundred and fifty years that anyone had called a member of the House al-Saud "king."

Abdulaziz spent two years in Mecca. During this time he devoted himself to the all-important business of bringing all the Hejaz under his control. His third son, a young man by the name of Faisal, who would later lead Saudi Arabia through one of its most difficult times, was appointed governor of the Hejaz.

The chief problem that existed was making the pilgrim routes to Mecca safe from Bedouin raiding. This was a slow, painful process, since the Bedouins of the area had considered it their God-given right to rob caravans that traversed the pilgrim routes. Characteristically, Abdulaziz tempered his ruthlessness with an equal portion of generosity—subsidizing the Bedouins so as to make their banditry unnecessary. However, if a tribe continued to disobey him, he took what he considered necessary action. One such "necessary action" resulted in the slaughter of some two hundred Bedouins at the hands of the Ikhwan.

However, the two years he spent ensuring the security of the pilgrim routes were at the expense of the Nejd, the home of the ever-restless Ikhwan. After the massacre at Taif, Abdulaziz had lost whatever confidence he had had in the Ikhwan; remembering the warning given him by Abdullah ibn-Jiluwi, he sent the majority of them home to the central desert. Whether or not Abdulaziz actually believed this would be the end of the Ikhwan is an interesting question. It is most probable that, like most people confronted with truly insoluble problems, Abdulaziz chose simply to ignore the issue and deal with something that could be solved.

Intoxicated with the successes they had achieved in the Hejaz, the Ikhwan could not bring themselves to return to the life of nomadic Bedouins. They had become God's warriors. They had been given a destiny that was larger and far more grand than merely herding camels and goats from oasis to oasis. Some historians argue that Abdulaziz should have recognized the monster he had created after the massacre at Taif and should simply have put the beast to merciful, eternal sleep.

Due to Abdulaziz's order forbidding the tribes of the Nejd to raid each other, the Ikhwan had to look elsewhere for their prey. They found as victims non-Wahhabi shepherds in the northern area of Arabia that borders Iraq. Several years earlier, Abdulaziz and the British had agreed on an arbitrary border between Arabia and Iraq. Until that time, the whole area had been a Bedouin no man's land where tribe raided tribe with a regularity that ensured that the same camel might change hands four or five times in a year, sometimes ending up in the possession of its original owner.

During 1924 and 1925 the Ikhwan made numerous raids across the imaginary line the British had drawn, absconding with sheep and goats and leaving in their wake the mutilated corpses of hundreds of Iraqi shepherds and a cacophony of lamenting women. In no way were the Ikhwan traditional Bedouin raiders. The Ikhwan were out to murder.

By the end of 1925 the Ikhwan had wreaked such havoc among the pastoral people of northern Arabia that the mere rumor of an impending raid was enough to send thousands of men, women, and children into panicked flight. Traveling no faster than their flocks of sheep and goats, these shepherds had little chance of escaping the mounted Ikhwan.

The raids, led by ibn-Humaid and the equally ruthless Sheikh al-Duwaish, followed a common pattern. Several thousand Ikhwan, mounted on camels, would suddenly appear and attack the shepherds without warning. The shepherds would make a vain attempt to save themselves by sacrificing a portion of their flocks. Ignoring the livestock, the Ikhwan would race after the terrified shepherds, cutting them down by the score and leaving the desert strewn with bloody corpses.

These border massacres might have continued indefinitely had it not been for an Englishman named Glubb. Despite his rather odd name, John Glubb (later known as Pasha Glubb) was in many ways the ideal of what the British liked the rest of the world to believe they really were. Glubb was a gentleman of the old school, regarding a rough-and-tumble tussle as perfectly acceptable as long as it was kept within honorable limits.

The Ikhwan, of course, knew no such honorable limits, and Glubb responded to their raids much as might an amateur boxer who suddenly finds his opponent's teeth sunk into his arm.

While still in the British army, Glubb unofficially mobilized a small British force to counter the Ikhwan threat. Despite the fact that Glubb's small force was mechanized, it did not have much immediate success against the Ikhwan. Glubb's initial failure was due to two important factors. First, the area that the British force was trying to patrol was too large for their meager numbers. Second, because the British were acting in an unofficial capacity, they could not call in reinforcements. More often than not, Glubb would be notified of a massacre only after it had taken place and after the Ikhwan had withdrawn from Iraqi soil.

It is relatively easy to poke fun at Glubb as the rather eccentric British adventurer who complained that the Ikhwan raids "weren't quite sporting." However, Glubb was far from an armchair moralist. His affection for the defenseless Iraqi shepherds caused him to resign his commission in the British army and take command of an Iraqi company charged with the task of repelling the Ikhwan. Even here Glubb was outnumbered by the hordes under al-Duwaish and ibn-Humaid, but the Englishman began to build an intelligence network which in later years allowed him to respond faster to the Ikhwan menace. Glubb's masterstroke, however, was convincing the Iraqi government to build a police outpost on the border.

Actually the police outpost wasn't on the border at all, but about eighty kilometers within Iraq. The location of the outpost didn't make much difference though, since the only man who knew where the border was, was Glubb himself. The Ikhwan did not know or care. Abdulaziz had seen a pencil line on a map and nothing more. The Iraqi government knew of the existence of a border but had no idea of where it was located.

For the six months prior to the construction of the police barracks, the Ikhwan had been relatively quiet, due in part to Abdulaziz's order that all raids on Iraq should cease. The construction of the police barracks was an open provocation, an irresistible target for the volatile Ikhwan. It is probable that Glubb foresaw this; it was this provocation, coupled with the "international incident" sure to follow, that he desired.

Predictably, the Ikhwan attacked and massacred the construction workers. However, this raid was somewhat different from those in the past. Glubb had succeeded by the raid in provoking the Ikhwan to openly defy an order from Abdulaziz. Glubb knew that the only force strong enough to destroy the Ikhwan was the force controlled by its creator.

If Glubb expected Abdulaziz to rise against the Ikhwan, he was disappointed, for Abdulaziz not only refrained from attacking the Ikhwan, he even defended the Brotherhood's right to attack hostile military outposts in a supposedly demilitarized area. But despite what Abdulaziz said publicly, there can be no question that the Ikhwan were again haunting him. His authority had been ignored. It is also very likely that the Wahhabi leader had heard the rumor that al-Duwaish and ibn-Humaid had made a secret agreement to depose Abdulaziz and divide Arabia between them.

Glubb was not idle. He trained the Iraqi shepherds to defend themselves against the Ikhwan. Glubb knew desert warfare and taught the shepherds to pitch their tents in a defensible pattern, how to hobble their livestock, and how to retreat so as to provide themselves with maximum protection.

Most important, Glubb widened his ring of spies, and his intelligence on Ikhwan activities grew more accurate. In many cases, Glubb was able to warn the shepherds in advance of an actual raid. But these tactics were all by nature defensive, and it was clear that no defensive maneuver would ever destroy the Ikhwan.

In early 1929 a large caravan of merchants, Bedouins, and camels began a journey from Kuwait to Egypt. The caravan was entirely Wahhabi, and all were loyal followers of Abdulaziz. They were aware of the problems that existed along the border, but as loyal Wahhabis they expected no trouble from the Ikhwan. The caravan, ten days' journey out of Kuwait, camped less than sixty miles from the imaginary line that separated Arabia and Iraq.

That same day, the Ikhwan, led by ibn-Humaid, launched a massive attack on the Iraqi shepherds. However, Glubb's spies had managed to forewarn him of the attack, and the shepherds escaped. The battle-frenzied Ikhwan found the oasis empty. Their disappointment was unbearable; they turned their blood-crazed attention to the nearest living things—the caravan of merchants and Bedouins.

The caravan was attacked with a vengeance. The Ikhwan set about slaughtering the males. Most of the men were shot or trampled beneath the hooves of the raiders' camels. The boys were chased and put to the sword. Babies were grabbed from their mothers' arms; their clothes were torn off, their genitalia examined, and, if male, their throats cut. When the Ikhwan finally rode off, the only survivers were women wandering aimlessly among the corpses of their men, their children, and their camels.

What might have been excusable had the victims been Iraqi shepherds was now intolerable, for the butchered were Wahhabis and loyal subjects of Abdulaziz.

Abdulaziz massed an army of still loyal Bedouins and immediately started the march north. At the oasis of Sibilla, Abdulaziz and his army met the forces of al-Duwaish. Abdulaziz did not attack; instead he signaled that he wanted an opportunity to speak with al-Duwaish. A tent was pitched equidistant from the opposing armies, and Abdulaziz and al-Duwaish rode forth to the tent alone.

The two men talked throughout the night. Abdulaziz employed logic, flattery, charm, and threats to win the rebel leader back to the al-Saud fold. But in this Abdulaziz failed, and just after dawn the two men returned to their own lines to prepare for battle.

The battle on March 29, 1929, at the oasis of Sibilla was the last true Bedouin battle ever fought. The two armies charged each other, wave after wave of camel cavalry followed by men on foot with rifles blazing and sabers flashing. Ancient war cries, noble names of tribes that traced their ancestry to the eldest son of the Prophet Abraham, filled the desert. Battle standards floated proudly above the sea of dust and warring humanity until their bearers were killed or wounded, and then these splashes of color in the brown desert wilted as fast as the short-lived desert wildflowers.

The battle was bloody but brief—less than fifteen minutes in duration. While the Ikhwan were unquestionably better warriors, they were hopelessly outnumbered. At first the Ikhwan retreat was orderly, but soon panic broke out and the Ikhwan found themselves running for their lives. Al-Duwaish was wounded in the abdomen and surrendered to Abdulaziz. Mistakenly believing the bloody wound to be fatal, Abdulaziz embraced his enemy and forgave him. Ibn-Humaid escaped but, upon hearing of the mercy extended to al-Duwaish, surrendered into the hands of Abdulaziz's cousin.

Ibn-Humaid was not executed but was kept in prison for the remainder of his life. He was jailed in Riyadh and then moved to dungeon caves just outside Hofuf. The labyrinth of caves still exists today, and although they are no longer used as a prison, the rumor exists that in one of the pitch-dark cul-de-sacs one may find the dried bones of the Ikhwan leader.

Spring, if such a season can be said to exist in Arabia, was punctuated by minor skirmishes between local Ikhwan bands and the armies of Abdulaziz. However, by late summer al-Duwaish's stomach wound had healed, and the old Ikhwan leader was again raising an army to rebellion. By the end of the summer months al-Duwaish was in command of an army ten thousand strong.

Abdulaziz, again in Mecca, decided on an unprecedented course of action. He decided to mechanize his army. This decision was made after consultations with various individuals including the Englishman, Philby. Philby encouraged the Wahhabi leader in this direction for two reasons. First, a camel cavalry stood no chance against a mechanized division; and second, Philby was the sole import agent for Ford motorcars in Arabia.

A large number of the vehicles never completed the journey and were simply abandoned along the route. However, those early Model T's and Chevies that did complete the seven-hundred-mile journey proved to be the deciding factor in the fate of the Ikhwan.

The mechanized, if not modern, army of Abdulaziz defeated the Ikhwan in every engagement. But more than anything else it was the sight of the motorcars being used in combat that seemed to crack the morale of the Ikhwan. The battles lasted for several months, but it soon became apparent that it was simply a matter of time before the Ikhwan would be annihilated. An impotent despair seemed to settle among them, draining them of their previous ardor and energy. It was almost as if the sight of Abdulaziz's armored motorcars was understood by them to mean the death of the old Arabia, in which the Ikhwan brotherhood could exist.

Soon the Ikhwan's despair turned to desperation, and the winter of 1929 found al-Duwaish pathetically searching for sanctuary for the women of his family. The sheikh of Kuwait, after consultation with the British, refused refuge to them. Rather ironically, al-Duwaish, at this point, asked Glubb to secure him sanctuary in Iraq. Glubb probably recognized that the Ikhwan was doomed and may even have felt compassion for his former enemy, but he refused to assist the aging Ikhwan leader.

In January 1930 a rumor arose that Abdulaziz's army was marching forth to put a final end to the Ikhwan. The Ikhwan panicked and made a desperate retreat into Kuwait. With their camels dying of exhaustion and their women dying of starvation, the Ikhwan were already defeated and could have offered no serious resistance to Abdulaziz's army.

The British in Kuwait took pity on al-Duwaish and attempted to convince the Ikhwan leader to surrender to them instead of to Abdulaziz. Finally al-Duwaish agreed to this if the British political agent in Kuwait would take personal responsibility for the safety of the women. The agent, a man named H. R. P. Dickson, dutifully took al-Duwaish's thirty-seven wives, sisters, daughters, cousins, and assorted other female relatives home to Mrs. Dickson.

Mrs. Dickson's astonishment quickly turned to concern and compassion when she saw the condition the al-Duwaish women were in. All were suffering from exhaustion, many were near starvation or ill, and their clothes were in rags. Mrs. Dickson bathed, clothed, and fed the destitute women.

Dickson went personally to plead with Abdulaziz for al-Duwaish's life. Dickson knew that Abdulaziz had already pardoned al-Duwaish once, and he knew the long odds against his mission of mercy. Dickson was to be surprised.

Abdulaziz was as magnanimous as he was charming. He agreed to spare al-Duwaish's life if the Ikhwan leader surrendered to him. When Dickson brought up the question of the safety of al-Duwaish's women, Abdulaziz was genuinely puzzled. "His daughters will be my daughters, his sisters my sisters," Abdulaziz was reported to have announced, adding, "Is it not so in your country?" Abdulaziz's promises to Dickson were never broken.

Al-Duwaish lived for about another year in prison in Riyadh, where he died of a hemorrhage in the throat. Just before he died, the old Ikhwan leader is said to have sent a verbal message to Abdulaziz—not asking forgiveness for himself but granting Abdulaziz his forgiveness. The Wahhabi leader was reported to have received the dying man's forgiveness with the sad, wry smile that was later to be captured in numerous photographs.

Two years later, in September 1932, Abdulaziz ibn–Abdul Rahman al-Saud was formally proclaimed king of the newly formed country of Saudi Arabia. The long journey that had begun at the water hole of Ain Heet in 1902 had reached its end. Abdulaziz had achieved his ambition—a united Arabia.

3

The Third Journey

Unlike most airports in the world, the one in Riyadh is busiest during the small hours of the morning. With hopelessly overcrowded facilities and a total absence of computers, the overworked air traffic controllers schedule all international departures and arrivals for these hours. But on the night of Wednesday, October 17, 1973, all airport activity came to an abrupt halt.

For most of the early evening the chief of airport security had been in his office overlooking the prefabricated customs hall. In every respect it had been a routine evening. Two Saudi nationals had been prevented from taking bottles of Scotch whisky through customs. A pregnant Bedouin woman had gone into labor and had been rushed to the British Military Hospital, and an American construction engineer had become verbally abusive when a customs officer confiscated his still only partly read *Playboy*.

The main preoccupation of the chief of airport security was his concern about his eldest son, who had only two days before been sent with a division of the Saudi army to Amman, Jordan. At five minutes to nine, the security chief tuned in Radio Riyadh to hear how the Arabs were faring in the fourth Arab-Israeli war.

At two minutes to nine the phone on the security chief's desk rang, and a voice he recognized as having far greater authority than his own informed him that he was to close the airport. A private jet would be approaching within the hour. The landing of the jet was to be afforded "top priority." The phone message ended with the unnecessary addendum: "This is the command of your King."

While that cliché is routinely used in the Saudi National Guard as a postscript to orders that range in importance from manning strategic radar posts to cleaning toilet bowls, the general on the telephone had meant it literally. King Faisal himself was awaiting the arrival of the private jet.

Before clearing the public from the airport and ordering the air traffic controllers to reroute incoming planes to Jeddah and Dhahran, the security chief checked the serial numbers of the private jet. He was surprised to find that it was not registered to a member of the royal family but to the Ministry of Petroleum and Minerals, the same ministry that would later be known as Petromin.

The private jet was flying in from Kuwait, and it landed just after ten o'clock. Two black Cadillacs were waiting at the side of the single runway to rush the passenger with a police escort down Shara Mathar (Airport Street) to King Faisal's palace.

The passenger, who at this point was nearing the end of the most important journey of his life, was neither a religious prophet nor an ambitious prince. He was a commoner by the name of Ahmed Zaki Yamani, Minister of Petroleum and Minerals.

Educated at both New York University and Harvard, Yamani was and is, with the possible exception of Hisham Nazar, the influential Minister of Planning, the most powerful commoner in the kingdom. Yamani's rise to power was swift. After finishing his studies at Harvard, he was appointed to the board of the Arabian-American Oil Company (ARAMCO). As one of the very few Western-educated Saudis on the ARAMCO board, it was not long before his talents came to the attention of the royal family, and Yamani was moved to the Ministry of Petroleum.

Privately, officials at Petromin say that a member of the royal family will never occupy the position of Minister of Petroleum. Their reasoning is that the entire issue of petroleum is too volatile and precarious and at any time may require a high-level scapegoat. Naturally, if this scapegoat proved to be a member of the royal family, a schism within the al-Saud clan could erupt.

Thus the minister has always been from outside the royal family.

Yamani will not become anyone's scapegoat. The evidence shows that while his influence in the Arab world outside Saudi Arabia has declined in the past few years, his position within the kingdom has remained remarkably secure.

Perhaps one of Yamani's most difficult moments came when King Faisal assigned his own son, Saud al-Faisal, now the Foreign Minister of Saudi Arabia, to the Ministry of Petroleum. Saud al-Faisal was supposed to be Yamani's deputy. However, the young Princeton-educated prince had higher ambitions than being merely a deputy of a commoner who had recently adopted the title "sheikh." Yamani was forced to present the problem to the king himself. King Faisal, to his credit, removed his son from the ministry.

Ahmed Zaki Yamani has been for the past dozen years the most visible Saudi to the Western media. He has also been the best thing that has ever happened to the Arab image in the West. Articulate, moderate, and soft-spoken, Yamani presents Western television audiences with a vastly different picture from that of the stereotypical Bedouin. Once outside Arabia, Yamani dons his three-piece Pierre Cardin suits and converses fluently and wittily in English but always remains an extremely conservative Muslim.

On the image Yamani has created for himself in the West, one of the sons of the late King Saud, himself an ardent supporter of the PLO, commented, "Arafat should take lessons from Yamani. If the PLO had Yamani they would be recognized by the United States in ten minutes. Yamani looks like [a] man you would want to invite to your home. Arafat looks like [a] man you would want to fumigate before allowing into your house."

On the night of Wednesday, October 17, 1973, Ahmed Zaki Yamani stepped from the private jet. In his left hand he carried a briefcase which contained a remarkable document. It was a single piece of unlined paper, handwritten in Arabic, with a host of barely legible penciled corrections, deletions, and additions crowding its margins. As unassuming as it might have appeared to ignorant eyes, it may have been the most important economic document of the twentieth century.

It announced that the Organization of Petroleum Exporting Countries (OPEC) would unilaterally raise crude oil prices by a whopping seventy percent and reduce oil production by not less than five percent per month from the September 1973 levels until Israel had withdrawn from all the occupied Arab lands taken in the 1967 war and the legal rights of the Palestinian people had been fully restored.

Yamani had been the author of this document. In constant consultation with King Faisal, he had put together a plan that would completely change the power structure of the world. It would make Saudi Arabia a superpower with at least as much economic influence in the world as either the United States or the Soviet Union.

The journey into superpowerdom really began in the early spring of that year. For some time King Faisal had been making pronouncements which strongly suggested that he was in the process of rethinking his own belief that oil and politics did not mix. It was natural and logical for Faisal to use oil as a weapon.

Why did Europe, Japan, and the United States ignore Faisal's warnings? In order to take a threat seriously, one has to believe in two things—the worthiness of one's opponent and the danger of the weapon he wields. Neither Europe nor the United States took Faisal or oil very seriously.

In the eyes of the West, Faisal was, if he was known at all, a mere desert princeling, uneducated in every Western sense of the word. He dressed in peculiar costumes and presided over a bizarre and at times brutal land.

Oil, while more familiar to the inhabitants of the West than Faisal was, was taken no more seriously. Oil had always been plentiful and reasonably inexpensive, at least since the end of World War II. What was not known was that the abundance of oil and its pricing were results of the manipulations and machinations of the seven largest oil companies, known in the trade as "the Seven Sisters."

Faisal was not to be taken lightly. He was a devout Muslim

whose austere life style contrasted sharply with that of his extravagant brother Saud. As a Wahhabi Muslim, Faisal was fiercely anticommunist and anti-Zionist. In fact, his dislike of these two ideologies often led him to equate them.

There is an old Arab proverb that says, "The enemy of my enemy is my friend, and the friend of my enemy is my enemy." The problem that Faisal faced was that, while the United States was the world's most tenacious foe of communism, it was, at the same time, the world's most generous supporter of Zionism. Quite understandably, Faisal was never sure whether the United States was a friend or an enemy—and with very few exceptions, those are the only categories that the Arab world understands.

Faisal's obsession was, of course, Jerusalem. As God's custodian of the First and Second Sanctuaries of Islam, the Holy Cities of Mecca and Medina, Faisal found it intolerable that Islam's Third Sanctuary should be barred to the vast majority of the Islamic world.

Understand that there is no such thing in Islam as consecrated ground. Mosques are not holy in and of themselves. They are merely meeting places where the men of a village gather for communal prayer. The validity of a prayer in Islam does not depend on the place in which it is said, nor does it gain potency from the rank or status of the individual who is praying. However, there are three places, at least to Sunni Muslims, that have become sanctified by their past associations with the actions of God and men inspired by God.

Thus, when a Muslim makes hajj, the once-in-a-lifetime pilgrimage to Mecca, when he circumambulates the Kaaba and kisses the black stone, he is doing so not out of any reverence for the stone itself but because the Prophet Muhammed performed the same action fourteen centuries ago.

To understand King Faisal's obsessive desire to pray in Jerusalem before he died, one must understand a little of the history of Jerusalem itself from the Muslim perspective.

Jerusalem was the city in which the Old Testament prophets wandered the streets and harangued crowds on the steps of the temples. These prophets were not simply Jews, just as the Patriarch Abraham was not simply the father of Judaism. These Old

Testament prophets were Semites and are considered to be the messengers of God not only by the Jews and the Christians but also by the Muslims. The Islamic world accepts the Old Testament and its prophets, although the Islamic view contends that the Jews have corrupted the teachings of the patriarchs.

A similar view is expressed about the Christian Gospels. While no Muslim will argue about the importance of Jesus of Nazareth as a prophet of God, the Muslims do not accept his divinity, and they are quick to point out how his teachings have been perverted by the Christian church.

Jerusalem is also home to Al-Aqsa, a sacred enclosure containing the Dome of the Rock, or Mosque of Omar, and the Mosque of Aqsa. Part of the wall of the mosque is believed to have been built with stones from the temple of King Solomon—this wall, known as the Wailing Wall, is also sacred to the Jews and a frequent location of trouble between them and Muslims.

Muhammed himself is believed to have visited Jerusalem and to have declared it a Holy City. Until the Prophet's dispute with the Jewish community in Medina, all Muslims were required to face Jerusalem while praying.

By early 1973 Jerusalem had also become an emotionally potent symbol of the homeless Palestinian Muslims. Driven from their land by Israeli terrorism, these Palestinians have represented for the past forty years the single largest group of displaced persons in the world. In numbers alone, there are more homeless Palestinians than all the refugees from Cambodia, Vietnam, Afghanistan, Central Europe, and Cuba combined.[1]

In the CBS documentary *The Palestinians,* televised on June 15, 1974, a wealthy Palestinian businessman who had fled persecution in Israel was interviewed at his fashionable home in Beirut. When the interviewer reminded the businessman of his good fortune while in exile, the Palestinian smiled and pointed to a glass jar half full of earth. The earth was from Jerusalem, and the businessman added that it was more valuable to him than anything else he possessed and that he would give up ev-

---

[1]*Newsweek,* April 28, 1980.

erything he possessed in order to be able to return to his homeland.

As a nation of immigrants, it might be hard for Americans to sympathize with or even understand the Palestinians' feelings of anger and sadness. It might be easier to imagine the resentment that would be felt by the residents of Vermont if their state were given as a national homeland to the persecuted Jews of the Soviet Union.

And so by spring 1973 Faisal felt it was time to do something about the lands occupied by Israel in the 1967 war. This was not his only motivation, but it was a strong one.

In April, Ahmed Zaki Yamani was in Washington reiterating King Faisal's warnings: "What we should do in our own interests to conserve our oil reserves is to produce exactly what we need to finance internal development. If you want me [i.e., Saudi Arabia] to produce more, I will only hurt myself. If you are not ready to help me, why should I hurt myself to help you?" Unfortunately, Yamani's question was assumed to be rhetorical and was lost in the verbiage that clutters the newspapers. His warning was ignored.

King Faisal himself then took center stage and granted an unprecedented interview to American television, during which he announced, "We do not wish to place restrictions on our exports to the United States, but America's complete support of Zionism against the Arabs makes it extremely difficult for us to continue to supply the U.S. petroleum needs and even to maintain friendly relations with America." What seemed like a plea rather than a threat was once more ignored.

The next act in this international drama took place in August of the same year. Egypt's president, Anwar Sadat, was in a predicament. His country, as always, was on the verge of bankruptcy; Israel still held the Sinai; and his sole source of financial aid, Qaddafi of Libya, was suggesting a union of Egypt with Libya.

Sadat was not so naïve as to believe that such a union would be of any benefit to his country; he saw the bid for what it was—an attempt on the part of the ever-mercurial Quaddafi to extend his power over Egypt. However, Sadat could not merely reject the suggested union out of hand, for to do so would have meant an end to the Libyan oil money that was flowing into Egypt.

During August 1973 Sadat secretly boarded a plane and flew to Riyadh to meet with King Faisal. Sadat knew of Faisal's antipathy to any form of Arab radicalism and of the Saudi monarch's personal—but private—hostility towards Qaddafi. Sadat patiently explained to Faisal how he was desperately trying to rid Egypt of the socialist trappings left over from the Nasser period and to have Egypt return to the conservative, true Islamic path. His problem, Sadat explained to Faisal, was that while accepting subsidies from Qaddafi, he inevitably came under the influence of the capricious and radical Libyan colonel.

While publicly reticent on the subject of Qaddafi, privately the Saudi royal family refer to him as "the mad colonel," so it is not at all surprising that Faisal should have decided to assist Egypt to free itself of Libyan influences. Sadat returned from Riyadh to Cairo with a promise from Faisal to double Saudi aid to Egypt. In addition, Faisal gave Sadat five hundred million dollars for military spending and six hundred fifty million dollars in long-term low-interest loans.

This Saudi money would finance the reconstruction of the Egyptian army and would allow it, in October of that year, to cross the Suez Canal and launch an attack on Israel. There is evidence that Sadat confided his invasion plans to Faisal; but apparently his talk was so vague that the Saudi monarch interpreted it as mere bravado.

In return for this massive Saudi military aid, Faisal secured a promise from Sadat that the Egyptian president would attempt to patch up his own relations with Jordan's King Hussein. Hussein had always been the victim of the Arab-Israeli conflicts and had recently isolated himself from the Arab world by carrying out a pogrom against the Palestinians in Jordan.

Soon after Sadat's return to Cairo, he invited the Jordanian king to a meeting. The conference turned out to be a nonconference at which words became separated from meaning and intentions became blurred in a smudge of cordiality. Like a scene from Ionesco, the meeting brought together Sadat, Hussein, and President Assad of Syria.

The Jordanian King immediately launched into a lengthy argument against any military action against Israel. Sadat nodded understandingly. Assad nodded understandingly. After two days King Hussein left Cairo with the mistaken impression that he had persuaded Sadat and Assad not to attack Israel.

As soon as Hussein left, Sadat and Assad began the real conference, during which they agreed to launch an assault to recapture their lost territory—and to do so before the end of the year.

August and early September saw a number of the Arab oil-producing nations issue warnings to the United States on its unrestrained support of Israel. On September 9 President Nixon decided that the situation was serious enough to warrant his attention. It was too little too late.

On that date, Nixon called for a full-scale White House conference to study U.S. energy supplies and needs. The conference concluded that the U.S. should embark on an immediate program of energy self-sufficiency. The study recognized that the United States was at the mercy of the Middle Eastern oil-producing nations.

Characteristically awkward, Nixon decided to threaten the Middle Eastern oil-producing nations with concerted action on the part of the Western oil-consuming nations should any production cuts be made. The threat was as empty as it was ill-advised. Saudi Arabia could stop producing oil tomorrow, continue with its massive development plans, and not feel a financial pinch for three years.

In early autumn 1973 U.S. imports of Arab oil provided about ten percent of its total petroleum needs. (Subsequently oil imports have increased threefold, so that now the United States relies on Arab oil producers for about thirty-one percent of its petroleum.)

No one in the Arab world took Nixon's threats very seriously. But there was another threat in the making that King Faisal did take very seriously. Six months later, after the oil embargo had been in effect for several months, Henry Kissinger, then Secretary of State, issued a thinly veiled threat to use American troops to secure the oil fields. American military personnel were being trained in New Mexico and Arizona for just such an operation, but the likelihood of the U.S. military's actually going into Saudi Arabia, the United Arab Emirates, or Kuwait was extremely remote.

King Faisal chose to take the threat seriously, however. Recognizing that the Saudi military was no match for the U.S. forces, Faisal announced that he had ordered the mining of all the eastern oil fields and would blow them up if any nation attempted military intervention.

We can be virtually certain that the oil fields were never mined. However, the fact that explosives were not attached to the oil rigs does not mean that Faisal was bluffing. In a statement to his people, Faisal announced that Saudi Arabs had lived in tents in the desert for five thousand years and had been free; if oil meant they were in danger of losing that freedom, he would order the oil destroyed, and they would all return to living in tents in the desert.

The response to this statement was overwhelmingly positive. Even now, less than a decade after it was made, most Saudis know it by heart and are only too ready to repeat it with absolute conviction.

The Western mind perceives of the desert in geographic or topographic terms. For the Bedouins of Arabia the desert is a state of soul. It represents perhaps the most complete sense of freedom that they will ever experience. Even today the desert Arabs cherish above all else this sense of freedom. The desert for them may be harsh, brutal, even life-threatening, but its borders are far away, and within this formidable sea of barren rock and sand dunes there is an exhilarating absence of man-made restrictions.

The modern Saudi Arab is too close in time to his desert-dwelling forefathers to be entirely comfortable within the four walls of an expensive villa or apartment. Even the young men who dash madly about the streets of Riyadh and Jeddah in their Mercedeses and Buicks relax once they have left the city limits.

They don't drive as rapidly. Their facial expressions change visibly. They have moved from the artificial time of business, commerce, and industry into the real time of the desert.

It was October, and Europe again prepared for a winter warmed by Arab oil. On Saturday, October 6, 1973, a delegation of American and British oil men began to assemble in Vienna to negotiate a price increase with OPEC. The oil men, led by George Piercy of Exxon, were aware of the militant mood of the Arab oil producers. They had read Yamani's remarks in the Western press and had heard Faisal's announcement on American television. In fact, the directors of Exxon, Mobil, Texaco, and SoCal (Standard Oil of California) had been personally warned by King Faisal in May 1973 that if the U.S. did not support a more balanced Mid-East policy, "You will lose everything."[2]

These oil men had many years of experience in dealing with Arabs, and, in part, it may have been this experience that blinded them to the reality of the situation. Certainly one of the most widespread pastimes in the Arab world is exaggeration. If an Arab signs a contract for one million dollars, one can fully expect him to announce that it was for ten million. If it hasn't rained in Riyadh for three years, one can fully expect that to be drawn out to at least ten. This exaggeration is not designed to deliberately mislead the listener; it is designed to entertain him. Storytelling is still very much a respected art on the Arabian peninsula, and so if the reality of a situation proves dull, it is quite acceptable, even expected, for one to exaggerate it.[3]

Western oil men interpreted Yamani's remarks and King Faisal's warnings as another case of Arab exaggeration. Joseph Sisco, then head of Middle Eastern Affairs at the State Department, shared the opinion that King Faisal was bluffing. His assessment was based on a secret CIA report that suggested that little attention need be paid to Faisal's warnings. The oil men who gathered in Vienna did not believe that oil and politics

---

[2]Anthony Sampson, *The Seven Sisters: The Great Oil Companies and the World They Made*, Viking, New York, 1975, p. 292.
[3]It is curious to note that the Prophet Muhammed approved of using exaggerated or false speech if it served any of three purposes—reconciling feuding persons, pleasing one's wife, or obtaining an advantage in conflicts with infidels.

would be mixed. After all, they were executives of multinational corporations. They had little to do with the making of American foreign policy. How could the continuing Israeli occupation of Arab lands be of any concern to them?

At three o'clock on Saturday, October 6, 1973, both the British Broadcasting Company and the United State's Voice of America reported that four divisions of the Egyptian Army had stormed across the Suez Canal using fire hoses purchased from the United States to blast their way through the huge sand escarpment the Israelis had constructed. At the same time, on Israel's northern border, seven hundred Syrian tanks broke through the barbed wire and advanced towards Kuneitra and Rafid.

At the OPEC offices in Vienna, delegates from the Arab oil-producing nations met for round-the-clock discussions. While the rhetoric was militant, the delegates could reach no consensus as to what action should be taken.

Iraq had already nationalized the minority American interest in Basrah Petroleum in southern Iraq but had secretly assured Exxon (then Esso) and Mobil that oil shipments would continue uninterrupted. Egypt was still trying to sell off-shore drilling rights to the big U.S. oil companies, and Saudi Arabia was merely hinting at a million-and-a-half-barrel-a-day production cut. Hardly a radical group. In fact, when a delegate began to sound too radical, Sheikh Ahmed Zaki Yamani, chairman of OPEC, would quietly remind him that they were in Vienna to "talk oil, not war."

On Monday, October 8, the OPEC delegates met with the delegates from the major British and American oil companies. Discussions lasted only an hour. The gulf between the price increase being offered by the oil companies and the increase being demanded by the producing nations was too great. While no figures were released publicly, it is generally thought that the oil companies were offering an increase in the neighborhood of twenty percent, whereas OPEC was demanding an increase of between fifty and one hundred fifty percent.

The following day, Tuesday, October 9, the oil companies and OPEC delegates met again. The oil companies submitted yet another price increase offer, which was promptly and unanimously rejected. At the close of the day's negotiations, the OPEC delegation issued a statement which said in part, "The price increase offered does not reflect the true market conditions."

The OPEC delegates had measured the situation correctly. The price increases offered by the Seven Sisters did not reflect the true value of oil. Saudi Arabian light crude, the OPEC price marker, was selling for $3.01 a barrel, or approximately seven U.S. cents a gallon.[4] These OPEC delegates, many of whom had been educated at such bastions of capitalism as the Harvard School of Business, understood only too well the theories of supply and demand, especially as they affect pricing.

Why should oil be artificially cheap? Why should nations who were themselves only at the very beginning of the development process make enormous sacrifices for the extravagantly wasteful West?

The problem was compounded by two other factors. The first was that the OPEC nations had come to recognize that their oil reserves were finite. They had begun to regard their oil as a one-time phenomenon. They understood that there would come a day when the last gallon of oil would be sucked out of the earth.

The second factor that made the price increase so important was that most of the members of OPEC are single resource nations: the vast majority of their revenue comes from the production of oil. Before King Faisal could organize an annual budget, he had to wait to see what the oil companies were offering. Before he could make plans for new hospitals and schools, he had to wait to see what Yamani could negotiate.

Even the development of the Saudi Arabian military, an issue as crucial as national defense, was dependent on the price of oil, which the oil companies had kept low for more than two decades.

A significant development occurred on Tuesday, October 9. After a long emergency session, the Kuwaiti Council of Ministers announced that they were organizing a meeting of the Organization of Arab Petroleum Exporting Countries (OAPEC) to discuss "the role of oil in the Middle East conflict." The Arabian

---

[4]A barrel of oil equals forty-two U.S. gallons.

Gulf oil producers were already scheduled to meet on October 17 in Kuwait, so the question of how to use the oil weapon most effectively against the supporters of Israel was placed on the agenda of that meeting.

The following day, Saudi and Egyptian oil experts met in Riyadh to discuss this delicate question. Faisal was aware that a unified Saudi-Egyptian position would in all likelihood be supported by the other Arab oil producers and would be a more moderate stand than the plans being suggested by Libya, Iraq, and Algeria. The question of how to use the oil weapon was delicate for the same reason that discussion of the use of nuclear weapons must be delicate—the weapons are really too powerful to be used. So, in essence, what was being discussed in Riyadh was the "nonuse" of the oil weapon.

A complete cessation of the oil flow from the Arabian Gulf would have produced the economic equivalent of nuclear war. This scenario of economic ruin for Europe and hardship for the United States was not in the self-interest of Saudi Arabia.

Why would a merchant deliberately bankrupt its largest customers, even for causes as passionately felt as the Palestinian one? Faisal was desperately looking for a moderate course in which oil would not really be used as a weapon, but one that would change European and U.S. policies toward the Middle East.

To this end, Faisal sent one of his closest and most trusted aides, Foreign Minister Omar Saqqaf, to Washington on Thursday, October 13, carrying a personal message from the Saudi monarch to President Nixon. The message asked, rather rhetorically, for clarification of the United States's position regarding the war in the Middle East. Again it warned that oil production cuts would ensue if the overtly pro-Zionist policy of the United States were not modified and balanced.

At one o'clock on the morning of Friday, October 14, while Foreign Minister Saqqaf's plane was still thirty-six thousand feet over the North Atlantic, the telephone rang next to the bed in Sheikh Ahmed Zaki Yamani's suite in the Intercontinental Hotel in Vienna. An Exxon executive told Yamani that the oil companies needed another two weeks before they could make a revised price offer. This conversation marked the end of cheap oil in the world. It was the last time that the oil companies and the oil-producing countries would negotiate oil prices.

Immediately after landing, Omar Saqqaf was whisked into private meetings with Secretary of State Henry Kissinger.

To be fair to Kissinger, it should be made clear that before he met with Omar Saqqaf, he knew that a massive financial and military aid bill for Israel was being drafted at the White House. Given the pro-Israeli mood of Congress, the aid package had every likelihood of swift passage. Kissinger, of course, could not tell Saqqaf about this aid package but he knew that the Saudis would soon learn about it. Kissinger had access to the same CIA report that influenced Joseph Sisco's opinion that Faisal and Yamani were bluffing.

Earlier in the day, Kissinger had received a letter signed by the four chairmen of ARAMCO, warning that increased American military aid to Israel "will have a critical and adverse effect on our relations with moderate Arab [oil] producing countries."[5] Thus Kissinger chose to be charming and cordial in his initial talks with Saqqaf but to dodge the issue of America's military aid to Israel.

If Kissinger's first meeting with Omar Saqqaf was tranquil, the OPEC meeting that took place in Vienna at noon was not. Sheikh Yamani reported that the oil companies asked for two additional weeks to prepare a new price offer. The news was greeted with words of anger, indignation, and resentment.

Yamani again tried to muster the dwindling forces of moderation. At the end of the meeting, a communiqué announced that OPEC would meet again in four days, on October 17, in Kuwait, "to decide on a course of collective action to determine the true value of the crude oil they produce."

This was the dramatic announcement the Western world never thought would be made. For the first time OPEC was going to set prices unilaterally. It was a declaration of independence that, I suspect, historians two hundred years hence will find as important as the one signed on July 4, 1776. It was an

---

[5]Anthony Sampson, *The Seven Sisters*, p. 300.

announcement that would, in the short span of five years, completely change the balance of power in the world.

Soon after the conclusion of the OPEC meeting in Vienna, Yamani flew back to Riyadh to meet with King Faisal. Before boarding his private jet, he repeated that there would be no further negotiations with the oil companies and that all future oil prices would be set unilaterally.

On Monday, October 15, just minutes before the Israeli counteroffensive was preparing to cross the Suez Canal, Egyptian Oil Minister Hilal arrived in Riyadh to meet with Yamani. The idea was that if the Egyptians and the Saudis could agree on a course of action, they could lead the meeting of oil-exporting nations to adopt the more moderate stance they desired. A unified Saudi-Egyptian position would ensure a unified conference.

The Egyptian oil minister wanted to take more radical action than Yamani could agree to. Faisal was still receiving Kissinger's reassurances via Omar Saqqaf in Washington, and the monarch was unwilling to impose a total oil embargo against the United States. Eventually Yamani convinced Hilal to accept a five-percent monthly oil production cutback.

The following day delegates from the producing nations gathered in Kuwait. They talked late into the night. On Wednesday morning the delegates issued an announcement that OPEC was raising the price of oil seventy percent. Saudi Arabian "light" crude rose from $3.01 to $5.11 a barrel.

Flush with success, the delegates were loath to break up without a further announcement on "the role of oil in the Middle East conflict." Wishing to dissociate himself from what would obviously be an anti-American resolution, the Iranian delegate left for Tehran to bring the news of the oil price increase to the ever-avaricious Shah. The remaining ten Arab oil-producing nations of OAPEC gathered at the Kuwait Sheraton at eleven o'clock to discuss how oil could be used as a weapon.

At nine-thirty that evening, a communiqué was issued by the OAPEC group. That it was moderate in tone was a tribute to Yamani. The communiqué was handwritten in Arabic and contained masses of penciled-in corrections and alterations, but its message was clear: for the sake of world cooperation and in the interests of the consumers, the Arab states were already making a sacrifice in producing more oil than was justified by their own budgetary needs.

The communiqué went on to contrast this sacrifice with the United States's continued military and economic support for Israel. The document ended by stating, "Because of all this, the Arab Oil Ministers...have decided to start immediately reducing oil production by not less than 5% per month from September levels. The same percentage will be applied in each month compared to the previous one until the Israeli withdrawal is completed from the whole Arab territories occupied in June, 1967, and the legal rights of the Palestinian people are restored."[6]

The five-percent production cutback was the amount agreed upon between Egyptian Oil Minister Hilal and Yamani, but it was no easy task getting the other Arab oil delegates to go along with it. The mood of the meeting in Kuwait was militant, and the proposed courses of action were far more radical than a mere five-percent cut in production. Compare the plan proposed by Iraqi Oil Minister Sadoon Hammadi, under which all American oil interests would be nationalized, all Arab investments in the United States would be liquidated, and all diplomatic relations between Arab oil producers and the U.S. would be severed.

King Faisal wanted to give the Americans time to reflect. He did not see it in the interest of Saudi Arabia to have the United States pushed into an economic corner. Privately, Faisal had met with James Akins, the U.S. ambassador to Saudi Arabia in Jeddah, and assured him that Saudi Arabia would not impose an oil embargo on the United States until at least the end of November.

On the same day as the Arab oil delegates voted for a five-percent monthly cutback in oil production, Omar Saqqaf crossed the West Lawn of the White House and joined President

---

[6]The Insight Team of *The Sunday Times, The Yom Kippur War,* André Deutsche, London, 1975, pp. 362–363.

Nixon in the Oval Office for a conference. Saqqaf's previous talks with Kissinger appeared to have been going fairly well, and it is likely that Saqqaf expected to hear from Nixon the beginning of a more balanced U.S. Middle East policy.

During the meeting, the president was asked what course the United States would follow in the Middle East conflict. President Nixon said that the United States was actively searching for a settlement in the Middle East that would be "peaceful, just, and honorable." Saqqaf, not understanding the character of this man who would be forced to resign because he was a liar, immediately reported Nixon's words to Faisal, commenting that he personally expected a major revision in U.S. policy toward Israel.

One day later the President asked Congress to provide Israel with 2.2 billion dollars in emergency military aid.

In Nixon's eyes this massive new military aid for Israel probably represented nothing more that a continuation of a preexisting policy. However, to King Faisal, who had been trying to soften Arab anger against the United States, this was a personal betrayal.

Faisal ordered an immediate and extraordinary meeting of the Saudi Council of Ministers on Friday, October 19.[7] The council met for most of Friday, adjourning for prayers but continuing their discussion late into the night. The following morning the announcement was made that oil exports to the United States were to be immediately suspended. "At the instructions of King Faisal ... a *jihad* [holy war] is declared. As *jihad* is the duty of all Muslims, every citizen in this country is called upon to back the freedom fight."

While theologically Faisal had no authority to declare the jihad, his call met with immediate and widespread support within the kingdom. It should be noted that this was the first time that the term *jihad*, historically associated with armed religious warfare, had been applied to economic conflict.

---

[7]While there is no prescribed day of rest in Islam, Friday is set aside as a day of communal prayer and worship. However, once the noon prayer and homily are completed, businesses are free to resume work. In practice, most Saudis do take Friday as a day of rest. Government offices and ministries close, and men use Friday as a day to be with their families.

Obviously, the United States would feel the petroleum pinch. Some 638,500 barrels of Saudi oil per day would stop flowing to the United States, and the energy crisis would, for the first time, reach the average American citizen. However, even more dangerous for the U.S. than the actual shortfall of oil was the example that Saudi Arabia had set for the rest of the Arab world.

The expressed purpose of the oil embargo was to force the United States to pressure Israel into withdrawing from the territories occupied in June 1967 and to have the world recognize the rights of the Palestinian people. However, when the embargo was lifted in March 1974, not a single inch of occupied land had been returned to the Arab world, and the Palestinian people were just as homeless as ever.

Was the boycott a failure? Faisal financed a huge new Egyptian army which he knew would soon attack Israel. Faisal further knew that the United States would continue to support Israel. This then provided the wily monarch with a perfect excuse in the name of Islamic support for the people of Palestine, to cut oil production and raise prices.

Faisal did feel deeply about the homeless people of Palestine and about the desecration, as he saw it, of the Holy City of Jerusalem; however, he also felt very deeply about the development of Saudi Arabia. When he first ascended the throne (figuratively, as there is no physical throne), his nation was one of the poorest in the world. The infant mortality rate was a staggering sixty to seventy-five percent. Diseases that had been virtually extinct in the West for decades were endemic to the Arabian peninsula. Medical care outside the major cities of Riyadh, Jeddah, and Dhahran consisted of applying red-hot coals to that portion of the body that was not functioning properly. Illiteracy in 1964 ran at about ninety percent of the population.

ARAMCO petrodollars had been flowing into the kingdom at a steady though artificially low rate since 1938. However, during the reign of King Saud, these funds had not been used to alleviate the scourge of poverty but to enrich a very few members of the royal family. Thus, when Faisal came to the throne he saw as his first duties the raising of oil prices and the more equal distribution of the oil wealth.

A rare photograph of King Abdulaziz's Bedouin army in 1911. It was this army that would later be transformed into the bloodthirsty Ikhwan. The photograph is attributed to William Shakespear. *(Photo credit: Geographical Journal)*

The Palace of King Abdulaziz, 1936: This was the King's palace in Muna, a village near the Holy City of Mecca. The automobile in the foreground is Philby's. Shortly after this photograph was taken, King Abdulaziz granted Philby the sole concession for importing Ford motor cars into Saudi Arabia. At present Ford cars are banned from the Kingdom due to the Arab boycott of companies doing business with Israel. *(Photo credit: Royal Geographical Society)*

Crown Prince Saud's tent, 1936: Crown Prince Saud is on extreme left, holding camera. Prince Khalid (who later became King) is third from left. The photograph was taken by H. St. John Philby. *(Photo credit: Royal Geographical Society)*

The Arabian delegation to the London Conference on Palestine, 1939: Here the Saudi delegation to the London Conference on Palestine is pictured visiting Northolt R.A.F. base. Unfortunately, the 1939 Conference on Palestine accomplished little. The Jewish delegation and the Arab delegation refused to meet in the same room, and the Conference broke up without making any significant progress towards a resolution of the problem. *(Photo credit: The Times, London)*

The desert camel: Once providing an almost exclusive source of food, milk, and transportation for the desert Bedouin, the camel has now been replaced by the supermarket and the four-wheel-drive jeep. *(Photo credit: Author)*

Execution square in Riyadh: The Clock Tower Square is in the heart of the old part of Riyadh, an area known as Dira. It is here that the public floggings, amputations, and executions take place after prayer on Fridays. *(Photo credit: Don McMunn)*

Qasr Al Hamra (The Red Palace): The Red Palace is the focal point of government in Saudi Arabia. It is here that the Council of Ministers met with Crown Prince Fahd to decide on the Kingdom's major internal and foreign policies. It was here that the assembled Al-Saud family took the oath of allegiance to King Faisal after the deposition of his half-brother, King Saud. *(Photo credit: Don McMunn)*

The Riyadh water tower: Originally designed to provide the capital city with water and a symbol of modernity, the Water Tower is now almost useless. The pressure of the water within the tower is too great for the underground pipes. In addition, the rooftop restaurant was closed because it provided a view into King Khalid's palace gardens. Thus the Riyadh Water Tower stands as a graceful but "empty" symbol of the Kingdom's race into the future. *(Photo credit: Don McMunn)*

Saudi women in purdah: The traditional seclusion of Saudi women remains virtually unchanged in Riyadh. Almost all women are completely veiled when they appear in public. Saudi women are forbidden by law to drive automobiles and have employment other than as nurses and teachers. *(Photo credit: Don McMunn)*

(Photo credit: Author)

The Plain of Arafat during the Hajj: Millions of pilgrims come annually from all over the world to pray in Mecca. Most camp in tents on the Plain of Arafat. The medical, sanitation, food, water, and transportation needs of the pilgrims are an annual challenge to the Saudi Government. *(Photo credit: Saudi Ministry of Information)*

Old Riyadh: Unfortunately not much remains of the old Riyadh of mud-baked houses, crenelated palaces, and narrow alleyways. Frequently the modern generation of Saudis sees these structures not as historic buildings worthy of preservation, but as embarrassing reminders of a poverty and backwardness that has only recently been escaped. *(Photo credit: Don McMunn)*

Diriyah Palace: The ruins of the ancestral home of the Al-Saud family. It was here in the eighteenth century that the preacher Muhammed ibn-Abdul Wahhab forged an alliance with Prince Muhammed ibn-Saud Al-Saud, which would result in the unification of the Arabian Peninsula. Diriyah was almost completely destroyed in 1818 by the forces of Muhammed Ali Pasha, the Ottoman Governor of Egypt. *(Photo credit: Don McMunn)*

Prince Faisal's visit to wartime Britain: The Emir Faisal (left) visited Britain in the November of 1943 on his way back to Saudi Arabia from the United States. Here Emir Faisal is greeted by Lord Fortescue (second from right) on behalf of the British King. To the right of Emir Faisal is Emir Khalid ibn-Abdulaziz, later to become King. *(Photo credit: The Times, London)*

Faisal envisioned the future of Saudi Arabia as linked politically and economically with the United States. There were two reasons for this. First, the United States was one of the few noncommunist countries that could supply the technology that Saudi Arabia desperately needed. Second, the U.S. was the only country in the world with an economic marketplace large enough to recycle the enormous Saudi petrodollar investments.

In Faisal's vision of the future, the welfare of the United States and the industrial development of Saudi Arabia were inseparable. But only slightly less pressing on the monarch's mind than the future of his own country was the idealistic—and for the most part completely mythic—quest for Arab unity. The Arab world had to present a united front against Israel and the supporters of Zionism, namely, the United States and the Netherlands.

Faisal resolved this dilemma by leading an embargo against the United States that, as far as Saudi Arabia was concerned, never really took place. As Fred Halliday points out in *Arabia Without Sultans*,[8] very little oil actually stopped flowing.

Saudi oil destined for the United States was rerouted across Europe or via refineries in the Caribbean to the east coast of the United States.

Faisal had no intention of damaging the economy of his single largest oil customer, and he must have given private assurances to Nixon to this effect, for diplomatic relations between the two countries did not deteriorate as expected. On April 30, 1974, merely a month after the embargo had been lifted, Kamal Adham, chief of Saudi Arabian Intelligence and brother-in-law to the king, referred in a letter to President al-Iryani of North Yemen to "our American friends."[9]

One of the major concerns of the United States during the 1973–74 Israeli-Arab war was to prevent the sophisticated military hardware that the United States had been selling to Saudi Arabia from falling into the hands of other, more radical and more pro-Soviet Arab nations like Syria or Iraq. Whether Nixon

---

[8]Fred Halliday, *Arabia Without Sultans*, Penguin, London, 1975, p. 19.
[9]*Ibid.*

and Faisal ever talked about this possibility, we do not know. However, Faisal sent into combat only a token force, equipped with none of this sophisticated weaponry.

What military sense does it make for a nation at war, as Saudi Arabia was, to deliberately choose *not* to employ its most effective weapons? None, unless, of course, there exists a tacit or even explicit understanding on the subject.

Note that negotiations for the sale of American military hardware remained unaffected throughout the entire embargo period and that President Nixon personally flew to Jeddah in mid-1974, only months after the supposed embargo was lifted, to formalize a billion-dollar-plus sale of American-made weapons and war planes.

In short, the Saudi oil embargo, when viewed against the backdrop of the Arab-Israeli war, was a pragmatic charade, orchestrated by King Faisal and Sheikh Ahmed Zaki Yamani. While it failed to secure a national homeland for the Palestinians, it unquestionably succeeded in bringing Saudi Arabia out of the backwaters of world influence. With craftiness and wisdom, Faisal chose to insulate and protect the United States from the oil embargo that he himself had initiated.

This, then, was the end of Yamani's journey, perhaps one of the most important milestones in the history of modern Saudi Arabia. Yamani's message to King Faisal, delivered in Riyadh late at night on Wednesday, October 17, 1973, was clear and unambiguous. The so-called balance of power in the world was changing. There was no longer just the United States and the Soviet Union to contend with. Soon there would be a third superpower with the ability at any time to annihilate most of the world's fragile and interdependent economies.

The Desert Kingdom had become a world power.

II

Camels, Cadillacs, and the Koran

"Morality is wonderful, but it is
my sad duty to report that it
sometimes is out of whack with the
realities of doing business in this
part of the world."

—*American businessman, The Milwaukee Journal,
Thursday, April 17, 1980*

"Every deed of the Muslim individual
or group of individuals must be inspired
and guided by the Law of God, the *Qur'an*,
which is the constitution chosen by God
for His true servants."

—*Hammudah Abdalati, Islam in Focus*

4

Islam

Any discussion of Saudi Arabia requires a discussion of Islam. For Islam, or perhaps more correctly the Wahhabi interpretation of Islam, pervades all aspects of Saudi life.

In Saudi Arabia, one finds remarkably few distinctions between the religious and the secular. It would not be an exaggeration to say that in most daily activities, the secular, as it is understood in the West, simply does not exist.

Five times a day the muezzin calls the faithful to prayer. Shops and stores are legally bound to close during the *salat* (prayer times). Taxi and truck drivers pull over to the side of the road, unroll their prayer rugs, and set about saying their devotions. Government offices, libraries, military installations, and hospitals come to a standstill. Everyone, from the chairman of the board down to the Pakistani floor sweeper, performs the necessary ablutions and then gathers together for prayer.

Islam is very much a way of life in Saudi Arabia. Fasting during the daylight hours of the month of Ramadan is rigidly enforced by the *mutawa* (officially the Organization for the Encouragement of Virtue and the Elimination of Vice, usually called the morals police), and any Muslim found eating, drinking, or smoking during this period is liable to receive a harsh flogging. The *mutawa* also enforce the strict public segregation of men and women and oversee public decency, which includes enforcing the Saudi dress code for women.

Not so many years ago, the *mutawa* armed themselves with paint brushes and dabbed green paint (green is the color associated with the Prophet) on the exposed ankles and arms of "indecently" dressed women in the *suq*. The *mutawa* have also been known to chase lazy Muslims into nearby mosques for prayer, despite the Koran's strict prohibition against enforced worship.

Islam saturates everything. Even mundane conversations are regularly spiced with pleas for the assistance of God. Anger is expressed with curses that more often than not suggest someone's fate on the Day of Judgment. Newspapers and television news will report yesterday's weather, but they will rarely predict tomorrow's—to do so would be considered arrogance. No plan for the future is uttered without the obligatory postscript *"Inshallah"* (God willing), and even Saudi Arabia's massive ($250-billion-plus) 1975–80 five-year development plan was instituted only after lengthy consultation with the powerful Ulema (religious leadership).

There is no aspect of Saudi life that is not affected by Islam. This is not to say that Saudi Arabs are any more religious or moral than people living elsewhere, only that that is the impression that *some* of them would like to give. And it is not to say that any more or any less hypocrisy exists in Saudi Arabia than it does elsewhere in the world. It is simply to emphasize the fact that Islam's influence in Saudi Arabia is social, economic, and political as well as religious.

There are several difficulties in writing about Islam. First and foremost is the notion, generally accepted among scholars of Islam and Arabic, that the Koran, the Holy Book of Islam, is untranslatable. While several worthy attempts at translation into English have been made, none of them adequately or accurately conveys the tone, nuances, subtleties, or charm of the original Arabic. Thus, many readers of English versions have found themselves brushing aside the Koran after one or two chapters as complete nonsense.[1]

Another difficulty with Islam is the sensitivity of the issue itself. Like most people who take their religion seriously, Muslims

---

[1] All the passages I have quoted from the Koran are taken or adapted from *The Koran Interpreted*, by A. J. Arberry, Macmillan, New York, 1973. Despite the title, this is a translation, one of the best available in English.

are loath to see yet another infidel, like myself, writing about Islam. Their sensitivity, when it is genuine, is quite understandable. There is no other major religion in the world that has suffered as much distortion, both accidental and deliberate.

However, much of Saudi sensitivity to criticism is not genuinely religious in nature, and at times the "protection of Islam" has been used as a screen to excuse and cover up inefficiency, corruption, various violations of civil rights, and, on least one occasion, coldblooded murder.[2] As it is difficult for some Americans to separate criticism of Israel's political policies from "anti-Semitism," so it is difficult for *some* Saudis to separate criticism of Saudi Arabia from an attack on Islam.

Nevertheless, I hope to achieve just such a separation.

The Revealed Word

The Koran is the Holy Book of Islam, but unlike the Old Testament and the New Testament it is not believed by Muslims to be written by men. The Koran is the Word of God revealed directly to the Prophet Muhammed, who in turn taught it to his followers. It was these followers who, two years after the death of the Prophet, compiled into book form the revelations that Muhammed had received.

The statement that the Koran is the Revealed Word of God is deceptively simple. It is not analogous to the Christian Gospels, for even the most devout Christian recognizes the Gospel writers to have been human beings despite their sainthood. Every word in the Koran, every mark of punctuation, every tone and rhythm, the Muslim believes was placed there by God, who used Muhammed, as He had used the prophets before the time of Muhammed, to bring the Divine Message to earth.

The Koran, unlike large portions of the Old and New Testaments, is not the story of a prophet's life, nor is it the history of Islam. It is, in the eyes of the faithful, a total spiritual, intellectual, and behavioral guide to life. It is considered to be the complete revelation of God's Message. Nothing further is needed, and nothing further is to be expected. It is the primary source of

---

[2]See chapter fourteen.

guidance for every choice and every decision—social, marital, political, economic—that a Muslim could possibly make.

Complementary to the Koran, but of secondary authority, is the Hadeeth (the Traditions of the Prophet Muhammed). The Hadeeth is a collection of teachings and interpretations of the Koran made by the Prophet and recorded by his closest followers. By far the largest number of traditions come from Ayesha, the Prophet's last and youngest wife.

The Hadeeth also contains stories from Muhammed's life that serve as an example of moral and spiritual excellence that all Muslims are called upon to emulate.

The authority of the Koran rests upon its authenticity as the Word of God. This authenticity is unquestioned and unquestionable to the Muslim. Even to suggest that the Koran might in some small way deviate from the Divine Message received by Muhammed is to commit a very serious heresy. Islamic scholars are quick to point out how individual portions of the Koran were passed orally from the Prophet to his followers until they were finally compiled in book form.

The historical authenticity of the Koran rests on three major points. The first is the relatively short period of time between the actual Revelation and its recording, only two years. The second and perhaps more important argument for historical accuracy is that Islamic scholars can trace almost all portions of the Message back to Muhammed himself.

The first caliph after the death of the Prophet, Abu-Bakr, was concerned that serious confusion about the Message might occur after the deaths of the companions of the Prophet who had memorized these Revelations. Abu-Bakr consulted the leading authorities and then commissioned Zayd ibn-Thabit, the chief scribe of the Prophet, to compile a standard and complete copy of the book. Ibn-Thabit worked under the supervision of the original companions of the Prophet, who checked and rechecked his work against their own collective memories.

The third argument to show the historical validity of the Koran is the fact that the original text in Arabic is still in existence, and one does not need to rely upon what might be a faulty or inaccurate translation. Islamic scholars are quick to contrast what they consider the corruption of the Christian Gospels due to the " irresponsible manner" in which they have been passed down, through translation, to the present day with the unquestioned veracity of the Koran.

The Articles of Faith

The fundamental and most important teaching of the Prophet Muhammed is faith in the oneness and unity of God. This is the bedrock of all Islam. It is expressed as *"La ilaha illallah"* (There is no god but God).

In theory, all a man has to do to become a Muslim is to utter *"La ilaha illallah"* with profound conviction. The simplicity of this faith is both attractive and deceptive, for it also implies the rejection of all forms of polytheism, pantheism, idolatry, sainthood (with the exception of the Shiites), the Christian concept of the Trinity, and humanism.

The second foundation of faith is the acceptance of the Prophethood, the messengers of God who have appeared to mankind throughout history to bring the Word of God to earth. This Prophethood includes Abraham (*Ibrahim* in Arabic), Noah, Moses, Ishmael, Isaac, Jacob, and Jesus. There is no hierarchy among these prophets; no prophet is any more important than any other, with the exception of the last prophet, Muhammed.

Muhammed's high position among the prophets of Islam does not stem from the fact that his message was any different from that of any of the other prophets but from the fact that the Revelations he received have survived to the present day uncorrupted by the passage of time.

It is important to understand that the Muslim believes that there is only one Message and that all the prophets throughout history have attempted to bring and deliver that same message. The Message, in a word, is "Islam" (literally, "submission and obedience to the Will of God").[3]

---

[3]It is important to understand that no such religion as "Muhammedanism" exists. The term is offensive to Muslims, since it suggests the worship of Muhammed, a mortal, rather than the worship of Allah or God. The term probably is a result of a misinterpretation of Islam by early non-Muslim traders.

While the Muslim categorically accepts only one God, he does believe in a panoply of angels, many corresponding to the Christian hierarchy, each assigned specific duties. However, unlike the Roman Catholic intercession of saints, the Muslim does not direct his prayers toward angels, nor does he accept that anyone or anything can intercede with God on his behalf.

The Muslim stands entirely alone on the Day of Judgment, completely responsible for his every thought, word, and action. The idea of having an advocate in Heaven, like Jesus Christ, is not accepted in Islam; neither is the concept of atonement.

The Muslim sees the advocacy of Jesus Christ and His atonement of sin as entirely contrary to the justice of God. This is for two reasons. First, Islam accepts no notion of "original sin." While the Koran's version of Adam and Eve's temptation is almost identical to that in Genesis, Muslims believe that Adam and Eve later repented of their sin and were forgiven by God. Thus the concept of hereditary sin is repulsive to Islam. Muslims further believe that a child is born in the state of *fitrah* (moral and spiritual purity), but should he subsequently sin, the expiation of that sin is his responsibility alone. Forgiveness is God's alone to grant.

The second reason why Muslims reject the concept of intercession and atonement is that they believe it deprives man of his responsibility and of his ultimate freedom. Individual responsibility is the cornerstone of Islamic justice. Every man is responsible for his own actions, and no other man, be he prophet or king, may deprive him of that responsibility.

The equation is existentially simple. To deprive a man of his responsibility is to deny him the consequences of his actions and thus to render those actions impotent and meaningless. In short, the Muslim believes that to stand between a man and his God, as a priest does, is to deny the individual access to the ultimate source of free will—God.

The idea of sin for the Muslim is simply defined as having the possibility of achieving perfection in God's eyes and choosing not to seek it. In Islam there is a hierarchy of sin, the most grievous being a sin against God; less grievous but still very serious is a sin against God and man; and at the bottom of the scale is a sin against man alone.

For the first two, forgiveness must be sought from God alone. The third is forgivable if the offended pardons the offender, if compensation is paid, or if punishment is applied. All sins in Islam are forgivable except one: Muslims do not believe that God will forgive the sin of *shirk* (polytheism, pantheism, Christian Trinitarianism, etc.).

Thus the Muslim is commanded to have faith in God, in righteousness, in piety, in the veracity of the Koran, and in the equality and brotherhood of all mankind. However, faith is not the end of Islam, it is only the beginning. Islam commands that the faithful Muslim prove his faith through actions. These actions are commonly referred to as the Five Pillars of Islam.

The Five Pillars

The First Pillar of Islam is a profession of faith. It is not enough to believe silently; the Muslim must take his belief out of the stasis of unspoken faith and proclaim it regularly. The profession of faith is *"La ilaha illallah. Muhammedun rasulu Allah."* (There is no god but God, and Muhammed is his Prophet.)

When one comes to think that this profession of faith is an essential part of each of the five obligatory prayers that nine hundred million Muslims say daily, it becomes quite probable that these are the most frequently repeated words in human history.

The Second Pillar of Islam is *salat* (prayer). In addition to the five daily prayers, the Muslim must join a communal prayer on Fridays at noon and must offer a funeral prayer over the corpse of a relative or friend. These prayers are obligatory, and their unexcused omission is a serious offense.

However, to be obligated to pray, the Muslim man or woman must be sane and responsible, above the age of puberty, free from serious illness, free from menstruation, and out of the confinement period due to childbirth and nursing.

The five daily prayers correspond to positions of the sun in the sky, and thus their times change from season to season. Early morning prayer (*Salatu-al-Fajr*) follows soon after dawn but before sunrise. The next prayer is at approximately noon (*Salatu-az-Zuhr*), followed by an afternoon prayer (*Salatu-al-Asr*). The last two prayers of the day are at sunset (*Salatu-al-Maghrib*) and in the late evening (*Salatu-al-Isha*). Men are encouraged to say their devotions communally at a local mosque, but private prayer, especially in the case of women, is permitted.

The individual prayers are prescribed and contain a recitation from the Koran. The Muslim prays not only with his vocal cords but with his entire body, changing his position from standing (*waquf*) to bowing (*ruku*) to prostrating himself with his forehead touching the ground (*sujud*). Old people, cripples, and the infirm are exempted from the physical rigors of prayer, and a devotion said while sitting is equally valid under these circumstances.

The five daily prayers are always preceded by a call to prayer. The words of the call to prayer (*adhan*) are prescribed, but the tone varies from muezzin to muezzin, ranging from a low, mournful dirge to a lighthearted chant to a fierce and almost threatening command. What follows is the call to *Salatu-al-Fajr* (the early morning prayer):

> Allahu akbar, Allahu akbar, Allahu akbar, Allahu akbar.
> Ashhadu an la illallah.
> Ashhadu an la illallah.
> Ashhadu anna Muhammad rasulu Allah.
> Ashhadu anna Muhammad rasulu Allah.
> Hayya ala-as-salah. Hayya ala-as-salah.
> Hayya ala-al-falah. Hayya ala-al-falah.
> As-salutu khayrun mina-an-nawn.
> As-salutu khayrun mina-an-nawn.
> Allahu akbar, Allahu akbar.
> La illaha illallah.
>
> God is great. (four times)
> I bear witness that there is no god but God. (twice)
> I bear witness that Muhammed is the Messenger of God.
>   (twice)

Come quickly to prayer. (twice)
Come quickly to success. (twice)
Prayer is better than sleep. (twice)
God is great. (twice)
There is no god but God.

When the Muslim hears the call to prayer, he sets about his ablutions. There are three kinds of ablutions in Islam: the complete ablution (*ghusl*), which entails a complete washing of the body and is mandatory after sexual intercourse, nocturnal ejaculations, menstruation, and the end of confinement of nursing women.

A partial ablution (*wudu*) entails the washing of the hands, feet, arms, and face, and must be performed after urination, defecation, passing gas, any flow of blood or pus from the body, vomiting, and awakening.

The third form of ablution is actually a substitute for the *wudu. Tayammum* allows the Muslim who finds himself where water is not available to substitute the use of sand for the purpose of washing.

Prayers must be said at the appropriate times. They may not be said prematurely, nor may they be stored up. The Muslim must also be facing the *qiblah,* the direction of the Holy Mosque in Mecca. This has presented some problems for Muslims in the United States and Canada. If the direction of Mecca is not known, the Muslim is told to use his best judgment. An error of this kind does not affect the validity of the prayer.

Some of the Wahhabi religious leadership took this directional problem so seriously that three years ago they suggested that all Saudi unversity students studying abroad be issued compasses with the direction of Mecca clearly marked. It is not known whether the government actually issued these compasses, but they are for sale in many of the souvenir shops in Riyadh, Jeddah, and Mecca.

Prayers are not considered valid unless the following steps have been taken: The *wudu* (partial ablution) is performed; the body and clothes are purified and the ground cleaned of all dirt and impurities; the individual is properly dressed (male covered from waist to knees, female entirely covered except for face, hands, and feet); declaration of the intention to pray is said; and the *qiblah* is observed (the person praying faces the Holy Mosque in Mecca).[4]

To the Westerner who has become used to watering down his religion with metaphors, symbols, and figurative interpretations, these specific prescriptions for prayer may appear superficial, empty, even meaninglessly legalistic. Christians often ask Muslims whether they really believe that God will turn a deaf ear toward the prayer of a person who has forgotten to wash his hands.

More often than not the Muslim's response is incredulity. "How could any man think of coming into the presence of Allah while unclean?" a student of mine replied. "God will never turn a deaf ear to a sincere man. But a man who prays while he is unclean is like a guest with bad manners: he dishonors himself and the host. Mr. Bill, is it that Christians come to their God while they are with dirtiness?"

On another occasion, during a camping trip with some students near Salbuk, some eighty-odd kilometers northwest of Riyadh, one of the students realized they had not brought enough water for both drinking and ablutions. While they had the option of *tayammum*—using sand instead of water—they chose to ration the drinking water so that there would be enough for the ablutions before prayer.

While my Arabic is far from fluent, I did catch the gist of what was being discussed, and so I imposed the same rationing upon myself. When the students discovered that I meant to limit my own drinking of water, they were genuinely shocked. "Do you mean to dishonor us, Mr. Bill? You are the guest. Nothing is ever limited to a guest. The Koran tells us that we must wash before we pray, but the Koran also forbids us to mistreat a guest. To save water by taking it from our guest would solve nothing—it would simply offend everyone, including God."

The Third Pillar of Islam is *sawn* (fasting) during the month of Ramadan. Ramadan is the ninth month of the Islamic calendar,

[4]Hammudah Abdalati, *Islam in Focus*, International Islamic Federation of Student Organizations, Holy Koran Publishing House, Damascus, 1977, p. 57.

but since the Islamic calendar is based on lunar months rather than solar months and is eleven days shorter than the solar calendar, Ramadan can come at any time of the year. The Muslim refrains from eating, drinking, and smoking during the daylight hours. Daylight, during Ramadan, is defined as the time at which a black thread can be distinguished from a white thread and is marked by a cannon shot in Riyadh.

In Saudi Arabia, it is traditional for the Muslim to break the fast at sunset by eating dates and drinking sweet tea. Most non-essential work stops during Ramadan, and most people sleep during the day and gather in family groups after sunset to enjoy large communal meals. Sexual intercourse is also forbidden during the daylight hours of Ramadan, but since most Saudis consider sex during the daylight hours unnatural and unhealthy, this prohibition causes little hardship.

The *mutawa* are especially vigilant during the month of Ramadan. Restaurants do not open until after sunset, and even the restaurant at the Intercontinental Hotel in Riyadh (which does open for non-Muslim guests) is required to ask for proof of religion before serving food to a guest during the daylight hours. An individual who publicly breaks the fast without a legal excuse is liable to be arrested and harshly flogged. While it is unlikely that a non-Muslim would be arrested for breaking the fast, the *mutawa* have been known to take the law into their own hands and administer instant justice with the camel-herding sticks they carry.

Many devout Wahhabi Muslims consider swallowing their own saliva to be a breaking of the fast. Thus many Saudis go through an entire day without any liquid to ease their parched throats. The *sawn* becomes truly agonizing when Ramadan falls during the blistering hot summer months.

The old and the sick, children, and pregnant women are usually exempt from the fast. Bona fide travelers are also exempt, but they must make up the fast at a later date on a day-by-day basis.

Many amusing anecdotes are told about Saudis traveling in Europe or North America during Ramadan. Marianne Alireza, the first American woman to marry a Saudi and to live in Saudi

Arabia, recounts the difficulties faced by Prince Faisal and his entourage while in London attending an international conference on Palestine.[5]

While the fasting could have been postponed, Prince Faisal insisted that his party observe it. At sunset, Faisal's retainers called down to the desk of their hotel to order food, only to find a very polite desk clerk who had never heard of Ramadan and who was very apologetic about the fact that the hotel's dining room was closed. The manager, no less polite and no less ignorant, arranged for the prince's entourage to be served insubstantial tea sandwiches, which the famished retainers devoured in such quantity that the kitchen staff could not keep up with the demand.

Ramadan is also a time of charity, generosity, and mercy. It is traditional for prisoners to be released for Ramadan into the custody of their families and then return to finish their sentences at the end of the month of fasting.[6]

It is a time during which Muslims are expected, even commanded, to give food and money to the poor. The end of the month of Ramadan is marked by the feast of Eedul-Fitr. The feast is a time of joyousness and gift giving, especially to children. It is traditional for families to slaughter many more sheep and goats than the family could possibly consume and to distribute the extra meat to the local poor.

The Koran specifically orders the Muslim to be charitable. In fact, the Fourth Pillar of Islam is the *zakat* (charity). The *zakat* is a voluntary alms-tax of two-and-one-half percent of an individual's net financial worth at the end of a year. If the Muslim has assets that exceed the equivalent of approximately fifteen dollars, he must contribute to the *zakat* (although, in Saudi Arabia, he is not legally bound to do so). The recipients of the *zakat* may be victims of poverty, men who have been deprived of a means to earn a living through illness or accident, new converts to Islam, or individuals who have incurred debts. They must be Muslim.

---

[5]Marianne Alireza, *At the Drop of a Veil*, Houghton Mifflin, Boston, 1971.
[6]This is true for both Muslim and non-Muslim prisoners, depending, of course, on the nature and severity of the crime committed.

The Saudi government has established an agency of the *zakat* that acts as a clearinghouse, accepting individual contributions and then distributing the aid to those in need.

Many Saudis distribute the *zakat* personally. One such individual is al-Rajhi, the multibillionaire Saudi banker, who is reported to have hired a team of twenty or so young men whose duty it is to search out families in real financial need. Once such a family has been located, al-Rahji personally makes a nocturnal visit, anonymously leaving a package of several thousand dollars on the doorstep or inside an open window—one of the more romantic ways of performing the *zakat*.

The Fifth Pillar of Islam is the hajj, the pilgrimage to the Holy Mosque in Mecca. The hajj is the duty of every Muslim throughout the world if health and money permit. The pilgrim comes to Mecca in a state of *ihram* (purity), symbolized by his or her donning special clothes. Female pilgrims wear long, simple all-white dresses, unadorned with jewelry or embroidery, and white cotton headdresses wrapped tightly around the hairline. For the majority of Saudi women, the hajj is perhaps the only time when they may appear in public unveiled.

Male pilgrims wear two long white seamless towels, one wrapped around their waists and tucked over a belt and the other crossed over one shoulder. Men in the state of *ihram* are always bare-headed.

The prohibition against seams or stitching in the towels worn by the men is an interesting one. One of the express purposes of the hajj is to remind the Muslim of the Day of Judgment on which he will stand before God. Stitching has come to be seen as a symbol of wealth and material prosperity which has no place in one's relationship with God. Thus the pilgrims, all dressed alike in simple seamless towels, are reminded of their equality in the eyes of God.

Before a pilgrim may be in the state of *ihram*, he must perform the greater ablution (*ghusl*) and must refrain from sexual intercourse for the duration of the pilgrimage. The pilgrim must also refrain from killing or damaging any animal or plant life within the precincts of the Holy Haram in Mecca. So strongly is this prohibition taken that many men will shave their heads to prevent even a single hair from falling out. Women do not shave their heads, but cropping the hair is common and encouraged.

Very few non-Muslims have personally witnessed the hajj. Mecca is strictly a Muslim city, and non-Muslims are not allowed to enter. On the outskirts of Mecca, the roads into the city are all blocked with what look like tollbooths manned by police officers. Every car, truck, and bus that enters Mecca is searched, and every person entering is required to produce proof of religion. In recent years, a ring road has been constructed around Mecca, appropriately named "the Christian Bypass," which allows non-Muslims to drive from Jeddah to Riyadh.

Probably the most famous non-Muslim to visit Mecca was Richard Burton, who in the nineteenth century disguised himself as a dervish and entered the Holy City. His adventures and experiences are recounted in his memoirs, *Pilgrimage to Al-Medinah and Meccah.*

In our own century, a few non-Muslim adventurers have attempted to visit Mecca, but to my knowledge none has succeeded in both entering and leaving.

There is a story told of a Muslim pilgrim who discovered that the person beside him in the Great Mosque in Mecca did not know the prescribed prayer. Assuming him to be a Christian he killed him on the spot. What makes the story doubtful is not that execution is too drastic a punishment for the violation of what Muslims consider the holiest place on earth, but simply that no bloodshed is tolerated within the Holy Haram. If the execution-murder of a non-Muslim did take place, it most certainly did not take place in the mosque itself.

The prohibition on non-Muslims' entering Mecca is absolute and without exception. Regular Saudia Airlines flights from Riyadh to Jeddah are not routed closer than fifty kilometers from Mecca because they often carry Christians. However, on a clear day Mecca is visible from the air.

During the construction of many of Mecca's large hotels, American and British engineers sat thirty kilometers outside the city, directing the construction of these buildings by way of closed-circuit television. Even during the "siege of

Mecca"[7] in November 1979, when a group of religious fanatics took over the Great Mosque, American and French security experts remained in Jeddah and gave their advice via telephone and walkie-talkie.

The hajj is significant to the Muslim because many of the actions he performs are reenactments of important events in the Koran. After entering Mecca in the state of *ihram*, the pilgrim goes to the Great Mosque which contains the Holy Kaaba, a square structure in the center of the huge courtyard.

The Holy Kaaba contains the black stone that Muslims believe was placed there by the prophet Abraham. The pilgrim circumambulates the Kaaba seven times, touching it at several spots while walking, and then kisses the black stone. Again, it is important to understand that the Muslim in no way worships this black stone, nor does he think about it as other than a stone. However, the pilgrim does respect the association of the Prophet Muhammed and the stone, much as a thinking Christian sees nothing magical in the idea of the Holy Grail but respects the connection between the cup and Christ.

Following the circumambulation of the Kaaba, the pilgrim runs or walks a prescribed course between two small hillocks, as-Safa and al-Marwah. This route is followed seven times, commemorating the course that Hagar ran after being abandoned by Abraham in the desert. Muslims believe that God took pity on Hagar and her son and provided them with a spring of water; thus marking the salvation of Abraham's eldest son, Ishmael.

The spring that Hagar drank from is believed to be the spring of Zam-Zam, regularly visited by pilgrims during the hajj. As Christian pilgrims to Jerusalem often return with vials of water from the Jordan River, so Muslim pilgrims often return with small bottles of water from the spring at Zam-Zam.

Most pilgrims camp in tents on the plains of Arafat near the Mount of Mercy. The plains become literally covered with hundreds of thousands of tents. The daily prayers said by the multi-

---

[7]Discussed in detail in chapter sixteen.

tude of pilgrims camped on the plains are often quite dramatically moving. The evening prayer is said on the Mount of Mercy itself, Jebel ar-Rahamad.

On the way back to Mecca from the plains of Arafat, pilgrims stop at the village of Mina to throw seven small stones at three pillars. Alternate interpretations of this action suggest that the pillars represent demons and the action is a symbolic rejection of evil, or that the action is a historical reenactment of Abraham's stoning of Satan.[8]

While not obligatory, pilgrims are encouraged to make a side trip to Medina to visit the Prophet's Mosque and the tomb of the Prophet Muhammed. This is the only "marked" tomb in Saudi Arabia. Wahhabi tradition opposes marking graves, as such tombs may become objects of veneration and thus encourage idolatry. Even the grave of King Abdulaziz is unmarked, and its location has been a closely guarded secret for the past twenty-eight years. Before the fall of Jeddah to the Ikhwan in the 1920s, a tomb existed on the outskirts of the city that was purported to be the burial site of Eve. Fanatic Wahhabi puritans, believing the tomb to be idolatrous, completely destroyed it after conquering the city.

The climax of the hajj is the feast of Eedul-Adha, which commemorates God's intervention in the salvation of Abraham's eldest son, Ishmael. Muslims believe that Abraham attempted to sacrifice Ishmael; Christians and Jews, on the other hand, believe the boy was Abraham's second son, Isaac. The Old Testament names Isaac but refers to him as "the only son" and "the eldest son" when only a few chapters earlier it describes the birth of Ishmael—fourteen years before the birth of Isaac. This may seem a trivial point, but Muslims often use it as an example of how the Old Testament has become corrupted. Muslim scholars suggest that the switch from Ishmael to Isaac indicates a prejudice in favor of Sarah, Abraham's legal wife,

---

[8]For a more complete version of the rules and regulations of the hajj, see *The Risala of ibn–Abi Zayd al-Qayrawani,* a partial translation of which is given in John Alden Williams's *Islam.*

and against Hagar, Ishmael's mother, who was a slave and might well have been black-skinned.[9]

Like the feast of Eedul-Fitr, the feast of Eedul-Adha is a time of celebration and gift giving. The Muslim must make an obligatory sacrifice of meat, usually sheep or goats, and give this meat in charity to the poor. A problem has emerged in recent years due to the enormously increased numbers of pilgrims making the hajj: there are simply not enough poor people in the vicinity of Mecca and Medina among whom to distribute the meat.

Tons and tons of meat have gone to waste. Pilgrims returning from the hajj tell of seeing the plains of Arafat covered with decaying carcasses. This waste is quite disturbing to Muslims, since the Koran expressly prohibits vain extravagance. Some Muslims question openly the utility and sense of such massive sacrifices. Although the Saudi government has, in the past, tried to provide refrigeration units to prevent meat spoilage, their efforts have been inadequate, and the waste remains a problem.

A problem many non-Muslim Westerners have when discussing Islam is the unofficial sixth pillar of faith, the *jihad.* Literally, *jihad* simply means "exertion." In common usage, however, in both the Islamic and the non-Islamic world, *jihad* has come to mean "holy war." It is the unquestioned duty of every Muslim, wherever he or she lives, to respond to the *jihad.* In this sense, Islam is very different from Christianity, which exhorts the individual to "turn the other cheek." The Koran expressly permits and even commands violence under certain circumstances.

> Prescribed for you is fighting, though it be
> hateful to you.
> Yet it may happen that you will hate a thing
> which is better for you; and it may happen that you
> will love a thing which is worse for you;
> God knows,
> and you know not.
> (*The Koran Interpreted,* II:212)

---

[9]Genesis 17–21.

It is possible to read the word "fighting" figuratively, although most Islamic scholars would believe that to be a corruption of the literal meaning, "physical violence." However, the Koran does limit when a Muslim can resort to physical violence:

> And fight in the way of God with those
> who fight with you, but aggress not: God loves
>   not the aggressors.
> And slay them wherever you come upon them,
> and expel them from where they expel you;
> persecution is more grievous than slaying.
> But fight them not by the Holy Mosque
> until they should fight you there;
> then, if they fight you, slay them—
> such is the recompense of unbelievers—
> but if they give over, surely God is
> All-forgiving, All-compassionate.
>   (*The Koran Interpreted,* II:187)

Thus the Koran does not permit aggression, but it demands retaliation. The key concept is that "persecution" (meaning here, I believe, religious persecution) is vastly more displeasing to God than is the killing of a man's physical body.

The reasoning here is twofold. First, religious persecution attempts to "kill" the Word of God, which in the Islamic hierarchy of values is the most heinous crime anyone can commit. Islam places much greater value upon the propagation of the Word of God than it does on the sanctity of human life. In fact, Islam does not accept that life is intrinsically sacred.

Second, although Islamic justice is certainly not devoid of mercy, it does demand punishment for crimes, and that punishment often takes a physical form.

One of the common misunderstandings among Westerners about the *jihad* has to do with its ultimate purpose. The purpose of the jihad is *not* to force people to convert to Islam. Such forced conversions are prohibited by the Koran. The one and only purpose for jihad is to protect Islam and its believers from persecution. But theory and practice are two separate entities. Thus King Faisal announced a jihad when he wanted popular support for an oil embargo that he never really meant to enforce, and Khomeini in 1980 declared a jihad against Iraq, a Muslim country itself.

Fortunately for both the Islamic and non-Islamic worlds, since Kemal Atatürk abolished the caliphate immediately after World War I, no one in the Muslim world has been able to agree on who, if anyone at all, should have the authority to declare the general jihad. One might say that the primary victims of this lack of Islamic unity have been the Muslims most in need of assistance and support, the homeless of Palestine.

Finally, it may be worth mentioning a few prohibitions placed on the Muslim by the Koran. No Muslim may force another Muslim to pray, an injunction which is frequently ignored in Saudi Arabia. No Muslim may eat carrion, swine, or the meat of any animal that has not been slaughtered according to the manner prescribed in the Holy Book. The prohibition on pork carries the weight of law in Saudi Arabia, and Westerners have been deported for attempting to smuggle into the country small quantities of bacon or ham. So strongly do the *mutawa* feel about the "pork issue" that on one occasion they raided a girls' school because a parent had complained that the girls were learning something about pigs. The ever-zealous *mutawa* searched the entire school without finding anything that bore any relationship to the quadruped. The complaints continued, however, and within a week the *mutawa* were back at the school. This time they found what they were looking for. In the basement kindergarten, surrounded by her uncomprehending five-year-old charges, was a middle-aged Egyptian woman blithely reading aloud in English the story "The Three Little Pigs." The offensive book was seized and destroyed. The offending teacher was told to seek employment elsewhere.

What may strike the Westerner as comic about the Saudi prohibition on pork is its intensity. Of the hundreds of Saudis that I have known personally, not a single one would willingly or knowingly eat pork. Those who have never tried it will quickly tell you how wretched the meat tastes. Those few who have inadvertently eaten it in Europe or the United States will describe in detail how they were ill for days afterwards.

Nevertheless, the Ministry of Information censors all incoming magazines and newspapers that contain recipes that call for pork or pork products. Even *The Muppet Show,* the very popular televised puppet show for children, is censored of all characters represented as pigs. This censorship becomes so meticulous during the periods of hajj and Ramadan that even the recipes on the sides of pasta packages are subject to the censor's black ink.

In contrast to the relative ease they have in enforcing the prohibition against pork, the *mutawa* and the regular police have their hands full with the ever-increasing flow of alcoholic beverages into the country.

Liquor, beer, and wine of every description are prohibited by the Koran, and, unlike Kuwait and the United Arab Emirates, the law in Saudi Arabia is rigorously enforced. The penalty for public intoxication is eighty lashes; the same is true for simple possession of alcohol. Smuggling liquor or manufacturing it in Saudi Arabia is punishable by three to five years in prison and three to five hundred lashes.

It is a myth that Westerners are exempt from such punishments. All Saudi prisons have their complement of Americans and Europeans who thought they could make a quick riyal or two making booze. These prisoners are flogged regularly.[10]

Despite these harsh penalties, one can find liquor for sale in Saudi Arabia. In Riyadh, black-market Johnny Walker Red Label sells for about fifty dollars a fifth, but just before Christmas the price may go as high as one hundred dollars. For the most part, liquor comes into Saudi Arabia in huge container consignments; customs officials are duly paid off. Some liquor is brought across the desert in the back of Bedouin pickup trucks. The vast majority of the smugglers are non-Saudis in the pay of a handful of degenerate princes who, due to their birthright, can smuggle and profiteer with relative impunity.

Just before Christmas, I had ordered a case of Scotch from our neighborhood bootlegger at the appalling price of 2640 Saudi riyals (about eight hundred dollars). On Christmas Eve, before the Scotch was due to be delivered, I received an apologetic tele-

---

[10]Saudi-Islamic justice is explained in chapter eight.

phone call from the bootlegger, explaining that the prince he worked for was himself throwing a big Christmas party and would therefore be using all the Scotch. After failing to wangle an invitation for myself to the prince's drunken revel, I resigned myself to a dry Christmas, but I was unable to forgive the Scrooge-like behavior of royalty.

Many of the Westerners in Saudi Arabia secretly brew their own wine and beer. Some have raised their brewing to the level of an art. At dinner parties in Riyadh, I have been served "burgundy," "chablis," "sauterne," and a particularly vile concoction billed as "date cider" which resulted in a forty-eight-hour bout with diarrhea. This malaise may in part have been psychological, since after dinner we discovered that the dates had been infested with worms which lay in a remarkable state of preservation at the bottom of each of the bottles we had drunk.

Vastly more satisfying than the yeasty homemade wines is a distillate the Saudis call *sadeeki* (literally, "my friend"). *Sadeeki*, the Saudi version of moonshine or white lightning, can exceed one hundred fifty proof and is excellent when mixed with tonic and lime.

Another prohibition in the Koran is the injunction against any representation of the human form. The argument here is a simple one. Since Muslims believe that man was made in the image of God, any representation of man comes perilously close to being a representation of God—a heresy on the magnitude of idolatry.

Private photography is tacitly permitted, and television is very much a reality of Saudi life but movie theaters are still strictly forbidden. Traffic signs indicating that pedestrians may be crossing utilize headless stick figures. Public photography, despite the Saudi passion for expensive cameras, remains unwise in Riyadh and downright dangerous in the desert.

Less than a year ago, a Finnish stewardess working for Saudia Airlines decided to capture in photographs the romantic mystique of the Dira *suq* in Riyadh. The only thing captured was her camera, which was seized by the police.

She was told that by taking photographs of old baked-mud buildings she was exporting a bad and primitive image of Saudi

Arabia. She was directed to the Ministry of Information for postcards of Riyadh's newest office buildings.

On another occasion, a professor of Arabic history at the University of Riyadh was photographing a natural sand arch in Riyadh for an article he was writing. His camera was confiscated, and he had to wait three days in jail before hearing the explanation about exporting a bad image of Saudi Arabia.

The cardinal rule in the desert is to photograph no person or thing without permission.

On a trip I made with some of my students, we came upon a herd of rare jet-black camels. With Pentax always ready, I asked the students whether they thought it would be all right if I photographed the camels. They laughed and assured me there would be no problem at all.

However, after no more than three frames, an ancient but remarkably agile Bedouin appeared over the top of a sand dune. With rifle raised overhead and cartridge belt strapped across his chest, and shouting at the top of his voice, the old man came running directly toward where I was standing. Being the only member of our party in Western-style dress and speaking Arabic poorly even when I am not frightened, I left dealing with this angry old man to my students.

It took nine youths to wrestle him to the ground and pry the antique single-shot rifle from his gnarled fingers.

The impassioned argument that followed was entirely incomprehensible to me. All nine students shouted at the same time. Some addressed the old Bedouin, some addressed other students, and a few seemed to be talking to themselves. The drama came to an abrupt halt when the old Bedouin reached beneath his *thobe*, produced an army-surplus revolver and leveled it directly at my head, shouting *"Allah akbar"* (God is great).

At this point, a sociology student named Moutlag—may it please Allah to provide him with only healthy sons—squatted in the sand next to the old man and whispered something to him. Slowly the old Bedouin lowered the revolver and actually broke into a sheepish and almost apologetic grin. Seconds later the old man was on his feet, commanding us to follow him to his encampment.

Within his tent we were served tea and warm camel's milk while he talked a mile a minute, frequently patting my shoulder and laughing. The only aspect of the scene within the Bedouin's black goat's-hair tent that was odd was the manner of the students. Usually gregarious and talkative, they were reserved and tense.

After politely declining the old man's invitation to dine with him (he had offered to slaughter a young camel), the students led the way back to where we had left the jeeps. As soon as we were out of earshot of the old man, I asked Moutlag what he had said that had calmed the old man.

At first he seemed reluctant to tell me. "He is an old man. He has lived all his life in the desert," Moutlag began. "There are many things he doesn't understand. You see, Mr. Bill, he thought you were a Korean. He has never seen a Korean, but he has heard stories about how Koreans steal the eyeballs out of camels. When he saw you pointing the camera at his camels, he thought you were going to shoot them and steal their eyeballs. We told him that you weren't Korean and that you weren't going to steal the camel's eyes, but that didn't satisfy him. When he pulled out the pistol, I felt I had no choice. I told him that even though you wore strange clothes, you were really a good Muslim, and that it was a great sin to kill a good Muslim."

The jeep erupted into laughter, my own included. "The old man thought we were very rude to refuse his invitation to eat," Moutlag continued, "but we had to get you away from his tent before prayer time. He would have expected all of us to pray together, and when you didn't pray he would have known the truth and would have killed you."

Again laughter filled the jeep—the laughter of relief, not mockery—and then the students began to talk in Arabic among themselves about the old man. "Did you feel how strong he was?" one of them asked. "Seventy years old and it took nine of us to knock him off his feet."

"He probably drinks camel's milk right from the udder."

"He was going to slaughter his best camel for us."

Then Moutlag turned to face me. Almost sadly he announced, "We are not like that old man. We are city Arabs. He is a Bedouin of the desert. He is more Arab than we are. If you are his enemy he will kill you without thinking twice. If you are his friend, he will kill his best camel to feed you. By God, Mr. Bill, it is not oil that makes Saudi Arabia special, it is old men like that one!"

5

The Family

One October evening I was chatting with Khalid, a Saudi friend, at one of Riyadh's many all-male cafés when we were joined by an old man I recognized as Khalid's father. After the never-omitted *"Salam alaikum"* (peace be upon you), Khalid's father took his son aside for a talk. When Khalid returned, I asked him if everything was all right with his family. He laughed.

"My father can't remember where he slept last night," Khalid replied. "He is getting old. He forgets many things now. He has four wives, and he must sleep with each of them in turn. He couldn't remember whose turn it was tonight."

Such are the problems of polygamy.

Actually only one form of polygamy is permitted in Saudi Arabia, namely polygyny. Polygynous marriage in Saudi Arabia allows a man to take up to four wives. Polyandry, the practice of a wife's having more than one husband, is unknown.

The Koran, the source of almost all civil and criminal law in Saudi Arabia, is somewhat vague on the question of polygyny. Before the time of the Prophet Muhammed, the period the Muslims call the *Gehenna* (ignorance), marriage practices were not regulated or restricted in any fashion. However, due to the constant warfare between rival Bedouin tribes, there was a pro-portionately larger number of women than men. This led to the practice of polygyny.

Before the revelation of the Koran, the status of women had fallen to the level of property. A man could take as many wives as he could pay for or win as plunder in battle. A man's wives were his property, not unlike his livestock, and he could do with them what he pleased.

If a husband grew tired of his wife, it was his right to sell her in the marketplace, trade her for a camel, or, if he preferred, beat her to death. The only limitation on the husband's conduct was possible retaliation by the wife's family if his treatment of her was brutal.

The Koran was responsible for the conceptualization of marriage on the Arabian peninsula. Women were no longer to be considered property, nor were they to be treated as such. Although women were obviously of secondary importance to men, they were to be acknowledged as human beings with certain undeniable rights. The man was charged with the duty of protecting his wife, providing her with shelter, food, and clothing, and treating her with kindness and respect. Some Islamic scholars have called the Koran "a woman's bill of rights."

The Koran prohibits a husband from discriminating among his wives. He cannot have a favorite wife:

> ...marry such women
> as seem good to you, two, three, four;
> but if you fear you will not be equitable,
> then only one...
> (*The Koran Interpreted,* IV:2)

A subsequent line (IV:129) reads: "You will not be able to be equitable between your wives, be you ever so eager..." Does this suggest that a direct prohibition upon all forms of marriage except monogamy? Such an interpretation is held by a small number of scholars, but the *sharia* (religious) law of Saudi Arabia allows a man to take up to four wives as long as he treats them absolutely equally.

Ironically, the emphasis on equal treatment is sounding the death knell on polygyny in Arabia. "Who can afford four wives?" Khalid asked rhetorically in reply to a question on the subject. "Fifty years ago, when everyone lived in tents, it was no problem. But now, each wife wants her own villa, her own car and driver, her own servants, her own month-long shopping spree in London and Paris. Who can afford it? Most young men can

only take one wife. The princes are different. They take more because they can afford more. In the royal family, the number of
wives a prince has had is a status symbol, like driving a Rolls
Royce."

Traditionally a bridegroom and his bride do not see each
other before the wedding. The marriage is arranged by members of the respective families, usually mothers, aunts, and
grandmothers. Although some of the more Westernized Saudis
do see their potential spouses beforehand, the arranged marriage is still very common.

In some liberal families the exchange of photographs is considered to be a suitable compromise.[1]

Sharia law demands that the bridegroom make a payment to
the bride's father which is kept in trust for the bride. The *mahr*,
or bride price, may run from a symbolic one riyal (thirty cents)
to a prohibitive five million riyals or more. The bride price is
customarily paid in gold, but money, land, clothing, cars, and
even livestock are acceptable.

The Hadeeth tells the story of a very poor man who came to
the Prophet lamenting that he was too poor to afford the bride
price required for marriage. According to the story, Muhammed
questioned the man at length and was convinced of the man's
poverty. The Prophet then asked the man if he knew any of the
Koran by heart. The man replied rather indignantly that just
because he was poor didn't mean he wasn't God-fearing.
Muhammed instructed the man to teach his wife what he knew
of the Koran—the teaching itself was to be the price paid.

When the *mahr* is of a more material nature, as it usually is in
Saudi Arabia, it becomes the uncontested property of the wife
and remains hers even if a divorce subsequently takes place.
The bride price is often the only property a woman truly owns,
and even then it is usually managed by her husband. However,
in the event of the death of the husband, the *mahr* is paid to his
widow before any settlements are made. Some Saudis explain

---

[1]On April 14, 1981, the practice of veiling the bride to her husband until marriage was
officially disavowed (*The New York Times*, April 20, 1981).

the custom of the bride price as "marriage insurance" for the woman.

Although family affairs like marriages never get into the Saudi newspapers, the amount of a specific bride price is often a subject of earnest gossip. Prince Abdullah, the commander of the National Guard and next in line to be crown prince, is said to have paid more than three million riyals (approximately one million dollars) for a woman whom he divorced eighteen months later because she bore him a daughter instead of a son.

The amount of a particular bride price depends to a large extent on the status of the bride's family. Familial status is extremely important in Saudi society. High status comes with economic success and political influence, but it is also closely related to the reputation of the family members. Families that enjoy a relatively high status in society will often demand an extremely large *mahr*, which in turn is only affordable by a family of similarly high status. Thus was created an inbred elite class, an aristocracy of noble families second only in power, wealth, and influence to the royal family itself.

Inflated bride prices are a major source of concern to young men, especially young men from the "noble tribes" who are expected to marry into other "noble tribes." One young prince shocked his family by rejecting three first cousins (such marriages are not considered incestuous in Arabia) who were running at just over a quarter of a million dollars apiece and choosing instead an illiterate fourteen-year-old girl from the Riyadh Orphanage[2] for whom he paid a mere fifteen hundred dollars.

Once the *mahr* has been agreed upon and paid, the couple becomes engaged. An engagement does not give the bridegroom the right to see his bride-to-be, but some of the more liberal Saudi families may grant the groom this privilege. Traditional Saudis argue that it is both undesirable and unnecessary for the bride and groom to become acquainted before the wedding—undesirable because this might result in some form of premarital indecency, and unnecessary because Saudi mar-

---

[2]See chapter six for details of the secret activities of this organization.

riages are not based upon preexisting emotional relationships. The bride and groom are expected to grow into love after the wedding, not before.

The love that may come to exist between a husband and wife is quite different from that which is considered ideal in the West. In Saudi Arabia, husband and wife are not seen as companions but as collaborators in the work of the family. It is not common for husbands and wives to socialize together; in fact, the opposite is more likely. The social lives of the husband and wife are usually separate. The wife may have close friends who are entirely unknown to her husband.

The ideal Saudi marriage is when the partners grow to respect each other, exhibit consideration for each other, and treat each other in a kind and compassionate manner. The romantic love that is so idealized in the West is virtually unknown in the rural areas. In the urban areas, romantic love is most often equated with Hollywood's worst products viewed via the videotape machine. Quite a number of Saudis openly scorn romantic love. They consider it as too volatile and too fragile a foundation for anything as serious as marriage. Saudis frequently cite the high divorce rates in the West as justification for their arguments.

The engagement period may be for any amount of time the groom and the bride's father agree upon. However, an engagement period of less than six months is not considered entirely respectable. Although Islamic law permits a Muslim man to marry "chaste women from among the People of the Book" (Christians and Jews), the Saudi government has recently passed a law forbidding Saudi men to marry non-Muslim foreigners. Saudi women have always been prohibited from marrying foreigners, regardless of religion. This prohibition may be waived by a *sharia* court, but exceptions to the rule are almost unknown.

No priesthood exists in Islam, so no one actually officiates at a wedding. All that is required is for bride and groom to exchange vows in the presence of at least two adult Muslim witnesses. It is also customary for a man who is knowledgeable in the Koran to recite one or more verses.

Usually there are two separate parties—one for the women and one for the men. At a prescribed point in the evening the groom and his retenue will invade the women's party.

The arrival of the groom is often performed with great ceremony. At this point he will ritually lift the bride's veil and stare, often for the first time, at her naked face. In theory, the groom has the right at this point to reject the bride. However, to do so would be a major breech of manners and an unforgivable insult to the bride and her family. In the past, such last-minute rejections have led to blood feuds between families.

While the bride has no such last-minute right of rejection, she cannot be forced to marry against her will. Although her mate is chosen for her by her family, her consent is legally necessary before the marriage can take place.

Vows are exchanged, and the bride and groom leave the party. Wedding parties usually start late in the evening and continue until dawn. The party itself is not for the bride and groom but for their families and guests, and it does not truly begin until the couple has left.

Traditionally, the wedding party for the women continues until the bride's mother enters with the bloody sheet on which the marriage has been consummated. This sheet is displayed to the assembled female guests both as proof of the bride's virginity and as proof of the consummation (and therefore legal validity) of the marraige. This custom seems to be dying out among middle- and upper-class Saudis, who see it as an artifact left over from a Bedouin heritage which they are eager to escape.

Weddings never take place in mosques. With the single exception of the Great Mosque in Mecca, women are forbidden to enter mosques in Saudi Arabia. Saudis explain this prohibition in numerous ways, but more often than not they tell foreigners that a mosque is a place of prayer and that "when a man and a woman are in a room together, the devil stands with them." Even during the great communal prayers on the Mount of Mercy during the hajj, men and women are kept apart.

It is a mistake to underestimate the value that Saudis place on the privacy of the family. Problems in the family stay within the family and are not discussed with outsiders, even good friends. While it is considered polite to ask a man about the welfare of his family in general, it is considered extremely bad manners to inquire about the health of his wife. The business of the family is always isolated from public view, usually behind high compound walls. Even the new high-rise apartments that are being built in Riyadh and Jeddah reflect this desire for privacy. Almost all the windows are frosted glass, of the type one might find in a bathroom in Europe or the United States.

Divorce itself carries no stigma in Saudi Arabia. It is not considered disgraceful, and there is no cause for individual or family shame. There are two reasons for this. First, no such thing as a "broken home" exists in Saudi Arabia, because almost all families are extended to at least three or four generations. Child-raising responsibilities are shared by the various generations of women. Thus the traumatic effect of divorce on children is diminished. Second, Islam not only permits divorce but considers it, in certain circumstances, a moral and righteous action. The Koran commands the spouses to treat each other with kindness and respect. If this should become impossible, then divorce is an accepted and dignified recourse.

Since divorce is cheap, simple, and quick, at least for the male, who need only announce his intention three times, one might expect Saudi Arabia to have a high divorce rate. Such is not the case. Although no statistics exist,[3] the divorce rate is low.

Since a husband is permitted more than one wife, he need not feel the claustrophobia he might experience in a monogamous society. If he can afford it, he can simply take a new wife.

The Saudi husband and wife also have different expectations of marriage than do their Western counterparts. The Saudi husband and wife do not see marriage as a recreational or social contract. They need not have leisure activities in common.

The opposite is so rare that one such case was reported in the *The Arab News* as a warning to other married couples. Apparently a husband in Jeddah had divorced his wife because

---

[3]Whatever statistics do exist are highly suspect. With the possible exception of surveys done by ARAMCO, statistics about Saudi Arabia come out of the fertile imaginations of ministry employees to serve the purposes of that particular ministry.

she insisted on cheering to victory a different football team than the one he supported. The wife contested the divorce in the *sharia* courts, and in due time the *qadi* (judge) overturned the divorce. While reminding the wife that it was her obligation to obey her husband, the *qadi* declared that football loyalties were too trivial a matter to be grounds for a divorce. (This is the only case I have heard of in which a woman succeeded in having a divorce overruled.)

Family pressure is also a factor against divorce. It is considered desirable for first cousins to marry. Thus, in many cases the family of the husband and the family of the wife are related. When such a marriage takes place, the family will often act as a mediating force in marital conflicts. Many divorces are avoided entirely, due to the support or pressure applied by the extended family. A divorce between first cousins could threaten the unity of the family.

Khalid, my Saudi friend, had been married to his first cousin. When he divorced her, his father became so furious that he took away the house Khalid had been living in, took away the Mercedes that his son had been driving, and quite arbitrarily ordered his son to pay his ex-wife half his monthly salary. Families in Saudi Arabia often act as judge, jury, and executioner. There is no appeal from a family ruling.

Servants become members of the Saudi family. Male servants have access to the harem and may view the women of the family unveiled. It is quite common in Saudi Arabia for ex-slaves to rise to positions of remarkable power and influence.

In some cases the loyalty between master and servant is even stronger than blood ties. I have been to dinner parties at Saudi homes where an old servant was seated next to the master of the house and was hand-fed throughout the meal by the head of the household.

Perhaps one of the more difficult master-servant relationships for the non-Muslim to understand is between a child and his wet nurse. When a woman suckles a child not her own, that child becomes her own. She becomes as much a mother to the child as the child's biological mother. When the child grows up, he is expected to treat his wet nurse with the same care and respect that he extends to his mother. He is not permitted to marry his wet nurse, nor is he permitted to marry the daughters of his wet nurse. Such a marriage would be incestuous.

Loyalty to one's family in Saudi Arabia remains the single most important duty a man or woman has. When an emergency arises, business meetings are canceled, multimillion-dollar contracts remain unsigned; it does not matter. Tomorrow is for business; today is for tending to the needs and desires of the family. And when you think about it, perhaps it makes more sense to value one's family above one's business dealings.

6

Women

There is an old saying in Saudi Arabia that a woman makes two outings in her lifetime: the first is from the home of her parents to the home of her husband; the second, from the home of her husband to the grave.

In Saudi Arabia's traditional families, this is still the expected pattern of a woman's life. However, the subject of women in Saudi Arabia is fraught with confusion, disagreement, and controversy. The confusion is genuine. I have yet to meet three Saudis who could agree on the proper status and role of women. Saudi women, especially those who have traveled abroad, themselves question what their position should be.

Saudis, both male and female, are hypersensitive to Western interpretations of the status of women in their country. They imagine, not altogether inaccurately, that most foreigners see the veiled, wraithlike figures of Saudi women simply as victims of social and sexual oppression. While common, this view of Saudi women is a gross oversimplification.

To understand the role of the Saudi woman, we must again look at the family. The population of Saudi Arabia, except for foreign workers, is composed of tribes that trace their ancestry back through the male line to a real or imagined individual. Arabs, in general, trace their descent back to the eldest son of Abraham, Ishmael. Quite a few Saudi tribes claim to trace their ancestry back to the Prophet Muhammed. Ancestry is a source of great pride.

Marriage was, until about thirty years ago, most often within one's own tribe. However, intertribal marriages did occur occasionally with the purpose of uniting two tribes in an alliance. The tribe was led by an old man, usually called a sheikh. The duties of the sheikh consisted of resolving conflicts within the tribe and leading the tribe in external affairs such as war. Either the sheikh was chosen by a group of male elders called a *majlis* (council), or he assumed the position through inheritance.

Most of these tribes were nomadic, wandering from place to place in the desert in search of grazing land for their camels and sheep. Land ownership, except in the coastal areas where agriculture was possible, did not exist. However, the Bedouin tribes of Arabia did recognize traditional grazing rights. Contrary to popular notion, the Bedouins did not wander throughout the desert. They moved in an understood and predictable area. Trespassing without first receiving an invitation was not merely bad manners; it could be considered an act of war.

The life of the nomadic Bedouin family focused on one thing and one thing only—survival. A trivial mistake in the desert could be fatal, and so each family member had specific duties, each necessary to the survival of the family unit.

Since a man could not survive in the desert without his tribe, tribal loyalty became a most important obligation. Similarly, a woman could not survive without a husband in this arid, forbidding land.

Women usually married soon after their first menstrual period, at the age of twelve or thirteen. A girl might be married at an even earlier age, but her husband was expected not to consummate the marriage until after she had entered puberty.

Women continue to be married at an early age in Saudi Arabia, although with the advent of women's education, it is not uncommon to find women still single in their twenties. Hassus, a woman of thirty who has six children, was married two weeks after her first menstruation. After living in the United States for five years, she has a different plan for her own daughters. "I suppose you may think it amusing," she told me, referring to her honeymoon. "No one had told me what to expect. I knew nothing about sex. I was twelve years old. When my husband started to touch my breasts, I hit him with my shoe. My daughters will not go through that kind of humiliation."

The ever-present concern for survival in the desert dictated not only the marriageable age of a woman but also her familial duties. She was responsible for the preparation of food, caring for the living quarters, raising the children, and tending to the needs of the livestock. She was also responsible for providing her husband with sons. Biological arguments aside, failure to give her husband a son was, and in some cases still is, grounds for divorce.

Despite the injunction in the Koran against holding women against their will, women were often taken as part of the spoils after a successful Bedouin raid. While a man could have only four legal wives, he could also have concubines and slaves for his sexual pleasure. Though this was not considered adultery, it was frowned upon by the more devout Muslims. It became traditional for a sheikh to give a slave woman her freedom if she bore him a son.

The tradition of treating women as loot lives on in some of Saudi Arabia's larger cities. A decade ago, the Saudi government began handing out taxis free of charge to nomadic Bedouins as an incentive to move to the urban centers and settle down. As a result, almost all the taxi drivers in Riyadh are Bedouin. But each year, the government found that they were losing more and more women, taxi drivers, and taxis. A driver would take a fancy to a woman passenger and simply drive her out into the desert. Neither driver nor woman would be seen or heard from again.

After an epidemic of such abductions in early 1980, Prince Naif, minister of the interior, announced that all taxi drivers had to be over the age of thirty-five and that no women were allowed to ride in taxis alone. The rule is not observed, and the kidnapings continue.[1]

---

[1]Under *no* circumstances should a foreign woman ride in a taxi alone in Saudi Arabia. Even a group of two or three women runs a risk when taking a cab. In January 1980 three Indonesian women got in a cab at the International Airport in Jeddah. None of them has been heard of since.

By far the most time-consuming of a woman's familial duties is child bearing and rearing. Women are told by the Koran to suckle their offspring for two years. Infant mortality rates among the nomadic Bedouins just twenty years ago ran as high as seventy-five percent, and to compensate, a woman would spend most of her child-bearing years either pregnant or nursing. During the nursing period, a woman was in an "unclean" state and was forbidden to pray or have sexual intercourse with her husband. Thus women won in battle served to satisfy the libido of the husband during the period his wife or wives were nursing.

Child bearing starts soon after marriage. It is not uncommon for fourteen- and fifteen-year-old girls to become mothers, and it is not at all unusual to find a woman of twenty-five with five or six children. On a recent trip to the Maternity Division of Shemasi Hospital in Riyadh, my wife encountered a fifteen-year-old Bedouin girl in intense emotional distress because she had received a negative pregnancy test result for the third time and was concerned that her husband would divorce her.

Women in Saudi Arabia have an important position within the family, but outside the four walls of the home they are virtually nonentities. The Koran is very specific when it comes to describing a woman's position within the family:

> Men are the managers of the affairs of women
> for that God has preferred in bounty
> one of them over another, and for that
> they have expended of their property.
> Righteous women are therefore obedient,
> guarding the secret for God's guarding.
> And those you fear may be rebellious
> admonish; banish them to their couches,
> and beat them. If they then obey you,
> look not for any way against them; God is
> All-high, All-great.
> (*The Koran Interpreted*, I:438)

The husband is the manager of the affairs of women. He is also a filter and a screen between his wife and the world outside the extended family. It is his duty to protect her not only from physical danger but also from the danger of exposure to publicity.

The Koran does not provide us with the reasons behind making men the managers of women's affairs, but Islamic scholars alternately suggest that business affairs are not in the "nature" of women or that women have no experience in public affairs and therefore should be protected from their own mistakes by being exempted from such responsibility.

Islam seems to suggest that such a thing as sexual "nature" does exist regardless of upbringing or environment. Thus the "nature" of women includes psychological characteristics which correspond to physiological ones. The male is seen as occupying the dominant position. It is in his "nature" to be the provider and protector. The woman's nature is seen to be more docile, more emotional, more submissive.

The woman is viewed as having a wealth of emotion but little intellect that is useful beyond the four walls of her home. The woman is also seen as being less practical and more capricious. Thus in this Islamic dualism the woman presides over the home but derives whatever authority she has from her husband.

A woman's status within the family depends on two factors, her age and the number of children she has had. Newly married couples often live with the husband's parents. Initially the new bride has little authority and comes under the direct guidance of her mother-in-law. Relationships between daughter-in-law and mother-in-law vary from affectionate to volatile, but the stereotypic antagonism of the West is notably absent. A woman receives greater status after the birth of a child, particularly if the child is male.

There is no such thing as a female public figure in Saudi Arabia. Women have little place in business and absolutely no place in politics. There is, or at least there seems to be, an unwritten law in Saudi Arabia that a man's wife's name shall only be known to her immediate family and a few female friends. Most Saudis do not know the name of King Khalid's wife, and a newspaper editor would lose his job if he dared to print it.

Women remain throughout their postpubertal lives in a state of *purdah* (literally, "seclusion"). Purdah is almost universally respected within the kingdom, despite the antics of some Saudi women once they arrive in Europe. Purdah is made obvious by the wearing of the *abaya* (a full-length black cloak) and veil, but the meaning of this seclusion or privacy goes beyond mere modesty. While a woman possesses no public self and correspondingly no reputation or honor, she is the repository of the honor of the family and the tribe. This fragile but most important treasure is too highly valued to permit a woman public exposure.

This sense of privacy diminishes slightly when a husband and wife have been exposed to European or American culture, and it may be dropped altogether in the company of Westerners in Saudi Arabia. However, purdah is always observed when other Saudis are present. My friend Khalid, for example, would bring his wife to parties given by Westerners, but only after he had been assured that no other Saudis would be present. On an occasion when both Khalid and his first cousin, Suleiman, were invited, Khalid refused to allow his wife to attend. Although Khalid and Suleiman were related by blood and were close friends, Suleiman had never seen Khalid's wife's unveiled face.

In Saudi Arabia, the legal status of women is confusing. Women seem both above and below the law at the same time. The Koran gives the woman a legal value of one half a man: "God charges you, concerning your children, to the male the like portion of two females..." (I:4:11). A woman's testimony in court is equal to half a man's. Where it requires one male witness to a contract, it requires two females. A woman is entitled to only half the inheritance of her brothers, and a widow may be left nothing other than her bride price.

Legal and social restrictions on women are quite severe, at least by Western standards, and are enforced. There are extremely few jobs that a Saudi woman may work at. A Saudi woman must have the written permission of her husband or male guardian before accepting employment.

While nursing is legally open to Saudi women, most consider it menial and beneath them. Teaching is a profession which quite a number of young Saudi women are entering, but the problem which arises here is with the very purpose of women's education. Why bother to educate girls who can do nothing with their education other than educate other girls?

There is a handful of young Saudi women who have a different vision of the future. They believe that the role of women is changing and that more job opportunities will open up for them. They cite as examples a women's clothing store in Jeddah that serves women and is run by women and the recent opening of an all-women's bank in Riyadh.

The debate on women working is a highly emotional one in Saudi Arabia. Sheikh Hisham Nazar, the powerful Minister of Planning, summed up the controversy in a statement reported in *Saudi Business*, a semiofficial government publication, on March 17, 1980: "It has been agreed that the issue of working women has significance. But there could be an unending discussion on whether a woman should or should not work. Yes, she must work, but within the bounds of Islamic Faith."

The Council of Ministers, together with the Ulema (religious leadership), are at present attempting to define where employment for women falls within an Islamic framework. However, it is highly unlikely that any dramatic changes will be forthcoming.

Some Saudis, both male and female, are even more outspoken. A young female teacher at the University of Riyadh was categorical. "The government likes to confuse the issue of Saudi traditions with Islam. It serves to keep the royal family in power. There is nothing in Islam that prohibits a woman from working, from having dignity, from seeking intellectual fulfillment. Anyone who says differently is lying to you."

At a dinner party attended by Sheikh Abdulaziz Muhammed Twaijairi, the second deputy commander of the National Guard, the subject of the status of women in Saudi Arabia came up. "The government," Twaijairi announced, "is studying the problem. Employment for women will increase in the future. But we will not make the mistakes that you in the West have made. There is nothing in Islam that forbids a woman from working; in fact the contrary is true. To arbitrarily prevent a woman from working is against Islam."

The most formidable obstacle facing women who seek employment in Saudi Arabia is the lack of transportation. Women are forbidden by law to drive. This law is not likely to be changed or modified in the near future, since to do so would be tantamount to allowing women to go unveiled in public. Women are also forbidden to travel within the kingdom without a male guardian (usually her husband or brother), although this is not rigorously enforced either by Saudia or by the airport police.

The Council of Ministers perceives that a problem facing the kingdom will be a shortage of trained manpower. Until now, it has been the policy of the government to import skilled labor. Young women are becoming increasingly vocal about their wish to enter the work force and thus alleviate part of this growing shortage.

On the other hand, the ruling princes are positively paranoid about preserving the Islamic status quo. They are beginning to have their doubts about sending young Saudis outside the kingdom for specialized training, since these same young people often return to Saudi Arabia corrupted by Western "decadence."

Prince Naif, the Minister of the Interior, recently ruled that there would be no scholarships for women studying outside the kingdom. In a lengthy interview in *The Arab News*, Prince Naif explained his ruling by stating that women were now welcome in all the university programs within the kingdom, and therefore there was no need for them to study abroad.

Sexual segregation in public is the rule. Although this can be considered part of purdah, Saudi Arabia carries it further than any other Islamic country.

Virtually all public places have special restricted areas for women. A small section of the public buses is partitioned off for them. Restaurants in Riyadh have special "family" dining rooms where women are welcome. Even the university libraries have one day a week set aside especially for women students. Hospitals have special waiting rooms restricted to women, and a portion of the waiting rooms at the Riyadh and Jeddah airports are restricted to "families."

This segregation is even extended into the home. Most Saudi houses have separate living quarters for the men and the women. The women of the household have their own living and dining areas—the modern equivalent of the harem.

With the exception of camping or picnicking in the desert, there are few recreational activities that a family can engage in as a group. Riyadh does have a zoo, but it is run by the *mutawa* and is open only one day a week for families. In fact, the problem of keeping men and women separate at the zoo became so difficult that the *mutawa* closed it altogether in 1979. The latest news is that the zoo has reopened with stricter safeguards for the segregation of men and women.

Public cinemas are completely illegal in the kingdom. Supposedly this prohibition comes from the Koran's injunction against representing the human form. However, television has become a way of life, as have videotape film parties. The continued ban on public cinemas really stems from the restriction on the mingling of the sexes.

When asked about the separation of the sexes, Saudis will often answer by retelling the story of Ayesha, the Prophet Muhammed's last and youngest wife. After the Prophet's death, Ayesha's father, Abu-Bakr, became the caliph, and when he died he was buried next to Muhammed beneath the floor of the hut that Ayesha was living in.

When the next caliph, Omar, died, his family came to Ayesha and requested her permission to have Omar buried next to the Prophet and Caliph Abu-Bakr. Ayesha granted her permission but moved out of the house. The Prophet had been her husband, Abu-Bakr had been her father, but Caliph Omar was no relation at all, and Ayesha could not share her house with an unrelated male, even though the man was dead.

Attitudes toward women in Arabia are paradoxical. A Saudi man is usually disappointed if his wife gives birth to a girl baby. The mother, no less than the father, considers a baby girl of little value. It is not uncommon for family members to commiserate with a father about the birth of a girl. The birth of a female will be forgiven if she is the firstborn, but each subsequent girl baby compounds the disaster. During the *Gehenna*, the period of ignorance before the revelation of the Koran, it was not uncommon for fathers to bury their newborn daughters alive in the sands of the desert. However, the Koran strictly forbids infanticide, and the tradition is virtually nonexistent in Arabia today.

One gauge of the value placed upon a boy baby is the fact that the father receives his name from the name of his eldest son. Soon after a man is married, he chooses the name of his eldest son even though his wife may be months or even years away from pregnancy. From then on, the husband is known as the father of his eldest son. For instance, Khalid has only a daughter, but is known as abu-Muhammed (the father of Muhammed) because when his wife gives birth to a boy, the boy will be named Muhammed.

The suggestion here is that the identity of the father, his public reputation, and his honor hinge on his eldest son. Thus the husband who is without a son is denied not only an heir to the family name but also an essential component of Arab manhood. This idea of coming to know the father through the son has some fascinating ramifications for the Christian, especially in light of the fact that Jesus, although he practiced Judaism, was a Palestinian Arab who, in all probability, understood this tradition.

A girl grows up in Saudi Arabia in a strictly domestic setting. Before the age of six or seven she may attend a coeducational school and have boys as playmates. At about the age of five or six, she assists in household duties and begins to learn what will be expected of her as a woman. Her education through secondary school is quite basic, concentrating on writing, reading, arithmetic, and lengthy memorizations from the Koran. At the onset of puberty, or before if she is tall, as many women from the Nejd are, she dons the *abaya* and veil.

Most girls take up wearing the veil and *abaya* upon graduation from primary school. Western teachers have commented on the trauma of the scene. "They knew they were locked in," commented one American teacher from the exclusive Riyadh Schools, "and that for the rest of their lives they would be imprisoned by the veil. My students wept openly.... Their childhood and their freedom was gone."

This kind of an interpretation does not agree with what Saudi women have told me. The first time a Saudi girl wears the veil, her family and her friends recognize her as a woman. It is a rite of passage into adulthood. As for the tears reported by the American teacher, I have attended few graduations anywhere in the world that were entirely without emotion. My own observation is that the majority of Saudi girls look forward to wearing the veil, in much the same way as American girls look forward to wearing lipstick or high heels.

The veil is a difficult thing for a great many Westerners to understand. Reactions range from patronizing amusement to maudlin sympathy to anger. Actually the veil deserves none of these responses. The Saudis alone among the Islamic world believe that the Koran commands the woman to be completely veiled. Thus, to many Saudi women, the wearing of the veil is in itself a fulfillment of a command from God. The Koran, however, does not call specifically for a woman to cover her face:

> And say to the believing women, that they
> cast down their eyes and guard their private
> parts, and reveal not their adornments
> save such as is outward, and let them cast
> their veils over their bosoms, and not reveal
> their adornments save to their husbands
> or their fathers, or their husband's father . . .
> (*The Koran Interpreted,* II:14:30)

This verse continues with a virtual laundry list of men that a woman may expose her "adornments" to, but never once tells us what exactly her adornments are. Variously, a woman's adornments have been interpreted to mean her mouth, her hair, her legs from the ankle up, her arms, her breasts, her neck, her nose, and—in the case of Saudi Arabia—all of the above. The only flesh a Saudi woman may expose publicly are her hands and feet.

Although the Koran instructed the Prophet Muhammed to veil his wives and daughters, we know that Ayesha did not veil her face. Most probably the veiling of the face came about as a form of identification: women who had accepted the revelations of the Prophet veiled themselves to signify they were Muslims.

This served two important purposes. First of all, it was a visible symbol of faith that served to bond the early Islamic community into a cohesive unit. Second, the veil served to identify a woman as a Muslim to would-be raiders and to warn the potential abductor of the revenge of the entire Muslim brotherhood. The Koran itself suggests that the veil is protective:

> O Prophet, say to thy wives and daughters
> and believing women, that they draw
> their veils close to them; so it is likelier
> they will be known, and not hurt ...
> (*The Koran Interpreted*, II:33:59)

The veil certainly provides a Saudi woman with modesty, but more than that, it provides her with a sense of security and protection. It is a symbol of her submission to the Will of God, a symbol of the respect her husband has for her, and a symbol of the honored position that she occupies in the family.

The symbolism of the veil and *abaya* must be of major importance to these women, for they are certainly most uncomfortable to wear during the summer months, when the temperature in the shade can break one hundred twenty degrees.

The *abaya* and the veil have become a way of life to the Saudi woman. She feels "naked" in public without them. Some Saudi women abandon the veil when they go on vacation to Europe or the United States. Others, however, carry their traditions with them. Some of London's prestigious Harley Street doctors report that Saudi women refused to unveil even during a gynecological examination.

Western women in Saudi Arabia are not required to wear the *abaya* or veil in public, although some have adopted the custom after growing tired of the barrage of whistles and sexual invitations that almost invariably greet the woman who ventures forth in public unveiled. Westerners in Saudi Arabia often see these crude overtures as products of bad manners, a lack of civilization, or general sexual frustration. They are in fact the result of nothing more than cultural differences: just imagine the absurdity of judging the civilization of America on the reaction of a group of teen-aged boys encountering a bare-breasted Polynesian woman in Times Square.

Women in Saudi Arabia are forbidden by law to socialize with unrelated men. Westerners are expected to respect and obey the laws of the kingdom, especially those that concern the position of women. A recent legal case in Jeddah illustrates this clearly. A British expatriate doctor and his wife, Richard and Penelope Arnot, gave a party in their apartment during which alcohol was served and unrelated men and women (all Westerners) danced and socialized together.

During the party, an unmarried European couple, only partially dressed, fell from the fifth-floor balcony to their deaths. The police arrived almost immediately and arrested Richard and Penelope Arnot. Dr. Arnot has been sentenced to one year in prison and thirty lashes for the alcohol offense and for allowing his wife to mingle with unrelated males. His wife was also sentenced to thirty lashes for the alcohol offense, plus fifty lashes more for giving false information to the court.

Ultimately, King Khalid pardoned the Arnots, and they were deported from the kingdom, but it should be noted that under Islamic law the Arnots could have been charged with murder, and had they been charged with murder, and had they been Saudi nationals rather than British they probably would have been executed.

Adultery is the most serious crime in Saudi Arabia. It is considered far more heinous than murder. Although the Koran specifically provides flogging as the punishment for adultery, Saudi law calls for the death penalty. On the other hand, it is difficult to get a conviction on an adultery charge, since the Koran dictates that there must be at least four witnesses to the physical act of unfaithfulness. However, a sworn confession can be used in lieu of witnesses. Convictions are rare but do occur from time to time.

A man convicted of adultery is either shot by a firing squad or hanged. Decapitation is considered too dignified a death for a man who would attack the virtually sacred institution of the family. The adulteress, on the other hand, is taken to the marketplace, placed in a burlap sack, and stoned to death by onlookers.

In some parts of Saudi Arabia, the woman may be buried waist-deep in sand before the first stone is thrown. The first stone is usually thrown by the imam (the religious leader), and, as an act of mercy, it is usually the size of a small boulder which produces at least unconsciousness if not instant death. The last stoning of an adulteress was reported to have taken place in the desert outside Jeddah in 1977.

Foreigners living in the kingdom are equally subject to the strict adultery laws (which cover premarital as well as extramarital sexual activity). A British woman and an American man served three years in Saudi prisons after they were found to be living together in Dhahran. There is one reported case of a foreign woman being executed for adultery. It is said that the woman was American and that her husband, in a fit of jealous rage, informed the police of her unfaithfulness. After extracting a confession from the woman, the *sharia* court, in deference to the fact she was an American and a first offender, sentenced her to be publicly flogged. However, her husband, not realizing the consequences of his action, signed an official complaint against his wife saying that her adultery had been repeated. The court reversed itself and imposed the death penalty. It is said that the woman was stoned to death. It is also reported that upon hearing the fate of his wife, the husband went mad and had to be deported from the kingdom in a straitjacket.

Saudi Arabia has its share of young, unmarried women who find themselves pregnant. In most cases, these women are part of the approximately thirty percent of the population which is still nomadic and desperately poor. In the majority of these cases, the family of the woman will decide her fate—usually death at the hands of her father or brothers. This is not considered murder in a strict legal sense, but it is frowned upon by the courts.

Recently a group of princesses formed an underground railroad to assist young unmarried Bedouin women who find themselves pregnant. Dodging the police, the *mutawa*, and the religious authorities, these princesses bring the pregnant woman to Riyadh, keep her in total seclusion and secrecy until after the baby is born, and then find her a position as a domestic servant in one of Riyadh's many palaces. The baby is secretly deposited at the orphanage which is part of the Al-Nahda Women's Club[2] in Riyadh, the only institution of its kind in Saudi Arabia. This covert home for unwed mothers has helped scores of Bedouin women and may have saved as many as fifty lives.

In Saudi Arabia recreation for women is limited. Most sports are prohibited, since they require special costumes that might expose too much of a woman's body. Swimming is extremely difficult for women, although attitudes in the Eastern Province seem to be a great deal more relaxed than in Riyadh and the Nejd. Probably the principal form of recreation enjoyed by Saudi women is watching television. Virtually all nonnomadic Saudis own televisions, and even the Bedouin tents on the outskirts of Riyadh sport TV antennas.

A recent survey done by the Saudi government shows that Saudi women are among the most fanatical television addicts anywhere in the world. On an average, the Saudi woman consumes a mind-staggering seven hours daily of Koran recitation, tear-jerking Egyptian soap operas, soccer matches, heavily censored news, and a phantasmagoric barrage of Japanese cartoons.

For families that can afford it, the high point of the year comes during Ramadan or the white-hot summer months when the family goes off to Europe, the Far East, or the United States for an extended shopping spree. Some of these shopping vacations have already become legendary in the Western press. For example, Sheikh Ahmed Zaki Yamani, who was staying at London's posh Carlton Tower, took his two daughters on an after-hours shopping binge at Harrod's. They spent just under one hundred thousand dollars in less than an hour.

---

[2]The Al-Nahda Women's Club was founded by Princess Sara, daughter of the late King Faisal and Queen Iffat. The club includes classrooms, lecture halls, a concert hall, and a large library. Entrance, naturally, is permitted only to women. This serves to protect the organization's clandestine activities.

A Saudi prince took his four wives to Tiffany's to buy "a few pieces" of jewelry. When the women had selected their trinkets, the salesman handed the bored prince a bill for $1,400,000, which he paid in cash from an oversized briefcase. On still another occasion, Sheikh Aharif al-Hamdan negotiated for several days in an attempt to purchase the Alamo in Texas as a birthday present for his son, only to discover that it was not for sale.

Not all Saudis are extravagant, but it seems that most love to shop, and they love to bargain-hunt. My friend Khalid justified a week-long shopping trip to London, during which his wife managed to spend twenty thousand dollars, with the following logic: "The cost of most things is at least a third higher in Saudi Arabia. Some items, such as clothing, are twice as expensive in Saudi Arabia as they are in New York, and three or four times as expensive as they are in Bangkok. Even with the added cost of airline tickets and hotels, I save money by shopping abroad."

Judging from the proliferation of shops specializing in women's items like perfumes, jewelry, and clothing, Saudi women have a virtually insatiable appetite for the very latest consumer goods. Fashion designers from New York, Paris, and Rome make annual trips to the palaces and villas of Riyadh, Taif, and Jeddah to peddle their high-priced wares. Interior decorators from Italy and Lebanon are in constant demand.

Based upon the criteria of utility, higher education for women in the kingdom is quite luxurious. Women may attend university free of charge. However, there is precious little they can do with their educations once they graduate.

No public education existed in Saudi Arabia before 1954. That was when Crown Prince Faisal ordered the formation of the Ministry of Education. This was the first attempt at a secular educational system, and, even though it was all-male, it met initially with great resistance from the Ulema.

Education for females was not established until Faisal, as king, ordered the formation of schools for girls in 1962. Female illiteracy was at ninety-eight percent when Faisal came to the throne only twenty years ago.

In 1962, the University of Riyadh admitted the first four women ever to study at the university level inside Saudi Arabia.

Their classes were separate from the men's, and to appease the archconservative Ulema, Faisal placed the entire administration of women's education under the auspices of the religious authorities. Female enrollment at the University of Riyadh grew at a breathtaking rate. The Center for Female University Education was established in 1976, and during the 1978–79 academic year there were more than three thousand women enrolled as university students in Riyadh alone.

Women's education remains segregated. Two burly *mutawa* members guard the entrance to the women's center, barring entrance to males. Women students are taught only by women teachers. On rare occasions, male professors will lecture to women students by way of closed-circuit television. Every desk is equipped with a numbered telephone so that the women may question the male professor, who in many cases is in a studio next door.

Women's education in Saudi Arabia is beset with problems. It is separate but far from equal. The physical facilities for women students are small and cramped, and different performance standards are set by the male and female colleges.

Many Saudis, both male and female, look upon women's education as an extension of their social life. Cheating is the rule rather the exception in both male and female education, bribery is commonplace, and administrative graft and corruption virtually ensure an inflated and extravagant annual budget. The 1980–81 budget for the University of Riyadh was 3,128,000,000 Saudi riyals (approximately one billion dollars). With an enrollment of only thirteen thousand students, the university spends about seventy-seven thousand dollars per student per year. Even granting that a portion of this budget goes to constructing the huge new campus at Diriyah, the per-student expenditure is easily the highest in the world.

In 1978 the grades of the women in the College of Arts at Riyadh University were arbitrarily lowered because statistically the women had performed better than the men. Since these statistics are passed on to UNESCO, the administrators considered the higher scores of the women to project a poor image of the kingdom.

All Saudi students, both male and female, receive a stipend of about two hundred fifty dollars a month while they are studying at a university. The government requires both male and female graduates to give two years of service to the kingdom following graduation or to repay the money invested in their education.

Women from the royal family or other families that can afford it usually pay their way out of this service. Nevertheless, hundreds of young women each year work off their university education in this way. Most are farmed out to rural primary and secondary girls' schools as teachers or teaching assistants. Some are placed in hospitals as nurse's aides, and a few are given secretarial work at women's hospitals or girls' schools. While the opportunities are still limited, a new consciousness is spreading among a few young Saudi women of a future career beyond the four walls of the home.

Walaa is a third-year university student, studying Arabic and English literature. She is twenty-one years old and is in the process of choosing between two men who want to marry her.

"The choice is difficult," she confided to me, "because before I marry, I want my husband to understand that I must be more than just a wife and mother. I don't think anyone in Saudi Arabia is questioning the importance of the family. The family is Islam. But the time has come for skilled women to enter the work force and serve their country."

I asked Walaa if she thought the government would change the employment regulations for women in the near future. "Of course the regulations will change. But they will change quietly. You will not find Saudi women shouting for rights as your women do in the United States. Saudi women are still quite shy, but they are ready to work, and they *will* work, *Inshallah.*"

7

Values and Paradoxes

The Saudi Arab is a creature of extremes. He knows no middle ground. He is either extravagantly generous or incredibly avaricious. He can be as patient as a caravan camel one moment and hysterical the next. His spectrum seems to lack the middle range of moderation. A word can provoke him to fury, but he is just as likely to laugh.

He will rarely tell the truth if an exaggerated version is available. He is spontaneous, irresponsible, fiercely loyal, not very honest, tiresome, delightful, dangerous, and playful. He offers the best and worst of human nature with tireless enthusiasm. Even his apathy is enthusiastic. The Saudi is so paradoxical that at times he seems to be deliberately caricaturing himself.

One of the most revered virtues in Arabia is generosity. A man's reputation depends largely on his willingness to give away what he has, and at times to give away what is not even his to give. In Arabia, generosity is more important than honesty, and the worst insult one can possibly make is to suggest that a man is stingy or cheap.

Generosity is a way of life, and at times an annoying one. It is a custom in Saudi Arabia to give away whatever someone admires. The custom is rigidly adhered to, and virtually nothing is too large or too costly to be exempt from this rule.

At a dinner party soon after I arrived in Saudi Arabia, I made the mistake of complimenting the host on a particularly large and attractive Persian carpet that covered the floor of his living room. "It is in your hands," he replied, promptly and seemingly without regret. I attempted to refuse his generous gift, but to no avail. I was told that the carpet would be delivered to my apartment the following day. It was not until after I had explained that my living room was too small for such a carpet that he finally accepted my refusal.

Marianne Alireza tells a similar story.[1] Her husband had spent several years designing and constructing a particularly magnificent house in Jeddah when it came to his attention that King Abdulaziz had admired the house. The house was promptly given to the king, who in turn gave it to his son, Faisal.

To admire or compliment another's possession in Arabia is the same as asking for it, and it is considered by most Saudis as poor manners. Ahmed, a close Saudi friend, announced one evening that he was going to stop wearing watches entirely. It turned out that he had hosted an American business delegation during their week-long stay in Riyadh. A discussion of Swiss watches had occurred, and by the end of the week, Ahmed had given away more than a dozen expensive watches.

Generosity is expected, but elaborate displays of gratitude are not. In fact, it is common for the recipients of gifts to act as if they had a right to the gift in the first place and express no gratitude whatsoever. Prince Sultan's weekly *majlis* (public meeting) is full of men petitioning him for a grant of land or money for the bride price. Few, if any, are turned away empty-handed.

There is an element of bravado in this tradition of generosity. It is almost as if the size and monetary value of the gift determine the manhood of the giver. The spirit in which the gift is given is of secondary importance to the price paid. One may be frugal in the private management of the family budget, but one must never seem ungenerous in public. In Arabia one is expected to give beyond one's means.

At a children's Halloween party at the Lockheed compound in Riyadh, my friend Khalid gave each of the two dozen costumed children a hundred-riyal note (thirty dollars) and the next day confided to me that he had lost his job the week before.

---

[1]Marianne Alireza, *At the Drop of a Veil.*

Saudis love to talk about money. Money occupies a more fa-vored position in conversation than even women and politics. Despite the injunction in the Koran against placing too high a value on money and riches (II:104), Saudis seem possessed by an all-consuming quest for financial gain. In business, they are openly avaricious and mean. They have, or at least seem to have, a mortal fear of being cheated, and they respond to this fear by cheating before they themselves are cheated.

It is not at all uncommon for foreign workers employed by Saudis to find their salaries reduced arbitrarily from a previ-ously agreed-upon figure. Neither is it uncommon for contracts to be inflated by ten or twenty percent in order to pay "commis-sions" to friends and family members.

The amount of graft and corruption in Saudi Arabia is a con-stant source of concern to the ruling members of the royal fam-ily, and late in 1979 an order was issued by the king banning "commissions" on all government contracts. Despite this ban, bribery remains widespread, and in many cases "paying off" is considered good manners.

The government's concern is political, not moral. The graft that exists on a large scale never filters down to the "average" Saudi, and those who are profiteering from this corruption are limited to several hundred princes and wealthy merchants. The majority of Saudis resent the corruption not so much because it is corruption but because they are unable to get what they con-sider their share of the action.

So widespread is graft that *The Arab News* ran a front-page news story on the startling case of a minor government official who refused a bribe from a foreign corporation. An editorial in the same paper called the government official "a new brand of hero."

Corruption stories have received wide publicity in the West. Adnan Khashoggi's multimillion-dollar "commissions" from Lockheed have already been investigated by both the press and the U.S. Congress.[2]

---

[2]It is alleged that Adnan Khashoggi received over two hundred million dollars from Lockheed for acting as a middleman with the Saudi government to secure huge military contracts for Lockheed.

More recently, multimillion-dollar corruption scandals have centered around Prince Muhammed ibn-Fahd, the son of the crown prince. With distinctions between the government and the royal family blurred beyond recognition, it has been easy, despite recent government regulations limiting the amounts that can be paid out as "commissions," for influential princes to reap hundreds of millions of dollars in bribes and kickbacks.

During the past three years, Prince Muhammed ibn-Fahd has been associated with a number of highly questionable business ventures.[3] It is reported that in 1977 he architected a seven-billion-dollar telecommunications deal between the Saudi government and the Dutch firm, Philips. Prince Muhammed's "commission" was reported to be in excess of one hundred million dollars.

The contract was eventually killed by the Saudi government because the Philips bid was considered inflated and Prince Muhammed's "commission" excessive.

In the same year Prince Muhammed became a partner in Arabian Bechtel, receiving a ten-percent equity share of the huge construction company. In 1978, barely a year later, Arabian Betchel was awarded a 3.5-billion-dollar contract for construction work on Riyadh's new international airport. Government officials privately alleged that Betchel could not possibly have gotten the contract without the prince's influence and assistance. Furthermore, they assert that Prince Muhammed received a large grant of land free of charge from the government. It was, curiously enough, this same piece of land just outside Riyadh that Betchel engineers chose as the "ideal" location for the new airport. Prince Muhammed is alleged to have sold the land back to the government for the astronomical sum of nine billion Saudi riyals (approximately three billion dollars).

Prince Muhammed has also been linked by the Western press to the Ente Nazionale Idrocarburi (the Italian state-owned energy company) corruption scandal. It was this scandal that resulted in the resignation of the Italian company's president. *The New York Times* reported that the publicity that Prince

---

[3] *The New York Times*, Wednesday, April 16, 1980.

Muhammed ibn-Fahd has received may force his father to appoint him to a government post so as to limit his future association with questionable business deals.

However, it is important to understand that what is considered corruption in the West may not be considered corruption in Saudi Arabia. For instance, Adnan Khashoggi was genuinely surprised when the Western press suggested that taking commissions from Lockheed was graft. The royal family was equally startled by the multitude of allegations concerning Prince Muhammed ibn-Fahd.

"What is this so-called scandal?" answered one official in the Ministry of the Interior when I asked him about Prince Muhammed's airport-land deal. "Many princes are given land by the government. It just so happened that in the case of Prince Muhammed the government decided to buy the land back from him. What is scandalous about that? To be perfectly candid with you, no one in Saudi Arabia cares what *The New York Times* says. Everyone knows that it is run by pro-Zionist Jews who never write anything complimentary about Arabs or Islam."

Not all Saudis are so complacent about the royal family's questionable business affairs. Yousif, a twenty-four-year-old university student, is angry about the abuses. "This entire country runs on influence. If you have a powerful prince for a friend, you can do anything. Is this Islamic justice? Of course not. The princes get richer and richer, and still the hospitals aren't built, still the schools aren't constructed. You tell me that King Faisal Hospital is the best-equipped hospital in the world. I am forced to agree with you. But try to get treatment there. You won't be admitted unless you have a letter from a prince. It is a hosptial for the royal family and for friends of the royal family.

"Do you wonder why Saudis don't complain more vocally? The answer is simple. Most of us are scared. The princes have all the power. To publicly criticize the royal family is to invite an accident. The desert is a very dangerous place."

Saud, an official at the Ministry of Planning, sees much of what the West views as corruption not as corruption at all, but simply part of the very personalized way in which Saudis conduct business. "Saudis do not hide behind policies and precedents. We deal between men." He continued, "The U.S. Army Corps of Engineers in Riyadh solves a problem by feeding all the information into a computer. A few seconds later they have their cold, impersonal answer. This is not the way Saudis do business.

"When my secretary comes to me and tells me his son needs an operation in London, should I tell him that the computer says he has used up all his emergency leave? Of course not. Here in Saudi Arabia, we sit down and talk, one man to another.

"Americans want to turn workers into machines. We will not copy that. America calls us corrupt because we help our friends, our brothers, our families. That is the thinking of a machine, not the thinking of a real man."

Equally important to manhood as generosity is hospitality. The Arab conception of hospitality gets its origin from the brutal terrain of the desert.

The Bedouin of Arabia will never turn away a stranger, will never withhold food, water, or shelter, even from an enemy. Traditionally, hospitality was obligatory for three days and nights, but as urban centers grow larger and the nomadic Bedouins become increasingly settled, the prescribed hospitality period is vanishing. The traditional Arab greeting to a guest is as follows: "O guest of ours, though you have come, though you have visited us and have honored our dwelling, we are truly the guests and you are the lord."

There is an old Arabian story that well illustrates the importance of hospitality. It is said that there once was an old man who was very poor. Other than his tent and his cooking utensils, the only thing of value the man owned was a magnificent Arabian stallion which was said to be the best of its breed anywhere in the world. A younger man had long desired to buy the horse from the Bedouin, but the old man had consistently refused to part with his horse.

The younger man now saw an opportunity for a doubly good deed to be done. He would offer the man more money than the horse was actually worth; thus he would be charitable and generous and at the same time acquire the horse that he had so long desired. The young man made his decision and set out on the journey to the old man's tent. When he arrived, the old man greeted him warmly and welcomed him to his humble tent. As it is considered extremely bad manners to talk business without first exchanging news and socializing, the young man sat, drank coffee, and had dinner with the old Bedouin without mentioning the purpose of his visit. It was only after they had finished eating that the young man expressed his desire to purchase the horse.

The old Bedouin smiled wryly. "What you have so long desired is already yours," the old man said. "Having nothing else to offer you to eat, I was forced, as your host, to slaughter the beast."

When one is invited to a Saudi dinner, one gets the distinct impression of the legacy the desert has left even in the heart of a major Arabian city. The egalitarianism of the Bedouin is ever-present. Hospitality is extended without regard to social or economic rank and is physically symbolized by a lengthy handshake and a kiss on both cheeks and, in some cases, a kiss on the nose.

Westerners are often made uncomfortable by the degree of physical contact Saudi men engage in. It is a common sight in Arabia for two or three men to walk down the street holding hands. This is simply a gesture of friendship and brotherhood, nothing more. Likewise, it is the custom for men who have not seen each other for some time to kiss each other on both cheeks. The kiss on the nose is usually reserved for someone older and is considered a gesture of great respect.

As a guest entering a Saudi house, one should remove one's shoes—this is especially true if the host himself is barefoot. At a formal dinner, each guest will be offered incense soon after arriving. The incense, usually sandalwood or frankincense from Yemen, is burnt in a traditional chalicelike ewer which should be raised to the face so that the fragrance of the smoke can permeate the beard and hair.

Soon after the incense has been passed around, a servant will appear with coffee. Unlike Turkish coffee, Arabian coffee is made from roasted green coffee beans mixed with cardamom and is served in thimble-sized cups. The coffee is a pale amber in color and is served without sugar, milk, or cream. Two or three cups of coffee are usual, and a guest's cup will be refilled automatically by a servant unless he signals that he has had enough. The common manner of signaling that no more coffee is desired is to hold the coffee cup in one's hand and shake it back and forth.

Dates and nuts are traditionally served along with coffee. As a guest in an Arab home, one does not wait to be invited to have one of this or one of that. One is a guest, and one is expected to act accordingly.

When the meal is served, it is usually spread out on the floor. While most urban Saudis now possess a dining room table, the majority of them prefer to continue to eat on the floor in the manner of the desert Bedouin. One should be cautious when sitting cross-legged on the floor not to expose the sole of one's foot to the person sitting adjacent. To do so is considered extremely bad manners.

The staple of the Arabian peninsula is still *kabsa*, roast or boiled mutton served with spiced rice. *Kabsa* is served on enormous trays, the mutton resting on top of mounds and mounds of rice. Knives, forks, spoons, and plates are not used. Guests and host alike are expected to use the right hand, as explained earlier, to tear off morsels of mutton and to mold the rice into a ball which can then be popped into the mouth.

For the untrained, this manner of eating can often be very messy. The guest or guests of honor are often hand-fed by the host. It is the very worst of manners to refuse some succulent tidbit that the host is trying to pop into your mouth.

Conversation, the principle form of amusement in Arabia, plays almost no role at all while eating. Saudis eat at breakneck speed, as if the first one finished were to receive some kind of prize. As soon as a guest is finished eating, he leaves the area of the floor where the food is arrayed. It does not matter that everyone has not finished. When the guest has finished, the meal is officially over, regardless of who else is still eating. The remains of the food are then devoured by the servants.

After dinner, tea and sweet cakes are usually served. This is the time for conversation, storytelling, political arguments, and, for Saudi women, discussions of matchmaking. Men and women rarely eat together when guests are present.

In some households the tea and sweet cakes may be accompanied by the *shisha*, a large pipe similar to a hookah. It may have four or even five hoses so that quite a number can smoke at the same time. A small quantity of an aromatic dried fruit medium is placed in the cup at the top of the *shisha*. The dried fruit is kept smoldering by hot charcoal, and the smoke is drawn through the hoses that lead off from the stem. Women from the Nejd, the central portion of Saudi Arabia, generally do not smoke either *shisha* or cigarettes. However, women from the more liberal Hejaz, the area in the west of the kingdom that borders on the Red Sea, are known to be great *shisha* smokers.

In contrast to Turkey, Morocco, and some other Middle Eastern countries, there is very little hashish or marijuana in Saudi Arabia. All intoxicating drugs are strictly prohibited by law, and the penalty for possession of even a small quantity of cannabis is severe.

The most commonly used illicit drug, other than alcohol, is *qat*. *Qat* is the leaf of a plant of the same name which is commonly grown in southern Arabia. The leaf contains a natural narcotic which is released when it is chewed. While *qat* is not legal in Saudi Arabia, its use is relatively common in the southern part of the kingdom, especially along the border with the Yemen Arab Republic. *Qat* is addictive, and the vast majority of its users are desperately poor.

Although hospitality is effusive throughout Arabia, it is tempered by an almost universal fear and hostility towards strangers. Saudi Arabia is one of the most xenophobic countries in the world. Foreigners are either welcomed with open arms or shot on sight, figuratively and, on rare occasions, literally.

No tourist visas are issued for entry into the kingdom. Likewise, the government rarely issues visas for foreign journalists or correspondents. Work visas are issued, but in the vast majority of cases these visas do not include the family of the worker. Pilgrimage visas are issued to Muslims wishing to make hajj, and the Ministry of the Interior spends the rest of the year tracking down the thousands and thousands of pilgrims who have overstayed their welcome.

Despite this, Europeans and Americans are generally well treated. They tend to make up a professional class of white-collar consultants, managers, technical experts, and educators. While respectful of the positions occupied by these Westerners, the Saudis are for the most part resentful of the intrusion of Western values and attitudes into the heart of their culture. This resentment is widespread and often appears to take the form of a national inferiority complex.

Saudis will often defend their country to Westerners even though no attack has been made. They find it difficult to believe that any European or American would find their country interesting or actually enjoy living in Saudi Arabia. Thus the majority of Saudis expect the Westerner to complain and criticize, and this expectation leads the Saudi to defend his kingdom by launching into lengthy criticisms of European and American values. It usually takes the Westerner quite some time to establish a relationship with a Saudi which can bypass this inane treadmill.

Paradoxically, foreign workers in Saudi Arabia who are not from Europe or the United States but from other Islamic nations are not well treated at all. The majority of imported manual laborers come from the two Yemens, Pakistan, Afganistan, Egypt, Jordan, and Indonesia.

The most downtrodden are the Yemenis, who make up the largest single group of foreign workers in the kingdom (some three hundred thousand). The Yemeni men gather at dawn at the Batha *suq* in Riyadh, huddled around charcoal fires in the winter and under the blistering sun in the summer, to wait for potential Saudi employers to arrive with trucks to haul them off, like cattle, to a job site in the desert. The average Yemeni working in the kingdom is completely illiterate and entirely unskilled. He works ten to fourteen hours a day and receives wages of less than one dollar an hour. He is usually not provided with housing, medical care, or food. He sends back most of his earnings to Yemen to support his family.

Most Yemenis living and working in Saudi Arabia reside in

shantytowns that cover every square foot of vacant land in and around the large cities. These shantytowns are constructed out of wooden packing crates, discarded corrugated iron, car fenders, and scraps of canvas that provide meager shade from the lethal summer sun. As many as a dozen Yemeni workers may share a tiny room, sleeping on a dirt floor. Diseases that have all but disappeared in the industrial world are common among Yemeni laborers. These include polio, cholera, and tuberculosis.

But by far the greatest suffering among the Yemenis is caused by malnutrition. Food prices in Saudi Arabia are among the highest in the world, and the grossly underpaid Yemeni is reduced to living almost entirely on rice. The life expectancy of a Yemeni in 1976 was less than forty years.

The reputation the Saudis have for generosity and charity apparently does not extend to their Islamic brothers from the south.

Despite the lip service the Saudis pay to the "suffering, homeless Palestinians," the lot of the Palestinians in Saudi Arabia is not much better than it is on the West Bank or in Gaza. While the Palestinian is not overtly persecuted in Arabia, he is treated as a second-class citizen. Even when employed and doing exactly the same job as a Saudi, a Palestinian—or, for that matter, an Egyptian—can expect a substantially lower salary.

The Ministry of the Interior is very strict about visas issued to Palestinians. Individuals with a history of political activism are banned from working in the country. Entry into Saudi Arabia is also barred to Palestinians who lack the technological skills the kingdom demands for its grandiose development plans.

Palestinians and Egyptians make up the majority of teachers and university professors in Saudi Arabia, but even occupying these generally respected positions does not ensure the non-Saudi Muslim decent treatment. A Palestinian professor of linguistics at the University of Riyadh, who resigned after teaching for only six months, was candid and bitter about what he saw as the exploitation of foreign Muslim workers: "I am a Palestinian. The Israelis stole our land. They are my enemy. But I never knew hatred, real hatred, until I came to this country and met my Muslim brothers, the Saudis."

An Egyptian professor of Arabic history also feels the scorn of the Saudis: "Money has come too fast to the Saudis. They have learned how to rule but not how to administer. When you sign a contract with a Saudi, he believes he has bought you, like a servant or a slave. The Saudi is frightened of Europeans and Americans. He is constantly comparing himself to them, and despite the ongoing development, the Saudi cannot help but find himself backward and materialistically inferior. There are two consequences of this national inferiority complex. The first is a rejection of materialism and a return to fundamentalist and fanatical Islam such as has taken place in Iran. The second consequence, however, is more common. Americans and Europeans are idealized, while [members of] the rest of the Arab world are scorned and treated like dogs. It is a paradox, but then all of Saudi Arabia is one enormous paradox."

The Saudis claim, with a certain degree of accuracy, that color prejudice is nonexistent in the kingdom. This is remarkable for a country that practiced slavery until only two decades ago. The vast majority of slaves imported into Arabia were black Africans from the Sudan and Ethiopia. They were auctioned off in slave markets, the largest of which was at the Buraimi Oasis—the site of an international conflict between Saudi Arabia and Britain. Most cities in Arabia had slave markets, and the poorest and oldest area of Riyadh is still known as Hilat al-Abd, the "area of the black man."

What made slavery in Saudi Arabia different from slavery elsewhere in the world was the institution of Islam. For a master to mistreat a slave was not only a sin against God but also a disgrace in the eyes of his own family and local community. A slave owner had the inescapable obligation to educate his slaves in the Koran, to treat them kindly and with generosity, and to free them if he could afford to do so. Thus racial tension based solely on skin color as the West has come to understand it does not exist in the kingdom.

The prejudice that does exist in Saudi Arabia, despite the egalitarianism of the Bedouins, is based on the rank of one's family and one's tribe. The usual division that Western Arabists make is between the "noble" and "ignoble" tribes. The former are descended from the warlike nomadic Bedouins, and the latter come from the agrarian tribes that settled in the arable coastal areas and oases. While this is a useful classification, it does not tell the whole story of family stratification in Arabia.

Perhaps the most important ingredient in family status is the size of the tribe one belongs to. If one comes from a large tribe, one is seen as having natural influence and power; if one comes from a small tribe, one is seen as having little strength and only a small amount of influence. On one occasion, while discussing Libyan politics with a group of Saudis, one of the Saudis present explained Muammer Qaddafi's seemingly psychotic policies as follows: "Qaddafi acts like a crazy man because he knows the truth. He is frightened because, although people obey his orders for the moment, he knows he has no real power. He comes from a very small tribe."

On the other hand, the siege of Mecca by political-religious rebels in late 1979 was doubly shocking to the Saudis, first because there had been violence within the Holy Haram and second because the leader of the rebels was a member of the al-Oteibi tribe, one of the largest and most powerful in the Middle East, numbering in the millions. There was general concern at the time that tribal loyalties would prove greater than religious and national allegiances.

Tribal loyalty is unquestionably strong in Arabia. Most large businesses are run along family or tribal lines, and nepotism is not only commonplace but actually considered a duty and an obligation. Of course, this does not necessarily breed efficiency, but in Arabia efficiency is of secondary importance to one's family and tribe. This all-important tribal loyalty has placed several large obstacles in the path of Saudi national development. Perhaps the most important obstacle is that, although the Saudi is fiercely proud of Islam and Saudi culture, he is devoid of patriotism and nationalism as these concepts are understood in the West.

Saudi Arabia is essentially an artificial political entity. Unity does not exist, despite a common language and common religion. For the most part, the people of the Hejaz and El Hasa (the eastern and western provinces) resent the inhabitants of the

Nejd, the central desert. They resent the fanatical Wahhabiism, the puritanism that they see as a corruption of Islam. More important, they resent the unequal distribution of oil revenues—the lion's share of which goes to the Nejd, the home of the royal family.

This resentment causes provincial and tribal loyalties to be traditionally stronger than loyalty to either the abstract concept of Saudi Arabia or the monarch himself. The one exception to this might have been King Faisal, who rescued the nation from the financial ruin left by King Saud and embodied most of the heroic virtues that are idealized by the Bedouins.

It is evident that the present ruling members of the royal family, while paying lip service to the virtues of patriotism, are openly opposed to any charismatic leadership. The delicate balance of power within the ruling family is so fragile that any prince who managed to enlist massive popular support would be considered an overt threat to the monarchy.

If you ask an average Saudi what he foresees politically in the next dozen years, he will almost automatically respond with a reference to the Will of God. While this deliberate vagueness makes excellent sense in a nation without any freedom of speech or press, it also illustrates an essential characteristic of the Saudi national character.

The peninsula Arab is among the most fatalistic of individuals anywhere in the world. Perhaps originally the life of the nomadic Bedouin was so fraught with hardship and suffering that the concept of a fate which would provide a release from suffering in the afterlife allowed the Bedouin a certain comfort in his day-to-day travails. Even as the Saudis have settled in urban centers, this fatalism remains strong. I have never met a Saudi, no matter how Westernized, who could speak about the future, even something that was arranged for the following day, without saying *"Inshallah"* (God willing). Even weather forecasting is prohibited, since it seems to represent an arrogant attempt to second-guess the will of God.

In some cases the use of *Inshallah* can be likened to the Western expression "knock on wood." There seems to be a traditional aversion to predicting the future, especially vocally, for to do so is to invite the trickery and malevolence of a capricious destiny. For this reason, children are rarely complimented in Arabia. To compliment the manners or intelligence of a child is believed to court accident, disease, and death.

Saudi fatalism is not merely superstitious in nature; it also reflects a sometimes deeply felt humility. Thus the word *Inshallah* also expresses an affirmation of faith in an all-knowing and all-powerful God and a corresponding recognition of the limitations and impotence of man.

Often this fatalism is carried to absurd extremes. For example, as a foreigner living in Saudi Arabia, it is entirely your responsibility to safeguard the health of those people employed by you, even temporarily. Should an electrician fail to turn off the electric current in your house or villa and hurt himself in the process of working on your wiring, you will be legally responsible for all his medical bills and the expenses his family incurs during the time he is out of work. The argument is that if you, as a foreigner, were not present in the kingdom, the accident would not have occurred in the first place.

The same logic is often employed in determining the guilty party in car accidents. Again, the foreigner's guilt is commonly a foregone conclusion due to the belief that the accident would not have happened had he stayed in his own country. The same convoluted logic applies to taxis that foreigners have hired. The advice often given newcomers to Arabia is that if one is riding in a taxi that has an accident, open the door and run as fast as you can.[4]

There is an anecdote, exaggerated I believe, told in the expatriate community in Arabia about a Dutch engineer who parked his car next to the construction site that he was supervising. A Saudi building inspector promptly fell off an I beam, tumbled nine stories, and landed on the roof of the Dutchman's car. According to the story, the Dutch engineer was forced by the court

---

[4]The horror stories about foreigners having accidents in Saudi Arabia are frequently exaggerated. One British chap who has had over a dozen accidents in Riyadh in the past five years would still rather drive in Arabia than in Britain. "By and large, the Saudis have a strong sense of justice, and no damned insurance companies keep you in court for years and years. If you're guilty you pay for the damage on the spot. It's that simple."

to pay the man-price (the price an individual must pay if he accidently kills someone—approximately fourteen thousand dollars for a man, less for a woman) to the family of the deceased. The logic behind the court's decision was that the Saudi building inspector might have had a greater chance of surviving had the Dutchman's car not been parked where it was.

Thus the Saudi is fatalistic, and yet his expectations for the future—*Inshallah*—are large and grand. The only limitation on his dreams is the fact that the oil reserves are finite.

Generous yet avaricious, fiercely loyal yet unpatriotic, libidinous abroad and a paragon of virtue at home, proud yet defensive, the Saudis are a people rich in paradoxes and contradictions. Wilfred Thesiger summed it up well when writing about the nomadic Bedouins that roam the edges of the Empty Quarter: "Probably no other people, either as a race or as individuals, combine so many conflicting qualities in such extreme degrees."[5]

[5]Wilfred Thesiger, *Arabian Sands*, Longmanns Green, London,1959, p. 167.

8

Crime and Punishment

On the afternoon of December 24, 1979, Bill T. left the villa he had rented in Olaya, a posh residential district of Riyadh. Bill and two other Americans had chosen the villa because there was a high percentage of American and European residents in the neighborhood. In the past there had been numerous confrontations between Westerners and the fanatical members of the Organization for the Encouragement of Virtue and the Elimination of Vice, better known to the foreigners as the *mutawa,* the religious or morals police. Now the Saudi government was openly discouraging the *mutawa* from patrolling the streets.

Bill had two errands to run. First he had to stop at the gold *suq* in Dira to buy his wife a necklace she had admired. It was the first Christmas in two years that Bill had been with his wife. It had taken him nine months to secure an entrance visa for her. The second errand was of a more commercial nature. He had a shopping list that included one hundred kilograms of sugar and a small six-ounce can of yeast. These ingredients were necessary to keep the large homemade still "cooking" in the villa's back yard.

---

[1]The case histories and information about Saudi prisons come from extensive interviews with the inmates of Malaaz, Diriyah, and Al-Kharj prisons. The interviews were conducted by my wife, who posed as a member of the inmate's family in order to gain access to the prison and supply the foreign inmates with food. All of the prisoners mentioned here are still incarcerated in the kingdom. For this reason, their last names have not been used.

At a hundred riyals (thirty dollars) a liter, Bill's *sadeeki* had been selling very well. He had been distilling for less than a year, but he had been able to buy a brand-new Volvo and put a down payment on a four-bedroom house in California. Bill would have been able to have paid for the house completely had he not been so cautious. He could only run the still on windy days when the yeasty fumes would dissipate quickly. Two of his friends had recently been deported for making wine.

Bill stopped at the gold *suq* in Dira, spent twenty minutes haggling over the price of the necklace, and then went on to Al-Sadhan Supermarket on Sitteen Street, where he purchased the sugar and the yeast. Al-Sadhan had a wholesale outlet where he could get the sugar at cut-rate prices.

Unknown to Bill at the time he was purchasing his supplies was the fact that the *mutawa* had only a week before made the rounds of Riyadh's supermarkets demanding information on anyone purchasing large quantities of sugar. So it was that Bill was followed back to his villa by two *mutawa* in an unmarked Toyota pickup truck.

At a quarter to seven in the evening, just as Bill was preparing to plug in the lights on the artificial Christmas tree his wife had brought with her from the States, the front doorbell rang. Before Bill could answer it, five Saudis, dressed in *thobes* and *ghutras*, had scaled the rear wall of the villa. At the same time, there was a loud metallic crunching sound from the side of the villa as a *mutawa* backed a jeep through the double gates of the compound. Within minutes, Bill was standing in the midst of seven stick-waving *mutawa*.

A question was barked at him in Arabic, and Bill responded with one of the four expressions he knew in Arabic: "I don't understand." A camel-herding stick, about the size of a broom handle, came down across his back. The question was again barked in Arabic. Again Bill responded by announcing that he didn't speak Arabic. This time three or four of the *mutawa* set about him with their sticks, knocking him off his feet. Bill made no effort to get up but simply attempted to protect his genitals and his head.

Much to his surprise, the beating stopped, but knowing that discretion is the better part of valor, he made no attempt to get back on his feet. After a few minutes, he found his wife crouching by his side, asking if he was all right. To his astonishment, the *mutawa* had all disappeared around the back of the villa to inspect the still he had constructed. Almost faster than thought, Bill was on his feet, half dragging his wife to the Volvo. They managed to get into the car and drive to a friend's villa. It was then that Bill understood why the *mutawa* had not bothered to guard him.

There was no place to go. He couldn't get out of the country without an exit visa, and the only way to get an exit visa was through the Ministry of the Interior. It was just a question of time before he was arrested. Bill's wife and his friend spent most of the night debating what he could do. Finally Bill decided to appear at work the following day, Christmas Day, and hope that he would only be deported from the country.

The regular police were waiting for him the next morning, and without so much as a word, slapped him into handcuffs. Bill was taken to the investigation prison in Dira, next to the Palace of Justice behind "Chop Square," the location of public executions. Bill was thoroughly searched and then placed in a cell with two Pakistanis who spoke no English. Later in the day he was moved to a larger cell, where he was confronted by three police officers, among them a captain who spoke halting English.

Bill was told to remove all his clothes and lie naked, face down on the floor. The captain asked him if he wished to confess to manufacturing and selling alcohol. Still hoping that he might simply be deported, Bill gave a full confession. The captain next demanded to know the names and addresses of everyone Bill had sold *sadeeki* to. Bill hesitated. The guard on the left brought a thin oil-soaked cane down on his buttocks. Bill screamed. Again the cane came down, this time cracking his skin. The flogging lasted only minutes, but when it was through, Bill was only half conscious.

In an hour the captain and the two guards returned to the

cell. A bucket of lukewarm water was poured over Bill before the questioning was resumed. It was not long before Bill was spouting names—not the names of people he had sold *sadeeki* to but names from a survey-of-literature course he had taken at UCLA—David Copperfield, Eliza Doolittle, Joseph Andrews.

Bill spent a week at the investigation prison in Dira and then was transferred to the prison in Diriyah, where he spent another month before coming to trial. At his trial, Bill was represented by a lawyer who pleaded guilty on his behalf. Bill was sentenced to three years in jail and three hundred lashes. As of this writing, Bill is still incarcerated and is being flogged regularly.

Like all other public institutions in the Kingdom of Saudi Arabia, the administration of justice is based strictly on the teachings of the Koran. The law of the land is religious in theory and in practice, and there is no distinction between civil and criminal cases, just as there is no distinction, at least in a Western sense, between religious and secular affairs. The system of law is referred to as the *sharia*, and the man who interprets the law is called a *qadi* (judge).

In theory, Saudi Arabia is a nation of laws, not a nation of men. In other words, no one is above the law. When a man stands before a *qadi*, he is, legally, an equal to the king. In practice, however, members of wealthy and powerful families rarely stand before a *qadi*. It is not at all uncommon in Saudi Arabia for a trial to be interrupted by a royal messenger who informs the court that the charges against a certain individual have been dropped on the instructions of this or that prince.

This double standard of justice results in some resentment and bitterness among the ever-growing numbers of young Saudis who have been educated in Europe or the United States. The corruption of the courts, at least in terms of who is actually brought to trial, is also a growing concern of the ruling members of the royal family. The al-Sauds vehemently reject that Saudi Arabia is an autocracy. The royal family receive their authority to rule, or so they frequently announce, by their exemplary adherence to Islam. Thus criticism of the behavior of an individual prince or princess (as in *Death of a Princess*) is also by implication an attack on the right of the royal family to rule in the first place.

While graft and corruption may be relatively common in Arabian business, violent street crime is almost nonexistent. The Saudis boast, with understandable pride, that there is no crime whatsoever within the kingdom. While this is obviously an exaggeration, Riyadh, Dhahran, and Jeddah are probably the safest cities in the world. Pickpockets, muggers, purse snatchers, burglars, and car thieves simply do not exist. When, on the extremely rare occasion, there is a robbery, one can be virtually certain that a foreigner, not a Saudi, is involved.

This lack of crime produces some remarkable sights that often surprise the newcomer to Arabia. Enormous public displays of cash are commonplace. In a country where credit is almost nonexistent (although American Express and Diner's Club are making some headway in Riyadh and Jeddah) and checks are looked upon with mistrust and suspicion, virtually everything is paid for with cash.

It is common to see unarmed payroll officers leaving the National Commercial Bank on Airport Street in Riyadh with two or even three large suitcases stuffed with millions of riyals. The gold market in Riyadh is composed of fifty or more small storefronts in a three- or four-block area. Even though these storefronts house millions and millions of dollars' worth of the precious metal, there is no more security than there would be if the stores were selling clothes or food. In fact, none of the banks or moneychangers in Riyadh even has a burglar alarm.

This is changing. The crime rate is rising, I believe, in direct proportion to the number of foreign workers brought into the country. Since the end of 1979 armed soldiers have been placed in front of many of the banks.

The most common crimes in Saudi Arabia are not even considered crimes elsewhere in the world. Drivers involved in serious car accidents make up a healthy portion of the prison population. If one is involved in a fatal car accident, one is bound by law to pay the man-price to the family of the deceased. This amount must be paid before the individual is released from prison. Saudi prisons also have their share of individuals who have violated the strict alcohol prohibition. The majority of these individuals are sentenced for either smuggling or manufacturing alcohol. Simple consumption, public intoxication, or possession is punished by forty lashes.

While alcohol was never legal for Saudis, it was permitted to foreigners in the kingdom until the 1950s. However, one night in 1952, a son of King Abdulaziz, Prince Mishari, stopped by the home of the British consul in Jeddah and asked for whiskey. Seeing that the prince was already quite intoxicated, the British consul refused the request. The prince left, only to return three hours later, even drunker than before, and repeat his demand for whiskey. When the British consul continued to refuse, Prince Mishari drew a pistol from his belt and shot the Englishman to death. In accordance with the *sharia* law, King Abdulaziz offered a life for a life: his own son's life in return for the life of the British consul. After consultation with the British government, which was not so much interested in justice as in good relations with the Arabian king, the family of the murdered British consul decided against asking Abdulaziz to behead his own son.

Abdulaziz did compensate the widow to the tune of about a quarter of a million dollars, and the drunkard Prince Mishari was imprisoned, but he was released in a sweeping amnesty order that accompanied the accession of his half-brother, King Saud, two years later.

Several months after the murder in Jeddah, King Abdulaziz issued a royal decree banning any alcohol whatsoever in the kingdom. There are, however, notable exceptions to this prohibition. Obviously, the diplomatic corps bring alcohol into the kingdom via the diplomatic pouches that cannot be touched by Saudi customs officers. Certain high-priority employees of the Saudi government are also granted alcohol privileges. The U.S. Army Corps of Engineers is granted both alcohol and pork privileges, and their compound is virtually the only place in Riyadh that one can get a ham-and-cheese sandwich. Restrictions on alcohol are somewhat more relaxed in the Eastern Province around the huge ARAMCO compound at Dhahran, and foreign corporations have actually opened speakeasys. However, in 1980 the regular and the religious police clamped down substantially on illicit trade in alcohol.

There is very little traffic in drugs in Saudi Arabia. Narcotics are strictly controlled by government prescription, and penalties for simple possession of hashish or marijuana are among the most severe in the world. Ken, an eighteen-year-old American, is currently serving fifteen years for attempting to bring two or three grams of hashish into the kingdom. In order to keep their son alive, Ken's parents have moved to Saudi Arabia so they can bring their son food on a weekly basis.

By far the most common infraction of the law in Saudi Arabia is debt. Individuals are held legally responsible for their debts and are imprisoned if they are unable to repay them on time. There is no such thing as bankruptcy in Saudi Arabia, and there is no distinction between civil and criminal proceedings. It is also important to note that an employee of a corporation in Saudi Arabia, no matter how low on the hierarchical ladder, is a legal representative of that company and is considered legally liable for the debts incurred by his employer. At present there are more than a dozen Europeans in Saudi jails because the companies they worked for went bankrupt and the owners fled the country, leaving financial responsibilities behind them.

Islamic justice is the harshest system of laws in the world. The penalties for breaking the law are brutal. Theft is punished by the public amputation of the right hand. Murder is punished by beheading, and, as previously mentioned, the adulteress is stoned to death. Due in part to the severity of the punishment, the actual process of justice is deliberate and cautious.

The *qadis* who preside over the *sharia* courts have gained a reputation for themselves, held by Saudi and foreigner alike, for honesty and impartiality. A man who is accused of a crime is always provided with an opportunity to defend himself and has the right to have a lawyer represent him at his trial. The accused is always confronted with any witnesses that testify against him. The penalty for perjury is one hundred lashes. Should a man be executed based on false testimony, the witness who has perjured himself is also executed.

The laws of the kingdom are enforced by four separate

agencies—the regular police, the *mutawa* (religious or morals police), the secret security police, and, probably most important of all, the family.

The regular police are predominantly concerned with traffic control and criminal investigation. They come under the authority of the Ministry of the Interior but are not directly concerned with the surveillance of political or religious subversives. The regular police are highly visible in the urban centers. They are armed with handguns, and their orders carry the weight of law.

The *mutawa*[2] come under the direct authority of the Ulema, the religious leadership, most of whom are from the al-Sheikh family, the descendents of Muhammed ibn-Abdul Wahhab, the eighteenth-century reformer. They are the most visible source of Islamic authority, patrolling the streets and markets of the major cities and ensuring that, at least in Riyadh, the shops all close for *salat* (prayer time).

While the authority of the *mutawa* has diminished somewhat in recent years, they are still very much a force to be reckoned with. In addition to ensuring the continued public segregation of men and women, the *mutawa* also enforce the prohibition in the Koran against any representation of the human form, and on at least one occasion have been known to stand at the customs counter at Jeddah airport and tear heads off dolls that Western children have tried to bring into the country.

The first and foremost duty of the *mutawa*, however, is simply to remind the people to pray five times daily. The reminder can be a vocal one or a less gentle prodding with the camel-herding sticks they carry. The *mutawa* in Riyadh become especially vigilant just before Ramadan and hajj, and on one occasion I witnessed three *mutawa* soundly thrashing a street vendor who was slow in closing his stall for prayers. The vendor was subsequently arrested by the regular police.

While the royal family supports the *mutawa* vocally and does consult with the Ulema over large questions involving the na-

---

[2]The *mutawa* publish a list of rules and regulations for foreign women living in Saudi Arabia. A copy of these rules can be found in Appendix F.

tion's development plans, some of the al-Sauds view the *mutawa* as ignorant, fanatical zealots—an anachronistic nuisance to modernization. This, however, is a view that is expressed only in private. Publicly, the royal family has never criticized the *mutawa* or the Ulema.

In 1978 friction developed between the *mutawa* and Prince Naif, the Minister of the Interior, over Christian worship services in Riyadh and Dhahran. Officially, religious observances other than Islam are banned by law in Saudi Arabia. Jews are prohibited by law from entering the kingdom; and, while Christians do form a large portion of the skilled work force, they are forbidden any form of public worship. However, the Ministry of the Interior does grant large corporations like ARAMCO and Lockheed visas to bring in "social workers." These so-called social workers are usually priests and ministers who covertly serve the spiritual needs of the expatriate community.

Word got out to the *mutawa* that Christian worship services were taking place in the ARAMCO compound in Dhahran. (This was with the knowledge and consent of Prince Naif.) The *mutawa* dutifully raided the service and dragged a Protestant minister off to jail. Naturally, ARAMCO officials were quickly on the telephone to Prince Naif, who after three or four days managed to secure the release of the minister. However, in order for the *mutawa* to save face, Prince Naif was forced to order the deportation of the minister, while at the same time issuing ARAMCO another visa for another "social worker." Much less gentle was the fate of two Egyptian Copts who were found handing out proselytizing pamphlets in Arabic in Riyadh. Both men have been in jail for almost a year and still have not come to trial.

More recently, the *mutawa* in Jeddah led a raid on several beauty salons. Such public institutions are considered by the fundamentalist Wahhabi Muslims to be indecently concerned with physical vanity. The *mutawa* succeeded in breaking apart the beauty salons and beating up a number of women—including the wife of a South American ambassador, which resulted in a minor international incident with humble apologies being issued by a number of powerful princes.

The secret security police are divided up among several branches of government and the military. It seems that every ministry has its own secret police, who spend most of their time watching the secret police from the other ministries. While that may be somewhat of an exaggeration, there is no question that internal security is fragmented at best and incompetent at worst. More later about the kingdom's secret police.

Perhaps the most important deterrent to crime in Saudi Arabia is the institution of the family. Family reputation is an all-consuming concern, and it would be virtually unthinkable to jeopardize it for mere financial gain. Aside from concern over reputation, the family actually polices itself internally, investigating and punishing family members who deviate from the Islamic norm. Punishments can range from a withdrawal of financial support to execution, although the latter is becoming increasingly rare in the urban areas.

Corporal punishment is often performed in public, usually in a central square near the marketplace. All public punishment is carried out on Fridays, after the communal prayer at noon. Westerners are not welcome witnesses, and photography is forbidden.

In Riyadh, executions take place in Dira Square, an open area in front of the marketplace. At about a quarter to twelve the muezzin calls the faithful to the large mosque next to the Palace of Justice. Here, hundreds of Saudi men listen to a sermon by an imam and then say a special prayer for the condemned man. Soon after the prayer is said, the regular police close off the roads leading into the square, and a crowd gathers.

A police van arrives with the condemned man, bound by the wrists. The condemned man, a convicted murderer or rapist, perhaps, is then taken to the center of the square and made to kneel. Several minutes later, a new chauffeur-driven Mercedes arrives, and from the back seat steps a huge man carrying a three-foot-long double-edged sword. He is the executioner.

All of the executioners in the kingdom are Sudanese ex-slaves. The executioner is always accompanied by an assistant or apprentice. At this point the assistant crosses the square and kneels next to the condemned man. Meanwhile the executioner positions himself some four or five paces behind them. When the executioner gives the signal, the assistant stabs the condemned man with a sharpened stick. The stick is thrust into the man's rib cage and causes an involuntary tightening of the neck muscles. As soon as the executioner sees the head jerk back, he takes three or four running steps and then brings the sword whistling down on the victim's neck. In most cases, the executioner manages to sever the head completely with one slice. The head, carried by the momentum of the sword, rolls several feet and is retrieved by the assistant. All that can be seen of the neck is a dark plum-colored cavity that spews forth a pulsating stream of blood for fifteen or twenty seconds before the muscles relax and the body collapses. On some occasions, more than one blow with the sword is necessary to remove the head, and a Saudi friend told me of one instance where the executioner was forced to hack the head from the shoulders.

As soon as the head is separated from the body, the crowd of onlookers begins to chant *"Allah akbar"* (God is great). The head and the body are promptly removed on a stretcher, and the crowd surges forward to spit into the victim's blood.

Any number of Westerners have commented, inaccurately I believe, on the "blood lust" of the crowd of onlookers. I believe that to comprehend the attitude of the crowd at a Saudi execution, one must remember that the execution is part of a religious observance. It is important here to understand the emphasis in Islam on justice. An execution is a public demonstration of the victory of virtue over evil—it is an extremely graphic affirmation of the sanctity of the law of God as revealed through the Koran. Thus when the crowd begins to chant "God is great" and people file forward to spit in the victim's blood, they don't do so out of titillation but rather with a dignity and solemnity that accompanies the witnessing of some potent sacramental ritual.

The amputation of the hand of a thief is handled in much the same manner. Again the punishment is preceded by a special communal prayer for the victim. After this, the condemned man is brought to the square and his right hand is carefully severed from his wrist. No pain-killing drugs are permitted before the amputation, although they may be administered afterwards.

The amputation is performed by a trained executioner who works swiftly so as to minimize the loss of blood. The incisions are made through the wrist joint, and once the hand is separated, the wrist is thrust into hot wax to prevent further bleeding and infection. At this point the victim is usually removed to a hospital for a medical examination and further treatment. The severed hand is publicly displayed, either nailed to a wall in the *suq* or, in Riyadh, tied to a rope and hoisted up the flagpole in Dira Square.

The first Westerner to suffer the amputation of his right hand will probably be Pierre C., a French national who was working in the kingdom with a large construction firm. Pierre was a drug addict when he arrived in Saudi Arabia and managed, for a short while, to sustain his addiction on his salary. However, it was not long before his need for heroin surpassed what he could afford, and Pierre was forced to turn to theft. Pierre embezzled several hundred thousand riyals from the company he was working for and was promptly arrested. He confessed to both the theft and his drug addiction and was given a date for his trial.

While waiting for trial, Pierre befriended a fellow inmate, an American, who told him that Muslims received much lighter sentences than did heathen, infidel Christians. Believing this to be plausible, Pierre requested that the *qadi* postpone sentencing until after he had converted to Islam. The *qadi* asked Pierre three times whether it was his sincere desire to become a Muslim, and Pierre replied three times in the affirmative. Finally, the *qadi* shrugged with resignation and ordered Pierre taken to Taif to the only mental hospital in the kingdom for a complete psychological examination.

Unfortunately for Pierre, Muslims do not receive lighter sentences than Christians. In fact, the opposite is true. Christians may be partially excused by ignorance, but no such excuse exists for the Muslim. Had Pierre not converted to Islam, he would probably have received five or six years in a Saudi prison and several hundred lashes. As it stands now, Pierre has been declared sane and has been sentenced to ten years' imprisonment and to have his right hand amputated at the wrist.

Saudi prisons must rank among the most unpleasant in the world. Almost all the prisons are old structures that contain none of the modern conveniences that the Western world has come to think of as necessities. It is not uncommon for ten or twelve men to share a tiny, ten-foot-by-ten-foot cell, sleeping either on the floor or on thin pads. Ventilation, especially during the hot summer months, is a constant problem, and heat prostration is a common medical complaint.

Food is provided daily, but the quality is so poor that many of the inmates cannot bring themselves to eat it. The staple of the prisoners' diet is rice, but the rice is often unwashed and is thus full of weevils and maggots. Saudi prisoners are brought food by their families on Thursday, the day set aside for visits by female family members. However, it has been the policy of the Saudi government to deport the families of foreigners who have been arrested, which leaves the non-Saudi prisoner with no access to food other than the substandard provisions provided by the prison. In order to assist these foreign prisoners, many of whom are guilty of no crime other than falling into debt, a group of women from the clandestine Riyadh Christian Fellowship have taken it upon themselves to visit foreign prisoners and supply them with food.

Sanitary conditions within most of the prisons in the central Nejd area are neanderthal. Inmates tell stories of being allowed to use toilet facilities only once a day during a prescribed time. The toilets themselves function irregularly, and the presence of fecal matter in the closely confined living quarters of the prison greatly increases the risk of a cholera outbreak.

Vermin are a constant source of annoyance and a health danger. Cockroaches, the large Saudi variety of which may grow to two inches in length, are plentiful. Rats and mice also infest the walls of the older prisons. Scorpions and camel spiders are a danger to inmates in prisons outside the urban centers.

Medical attention for prisoners is erratic. Most of the prisons have a full-time male nurse on duty to dispense medication. A prisoner may request to see a bona fide doctor if his condition is judged serious enough. Since drinking water must be purchased by the prisoners, dehydration is quite common. Equally common, and virtually impossible to get rid of, are internal parasites. A number of European prisoners being held in the prison at Diriyah have taken to eating cigarette tobacco in an attempt to rid themselves of these intestinal worms.

The story of a Swiss businessman, Claude P., is illuminating in regard to both the theory and actual application of Saudi-Islamic justice. Claude P. owns a small exporting firm based in Bern. For the past five years, Claude P. has been doing business in Saudi Arabia. In accordance with Saudi law, any foreigner doing business within the kingdom must have a Saudi national as a partner. Claude P. had two such Saudi partners. In September 1979 Claude flew into Riyadh to examine the state of his business interests and to collect his share of the previous year's profits.

When Claude first attempted to contact his two Saudi partners, he was told that neither was available. After some days and more than twenty phone calls, Claude finally managed to speak with one partner on the phone. He was informed that there were no profits and that the accounts of the business were not available for his inspection. Claude, quite understandably, protested, and after a lengthy argument the two Saudi partners finally agreed on a face-to-face meeting at the Al-Yamamah Hotel.

Claude arrived at the hotel fifteen minutes early and was quite surprised to see that his partners were already present. He was even more surprised to see that they were accompanied by two police officers. Claude was arrested on the vague charge of "improper business practices."

Claude P. spent five and a half months in the Malaaz prison before coming to trial. During this time, he was flogged each week. When he finally arrived in court, his trial lasted all of twenty minutes.

The *qadi* declared him completely innocent of all charges and ordered his immediate release. However, the two Saudi partners filed an appeal to the *qadi*'s ruling, and since no such thing as bail exists in Saudi Arabia, Claude P. was returned to jail, flogged weekly, pending the appeal.

Saudis who have heard the story of Claude P. dismiss it as an exceptional miscarriage of justice, which, they are quick to point out, occurs under any legal system. This is undoubtedly true, but what is exceptional is the Saudi practice of inflicting physical punishment on a man before he has been to trial, before he has been convicted of any crime, even after he has been declared innocent. This is not only a violation of justice in a Western sense, but it is also contrary to the letter and spirit of the *sharia* law on which all Islamic justice is based.

The use of torture in extracting confessions is common. Eyewitness accounts of beatings in police stations abound. During his stay in the Malaaz prison, Claude P. witnessed a Yemeni man brought in on the charge of theft. According to Claude, the Yemeni was kept in solitude for ten days; each day one of his toenails was removed until, at the end of this period, the Yemeni prisoner lost control of his mind and had to be sent to the mental hospital in Taif.

The floggings that are administered in the prisons vary in severity, depending on their purpose. There is a myth that is widespread in Arabia that the man administering the flogging must keep a copy of the Koran beneath his arm, thus allowing him to swing only from the elbow. The myth concludes that if the Koran falls from beneath the man's arm, the prisoner must be pardoned. There is absolutely no substantiation to this story. While some floggings are more ceremonious than serious, others are downright brutal. Inmates at various Saudi prisons concur that the most debilitating flogging is administered to the soles of the feet. The prisoner is hung up by his arms, and the guards lash the soles of his feet until the individual either confesses or slips into unconsciousness.

It is important to understand that while Islamic justice is harsh, it in no way condones torture. The incidents of torture within the Saudi prisons, while they are relatively common, are outside the framework of the *sharia* and are completely illegal as such. There are, however, quite a number of Saudis in powerful positions in the Ministry of the Interior who choose to turn a blind eye toward the methods used by the police. Internal security appears to outweigh all concern for the protection of individual rights.

It is also important for the foreigner in Saudi Arabia to understand that most foreign embassies will do little or nothing to assist their citizens who find themselves in legal difficulties. While the consular offices, especially those of the United States, will claim that they are helpless to intervene, this is not the case at all. The German consulate in Jeddah put pressure on the Saudi government in the spring of 1980 and managed to secure the release of more than a dozen German nationals who were languishing in Saudi debtors' prisons. The reluctance of U.S., British, and French consulates to do the same is based on their phobia about offending the Saudis and thus disturbing the multibillion-dollar business deals their big national corporations are engaged in.

If the crime rate in Saudi Arabia is rising, much of the increase can be traced directly to the fabulous amounts of cash that are flowing into the country from oil revenues. Materialism is unquestionably the single greatest challenge that has ever faced Islam. As Jules Archer put it,[3] the future of Saudi Arabia can be seen as a confrontation "between Mecca and mechanization." It is therefore important for us to examine how the Saudis are handling their unbelievably large development plans for the modernization of the desert kingdom.

---

[3]Jules Archer: *Legacy of the Desert,* Little, Brown & Company, Boston, 1976.

9

Modernization

In order to understand the vastness of Saudi Arabia's development plans, let us make an analogy to the United States. If we took all the land east of the Mississippi River and bulldozed it so that all that was left standing were a dozen or so small communities of wattle huts and a few clumps of trees, and then we populated this wasteland with several million illiterate, fundamentalist Calvinists who almost universally mistrusted "newfangled gadgetry," we would have a picture not too dissimilar from what existed in Saudi Arabia thirty or forty years ago.

The challenge of turning these eight hundred fifty thousand square miles of desert into a modern nation in less than half a century is probably the most dramatic and courageous social undertaking in modern history. What makes the modernization of Saudi Arabia truly remarkable is not only the speed at which it is taking place but also the unshakable determination of the vast majority of Saudis not to sacrifice their traditional Islamic values in the process.

Whether or not the Saudis will be successful in improving the quality of life on the peninsula by importing modern technology and at the same time maintaining thousand-year-old religious values is an open question.

The history of Saudi Arabian modernization began with an American philanthropist named C. R. Crane. Crane was a multimillionaire who had become fascinated with the Arab culture of the Middle East. In 1931 Crane expressed a desire to Henry St.

John Philby to meet the already legendary monarch of Arabia, King Abdulaziz.

Philby arranged the meeting to take place in the king's baked-mud palace in Riyadh. In keeping with the accepted behavior of foreigners in Riyadh at that time, Crane donned the traditional Arab *thobe* and *ghutra* before entering the city. The purpose behind Crane's visit was to discuss with the king the possibility of having one of his employees, a geologist named Twitchell, prospect for oil.

The American philanthropist's plan was reported to have amused King Abdulaziz, who on any number of previous occasions had announced that he was convinced that no oil whatsoever lay beneath the sands of his kingdom. However, when Crane had explained what exactly a geologist was, Abdulaziz had an idea of his own. What his people had always lacked was water. If a geologist could find oil, why couldn't he find something truly valuable and useful like water?

Abdulaziz agreed to Crane's proposal, and within weeks, Karl S. Twitchell was dispatched to the Arabian peninsula. Between his frequent searches for water, Twitchell was also able to prospect for oil, and within several months of his arrival, the American mining engineer had found the clues he was looking for.

However, when Crane approached American oil companies, none of them was particularly interested in purchasing exploration rights. In fact, Twitchell's discovery was treated with condescension and ridicule in corporate boardrooms. Nevertheless, Crane persisted, and finally he convinced Standard Oil of California (SoCal) to bid on a comprehensive oil concession.

King Abdulaziz's amusement over oil faded notably when he came to Jeddah to negotiate with the representatives of Socal. At first the Arabian king demanded one hundred thousand British pounds, but after several days of bargaining, Abdulaziz finally agreed to let the concession for oil go for thirty thousand pounds. The amount was paid in gold sovereigns, which were counted by hand, on May 29, 1933.

Standard Oil of California, unbeknown to itself at the time, had gotten in on the ground floor of what must be considered one of the best deals in history. Taking inflation and exchange rates into account, the thirty thousand gold sovereigns translate currently to no more than two million dollars—hardly much of an investment when one considers that Saudi Arabia is now earning more than three hundred and thirty-six million dollars in oil revenues every day.

It took five years before the first oil was actually exported—a half million barrels in 1938. The following year saw oil production rise to 3.9 million barrels, about one third of Saudi Arabia's present daily production capacity. Oil production was interrupted by World War II, and the flow of crude did not become steady again until 1946. From that year onward, skyrocketing oil revenues started the leaders of the al-Saud family thinking about the technological future of their country.

The first five-year development plan for Saudi Arabia was formulated in 1970. The cornerstone of this plan may strike some Westerners as ironic. Its express purpose was to help liberate Saudi Arabia from economic dependence on its own oil.

If the U.S. government is concerned with its growing dependence on Arab oil, then Saudi Arabia is twice as concerned about its own dependence on U.S. and European oil revenues. Saudi Arabia has never had any illusions that oil was an infinite resource. And most Saudis are fully cognizant of the fact that the oil will run out in the future. The goal of the first five-year plan was to diversify Saudi Arabia's income-producing industries, while at the same time to begin a massive program to construct hospitals, schools, universities, and government ministries to administer the growing nation.

Naturally the influx of new technology met with substantial resistance from the more conservative elements of the population. The advent of television in the kingdom produced bloody street riots, automobiles were stoned by angry crowds of Wahhabi Muslims, and nomadic Bedouins would routinely take pot shots at ARAMCO aircraft. But the real confrontation between development and Islamic traditionalism was not felt until modernization had reached the level of the individual. It is the massive importation of American and European luxury consumer goods that truly threatens the austere and puritan Muslim society.

Adam Smith, in a recent article in *Atlantic*,[1] summed up the tension between traditionalism and development in Saudi Arabia as follows: "A well-designed car may start to shake at a hundred miles an hour, and shake apart at some speed above that. Saudi Arabia is already traveling at a hundred miles an hour."

Interestingly enough, the three men who currently head Saudi Arabia's massive development plans are not members of the royal family. Within the kingdom, they are referred to as "the three technocrat princes," unquestionably the three most powerful commoners in the country. The first is the highly visible and articulate Sheikh Ahmed Zaki Yamani, minister of Petromin, dean of OPEC, and indisputably the most reliable political spokesman in the kingdom.

Yamani is virtually an honorary member of the al-Saud clan. He was close friends with King Faisal and weathered the change of monarchs remarkably well. Yamani's Western education has influenced his ideas about his country and brought him into the powerful orbit of Crown Prince Fahd, the strongman behind the throne. Yamani may run into political problems should Prince Abdullah, the second deputy prime minister and commander of the National Guard, come to power. Prince Abdullah is known to be an archconservative who has privately advocated slowing the development process and cutting back oil production.

The second "technocrat prince" is Sheikh Hisham Nazar, minister of planning, whose office on University Street in Riyadh is perpetually littered with computer printouts and enormous wall graphs. Nazar is the architect of the future of the kingdom. It is his ministry, in consultation with the Council of Ministers (the ruling al-Sauds) and the Ulema, that plots the course of development for the kingdom and attempts, sometimes successfully, to anticipate problems.

---

[1]Adam Smith, "Superinflation," *Atlantic*, December 1978.

Nazar has increasingly come under fire from the ultracon-servatives in the country for confusing Islamic development with Westernization, the latter being viewed as merely copying the materialistic degeneracy of the West. Unquestionably, Hisham Nazar occupies the most difficult and thankless posi-tion in the kingdom, but, at least publicly, his calm stoicism seems well suited to the extreme pressures of navigating a country in a flat-out race against the day the oil wells run dry.

Nazar is candid about the pressure he sees being placed both on Saudi Arabia and on himself personally. Speaking to two American journalists, he was quoted as saying with no small touch of irony, "Frankly, I wish you could find some other sources of energy to take the pressure off us."

The third "technocrat prince" is the multimillionaire mer-chant, hotel owner, and foreign investor, Ghazi al-Gosaibi, min-ister of industry and electricity. When Gosaibi is not engaged in displaying the Saudi national inferiority complex by ridiculing the United States with what one assumes he considers wit, he can be a powerful and intelligent exponent of the uniqueness of the development of Saudi Arabia.

In an informative speech given to the Arab-American Associ-ation in Washington, Gosaibi questioned the very foundations of the most cherished notions about Third World modernization. He categorically rejected the idea that 'Saudi Arabia was "copying" the West, and he went on to criticize the popular no-tion held among so-called experts that the industrial and technological development of a country must be paralleled by a corresponding change in values.

Gosaibi, like most Saudis, was adamant that, regardless of the technological tools used by Saudi Arabia, regardless of industrial or social development, the nation's values would remain unshakably Islamic.

The physical signs of development are everywhere. The sky-lines of Riyadh and Jeddah are dotted with cranes, and partly constructed buildings adorn virtually every block of the capital. Bulldozers and backhoes are as plentiful as taxis, and the air in the urban centers is perpetually clogged with construction dust.

The major news reported in Saudi newspapers is the daily signing of multimillion-dollar contracts for even more construction. Curiously enough, American firms are receiving only a small share of these huge contracts. This is due in part to the fact that American workers abroad are required to pay U.S. income tax on their earnings. It was recently estimated that it costs a U.S. construction firm three times as much to keep a construction engineer in Saudi Arabia as it does for a Korean or European company.

Industrial development is booming within the kingdom. Yanbu, until recently a small town on the Red Sea some three hundred kilometers north of Jeddah, is scheduled to become one of the largest industrial port cities in the world. Literally billions and billions of dollars have been poured in the construction of this superport, which will also be the terminal site of a trans-Arabian oil pipeline.

While oil is ridiculously plentiful (gasoline sells for approximately eighteen cents a gallon), water remains a constant problem in the desert kingdom. Huge desalination plants have been constructed along both the Arabian Gulf and the Red Sea to provide fresh water for the city dwellers. The largest desalination project is the one in Jeddah, where millions of gallons of sea water are pumped through an elaborate process and rendered fresh daily. This desalination program is headed by Prince Muhammed ibn-Faisal, the eldest son of the late King Faisal and his favorite wife, Iffat.

Prince Muhammed ibn-Faisal was also the architect several years ago of a plan to lasso icebergs in Antarctica and tow them to the kingdom as a means of providing the nation with additional fresh water. His plan was widely ridiculed in the Western press, immediately written off as another lunatic extravagance of some oil-rich Arab.

The ridicule was and is more indicative of the level of ignorance of Western journalists than of the merits of the plan itself.

As oil is indispensible to the continued growth of American industry, so water is indispensible to the development of the desert kingdom. Why then should it be any more ridiculous for the Saudis to tow icebergs from the South Pole than for the United States to ship crude oil halfway around the world?

According to a recent interview in *Saudi Business*, Prince Muhammed has not given up on his iceberg scheme, and he is currently working on plans to make it cost-effective. For the Westerner who has taken abundant supplies of water for granted, it may be difficult to comprehend what a paucity of water means. A high-ranking official at the Ministry of Planning put it concisely when he said, "Water, not oil, is the lifeblood of Saudi Arabia's future."

One of the highest priorities during the first two five-year development plans was agriculture. Saudi Arabia imports more than ninety percent of the food it consumes. Such dependence on foreign nations worries the ruling members of the royal family.

Huge agricultural projects have been started both at Al-Kharj, an oasis some fifty kilometers south of Riyadh, and at Hofuf, the kingdom's largest natural oasis. The initial problem that hindered agricultural development was the extreme shortage of water. This problem has been overcome, at least partially, in Hofuf and Al-Kharj by tapping huge underground reservoirs. The problem now, of course, is that these huge underground lakes, like the oil reserves in the Eastern Province, are finite resources which cannot be renewed.

The primary agricultural thrust so far has been in truck farming. The farms in Al-Kharj are producing melons, tomatoes, lettuce, and a variety of other quality fruits and vegetables as well as the Arabian staple, dates. However, the cost of irrigation and manpower to work the farms has priced domestically grown fruits and vegetables at least equal to if not higher than imports from Cyprus and Lebanon.

A similar problem confronts Saudi Arabia's small dairy industry. A liter of domestically produced milk sells in the Riyadh markets for about $1.70, more than twice the price of a liter imported from Holland. In addition, American food analysts in the employ of the Saudi government have been openly critical of the lack of sterile procedures in the bottling of milk.

By far the most serious obstacle facing agricultural development in Saudi Arabia is the shortage of manpower. Saudis consider manual labor beneath their dignity. Thus, almost all the nation's farm workers are brought in from the two Yemens, Pakistan, and Taiwan. One ten-thousand-hectare[2] farm just outside Hofuf is worked by several hundred imported Chinese from Taiwan.

The manpower shortage extends into every facet of Saudi development. A shortage of skilled labor is certainly an integral part of the problem. But the basic problem is an attitudinal one. The government has recognized this only recently.

Despite the puritanism of Wahhabi Islam, there is absolutely no work ethic among the Saudis. The Saudi sees no virtue in hard work, nor does he believe that honest labor is particularly pleasing to God. In fact, just the opposite seems to be the case. There seems to be an antiwork ethic in Saudi Arabia. This should not be confused with ordinary laziness or sloth. While a Saudi will commonly scorn some business-related task and put it off to an endless *bokra* (tomorrow), he will work tirelessly around the clock at solving a family problem.

The Saudi attitude toward labor has won him the ambiguous label "the aristocrat of the desert." There is an old Bedouin proverb that sums up the antipathy the Saudi feels toward work: "When the plow crosses the threshold, manhood departs."

While the dignity of the Saudi may still be intact, the very real needs of the modern state remain unfulfilled. Virtually all skilled labor in the kingdom has to be imported. In fact, the entire infrastructure of modern technology is based on employing large numbers of foreign, and in many cases non-Muslim, technicians.

For the past twenty years, the Saudi government has actively encouraged Saudis to enter technical training programs. With the possible exception of ARAMCO's training program in

---

[2]One hectare is equal to ten thousand square meters or 2.47 acres.

Dhahran, these programs have failed to overcome the stigma the average Saudi sees attached to manual labor.

The Saudi aversion toward labor is naturally reflected in students' curriculum choices at the kingdom's universities. University tuition within the kingdom is free to Saudis, and the student is entirely at liberty to select his area of specialization. For the 1979–80 academic year, the University of Riyadh accepted more than one thousand students in the supposedly glamorous field of mass communications. The vast majority of these students see themselves as future television producers. If this trend continues, in ten years there could be one television producer in Saudi Arabia for every five hundred people!

Another major problem facing education in the kingdom is the fairly rigorous censorship of textbooks. At the beginning of each semester, new textbooks brought in from Europe and the United States are routinely censored of any material that might conceivably be offensive to Islam. The pages removed may contain educationally trivial material—for example, a reference to astrology. However, in a number of cases, the material censored is of critical importance to the student's comprehension of his subject. For example, the medical school of the University of Riyadh was ordered to cut out of one of its textbooks a chapter on Darwin's theory of evolution because it contradicted the creation story told in the Koran. In another case, the department of sociology decided to avoid teaching theories of social stratification because the idea was offensive to the Islamic concept of equality.

Officially, Saudi Arabia claims to have no appreciable "brain drain." In other words, very few of those Saudis sent abroad to study for advanced degrees remain abroad to practice their expertise. This is substantially correct. The vast majority of Western-educated Saudis do return to the kingdom to work. However, what the Ministry of Information does not publish is the rate of internal intervocational brain drain. For example, Western-educated Saudi doctors who return to the kingdom receive a starting wage of approximately six thousand Saudi riyals a month (about eighteen hundred dollars). While the government does provide the new practitioner with free housing, this salary is about a quarter of what the doctor could make if he went into private business. Thus, one finds great numbers of skilled doctors rejecting the field they have been trained in and opting for a career in the booming private sector.

The development of modern medical facilities in the kingdom has been both dramatic and problematic. Unquestionably the finest-equipped hospital in the world is the King Faisal Hospital in Riyadh. Hundreds of millions of dollars have been spent on the very latest medical technology—much of which remains in crates because the hospital lacks the skilled technicians to operate it.

Nevertheless, the kingdom as a whole has moved with remarkable rapidity toward modern health care. Life expectancy has soared from a mere forty years in 1968 to fifty years at present. Infant mortality rates have dropped substantially.

Health care facilities are being built in numerous small towns and villages. Vaccinations and inoculations have virtually eliminated certain diseases in urban centers and reduced their prevalence in the outlying regions.

Health care in the remote desert areas remains extremely primitive. In the desert regions of El Hasa, the oil-rich Eastern Province, cutaneous leishmaniasis is epidemic. Cutaneous leishmaniasis is parasitic disease transmitted by the sandfly. The organism, *Leishmania orientales,* burrows under the skin and multiplies, causing suppurating sores. To this day, the Bedouins in the area treat these sores by inflicting themselves with third-degree burns with red-hot coals. Peter Iseman reported, in an article in *Harper's,*[3] that in the southwestern region of the Asir, the belief prevails that boys menstruate, because bloody urine, a symptom of bilharzia, is so common.

One of the most difficult medical problems facing Saudi Arabia, and for that matter most of the developing world, is the fact that many of the huge American and European pharmaceutical corporations are using Saudi Arabia as a testing ground for drugs which have not yet been approved for use in the United States or Europe. The Saudi government has not yet developed a

---

[3]Peter Iseman, "The Arabian Ethos," *Harper's,* February 1978.

screening process to isolate dangerous medications, and medical expertise is such that a doctor might not recognize the hazards of prescribing an untested medication. Saudi Arabia, like many of the developing nations, has not yet developed legal recourse for an injured party.

The Saudi government, advised by the doctors at King Abdulaziz Teaching Hospital in Riyadh, has come to recognize this problem and has set up a team of foreign-educated food and drug experts to screen the products brought into the kingdom. However, this program, called Comprot, is years away from being truly effective.

Along with its advances in medical care, Saudi Arabia has developed one of the most ambitious social welfare programs anywhere in the world. Any man who is out of work or is unable to work because of poor health is provided with approximately sixteen hundred riyals (about five hundred dollars) a month. The unemployed man's wife or wives and his children are each provided with similar subsidies. Thus a man with two wives and five children would be paid approximately four thousand dollars per month, or forty-eight thousand dollars annually. And there are no income or sales taxes in Saudi Arabia.

Education at all levels is entirely free. Scholarships for male students are available for foreign study in certain specialized areas. A Saudi studying for an advanced degree in the United States not only has his tuition, room, and board paid for by his government but also receives a generous monthly stipend for incidental expenses.

In early 1980 the Ministry of Education initiated a free lunch program for all the boys' schools in the kingdom. The program failed, due in part to poor planning and lack of refrigeration units at many of the schools, so the government decided to compensate every school child, both male and female, by paying each a luncheon allowance of about sixty dollars a month.

Every male Saudi is eligible to apply for a government-sponsored housing loan. The loan is for any amount up to three hundred thousand riyals (about ninety thousand dollars), and under Islamic law this is entirely free of interest charges. (Usury is forbidden in Saudi Arabia. However, commercial banks are allowed to pay small "commissions" to customers having savings accounts.) If these housing loans are repayed in twenty-five years, the government automatically deducts twenty-five percent of the original loan. A large number of Saudis are using these government housing loans not only to construct primary residences but also to build large investment properties.

Above and beyond these benefits is the legendary, though quite real, generosity of the royal family. Almost every Saudi one meets has a story of some prince helping the poor. While the vast majority of these stories are exaggerated, many have a firm grounding in truth. The royal family is expected to use its power, influence, and wealth for the common good; thus, a poor man has every right to expect generosity. In fact, he would be surprised if he were treated any other way.

One of the more amusing tales is told about the present King Khalid. An extremely poor Bedouin walked over a hundred miles to ask the monarch for money. According to the story, the poor Bedouin had taken four wives in the course of his long life in the hope of being blessed with a son. Instead, the virile nomad had had eleven daughters, and the entire family had accompanied him on his trek to King Khalid's *majlis* (public meeting). It was thus with astonishment that King Khalid entered the *majlis* chamber (traditionally an all-male preserve) to discover it filled with the Bedouin's eleven daughters and four wives.

"Khalid," the Bedouin is said to have bellowed at the king (any Saudi may address the king by his first name), "I am poor. I have no house. You must give me a house, or I will give you all my wives and all my daughters. Allah knows no greater curse than the plague of women that surround me."

King Khalid was reported to have responded, with a twinkle in his eye, "Your women are a curse of your own making, but your poverty is not. A house and a car are yours." The following day the old Bedouin and his four wives and eleven daughters were taken by government Mercedes to a half-constructed house on the outskirts of Riyadh, which they promptly moved into. That same afternoon two Toyota pickup trucks were delivered, accompanied by a note written by the King, "For you and your curse."

The problems of development in Saudi Arabia are many, but it would be naïve to expect them to be otherwise in light of the grand scale of the planning that is currently underway. It is probable that Saudi Arabia will spend over 150 billion dollars in the next five years on modernization, or the equivalent of twenty-five thousand dollars for every man, woman, and child.

The primary problem is training native manpower. The government has proposed military conscription of all males over the age of eighteen as a possible means of overcoming the Saudi aversion to manual labor.

Some of the failures in modernization are more glaring than others, but perhaps the most embarrassing to the Saudis was the construction of the Riyadh water tower. The water tower is an enormous mushroom-shaped structure in the center of Riyadh, surrounded on four sides by immaculately cared-for gardens.

It was designed to supply water to a large portion of the capital city and also as a symbol of the progress the kingdom was making toward modernization. Soon after its completion, the Ministry of Information produced several hundred thousand posters and color postcards of the water tower and its surrounding gardens which they distributed widely both inside and outside the kingdom.

Then the engineering firm decided to fill the tower with water. The pressure was too great and a large number of the underground pipes burst. After consultation, it was decided that the necessary modifications were too expensive and that the huge tower should remain empty.[4]

The Ministry of Information, fearful of losing its symbol of modernity, invited school groups to use the observation deck of the tower for class trips and picnics. Unfortunately, it was soon discovered that the observation deck overlooked the garden of King Khalid's palace and thus could not be used by school chil-

---

[4]The Riyadh water tower is now filled with water but is being used only two hours a day due to water pressure problems.

dren or, for that matter, anybody else. And so the Riyadh water tower has become not a source of pride but a symbol of a nation's race against time.

It is almost too easy to find fault with Saudi Arabia's ambitious plans. One must always bear in mind the centuries of nomadic isolation that preceded its startling entrance into the twentieth century. Dr. Ali Jad, dean of the College of Arts of the University of Riyadh, expressed the magnitude of change well. He was responding to a delegation of Western teachers who complained that their passport and visa affairs were being handled by an illiterate Bedouin who spoke not a single word of English.

"Look for a moment at the situation from a different point of view," Dr. Jad said. "The man who handles your passports is unquestionably illiterate. Fifteen years ago, he was following sheep and goats around in the desert. Today, he lives in an air-conditioned apartment in Riyadh and works at a desk. Certainly, he makes mistakes. Certainly, there are things he fails to understand. But there is one thing you Westerners fail to understand. You don't yet understand the miracle of change that is taking place."

III

The House al-Saud

"Despite their altruistic and quasi-
religious claims to the contrary,
the primary concern of the Saudi
royal family has always been keeping
itself in power. The history of modern
Saudi Arabia is a bloody chronicle of
how one family imposed tyranny upon
an entire nation."

—*A student of political science,*
Aden, People's Democratic Republic of
Yemen, 1979

"In Saudi Arabia, we do not believe in
the so-called divine right of kings.
My uncle is not king because of some
magic authority he received at birth.
No, in Saudi Arabia the king receives
his authority because of his exemplary
obedience to the Will of God. We al-Sauds
are all servants of God and servants of
our people."

—*Prince Khalid al-Saud, university*
student, Riyadh, 1979

10

A Desert Clan

It is unlikely that during the last quarter of the twentieth century the world will see any single family as wealthy or as powerful as the House al-Saud. Numbering approximately five thousand strong and growing larger daily, this family owns, controls, and reaps the profit from the single largest oil reserve in the world. This is a family with multibillion-dollar investments around the world, a family that owns a nation, a family that controls the destiny of most of the Western world's economies.

On one occasion a student of mine, a minor al-Saud prince, invited me to accompany him to the airport to visit the Boeing 727 his father owns. The tour was enlightening on several levels. The jet was fully customized, seating approximately fifty passengers in loungelike luxury. The dining room boasted a long table that could seat thirty dinner guests, and the wet bar in the lounge was fully stocked with everything from Johnny Walker Black Label to Irania Caviar. In the rear of the jet were three bedrooms, each complete with a king-sized bed and a fireplace filled with plastic logs.

On leaving the jet, my student explained that his father used the 727 only for long business flights. "On short flights within the kingdom, my father prefers the Lear jet." At which point my student pointed to the smaller jet that sat alongside the 727. "He saves money on jet fuel."

From the marble palaces of Jeddah to the hundreds of summer villas that dot the coastline of the Mediterranean, the wealth of the Saudi royal family is as fabulous as it is conspicuous. Prince Khalid, a middle-grade officer in the Saudi National Guard, retains a dozen full-time Pakistani mechanics to care for his seventeen Rolls Royces.

Prince Abdullah, a Jeddah businessman, owns houses in London, Paris, Casablanca, Monte Carlo, New York, and Los Angeles in addition to his three forty-room palaces within the kingdom. It is reported that Prince Abdullah employs over a hundred servants to staff his various palaces and vacation homes.

Al-Saud wealth is a new phenomenon. Until about thirty years ago, the al-Saud family fought a continual battle against its own poverty. The political influence of the al-Sauds extends into the history of the Arabian peninsula a mere three hundred years. The Saudi royal family is part of the Anaza tribe, the largest Arab tribe in existence today. The al-Sauds trace themselves back to the Masalikh branch of the Anaza tribe, who originally came from the plains in northern Syria.

Sometime prior to the dawn of the eighteenth century, the al-Saud clan migrated south to the central Arabian desert, an area called the Nejd. The al-Sauds settled in a wadi, a dry river bed, some twenty miles from the present site of Riyadh. Here in Wadi Hannifa, the ancestors of the Saudi monarchs built the adobe village of Diriyah. Like most of the inhabitants of the Nejd, the al-Sauds were farmers who waged a perennial battle against the rocky, infertile desert that surrounded them. Their major crop and the staple of their diet was dates.

In addition to the ever-present difficulties of farming some of the most arid land in the world, the early al-Sauds also contended with hostility from the neighboring tribes. Raiding one's neighbor's livestock was not only commonplace but a firmly established practice of desert life. In the central Arabian desert, there was no legal system. Each extended family was ruled by its own customs and traditions.

It should be noted here that although Islam was the common religion of the Arabian peninsula, isolation in the desert mitigated against uniformity in either Islamic doctrine or theology.

By the middle of the seventeenth century, Islam had become so diversified that its practice varied greatly from region to region.

In some places, Islam disappeared. It was replaced by animistic worship of sacred trees and shrines. In other areas, amulets were worn to ward off evil. Astrology proliferated, miracles were said to be performed at the tombs of holy men, and other rituals usually associated with magic were practiced. In general, Islam had become synonymous with oracular predictions, various forms of fetishism, and superstition.

The rise to power of the al-Saud family can be traced to 1720, when Saud ibn-Muhammed ibn-Mugrin became the emir of Diriyah. Diriyah was a small village, composed of narrow winding streets and dried-mud houses, surrounded by a fortified wall. Beyond the village wall were groves of date palms cultivated by the villagers. Unlike most of the surrounding desert, Diriyah was located above a relatively large source of underground water.

In 1725, after five years of comparatively peaceful rule, Saud ibn-Muhammed ibn-Mugrin died, and the position of emir fell upon the shoulders of his cousin, Zaid ibn-Murkham. Emir Zaid was no sooner granted his title than he was murdered by in-family rivals. Within six months of Zaid's murder, Muhammed ibn-Saud emerged as ruler of Diriyah.

Muhammed ibn-Saud was a truly remarkable leader. Like his descendant, King Abdulaziz, Muhammed ibn-Saud combined the qualities of piety, ruthlessness, cunning, and great personal bravery with a profound sense of historical and religious destiny. It was with the emergence of Muhammed ibn-Saud that the influence of the al-Saud family took a quantum leap forward.

In 1744 an itinerant preacher arrived at the gates of Diriyah and asked Emir Muhammed for sanctuary. His name was Muhammed ibn-Abdul Wahhab, and the task he saw before him was the elimination of idolatry that had come to corrupt Islam. He had a vision of a return to the pure and original message of the Koran. Initially, Wahhab's homilies had met with great resistance and hostility. Not only had he been driven from towns and villages, but on at least two occasions he had been beaten unconscious.

Unlike most of the surrounding towns and villages that had driven the itinerant preacher away, often with stones and rocks following his retreating figure, Diriyah and its emir welcomed the austere, cold-eyed reformer. Muhammed ibn-Abdul Wahhab continued his impassioned vocation in the village of Diriyah, preaching to all who would listen about how the message of the Prophet Muhammed had been perverted and how Islam was in desperate need of purification.

History does not tell us what the average Diriyah villager's reaction was to the spirited harangues of Wahhab. It does tell us not only that Emir Muhammed was impressed by the reformer but that in a very short while he became convinced of the veracity of the man's preachings. In short, within a year of seeking sanctuary in Diriyah, the reformer Wahhab had managed to convert the town's ruler to his own fanatical and iconoclastic vision of puritan Islam.

An alliance was formed between the prince of Diriyah and the preacher Wahhab, who together launched a campaign to cleanse Islam of the falsehoods and misconceptions that had crept into it though the twelve centuries of isolation and ignorance since the Prophet Muhammed had originally revealed the Message.

Wahhab's alliance with Emir Muhammed ibn-Saud of Diriyah marks the turning point of what would later be referred to as the Wahhabi Reformation of Islam. Wahhab had a vision of a reformed Muslim world, and Emir Muhammed had the means to make that vision a reality—the sword. While Emir Muhammed's religious conversion to Wahhabi Islam appears to have been genuinely motivated by spiritual concerns, there can be no question that the cunning prince also saw the Wahhabi Reformation as a golden opportunity to expand and enlarge the political power and influence of his own family.

Thus the Wahhabi Reformation started in the central Nejd and was carried forward into the Arabian desert by the energy and enthusiasm of the fanatical preacher Wahhab and the armies of Emir Muhammed ibn-Saud. From village to village the preacher and the prince went, exhorting crowds to return to the true message of the Koran, felling so-called sacred trees, destroying the tombs of supposed holy men, and demolishing idols that had been receiving veneration.

There is a story told of how Wahhab, several days in advance of Muhammed ibn-Saud's armies, entered a village and began to preach reformed Islam. The villagers, content with their mixture of pagan and Muslim beliefs, were hostile and insulting to the preacher.

Soon after Wahhab had begun his harangue, he was interrupted by a village elder who demanded to know what Wahhab would do with a confessed adulteress. The crowd of villagers understood that Wahhab was being tested and immediately increased their mockery of the reformer.

According to the story, Wahhab was silent for a short while, seemingly impervious to the insults that rained from the crowd. Suddenly, he demanded that the offending woman be brought before him. Within minutes, the adulteress was brought to him and thrown into the dust at his feet. Three times Wahhab demanded a confession from the woman, and three times the woman acknowledged her adultery. Finally, amid the continuing taunts from the crowd, Wahhab seized a small boulder and, unlike Christ when faced with a similar situation, dashed the poor woman's brains out.

Far from provoking the rage of the villagers, Wahhab's action earned him their profound respect. Here then was the true believer, a man who not only talked but acted. This was not just another itinerant charlatan soothsayer full of flattery and false prophecies.

Military success followed military success, and soon a large portion of the central Nejd was under the political influence of the al-Sauds and the religious influence of the ever-zealous Wahhab.

A problem facing the Wahhabi Reformation at this point was the capricious nature of the desert Bedouin. It was not uncommon for a tribe to pledge unswerving loyalty to Wahhabi Islam and the al-Sauds one week and a week later retract the pledge and launch an attack on Muhammed ibn-Saud's armies.

This unpredictability was not so much a product of indecision as it was an expression of the anarchy of desert life. The desert Bedouin of the period valued his independence and thus found it easy to reject the authoritarian precepts of Wahhabiism, which sought to establish an orderly society of laws. Battle after battle was fought and refought.

In 1765 Emir Muhammed ibn-Saud died, and his son, Abdulaziz ibn-Muhammed, assumed leadership of the al-Saud clan. With continued advice and guidance from Wahhab, Emir Abdulaziz continued his father's military campaign. In 1773 Riyadh fell to the al-Saud armies, and within three years Emir Abdulaziz had added the regions of Sudair and Washm to the Wahhabi fold.

Emir Abdulaziz was a wise and prudent ruler, inheriting his father's cunning and military craftiness. By 1789 all of the Nejd had been subdued and was subject to the rule of the al-Sauds.

In 1792, at the age of 89, Muhammed ibn-Abdul Wahhab died. The aged preacher-reformer did not live to see the fruition of his vision—the taking of the Holy Cities of Mecca and Medina, but he left a legacy of stability, orderliness, and zeal that would serve the al-Saud family well in the turbulent decades of the nineteenth century.

While that century was just beginning, in 1803, Emir Abdulaziz died and was succeeded by his son Saud.[1] By this point the al-Sauds contolled most of the Arabian peninsula. Al-Saud armies had captured Mecca and Medina and were in control of most of the Hejaz. To the southwest, the al-Saud armies had taken most of present-day Oman and even portions of Yemen.

For the first time, the military successes of the al-Saud armies attracted attention beyond the perimeters of the Arabian desert. At this time the predominant force in the Middle East was the

---

[1]See Appendix C for the eighteenth- and nineteeth-century al-Saud family genealogy.

Ottoman Empire, which claimed the Arabian peninsula as its own. The Ottoman sultan became concerned about the growth of Saudi power and influence and considered the al-Sauds a threat to the prestige of the Ottoman Empire.

The sultan's concern turned to blind rage when he learned that the Wahhabis in control of Mecca had removed his name from the list of prayers on Friday. This action represented a direct challenge to the authority of the sultan. The sultan decided to reclaim the entire region of the Hejaz from the Wahhabis in order to reestablish the prestige of the Ottoman caliphate.

The sultan's governor in Egypt, Muhammed Ali Pasha, was ordered to invade the Arabian peninsula. Muhammed Ali Pasha saw himself ruling an Arab empire that included Egypt and the Sudan and stretched beyond the Red Sea across Arabia, Syria, and Iraq. This ambition would put Muhammed Ali Pasha in direct conflict with the Ottoman sultan. However, at this point Muhammed Ali Pasha chose to consolidate his power at home in Cairo and use the military adventure into Arabia to his own future advantage.

Muhammed Ali Pasha named his son, Toson, to lead his armies into Arabia. These armies were a motley assortment of Egyptians, Albanian officers, European mercenaries, and other political undesirables whom Muhammed Ali wanted out of Egypt. In October 1811 Toson's armies landed at Yanbu, a small port some three hundred kilometers north of Jeddah. The Saudi army offered no resistance to the invasion, choosing instead to draw Toson's forces into the interior desert so as to lengthen their supply lines and to have the advantage of fighting on familiar terrain.

The Saudi battle plan succeeded. When Toson's forces arrived at Wadi Al-Safra, just outside Medina, they found themselves completely surrounded by the Saudi army.

The battle lasted three days and claimed nearly five thousand of Toson's troops. The Egyptian army, or what was left of it, retreated to Yanbu, on the Red Sea. Toson sent a message to his father in Cairo, requesting reinforcements. Muhammed Ali Pasha responded by sending an additional five thousand men. These arrived in Yanbu in the spring of 1812. Toson renewed his attack on Medina. The siege lasted almost three months, but eventually the Saudi defenders were forced to surrender.

Toson learned an important lesson during the siege of Medina. The very length of the siege and the tenacity of the Wahhabi defenders illustrated to him that mere military might could not hope to take, let alone control, the entire peninsula. At this point Toson launched a campaign of bribery, buying the loyalties of influential tribal chieftains.

Sensing a change in Tosons tactics, the Saudi forces again resorted to their original strategy of drawing the Egyptian army farther and farther into the harsh desert. Not only was the terrain more familiar, but the tribes of the Nejd were more likely to be loyal to the House al-Saud than those in the Hejaz.

In 1813 Muhammed Ali Pasha landed with a large army of reinforcements at Jeddah. He personally planned the invasion of the Nejd. The Egyptian plan was essentially a simple one. The army, in three spearheads, would attack Turabah, Qunfuda, and the Nejd.

With this plan, Muhammed Ali Pasha hoped to bring the entire peninsula under his control. However, like his son, Muhammed Ali Pasha had underestimated the tenacity of the Saudi forces. The Egyptian army was defeated at Turabah, and Toson's army was forced into retreat at Qunfuda. Muhammed Ali Pasha was forced to send back to Egypt for more troops.

At this point, the Saudi forces were outnumbered by the Egyptian army and avoided direct confrontation. Instead, the Saudi army fought a guerrilla war, striking at the Egyptians suddenly and then retreating before the Egyptian army could retaliate. Although such guerrilla warfare wasn't decisive, the Saudis succeeded in harassing and demoralizing their enemy. The army of Emir Saud ibn-Abdulaziz might have even been victorious if Saud had not died.

Emir Saud was succeeded by his eldest son, Abdullah ibn-Saud. Emir Abdullah was young and relatively inexperienced in the arts of desert warfare. He charted a new course for the war against the Egyptians. Instead of using guerrilla tactics,

Abdullah sent his army to confront the enemy directly. What followed was a series of large battles in which the smaller Saudi army was devastated by the Egyptian forces.

Following the arrival of Egyptian reinforcements in Jeddah, Muhammed Ali Pasha personally led an army of over seven thousand strong to a position about halfway between Taif and Turabah, where he met the Saudi army, led by Abdullah's brother. It was here that the Saudis encountered their first major defeat. Muhammed Ali Pasha marched his army to the southeast, capturing Turabah and Ranya, and in a short time gained control over the entire Asir, the fertile southwestern region of the peninsula.

Recognizing that more men were necessary, Muhammed Ali Pasha returned to Cairo and raised another army. This one went to Arabia with Muhammed Ali's son, Ibrahim, at its head. The new Egyptian army under Ibrahim Pasha proved to be the deciding factor. Ibrahim marched his army directly into the Nejd, destroying each and every village in his path.

By early 1818 Ibrahim Pasha and his army had marched into Wadi Hannifa and were within eyesight of Diriyah, the home of the al-Saud family. For five months the Egyptian army laid siege to Diriyah, employing heavy artillery left over from the Napoleonic wars. Finally the inhabitants of Diriyah were forced to surrender on September 9, 1818.

During the process of securing the surrender of Diriyah, Ibrahim Pasha had promised to guarantee the safety of the inhabitants if the al-Saud family surrendered and went into exile. However, as soon as the residents of Diriyah had opened their gates to the Egyptian army, Ibrahim Pasha violated all the surrender terms he had offered. He seized all the lands of the al-Saud and Wahhab families, executed large numbers of townspeople, and razed the town. Emir Abdullah was sent to Constantinople, where, on the orders of the sultan, he was beheaded.

This, then, would seem to be the end of the al-Saud clan. The emir had lost his head in Constantinople. Most of the male members of the family had been captured by Ibrahim Pasha.

The ancestral home of the family had been reduced to ruins, and the vision of a unified Arabia would seem to have been buried beneath the rubble and carnage of defeat.

However, another branch of the family emerged, led by a second cousin of the executed emir, Turki ibn-Abdullah. This branch of the House al-Saud provided a direct line to the present rulers of Saudi Arabia.

After an abortive attempt to recapture the family seat at Diryah, Turki ibn-Abdullah established himself in Riyadh, where he ruled for ten years. Turki, the great-grandfather of Saudi Arabia's first king, Abdulaziz, rebuilt the city of Riyadh and provided it with a decade of peaceful and stable prosperity.

Among the buildings that Turki built was the Qasr, a large fortified palace that would serve as the seat of government and the al-Saud royal residence for more than a century. Turki also reestablished the bond between the House al-Saud and the family of Muhammed ibn-Abdul Wahhab by inviting the reformer's grandson, Abdul Rahman ibn-Hassan to come to Riyadh as the city's chief *qadi*.

At the same time, a cousin, Mishari ibn–Abdul Rahman al-Saud, escaped from Muhammed Ali Pasha's prison in Cairo. Mishari had been taken to Cairo following the fall of Diriyah in 1818. Mishari came back to Arabia and made his way across the peninsula to Riyadh. His entrance into Riyadh marks the beginning of the most ignoble period in the history of the al-Saud family, a period characterized by deceit, treachery, and fratricide.

Mishari ibn–Abdul Rahman was an ambitious man who believed that he should have been the leader of the al-Saud family and the ruler of Riyadh. He was publicly loyal to Turki ibn-Abdullah, but privately he was discontented with the political appointment granted him by Emir Turki.

Soon after Mishari's return to Riyadh, Emir Turki discovered a conspiracy to oust him from power. Mishari was the prime mover behind the coup attempt. Instead of punishing Mishari for his treachery, Emir Turki forgave his cousin and even made him a present of a large house in Riyadh. Again Mishari publicly declared his loyalty to his cousin Turki. However, four years later

Mishari financed the assassination of Emir Turki as he left the Great Mosque after Friday prayers. Mishari then promptly declared himself the emir of Riyadh and moved himself into the Qasr palace.

Turki's son, Faisal, was away from Riyadh at the time of his father's murder, but as soon as he received the news, he began plotting his revenge on Mishari. Faisal ibn-Turki was a popular figure among the townspeople of Riyadh and had no difficulty in getting inside the dried-mud walls of the city. Mishari, upon hearing of Faisal's return to Riyadh and knowing of his support among the townspeople, retreated to the Qasr, where he prepared for Faisal's attack.

Faisal did attack the Qasr, but not as Mishari had expected him to. During the night, Faisal's men were able to lower ropes over the walls of the fortified palace, enabling several dozen of his men to scale them. A fierce and bloody battle ensued between those loyal to Mishari and those loyal to Faisal. In the end, Faisal was victorious, and Mishari lay headless in one of the courtyards of the palace.

Faisal declared himself the emir of Riyadh and set about the job of ruling the desert town. However, Emir Faisal was destined to have many more problems with dissident family members. Less than a year after Faisal had killed Mishari, a large Egyptian army marched toward Riyadh. Leading this force was Khalid ibn-Saud, the younger brother of Emir Abdullah, who had been beheaded in Constantinople. Primogeniture is not practiced in Arabia regarding the succession of monarchs. It is common for the crown to be passed from brother to brother so that Khalid's claim to the throne was legitimate and divided the popular support that had previously been directed toward Faisal.

Khalid's bid for power was successful, and he too declared himself emir of Riyadh and moved himself into the Qasr. Faisal was exiled to Cairo, where he was imprisoned.

Khalid didn't last long. He too was soon faced with another claimant to the official seat of the House al-Saud. Abdullah ibn-Thunaiyan al-Saud, whose descendant Ahmed was destined to play an important role in the shaping of modern Saudi Arabia, marched his army against Riyadh. At the same time as Abdullah ibn-Thunaiyan was laying siege to the Qasr, Faisal ibn-Turki was escaping from prison in Cairo and making his way back across Arabia to Riyadh.

Khalid fled Riyadh, leaving Abdullah ibn-Thunaiyan victoriously declaring himself emir of Riyadh and moving himself into the Qasr. However, Abdullah ibn-Thunaiyan was ousted from the palace and from Riyadh by the return of Faisal ibn-Turki.

In May 1843 Faisal again declared himself emir of Riyadh. As can be easily imagined, the townspeople of Riyadh were tired of the constant vying for power which had turned their city into a battleground for twenty years.

For this reason, the people of Riyadh rallied around Faisal in the hope that he would prove to be strong enough to provide Riyadh with stability and peace. In this the people of Riyadh were not disappointed. Emir Faisal ruled over Riyadh for twenty peaceful years.

The cholera epidemic that hit Riyadh in 1854 was the worst in the town's history. No one escaped illness, and some historical sources place the mortality rate as high as one in three persons.

The Wahhabi inhabitants of Riyadh interpreted the epidemic as a symbol of God's displeasure. They sought and found the cause of the disease in the decadent manner in which they had come to live. In order to prevent such a plague from happening again, the people of Riyadh, with the active support of Emir Faisal, founded the *mutawa* to enforce the many prohibitions of Wahhabi Islam.

After Faisal died in 1865, the al-Saud family went back to bickering and battling for control of Riyadh. Faisal's two sons, Abdullah and Saud, waged a civil war in Riyadh that lasted nine years, each alternately claiming to be the true emir. During this struggle, Abdullah built a new fortress in Riyadh—Al-Masmak, the very fortress that Abdulaziz would attack in 1902 when he killed the Rashidi governor of Riyadh.

During this civil war, much of the region ruled by the al-Saud family was whittled away by the Ottomans and the Rashids. El Hasa, the eastern province of Arabia, was lost to the Turks, and land in the north was snatched by the Rashids.

In 1875 Saud died, and the youngest son of Emir Faisal became the ruler of Riyadh. His name was Abdul Rahman ibn-Faisal al-Saud. Abdul Rahman was faced with the problem of Saud's sons, who joined together to oppose him. So outnumbered was Abdul Rahman that he was forced to call on the traditional enemy of the al-Sauds, the Rashid family, for help in staying in power. The Rashid family viewed this invitation as an opportunity to extend their authority into the Nejd. So, while agreeing to support Abdul Rahman, their intention was to take Riyadh for their own.

In 1887 Rashidi forces entered Riyadh, ostensibly in support of Abdul Rahman. However, their design soon became clear. Abdul Rahman and his family were rounded up and stripped of all authority and power. A Rashidi governor was installed in Riyadh.

Two years later, Abdul Rahman returned to Riyadh and was reappointed emir. He had little power. The authority in Riyadh continued to be the Rashidi governor, a brutal and cruel man by the name of Salim ibn-Sakhan.

Abdul Rahman learned that Salim was planning to murder the entire male line of the al-Saud family. He attacked the Rashidi representative and murdered him and many of his officers.[2] When the news of Salim's murder reached Hail, Muhammed ibn-Rashid, the ruler of the Rashid family, marched his army to Riyadh and laid siege to the al-Saud capital. It was not long before Abdul Rahman recognized that his position was hopeless, and in 1891 he and his wife Sara and their two children, Abdulaziz and Nura, abandoned Riyadh to the Rashidi army and made their way across the desert to a lonely and humble exile in Kuwait.

This would again seem to be the ignominious end of the House al-Saud. In a single century, the al-Sauds had dwindled from a family of rulers of the entire Arabian peninsula to one exiled and defeated man and his next-of-kin, living on the good graces of the sheikh of Kuwait. And it would have been the end

---

[2] A complete description of Abdul Rahman's attack on Salim and his exile from Riyadh was given in chapter three.

of the al-Sauds had it not been for Abdul Rahman's son, Abdulaziz, who a decade later would launch an epic journey to attain the position he believed to be his birthright—king of all Arabia.

11

Abdulaziz's Later Years

It is unnecessary here to repeat the chronicle of Abdulaziz's heroic attack on Riyadh, his creation of the bloodthirsty Ikhwan, his wars with the Rashids and with the sherif of Mecca, and his final unification of Arabia. It is, however, worthwhile to look at the years following the unification, the years between Abdulaziz's ascension to the throne in 1932 and his death in 1953.

Unlike the previous fifty-one years of his life, these last twenty were neither heroic nor particularly happy for the aging king. They were filled with problems that the desert king was ill-equipped to solve. Abdulaziz was a great ruler—and a miserable administrator.

The greatest problem Abdulaziz faced in the last half of the 1930s was financial. The income for the newly formed Kingdom of Saudi Arabia came from a tax that was levied on the pilgrims making the annual hajj to Mecca. But that revenue was minuscule in relation to the squalor and poverty that existed in Arabia.

It was a tradition for the king to give gifts to all those who visited him. This mandatory gift giving insured that the Saudi treasury (which was at this point a brass-studded bridal chest that Abdulaziz used to carry in the trunk of his motorcar) was always on the verge of being empty.

The greatest strain on the tight Saudi economy of this period was food. Almost nothing could be grown in the arid soil of the peninsula, and all produce had to be imported. Thus there existed during the thirties and forties an enormous balance-of-payments deficit: large amounts of money were being drained out of the kingdom in return for foodstuffs, while there was only a trickle of revenue flowing into the kingdom from oil production and the tax on pilgrims.

Abdulaziz was not ignorant of the problems his people faced; he was simply financially unable to do anything to alleviate them. In addition, Abdulaziz was not an administrator in any sense of the word. He made all decisions personally. He had no opportunity, in the isolation of the Arabian desert, to understand how a government could be a vehicle for social change.

If a sick man came to Abdulaziz's weekly *majlis*, the monarch would give the man money, but it would never enter his head to set up a Ministry of Health.

Up to this point in the history of Arabia, there had been very little foreign influence in the interior desert. Abdulaziz had only been out of his kingdom on one occasion, and that was for a brief stay in Iraq.

Englishmen, like Shakespear, Cox, and Philby had befriended and even advised the king, but essentially the interior desert remained an isolated island of Wahhabi customs and traditions untouched by Western ways. This remained so during the thirties despite the presence of American oil men in the eastern oil fields. Abdulaziz, while personally liking the Americans he had met, made it all too clear that foreigners, especially non-Muslims, were not welcome in Riyadh. On the rare occasion that he did invite foreigners to Riyadh, Abdulaziz insisted that they wear full Arab dress.

It should also be noted that at this period no coherent foreign policy existed. Abdulaziz's desert instinct suggested to him that his internal problems could only be complicated by the outside world, and his response was isolationism. Only the growing demands on his treasury forced him to allow more American oil men into the kingdom.

Abdulaziz's financial plight was destined to get even worse before it improved. September 1939 saw the beginning of World War II and with it a cutback in oil production in the Eastern Province. Even the traditional mainstay of the Saudi economy, the pilgrim tax, shrank as foreign pilgrims became fewer because of the war.

The king faced a dilemma. His political savvy told him that the only sane position for Saudi Arabia in the world conflict was neutrality. However, the economic ruin that waited on his doorstep made him decide to enter the war on the side of the Allies. He hoped to receive aid from the United States.

There is a report that the Germans attempted to buy Abdulaziz's loyalty. Through a contact in Baghdad, they sought to discover how much money it would take to bring Abdulaziz into the war on the Axis side. The Germans believed the stereotype that all Arabs can be bought. They learned that King Abdulaziz wasn't for sale.

Abdulaziz's attitude towards World War II was probably colored by Philby, who had become an ardent pacifist advocate of international isolationism. In fact, Philby had gone off to the United States on a lecture tour, urging the American people not to let the "war-mongering" Roosevelt lead them into the European conflict. When Philby returned to England following the lecture tour, he was arrested as a "political undesirable" and imprisoned for several months.

After World War II, America showed renewed interest in Saudi Arabia. President Roosevelt was aware of the importance of the relationship between the United States and Saudi Arabia due to the role petroleum had played in the war.

Also, the Soviet Union was expanding its empire in Europe and attempting to extend its sphere of influence in the Middle east.

Roosevelt met with Abdulaziz in 1945. He desired a continuation of the warm relationship between the United States and Saudi Arabia that had existed through the offices of ARAMCO. He desired to check whatever Soviet influence existed in the area, and he wanted to convince Abdulaziz to be a force of moderation in the growing problem of Jewish immigrants moving from Europe to Palestine.

The meeting between the American president and the Saudi monarch was cordial. Roosevelt told Abdulaziz that the United

States "would take no steps on Palestine without consulting him."[1] Roosevelt went on to urge Abdulaziz to meet with Jewish leaders so that he and other Arab leaders could come to a mutual understanding of the problem. Roosevelt attempted to arrange a meeting between the Saudi king and Zionist leader Chaim Weizman, but Abdulaziz refused the invitation, explaining that he was not a spokesman for the Arab world.

Abdulaziz expressed to Roosevelt great sympathy for the suffering of European Jewry. However, he asked why Palestinians should suffer for the crimes of the Nazis. Abdulaziz was not opposed to the idea of a Jewish state, but he thought that justice would be better served if such a state came into being in Germany.

Following the meeting between Roosevelt and Abdulaziz, ARAMCO went back to full-scale oil production, and the oil royalties again flowed into Abdulaziz's brass-studded bridal chest. ARAMCO was now producing petroleum on a large scale to fuel the postwar industrial boom. The size of the royalty payments reflected this increased production; from 1947 onward, Saudi Arabia would not have to worry about bankruptcy. It would not have to concern itself with courting foreign powers in order to receive financial aid. It would be financially self-sufficient.

This resolution of the kingdom's financial worries should have been a triumph for Abdulaziz. It was not. Instead, it created problems of a new and different kind, problems that the monarch was not equipped to handle. It should be understood here that throughout his reign, Abdulaziz *was* the government of Saudi Arabia. There were no ministries, no cabinet, no consultative assemblies. There were no agencies of government to oversee or administer things like budgetary planning. When ARAMCO paid its oil royalties, they paid them directly to the king. While a number of Abdulaziz's sons were in positions of regional power, none exerted influence over the central authority of the kingdom, the king himself.

---

[1]Thomas A. Bryson, *American Diplomatic Relations with the Middle East, 1784–1975: A Survey*, The Scarecrow Press, Metuchen, N.J., 1977, p. 125.

By 1947 the oil royalties were beyond anything the al-Saud family had ever dared dream of or hope for. Abdulaziz continued to give lavish gifts to his visitors and instituted an extremely generous allowance system for members of his own family. Even after all these expenditures, there was enough surplus revenue to initiate a 270-million-dollar development program, the first program of its kind ever in Saudi Arabia. The 270 million dollars were earmarked for the construction of railroads, roads, ports, schools, hospitals, and most important, irrigation systems.

However, Abdulaziz and his family had no experience in handling large sums of money. Suddenly, the age-old scourge of poverty was gone for the royal family. Suddenly, material luxury was theirs. The pleasures and treasures of Europe and the United States of America were only a jet ride away.

Young princes took to spending more and more time outside Saudi Arabia, away from the puritanical Wahhabi rules and regulations. London and Paris became playgrounds for the princes, who donned Western garb and spent lavishly at hotels and nightclubs. Like children away from strict parents for the first time, these young princes indulged in everything that was forbidden in Saudi Arabia. They were free to buy women and free to drink alcohol.

Stories of debauchery filtered back to the kingdom, and Abdulaziz heard about his sons' escapades.

The crisis came to a head in Paris. A son of Abdulaziz, Prince Mousaad, was arrested in Paris for dancing naked in a fountain, brandishing a sword. Perhaps if Mousaad's mother had been a slave or a member of an obscure family, Abdulaziz might have chosen to ignore the incident. However, Mousaad's mother was an al-Sudeiri, the most powerful family on the Arabian peninsula after the al-Sauds themselves. Abdulaziz ordered Prince Mousaad to return to Saudi Arabia immediately and placed him under house arrest. Prince Mousaad's reaction was one of bitterness, a bitterness that his own sons would share, a bitterness that twenty-five years later would stun Arabia and change the course of Arabian history. We shall learn more of Prince Mousaad and his sons when we look at the character of King Faisal.

Only a short while after Prince Mousaad had performed in the Paris fountain, another of Abdulaziz's sons, Prince Mishari, murdered the British consul in Jeddah because the man refused him whiskey. If Mousaad had shocked Abdulaziz, Mishari succeeded in shattering the old man. Earlier I described how, true to Islamic law, Abdulaziz offered the family of the British consul Mishari's life and the British declined to ask for Mishari's execution.

Nevertheless Abdulaziz insisted that his son be punished. He jailed Mishari, who remained in prison until, after Abdulaziz's death, he was pardoned by his brother, King Saud.

With the moral fiber of his family seemingly disintegrating all around him, Abdulaziz became morose and depressed. The final years of his rule were particularly unhappy ones.

In early November 1953 scores of messengers left the Qasr al-Qarwah, Abdulaziz's palace in Taif. Their destinations were the royal palaces of El Hasa, the Hejaz, the Nejd, and the Asir. Their message was simple and brief: "Abdulaziz is dying. The King commands his family to attend him."

From all over Arabia, Europe, and the United States, Saudi princes made their way to the old king's palace in Taif. On November 9, 1953, King Abdulaziz ibn–Abdul Rahman al-Saud died, surrounded by forty sons and more than sixty grandsons.

In accordance with his wishes, only minutes after the king had been declared dead, the princes filed past their oldest brother, Saud, each in turn announcing, "*Nubaik ala Kitab Allah wa Sinnat a rasoul Allah*" (We pledge loyalty to you on the Book of God and the Traditions of His Messenger).

Faisal embraced his brother Saud, kissing the new monarch's shoulders and the bridge of his nose, a gesture of affection and respect.

The corpse of King Abdulaziz was transported to Riyadh and buried in the desert at Miqbarat al-Oud. The grave was unmarked by any inscription—as is the Wahhabi custom. Two flat, upright stones indicated the head and foot of the burial mound. Next to the grave was the grave of Nura, Abdulaziz's favorite sister, who had, sixty years before, shared a camel saddle-bag with her brother on their way to exile in Kuwait.

Today the graves have disappeared. Wind and sand storms have covered up the stones, and all one sees is an expanse of lonely sand. The desert has reclaimed its king.

12

King Saud

Of all the monarchs of Saudi Arabia, King Saud may have been the most human, the least heroic, and correspondingly the least understood. The handful of history texts that cover the period write Saud off in a single tersely written paragraph. He is described as "incompetent," "extravagant," and "degenerate."

Today, King Saud is considered a national disgrace in Saudi Arabia. His portrait is not displayed anywhere in the kingdom. All references to him or his reign are automatically purged from books entering the kingdom, and extremely few Saudis are willing to talk about the "black sheikh of the family."[1]

Linda Blandford sums up the Saudi view of King Saud in her gossipy exposé of Arab oil wealth.[2] "King Saud of Saudi Arabia had forty sons and a bad image. He went in for gold-plated Cadillacs, watches for visitors, concubines and morphine."

Peter Hobday is equally condemning: "It is said that while Saud never had more than the permitted four wives at any one time, he has left nearly a hundred children, among them 45 sons. He had up to 100 concubines, and spent most of the Kingdom's income or about $200 million a year—on lavish palaces, cars and jewelry."[3]

---

[1]Just before publication, there was an effort inside Saudi Arabia to reinstate Saud in the history books. His portrait has reappeared and the University of Riyadh has been renamed King Saud University.

[2]Linda Blandford, *Super Wealth: The Secret Lives of the Oil Sheikhs*, William Morrow & Co., New York, 1977.

[3]Peter Hobday, *Saudi Arabia Today*, Macmillan, New York, 1978, p. 69.

While these accusations against Saud may be essentially accurate, they in no way convey a complete picture of this complex and tragic man. It is doubtful that anyone would argue that Saud was other than a failure as a monarch. However, to attribute his failure to greed, lechery, or mere self-serving ambition is to ignore the extremely difficult and complicated time of his reign.

Compare a description of King Saud, written during his reign as monarch by Wanda Jablonski, an editor of *Petroleum Week*: "He [Saud] is a good man, with a simple straightforward manner, who tries hard to be a good father to his people.... He is powerful but he is no dictator. His position has been aptly described as 'autocratic in theory but democratic in principle' ....He is deeply religious—with no sham about it.... He has emerged as an Arab ruler who keeps his feet on the ground, a staunch opponent of communism, a friend of America."[4]

The contradictions become starkly evident. How can one reconcile the image of King Saud as an extravagant degenerate with a hundred concubines and a morphine habit with an image of him as a deeply religious man who kept his feet solidly on the ground?

The truth about King Saud is intricately bound up in the character of the man himself and the changes that swept through the Middle East.

Saud ibn-Abdulaziz al-Saud was born in 1902. His mother was Wadha bint-Hazami,[5] a member of the Bani Khalid tribe that was large and powerful in El Hasa. Saud was not the firstborn son. His brother, Turki, had been born several years earlier, and thus Saud was relegated to the subordinate position of the second-born.

Abdulaziz saw to it that his sons received a typical court education. This included memorizing the entire Koran (something that Saud managed to accomplish before his fourteenth birth-

---

[4]Grant C. Butler, *Kings and Camels*, The Devin-Adair Company, New York, 1960.
[5]As *ibn* means "son of," so *bint* means "daughter of."

day), basic instruction in reading, writing, and arithmetic, plus extensive lessons in the art of desert warfare.

Turki ibn-Abdulaziz was a joy for his father to behold. By the time he was twelve, Turki was an expert horseman who had already proved himself to be a cunning and courageous warrior. Saud, while growing as tall as his father—over six feet—suffered from indifferent health and weak eyesight. He was no match for his elder brother's physical agility.

It is virtually certain that Abdulaziz would have named Turki his successor to the throne had his eldest son not been one of the many victims of the so-called Spanish flu that swept the world following World War I, claiming more casualties than the war itself. The al-Saud family was hit particularly hard by this epidemic. The fatal disease entered the Arab world in December 1918 and soon claimed Turki and his two younger brothers, Fahd and Saad. Shortly thereafter, Al-Jauharh bint-Musaad al-Jiluwi, a wife of Abdulaziz and mother of the present king, Khalid, also perished of the disease.

Abdulaziz was particularly distressed by the death of his eldest son, but he soon elevated Saud to that position, even though Saud was not the warrior or horseman that Turki had been. However, Saud soon proved himself to be a courageous warrior when he rode with his father in the 1921 war against the House al-Rashid.

Saud rode again with his father during the war in 1926 against the Hashemite sherif of Mecca. A curious—and unsubstantiated—story is told about Saud during this time. It is curious because the image of Saud in the story is quite out of character with the image of him as "an extravagant degenerate."

Soon after Mecca had learned of the Ikhwan massacre at Taif, the Holy City surrendered without a fight. Abdulaziz and Saud entered the city in the requisite pure state of *ihram*. Naturally, both father and son were unarmed at the time. According to the story, there was treachery abroad in Mecca, and soon after Abdulaziz and Saud had begun to pray in the Great Mosque, they were attacked by four knife-wielding assassins. Abdulaziz was instantly knocked unconscious. Saud threw himself between the would-be assassins and the body of his father and fought with them until help arrived. It is said that Saud managed to kill one of the attackers before he was rescued.

If the story is accurate, one is forced to see Saud, at least within the context of this one incident, as a loyal and courageous son risking his own life to save that of his father. One is also forced to speculate what bearing, if any, this incident might have had upon Abdulaziz's choice of Saud to succeed him as king.

After the fall of Mecca, Abdulaziz turned his attention to the rest of the Hejaz, which was still held by the Hashemites. He appointed Faisal to lead the Ikhwan invasion of the Hejaz and ordered Saud to return to Riyadh to be viceroy of the Nejd. It is at this point that we encounter the first friction between the two brothers.

Faisal was a logical choice to head the attack on Jeddah. He had traveled outside Saudi Arabia and would have been familiar with the ways of the foreign diplomatic community that existed in Jeddah. Nevertheless, Saud felt slighted by Faisal's appointment, and the following year he wrote to his father in Mecca expressing his disappointment and bitterness. "The honorable post is not here in the Nejd, but as commander in the war. You taught us to speak frankly and I will do so. I will not stand for it."[6]

Saud's letter probably filled Abdulaziz more with paternal pride than with annoyance at his son's insubordination. It was a letter that Abdulaziz himself might have written, a letter that contained within it the essence of Bedouin manhood—a desire to prove oneself courageous in battle coupled with the frankness and candor of speech that is so respected among the desert dwellers.

Abdulaziz resolved the situation by dividing the command of the Ikhwan between two of his sons in order to avoid either one's receiving all the glory. Faisal was appointed to lead the siege on Jeddah, and Muhammed, Abdulaziz's third-eldest son, was given command of the Ikhwan attack on Medina. Saud however, was left in Riyadh as viceroy of the Nejd.

---

[6]Gerald De Gaury, *Faisal: King of Saudi Arabia*, Frederick A. Praeger, New York, 1967, p. 39.

Saud was annoyed at his father's decision, but, after making his written protest, he never brought the subject up again. Saud functioned in Riyadh as its local governor, holding a weekly public *majlis*, resolving tribal disputes, and earning himself a reputation for charity and generosity. Saud had had ample opportunity to watch his father uniting the diverse and often hostile tribes of Arabia, and he had learned from his father the political value of generosity and magnanimity. Here in Riyadh, Saud attempted to emulate his father, but what the son lacked was his father's charm and intelligence.

It is interesting to note, especially in light of Saud's later characterization as a moral degenerate, that part of his duties as viceroy consisted of enforcing the strict Wahhabi code of behavior. Not only was Saud vigilant in the enforcement of Wahhabiism, but he also gained for himself a reputation as a pious, God-fearing man. Saud's reputation became such that a few years later, al-Duwaish and ibn-Humaid, the renegade Ikhwan leaders, sent Saud a letter complaining that Abdulaziz was working for his own ambition rather than for the propagation of Islam. They further went on to demand a *jihad* against Iraq.

What this letter was supposed to accomplish isn't known. However, the fact that it was sent to Saud is enlightening. Perhaps al-Duwaish and ibn-Humaid thought that Saud was a puritan zealot like themselves who would ignore family loyalty in order to join the rebel forces in spreading the true faith. On the other hand, al-Duwaish and ibn-Humaid may have simply been looking for someone they knew to be deeply religious and who was also close to Abdulaziz to act as their advocate with the king. In either case, the fact that al-Duwaish and ibn-Humaid sent their letter to Saud suggests strongly that, at least at this point in his career, Saud had a relatively widespread reputation as a devoted Wahhabi Muslim.

Saud neither sided with the rebel Ikhwan nor acted on their behalf with his father. He promptly forwarded their letter to his father without any comment of his own. Soon after, Abdulaziz raised his own army against the marauding Ikhwan.

In 1934 there was military trouble in the southwestern province of the Asir. The Asir is mountainous but fertile and is bordered by Yemen to the south. The imam of Yemen had, for a number of years, allowed tribes under his command to raid northward across the border into Saudi Arabia. On several occasions, Abdulaziz had protested these raids to the imam, a man by the name of Yahya. There had followed a brief period of negotiation between Imam Yahya and Abdulaziz, but no resolution. The raids continued, and Abdulaziz felt they had come to represent a direct threat to his authority. Once again he ordered his sons into the saddle.

Abdulaziz appointed both Faisal and Saud as his commanders in the field. Faisal was ordered to move his army south along the coast, while Saud was ordered to move his forces south through the mountains. Faisal's campaign in the Asir was a success for the al-Sauds. The imam of Yemen had completely underestimated both the resolve of Abdulaziz and the strength of the al-Saud army. Within a matter of weeks, he was forced to petition Abdulaziz for peace. Faisal handled the negotiations with the beleaguered imam, and for twenty years thereafter no fortifications were needed along the Saudi-Yemeni border.

Saud and his army had become bogged down in the mountains, and he was unable to share the glory of his younger brother's victory. In many respects Saud lived his entire life under two shadows, constantly comparing himself with his father and his younger brother Faisal. Neither of the comparisons was particularly favorable to Saud. He was neither a charming desert warrior nor a sophisticated diplomat.

Abdulaziz's choice of Saud as his successor becomes even more puzzling in light of the fact that he offered Saud virtually no training in international relations. In fact, it would seem that Abdulaziz attempted to keep Saud as isolated as possible from the international community.

Perhaps Abdulaziz could not foresee the international position that a modern Saudi monarch would occupy. Unlike Saud, Faisal traveled extensively in Europe and the United States. He became well versed with Western ways and fluent in English. Saud, on the other hand, did not leave the kingdom until after he was forty-five.

In May 1942 Alexander Kirk, an American diplomat, visited Saudi Arabia. During his visit, Kirk stopped in Riyadh for talks with both Abdulaziz and Saud. It was at this time that Kirk heard of Saud's desire to visit the United States. Even though it was wartime, or perhaps because of it, a year later the State Department issued a formal invitation to King Abdulaziz or his representative to visit America.

Kirk and the State Department had thought that Abdulaziz would naturally send his eldest living son, Saud. However, Abdulaziz chose to send Princes Faisal and Khalid to represent him, announcing that Prince Saud was to remain in Riyadh because of very important business. Once again Saud may have felt slighted.

Saud finally did visit the United States in 1947. Relations between the two countries had become strained over the question of Palestine. President Truman had chosen to ignore Roosevelt's promise to Abdulaziz that the United States would take no position on Palestine without first consulting with the Saudi monarch. The situation was not helped either by Saud's lack of diplomacy or by Truman's patronizing attitude toward the future king.

Truman treated Saud rather like the small child of an important client, secretly amused by the odd garb of the Saudi entourage and indulgent of their curious mannerisms. He dodged the issue of Palestine, and Saud may have lacked the expertise and self-confidence necessary to force the American president into a serious discussion of the issue. Instead, Truman presented Saud with a ridiculous decoration for "meritorious service to the Allied Cause during World War II."

Given the fact that Saudi Arabia entered the war only two months before it was over and that not a single Saudi national saw combat, one can only wonder what service Saud performed. What is much more likely is that some low-level bureaucrat in the State Department believed, as the British had when they presented Abdulaziz with a knighthood, that all Arabs were in awe of glass beads, trinkets, shiny coins, and colored ribbons. It is doubtful whether anyone viewed Saud's trip to the United States as a diplomatic triumph. However, as a result of Saud's visit, the United States raised the American legation in Jeddah to the status of an embassy in 1949.

With the dawn of the 1950s, winds of radical change began to blow across the Middle East. Behind this radicalism was the growing regional awareness of the exploitation the Middle East had suffered under British and French colonialization. This was made painfully evident by the creation of Israel.

The Arab world regarded this as the theft of Arab land and as the starkest of betrayals. Abdulaziz could not understand how his old friends, the British, could support such an injustice.

An old Bedouin proverb says, "A man betrayed once is a man with one hundred eyes." Like the betrayed man, the Arab world began to focus its one hundred eyes to determine how else it had been deceived.

It was not long before a seventy-one-year-old Iranian put together the pieces of the petroleum jigsaw puzzle and came to the indisputable conclusion that his country was being robbed by Britain and the United States. Muhammed Mossadegh came to see clearly how the international oil companies and the British government were keeping the price of petroleum artifically low so as to create an industrial boom in the West while at the same time retarding the development and modernization of most Middle Eastern oil-producing nations.

Mossadegh, then leader of the National Front Party in Iran, was elected premier in 1951 and almost immediately nationalized the British-owned oil industry. Diplomatic relations with Britain were broken, and Mossadegh prepared to lead his country to prosperity and renewed pride in itself.

Mossadegh's great failure was that he underestimated the reaction in the West. In 1953 he was ousted from power by a CIA-directed coup.

Even before Mossadegh was ousted and imprisoned, radicalism had broken out elsewhere in the Middle East. King Abdullah, son of the sherif of Mecca, was assassinated in Transjordan in 1951.

In Egypt, a group of military officers overthrew King Farouk in 1952 and placed his infant son, Fuad II, on the throne. After King Fuad II had reigned for only a year, the same officers declared Egypt a republic.

The events in Jordan, Iran, and Egypt had a curious effect within the Kingdom of Saudi Arabia. In addition to being an understandable reaction to colonial exploitation, these outbreaks of radicalism were harbingers of the pan-Arab movement that would become a real force in the Middle East within five years. Throughout his later years, Abdulaziz was a public advocate of Arab and Islamic unity. Although the old Saudi king did not perceive Arab unity in the same terms that Gamal Abdel Nasser would come to, Abdulaziz did appreciate that it was in the best interest of Arab nations to stand united on issues of common concern.

However, the assassination of King Abdullah in Transjordan, the coup in Egypt, and Mossadegh's nationalization of the Iranian oil fields were all essentially antimonarchical movements, and as such they represented, by way of example, a direct threat to the Saudi royal family.

Abdulaziz could not support or recognize the radicals; nor, in the interest of Arab unity, could he condemn them. His only option was to ignore them and hope they would go away. Thus Abdulaziz withdrew even further from internationalism and deeper into his desert isolation.

Such was the state of Saudi Arabian foreign policy when Abdulaziz died in 1953. Saud was proclaimed the new king the same day, and Faisal dutifully pledged his loyalty to his older brother. King Saud confirmed that Faisal would continue as viceroy of the Hejaz and as foreign minister. However, Saud retained the position of president of the Council of Ministers for himself.

The fact that Saud became his own prime minister suggests the kind of ruler he envisioned himself to be. Unquestionably, Saud saw himself following in his father's benevolent but autocratic footsteps. As his father had made decisions personally, so

Saud would make decisions personally. Like his father, Saud could not understand how the millions of petrodollars that were pouring into the kingdom annually might necessitate the need for reform in government.

If Saud's internal policy was similar to his father's, his foreign policy was its antithesis. Rather than continue Saudi Arabia's political isolation from the rest of the world, King Saud, almost immediately upon being declared king, embarked on numerous visits to other Arab and Islamic countries.

It has been argued that Saud's insatiable ego was not satisfied with merely being the king of Saudi Arabia but that he also wished to lead the entire Arab world. Whatever the truth of this argument, one can say with confidence that Saud could not understand the radicalism that was spreading throughout the Arab world.

During the spring of 1954 Saud went to Cairo, where he met with the newly elected president of Egypt, Gamal Abdel Nasser. This visit was bizarre. Saud was the most politically and religiously conservative of the Arab rulers. Nasser, on the other hand, was a revolutionary socialist, actively supporting antimonarchical organizations in Jordan and later in Yemen and Saudi Arabia.

The reason for Saud's visit to Cairo may have come out of a border dispute with Britain that had been simmering for several years. The sheikhdoms on the Arabian Gulf that now comprise the United Arab Emirates were at the time protectorates of Britain. Both Abu Dhabi, one of these sheikhdoms, and Saudi Arabia claimed sovereignty over an oasis located on their common border. The Buraimi Oasis was internationally insignificant in all respects except one: it was one of the largest Saudi slave markets on the peninsula.

The British press had a field day with this, and soon British public opinion was inflamed over the prospect of Britain's sitting idly by while Saudi Arabia reclaimed its human meat market. Whitehall was pressured into supporting Abu Dhabi's claim to the Buraimi Oasis.

Saud probably saw the crisis with the British as another example of British colonialist intervention in the Arab world and himself as yet another victim.

Saud had a knack of perceiving things exactly as they were not. Thus the most politically and religiously conservative leader in the Arab world attempted to join the radical Arab movement by forging a bond of friendship with Nasser. Needless to say, Saud's attempt was doomed from the start, but the devastating consequences were still almost a decade away.

Nasser commiserated with Saud over the Buraimi Oasis, and during the summer of 1954 he made the hajj to Mecca. Nasser then met again with Saud to seek his support for his own concept of Arab neutrality coupled with pan-Arab unity. Saud had no problem supporting pan-Arab unity at least theoretically. However, Nasser's idea of "neutrality" worried the Saudi king. Nasser envisioned the Arab world as linked exclusively neither to the capitalist West nor to the communist East, but maintaining healthy relations with both. Saud, with his ingrained fear of communism, could not bring himself to support any relationship whatsoever with the Soviet Union.

Saud's support of Nasser continued for the next several years, although he did publically criticize Egypt for purchasing military hardware from the Soviet Union. In the July of 1956, Nasser nationalized the Suez Canal. As in the case of Mossadegh's nationalization of the Iranian oil fields, the West responded with shock, anger, and finally military force. Britain, France and Israel joined together and launched an attack on Egypt. Saud supported Egypt's right to nationalize Suez, and broke diplomatic relations with both Britain and France following their aggression against Egypt. However, what Saud did not or could not foresee was that the Suez crisis was seen in Moscow as the explusion of British and French influence in the Middle East. Correspondingly, the Kremlin perceived a power vacuum in the Arab World which it soon set about filling itself.

Even if King Saud did not see the expanding Soviet role in the Middle East, President Eisenhower and John Foster Dulles thought they did, and it worried them to the point where they intervened in the Suez crisis to pacify the area. However, as far as Eisenhower was concerned, the damage had been done. The Soviets had secured a foothold in the Middle East—Nasser's Egypt.

It is at about this time that Saud found himself in financial difficulties. He had been spending lavishly, but at a level which in his own mind befitted the king of Saudi Arabia. Saud turned to the goose that laid the golden egg, ARAMCO, and demanded more money. ARAMCO, unwilling to part with any of its own profits but also unwilling to offend Saud, worked out one of the most audacious confidence schemes in U.S. history, whereby American taxpayers would end up subsidizing King Saud's private bank accounts.

The scheme worked as follows: the powerful oil lobby in Washington won passage through Congress of a bill which allowed ARAMCO to deduct the subsidies paid to King Saud as a direct tax credit from the amount ARAMCO owed the United States Treasury, on a dollar-for-dollar basis. In other words, ARAMCO paid nothing extra, King Saud received a massive subsidy, and the revenues that the U.S. Treasury did not receive from ARAMCO were simply made up by increased taxes on the American people.

So large was the American taxpayer's subsidy to King Saud that one member of the royal family claimed that upon completion of his fifty-million-dollar Nasseriah Palace, Saud joked that he should send a card of gratitude to the American people.

President Eisenhower had been a silent advocate of the passage of the ARAMCO "tax credit" bill. Eisenhower's "containment" policy of Soviet expansionism had been sorely stung by the Suez crisis, and he certainly wished to avoid offending the wealthiest of the Arab leaders. Eisenhower also saw Saud as a possible alternative to Nasser as leader of the Arab world.

On January 5, 1957, Eisenhower announced a major new foreign policy. In years to come, it would be referred to as the "Eisenhower Doctrine." In reality there was nothing very new about the doctrine at all. It was merely an extension of Eisenhower's attempts to contain Soviet expansionism. The

Eisenhower Doctrine provided U.S. military and financial assistance for nations whose national sovereignty was threatened by communism.

Congress provided the president with the extraordinary power to send American troops into a foreign nation without prior consultation or approval. All this may have sounded quite reasonable in Washington, but few State Department officials were willing to speculate how the Eisenhower Doctrine would be received in places like Cairo, Damascus, Tunis, Algiers, or Riyadh.

Eisenhower needed an Arab advocate to explain his doctrine to the leaders of the Arab world. The advocate he had in mind was none other than King Saud.

The American plan was simplistic, and it ignored both the real events in the Middle East and the limitations of Saud's own character. The Americans perceived Saud as the wealthiest and most conservative Arab leader, and they believed that he could be fashioned into a rival to Nasser's growing leadership.

Eisenhower invited Saud to visit the United States. The American purpose behind the visit was to explain the Eisenhower Doctrine to Saud and enlist his aid in popularizing it among other Arab leaders. Saud accepted the American invitation, but he had not forgotten the patronizing treatment he had received ten years earlier from Truman.

Saud came on January 30, 1957, armed with designs of his own. His reception in New York left much to be desired. New York's pro-Zionist mayor, Robert Wagner, made no secret of his refusal to greet the Saudi king. Saud visited the United Nations and then flew on to Washington, where he was met by Eisenhower and Dulles at the airport.

Eisenhower and Saud met at the White House for lengthy discussions of "the doctrine." Neither man wanted to predict the effect it would have in the Middle East. Eisenhower was concerned with containing the Soviets, while Saud was interested in what he could wring out of the United States in return for his services.

Saud argued that if the Eisenhower Doctrine was to be successfully received in the Arab world, it would have to be at least as attractive to Arab leaders as Nasser's Soviet-financed pan-Arabism. Eisenhower announced that Saudi Arabia would receive American tanks, aircraft, arms, ammunition, and the services of American military personnel in training the Saudi armed forces. This was sweetened by a loan of 250 million dollars.

Saud left the United States feeling that his visit had been an unqualified success. Not only had he won military aid for Saudi Arabia and secured a quarter-of-a-billion-dollar loan, but he had also convinced the U.S. to put pressure on Israel[7] and, he thought, improved his own standing in the Arab World. He was no longer just the king of Saudi Arabia, he was the leader of an American-backed program of Arab unity.

On his way back to Saudi Arabia, King Saud stopped in Morocco, Tunisia, Libya, and Egypt, acting as an agent for the Eisenhower Doctrine. The monarchs of Morocco and Libya and President Habib Bourguiba of the newly independent state of Tunisia responded cautiously but on the whole favorably to the American plan. Saud's real problems did not begin until Cairo.

In Cairo, Saud met at the Abdin Palace with President Nasser, President Shukhri Kuwatli of Syria, and King Hussein of Jordan. The meeting was characterized by discord, raised voices, and lack of agreement. Gerald De Gaury traces much of the split between the conservative Arab monarchies and the radical socialist states to this meeting. In his biography of Faisal, De Gaury writes, "It was soon clear that if the Arab world was not already divided between the arch-conservative monarchies and the radical socialists, the so-called 'Eisenhower doctrine' was going to produce just such a split."[8]

King Saud's flirtation with Nasser's radical socialism came to a momentary end. Nearly a decade later, Saud again tried to befriend the wily Egyptian leader. But in late 1957 and early 1958 both King Hussein of Jordan and King Saud of Saudia Arabia felt distinctly threatened by radical socialism.

---

[7]On February 2, 1957, the U.S. Ambassador to the United Nations, Henry Cabot Lodge, supported two resolutions calling on Israel to withdraw completely from Gaza, and calling on both Israel and Egypt to observe an armistice.
[8]Gerald De Gaury, *op. cit.*

King Saud attempted to architect and finance a plot to assassinate Nasser and break apart the newly formed United Arab Republic, a union of Egypt and Syria. The plot was first revealed by Nasser himself in a speech in Damascus on March 5, 1958, and the full, amazing details of the conspiracy were published that day in the semiofficial Egyptian newspaper *Al Ahram.*

The manner in which the alleged conspiracy was revealed has led some Middle East observers to wonder whether the plot wasn't entirely a product of Nasser's own fertile imagination, to discredit King Saud in the Arab world. However, most historians seem to agree that the evidence points to a real conspiracy.

According to *Al Ahram,* King Saud had approached Colonel Abdul Humaid as-Sarraj, head of Military Intelligence of the Syrian army, and offered him two million pounds and the presidency of Syria if he could arrange the assassination of Nasser. Saud's alleged plan called for the sabotage of Nasser's private aircraft. Colonel Sarraj refused. According to Colonel Sarraj, Saud then offered two million pounds plus an additional twenty million if the assassination was successful. The plan discussed between the two men and later revealed by Colonel Sarraj called for Nasser's chauffeur to flood an area of roadway with gasoline and ignite it just as Nasser was passing.

To prove his allegations against King Saud, Colonel Sarraj produced photocopies of three checks from Riyadh, drawn on the Arab Bank of Beirut, totaling just under two million pounds; a letter to himself written on King Saud's private secretary's letterhead; and a tape recording of himself discussing the conspiracy against Nasser with King Saud's alleged agent, a widow of King Abdulaziz.

Saud further brought suspicion upon himself by responding to the accusations by ordering a full commission to investigate and then never naming anyone to the commission. Naturally, no investigation followed.

If King Saud's image abroad was declining, his image within the Kingdom of Saudi Arabia was no better. During his five years as ruler, Saud had brought about no reforms and had initiated not a single development plan.

On the other hand, Saud had a reputation for decadence and extravagance. He ordered the Nasseriah area of Riyadh turned into a "forbidden city" of palaces. The Nasseriah Palace complex cost fifty to one hundred million dollars. It included four separate palaces for his four reigning wives, thirty-two mansions to house his concubines, thirty-seven villas to house his sons, as well as schools, a hospital, a museum, a zoo, and the largest air-conditioning plant in the world.

The palaces, mansions, and villas were garishly furnished with imitation Louis XIV furniture, Chinese wardrobes, Syrian tables inlaid with silver, gold, and mother-of-pearl, vast crystal chandeliers, and oversized Persian carpets. One such carpet was recently sold in Riyadh at an auction. Eighty meters long and forty meters wide, the carpet was bought by an American for sixty-five thousand dollars. The price reflects the fact that the carpet was damaged. In perfect condition the same carpet might have fetched a million and a half.

The Nasseriah Palace complex was only one of the many palace complexes built by Saud during this time. The actual number of palaces that Saud built may be as many as fifty. In Al-Kharj, Saud renovated one of his father's Ikhwan fortresses into a five-hundred-room weekend palace. Today, the Al-Kharj weekend palace is deserted and falling into ruin. The Nasseriah Palace complex in Riyadh was bulldozed to the ground on the orders of Faisal soon after he became monarch.

King Saud was as extravagant toward others as he was toward himself. At the end of his Washington visit, he presented every member of the hotel staff with a crisp new five-hundred-dollar bill. The tips he gave to the staff of the transatlantic liner on his return voyage are reported to have been in excess of fifteen thousand dollars. Saud was generous at home, too. He gave away hundreds of thousands of riyals weekly. A poor family could safely expect ten thousand riyals (three thousand dollars) just for making the trip to his weekly *majlis,* and even more if they had a special need.

Saud had earned himself a reputation for economic reckless-ness. By extension, the entire royal family suffered the same reputation. It was not until early 1958 that the senior al-Saud princes realized how serious the financial situation was. The country's treasury contained only twenty thousand riyals ($6,700), and the national debt was approaching four hundred million dollars.

On March 24 twelve senior princes, led by Fahd ibn-Abdulaziz (the present crown prince), entered Saud's Nasseriah Palace and made their way directly to the monarch's huge *majlis* chamber. King Saud was there with his younger brother, Crown Prince Faisal, and his uncle, Prince Abdullah ibn–Abdul Rahman. There was an ominous silence while the twelve senior princes filed into the large hall.

Prince Muhammed ibn-Abdulaziz (later known as "Muhammed of the Twin Evils"), speaking for the group, ordered the king's bodyguards from the chamber. The bodyguards remained motionless, their eyes riveted to the monarch. Finally, after a tension-filled silence, King Saud nodded to the bodyguards, and they withdrew.

"We have sworn and pledged ourselves to save you and in accomplishing that so to save ourselves and the kingdom," Prince Muhammed announced.

"What do you want me to do?" Saud is reported to have replied.

"We decided to demand your abdication, but your brother Faisal opposed the idea and asked that you remain on the throne. We have accepted on one condition: that you hand over all your power to Faisal."

King Saud remained silent for several minutes with his eyes shut. Finally he reopened his eyes, nodded thoughtfully, and replied: "I accept the conditions."

This then should have been the end of any real authority King Saud might have enjoyed, and it might have been a good thing for the kingdom if it had been. However, King Saud was not the kind of man who would allow himself to be a figurehead monarch, and it was not long before Saud was mustering support for a comeback attempt.

Crown Prince Faisal took over immediately as the kingdom's prime minister. Faisal's two immediate tasks were to reestablish the nation's position in the Arab world and to reestablish the national economy. Faisal declared that it was Saudi Arabia's policy to be neutral in international affairs. This was in direct conflict with Saud's acceptance of the Eisenhower Doctrine, but Faisal hoped to still some of the critics of Saudi Arabia who were charging that the kingdom was nothing more than a United States puppet.

Reestablishing the national economy was a more difficult task. Faisal first borrowed half a billion riyals from a wealthy Saudi banker, al-Rajhi, and then brought in the financial wizard Anwar Ali to head the newly formed Saudi Arabian Monetary Agency (SAMA). Although Anwar Ali and Faisal were eventually able to see the kingdom to solvency, it was not before the riyal was devalued by forty percent against the dollar.

July 1958 again saw Nasser's influence at work in the Middle East. A group of pro-Nasser revolutionaries in Iraq, led by Abdul Karim Kassem, overthrew the monarchy and executed before firing squads the entire Iraqi Hashemite royal family. If the House al-Saud had any doubts about the plans Nasser had for the monarchies of the Middle East, they entirely vanished with the bloody mass murders in Iraq.

Spring and summer of 1958 saw the tensions between Egypt and Saudi Arabia increase. Radio Cairo regularly broadcast virulent attacks on the Saudi royal family, and rumors were rife that Nasser was secretly supplying republican rebels in Yemen with arms and ammunition. The situation became so tense by August that Faisal secretly flew to Cairo to meet with Nasser.

During the next year, the friction and rivalry between King Saud and Crown Prince Faisal emerged as a divisive force in the royal family. As king, Saud still had single-handed control of the elite White Army, a crack force of Bedouins whose duty it was to protect the monarch. Faisal, on the other hand, had the loyalty of the vast majority of the House al-Saud, including the powerful al-Sudeiri and al-Jiluwi tribes. In a bid to break the deadlock in this internal power struggle, Faisal had himself appointed minister of the interior.

Of all the ministries that comprise the Saudi government, none wields such internal power and authority as the Ministry of the Interior. The minister of the interior is responsible for the majority of security operations, including the secret police. Faisal saw his appointment as an opportunity to balance his own power aginst Saud's control of the White Army.

Reports in the Western press during this period suggested that the quarrel between Faisal and Saud was intensifying. It seemed that both brothers were keeping each other under close surveillance, and one article published in the autumn of 1959 suggested that Saudi Arabia was on the brink of civil war.

During the spring of 1960 Crown Prince Faisal's health deteriorated rapidly until in May he was forced to leave Saudi Arabia for treatment in Switzerland. Saud saw his opportunity and moved quickly to consolidate his power while his brother was out of the country. However, Faisal's agents at the Ministry of the Interior discovered Saud's plans, and met Faisal's plane in Cairo. Faisal did not get to Switzerland on this trip; instead he returned immediately from Cairo to meet the challenge posed by his elder brother in Riyadh.

Faisal's physical presence in the kingdom temporarily postponed whatever plans Saud may have had, but it soon became clear to Faisal that his power struggle with his elder brother was moving closer and closer to armed conflict.

When Faisal finally flew to Switzerland, Saud and his supporters moved to return to power. In order to assist the economy, Faisal had reduced the allowances paid to powerful tribal leaders. In Faisal's absence, Saud and his sons nurtured discontent among these important tribal groups and won much support. In addition, Saud allied himself with a group of reformers. The alliance was opportunistic on Saud's part.

Included in the odd collection of radical reformers was Prince Tallal, son of King Abdulaziz and the vivacious and troublesome Munayir. Prince Tallal had traveled abroad and witnessed how governments in Western Europe conducted themselves. The radical prince called for a constitution and free elections for Saudi Arabia.

Also among Saud's radical supporters was Sheikh Abdullah ibn-Hamud Tariqi, who became the first Saudi minister of petroleum. Tariqi, like Iran's Mossadegh, was a nationalist who saw his country being systematically robbed of the lion's share of the oil profits by the Western oil companies. Tariqi wanted total Saudi control over the production, transportation, and marketing of oil.

With this motley assortment of traditional tribal leaders and radical reformers, King Saud reestablished his authority. He dismissed Anwar Ali and appointed Prince Tallal as minister of finance. When Faisal returned from Switzerland in December, he withdrew from the government.

Prince Tallal was a short-lived minister of finance; he either resigned or was dismissed in July 1961.[9] He was replaced by his younger brother, Prince Nawaf. However, Prince Tallal's republican activities did not end with his ministerial duties but continued through the next several years.

By autumn of 1961 King Saud's health was in a state of decline, and the monarch was forced to leave the kingdom for medical treatment in Europe and the United States. During Saud's absence, Faisal took over the duties and responsibilities of the head of state.

This was a time of great confusion in Riyadh. Not even the senior members of the House al-Saud were certain from day to day who had power. The government was divided into camps loyal to Saud or to Faisal, but from week to week members of these camps shifted back and forth according to the latest rumors. In addition to the discontent of the powerful tribal leaders and the antics of the radical reformers, there was concern among the al-Sauds over Nasser's continuing military support for the republican rebels in the mountains of Yemen.

Yemen was ruled by an autocratic, archconservative imam who enjoyed the support of the Saudi royal family. The al-Sauds viewed Nasser's support of the Yemeni rebels as an attempt by Egypt get a foothold on the Arabian peninsula and, as such, a direct threat to themselves.

Faisal seized the opportunity of his brother's absence to replace several of King Saud's sons, who had risen to powerful po-

---

[9]At the time, Prince Tallal was said to have resigned. However, later, in a press conference in Beirut, he announced that he had been "dismissed without explanation."

sitions in government, with more competent and more loyal senior princes. One of the two most important changes was the dismissal of King Saud's son Saud from the leadership of the National Guard (the White Army) and his replacement by Abdullah ibn-Abdulaziz (who, although a potential threat to the unity of the House al-Saud himself, still holds the position today). The second important change was Faisal's dismissal of Prince Badr ibn-Saud (another son of King Saud) as governor of Riyadh and his replacement with Prince Salman ibn-Abdulaziz, one of the seven sons of King Abdulaziz and Hussah al-Sudeiri, referred to as the Sudeiri Seven. Prince Salman continues as governor of Riyadh to this day.

Essentially what Faisal was attempting to do was break Saud's stranglehold over the Saudi government by bringing into positions of power members of the royal family whose maternal lineage traced back to the powerful and loyal al-Sudeiri, al-Jiluwi, and al-Sheikh families (the last were the direct descendants of the eighteenth-century religious reformer Sheikh Muhammed ibn-Abdul Wahhab). In addition, Prince Abdullah ibn-Abdulaziz's appointment as commander of the National Guard assured Faisal the loyalty of the Bedouin White Army, leaving only the eight-hundred-strong palace guard loyal to King Saud.

With an eye to both Saud's reaction to these changes and Nasser's support of the Yemeni rebels, Faisal embarked on a program to strengthen the National Guard. An elite, hand-picked corps was formed which was informally known as the *fedayeen* ("devotees until death"). The *fedayeen* numbered approximately five thousand and were trained as guerrilla commandos. Their loyalty was to Faisal.

The internal power struggle in Saudi Arabia was readily apparent to most observers in the Middle East, and many saw it as a sign that the al-Saud family was disintegrating and that the kingdom was ripe for revolution.

Toward the end of the summer, Prince Tallal, on his way back to Saudi Arabia from a trip to Europe, stopped in Beirut and heard that his villas and palaces in Riyadh, Mecca, and Taif had been searched by the royal palace guard, who were loyal to

Saud, and that one of his palaces had been seized by his full brother, Prince Nawaf. Assuming, correctly, that the royal palace guard would not enter the palaces of a senior prince without the express permission of the king, Tallal realized that his fall from grace was near complete. He halted his journey in Beirut and, the following day, gave one of the most remarkable press conferences in the history of the Saudi royal family. A portion of it follows:

> I believe that public opinion, both in the Arab world and abroad, was astonished to learn about the seizure of my property in Saudi Arabia. The Koran forbids homes' being entered, let alone occupied, without their owner's permission, as do the laws of all nations. But in our country, there is no law that upholds the freedom and rights of the citizen. For a long time now we have been demanding the introduction of a system of government which would protect the rights of the individual and define the responsibilities of the rulers within a democratic and constitutional framework. If a person like myself, who is considered to have some influence, is treated with such harshness, what must be the position of the ordinary man?

Prince Tallal concluded his prepared remarks by announcing:

> I also wish it to be fully understood that I belong to no group but only to my people, and it is in their interest alone that I work. If in the course of doing my duty I am faced with trials and tribulations, this will only strengthen me and make me more patient and confident in the cause which I have espoused. All my property means nothing to me now that I have dedicated myself to my country's welfare. Peace be with all who are just, who uphold right and renounce falsehood.

After Tallal's press conference, *Al Ahram* reported that King Saud became hysterical and threatened to have Tallal executed should he ever dare return to Saudi Arabia. Prince Abdullah ibn-Abdulaziz, the newly appointed commander of the National Guard, who was himself in Beirut at the time, issued a public statement refuting Tallal. This was published on August 18, 1962, in the Beirut daily newspapers *Al Safa* and *Al Hayah*.[10]

---

[10]The full text of Prince Tallal's press conference and Prince Abdullah's reply appear as appendices G and H.

Unquestionably the most important reaction to Tallal was that of Nasser. It is more than probable that Nasser assumed that Tallal's public criticism of the Saudi regime indicated that Tallal felt secure enough of his support within Saudi Arabia to risk such a public disclosure. Tallal's naming of the four senior princes as his supporters also lent credence to the notion that radical republicanism was a widespread movement within the kingdom. From Nasser's vantage point in Cairo, it must have seemed that the House al-Saud was destroying itself from the inside out.

On August 17 armed guards accompanied by officials from the Saudi Arabian embassy arrived at Beirut's Hotel St. George. They promptly and unceremoniously confiscated Prince Tallal's passport. Their authority, they announced, came directly from His Majesty King Saud ibn-Abdulaziz. Three senior princes in Riyadh, Badr ibn-Abdulaziz, Fawaz ibn-Abdulaziz, and Saad ibn-Fahd, handed in their passports in sympathy with Tallal.

On August 19 Prince Tallal arrived in Cairo. On the same day, although on a later flight, Prince Badr, Prince Fawaz, and Prince Saad also went into an Egyptian exile. The following day Prince Tallal had a lengthy meeting with President Nasser.[11]

A year later, Tallal and his three supporters applied at the Saudi embassy in Cairo for passports. By January 1964 the passports had been issued, and the four dissident princes were on their way back to Saudi Arabia. It may be that the royal family considered the safest place for Tallal was inside the kingdom. Prince Abdullah ibn-Abdulaziz, in his reply to Tallal's press conference, had written: "I wish Tallal had never left and now I wish he would return. He who desires to serve his country should

---

[11]Accurate information about the "Tallal affair" is extremely hard to come by, despite the fact that most of the participants, with the obvious exception of Nasser, are still alive. Prince Tallal, who is back in the good graces of the House al-Saud, currently resides in New York City and functions as a special envoy for the United Nations Children's Fund (UNICEF). However, Tallal has refused to respond to questions about this period of his career, especially as to the subjects discussed with President Nasser on August 20, 1962. It is possible that one of the conditions Tallal had to accept before being welcomed back into the al-Saud family fold was that he would make no further public comments on this turbulent period.

not take the struggle outside its borders, especially if he claims a large following, as Tallal does."

What becomes historically significant in the Tallal affair is that Nasser may well have believed that a schism existed within the Saudi royal family. This belief may well have motivated Nasser to step up military support for the Yemeni rebels.

Less than a month following Tallal's meeting with Nasser in Cairo, reports began filtering into Riyadh that Imam Ahmed Ibn Yahya, the autocratic ruler of Yemen, had died. Prince Fahd Ibn Abdulaziz was immediately dispatched to Sanaa to carry King Saud's condolences. However, in less than a week, on September 26, Ali Abdullah Salleh, an army officer who subsequently promoted himself to the rank of Field Marshal, announced that a successful coup had taken place and that Yemen was now a republic. Salleh also announced that the new Imam, Muhammed al Badr, had been executed. This last announcement turned out to be entirely false.

Ali Abdullah Salleh was the son of a Yemeni blacksmith, who had won a scholarship to study military science in Baghdad. Following the assassination of the Iraqi Royal Family, Baghdad had turned into a hotbed of pro-Nasser revolutionaries. Unquestionably, Ali Abdullah Salleh had come under the influence of these revolutionaries and had returned to Yemen with the idea of fermenting revolution.

It was obvious to the Saudi royal family in Riyadh that Ali Abdullah Salleh, the self-appointed Yemeni army field marshal, and his republican followers were being generously supported by Nasser. In fact, it is now quite obvious that Nasser had prior knowledge of the coup attempt Salleh was planning. Egyptian troops were waiting near the Yemen coast. On September 26 these troops landed and marched on Sanaa, where they insured Salleh's successful takeover.

The new regime was immediately recognized by Egypt, the Soviet Union, and several Western European nations. Crown Prince Faisal was in New York, leading the Saudi Arabian delegation to the United Nations, at the time of the coup. He flew to Washington to meet with President Kennedy. Faisal argued that the United States should withhold diplomatic recognition from

Salleh's regime since it "did not reflect the will of the people" but was rather a conspiracy financed by Cairo. Faisal also asked Kennedy to withhold food assistance to Egypt since the funds earmarked for food were being used instead to purchase Soviet-made weapons. These were being trans-shipped to the rebel forces in Yemen.

Kennedy was as concerned about Soviet "containment" as his predecessor had been, and therefore insisted that U.S. aid to Egypt would continue.

On December 19 the United States extended diplomatic recognition to Salleh's government. Nasser, who no longer had to concern himself about a cutoff of U.S. aid, immediately began to use Salleh's government against the Saudi Arabian royal family.

It was at this point that Egyptian jets (Soviet-made MIGs) began to cross the border from Yemen into Saudi Arabia and bomb towns and villages in the southern province of the Asir.

Faisal again met with Kennedy in Washington and again requested that the American president discontinue financial aid to Egypt. Again Kennedy refused.

Meanwhile, the situation in Riyadh was getting worse. With Faisal out of the country, his supporters in the government were impotent to act on the Egyptian threat in the south. King Saud seemed unable to cope with the situation. In early October a group of senior princes got together and cabled an appeal to Faisal to return and take over the position of prime minister.

Faisal returned to Riyadh on October 25. It didn't take him long to act. Faith in King Saud was low, and groups of princes had begun to plan how best to save the kingdom. Faisal appointed Prince Khalid (the present king) to lead the White Army, Prince Fahd (the present crown prince) as minister of the interior, and Prince Sultan as minister of defense and aviation (a position he still holds today).

Faisal's appointments followed tribal maternal lineage. Prince Khalid was an al-Jiluwi on his mother's side, and both Prince Fahd and Prince Sultan were al-Sudeiris. All three were loyal to Faisal.

On November 6, 1962, Faisal issued his now famous Ten Points of Policy. This statement described the first specific government reforms in Saudi Arabia's history. To the Western reader, this document may seem conservative, but to the puritan population of Saudi Arabia it came as a radical departure from custom and tradition.

On November 10 Muhammed al-Badr, imam of Yemen, crossed the border into Saudi Arabia. The public announcement of his arrival incited the Yemeni tribes still loyal to the imam to redouble their efforts to oust the new republican regime under Ali Abdullah Salleh. By the end of November Faisal had broken diplomatic relations with Egypt, and Yemen was embroiled in an all-out civil war. The Egyptian-backed forces of Ali Abdullah Salleh held most of the cities and towns in Yemen, whereas the countryside was under the authority of tribes still loyal to the exiled imam.

During December 1962 Egyptian air raids into Saudi Arabia increased. Targets were frontier towns and villages which Saudi Arabia would have to use as staging areas for any future invasion of Yemen. At the end of the year an American CIA report placed the number of Egyptian troops in Yemen at about thirty thousand. On January 3, 1963, Prime Minister Faisal ordered a Saudi military mobilization.

One might have imagined that, confronted with a common enemy, such as Egypt, the senior princes of the al-Saud clan would have rallied together around Faisal for their mutual defense. However, the events of the autumn of 1962 indicate that such was not the case. Rather than reuniting King Saud and Crown Prince Faisal, the conflict in Yemen appears to have driven them even further apart. Saud had reached the nadir of his authority and influence. He knew that Faisal had been recalled from the United States because the senior princes had perceived the monarch as incompetent. In late November palace guards discovered a conspiracy against the king. Seven Saudi air force pilots, minor members of the royal family themselves, had planned a coup in Riyadh. Before the conspirators could be arrested and beheaded, the pilots caught wind of the fact that their plot had been detected. All seven took off in their American-made planes and defected to Cairo. According to sources in Riyadh, King Saud was so rattled by this coup attempt that he ordered the storage batteries removed from the tanks of the royal guard in Riyadh lest they should be turned against him.[12]

By January 1963 the republican troops in Yemen had managed to capture and display an array of American-made arms. The conflict was intensified since these American-made weapons proved the Egyptian claim that Saudi Arabia was actively supplying the loyalist forces with arms.

In March Dr. Ralph Bunche, the United Nations' Undersecretary General, embarked on a fact-finding tour of the region. Bunche stopped in both Cairo and Riyadh, meeting with Nasser and Faisal. It is a tribute to Bunche's patience and intelligence that he returned from his tour announcing that both Cairo and Riyadh had accepted his "disengagement plan."

The U.N. plan called for Saudi Arabia to stop aiding and supporting the forces loyal to the Yemeni imam and for Egypt to withdraw its troops completely from Yemeni soil. In order to oversee the orderly disengagement of troops, the U.N. ordered in two hundred observers, predominantly Yugoslavs and Canadians, to patrol the border between Yemen and Saudi Arabia.

The observer force was doomed from the outset. Two hundred men could hardly hope to patrol a border in such difficult mountainous terrain. Further, being located on the border of Yemen and Saudi Arabia, the U.N. observers had absolutely no way to monitor Egyptian troop movements by way of the Red Sea. The conflict continued.

By June 1963 there were reports that the Egyptians were using Soviet-made poison gas against the loyalist forces. U.N. observers were unable to confirm such reports because they were bound to the northern border region of Yemen.

A ten-year-old Yemeni boy was flown to London for medical treatment. The British hospital's diagnosis, coupled with the boy's own testimony, confirmed that the Soviets were using Yemen as a testing ground for chemical warfare.

---

[12]Robert W. Stookey, *America and the Arab States: An Uneasy Encounter*, John Wiley & Sons, New York, 1975, p. 184.

In part as a result of these claims and counterclaims, General von Horn, the man in direct charge of the U.N. observer force, resigned in August, giving his reason as a complete and utter "lack of support" for his mission.

Although the United Nations appointed General Gyani of India to continue the work of General von Horn, the conflict in Yemen continued unhindered by the U.N. observers.

All during the conflict in Yemen, there existed a great confusion of leadership in Riyadh. Just because Faisal had returned from abroad did not mean that he was in control of the government. While he had consolidated some power by way of his strategic appointments, King Saud's supporters still occupied important posts in the government. As Faisal began to act more and more decisively in the Yemeni crisis, King Saud became more and more aware that he was being pushed into political oblivion. Tensions between the supporters of Faisal and Saud grew stronger as royal decrees were contradicted, orders were countermanded or ignored, and the business of government virtually ground to a standstill.

During the spring of 1964 tensions in Riyadh drew so intense that Saud's sons were openly encouraging their father to consolidate his power and oust Faisal. Rumors of conspiracies and counterconspiracies abounded. In mid-March, the secret police (loyal to Faisal) arrested the commander of the royal guards, a man known to be an ardent supporter of King Saud. Subsequently, the eight-hundred-member royal palace guard was dispersed, and the last vestige of Saud's military support vanished. However, the dispersement of the royal guard did not act to calm the tensions. King Saud's sons were still actively supporting Faisal's ouster, and the Ministry of the Interior had its hands full throughout the summer of 1964 arresting and beheading "subversives."

On October 24, 1964, Crown Prince Faisal left the Red Sea port of Jeddah for a week's overland journey to Riyadh. It is very probable that Faisal knew full well what was going to occur and deliberately chose to be out of touch. On the day Faisal left Jeddah, princes from all over Saudi Arabia arrived in Riyadh to deal with the worsening crisis of leadership. More than one hundred al-Saud princes and members of the Ulema assembled in Riyadh and debated the situation for three days.

On October 28 they reached the unanimous decision to ask King Saud to abdicate in favor of Faisal.

Accordingly, a delegation of senior princes and members of the Ulema (predominantly of the al-Sheikh family) went to Saud's Nasseriah Palace and asked Saud to abdicate. Saud would be allowed to remain in Saudi Arabia following his abdication if he refrained from political activity. Saud refused.

The princes and the Ulema continued to meet in the heavily guarded Sahara Hotel in Riyadh. The meeting was chaired jointly by Abdullah ibn–Abdul Rahman, the brother of the late King Abdulaziz and the oldest al-Saud male, and Muhammed ibn-Ibrahim al-Sheikh, grand mufti of Saudi Arabia and direct descendant of Muhammed ibn–Abdul Wahhab. Everyone present agreed that Saud had to go. The talk centered on how he could be forced to resign. On the morning of October 29 it was decided to insist upon King Saud's abdication and to proclaim Faisal the new king.

A small group of senior princes went by motorcar to intercept Faisal on his way to Riyadh to tell him of their decision. By late afternoon they found Faisal camped in the traditional Bedouin style some one hundred kilometers due west of Riyadh. The traditional greetings were exchanged, and then Faisal asked for the latest news.

The senior princes fell silent while the letter they had drafted was handed to the crown prince. Faisal read the message, walked a short distance from the delegation, turned his back to them, and said his afternoon prayers.

The delegation of senior princes was forced to wait until late evening before Faisal responded to their message. Faisal was a realist, and realistically he was their only choice. However, he had sworn a solemn oath before his father and brother that he would not dispute Saud's right to rule. Faisal was faced with the dilemma of having to choose between what was clearly best for his country and what was clearly best for his own sense of honesty and honor.

By the light of a dozen campfires, the senior princes pressed Faisal for an answer to their message. Would he become the new king?

Finally Faisal, his narrow face made even more gaunt by the flickering light of the campfires, did respond.

"It is my right," the crown prince announced, "to ask you how you propose to carry out this decision."

"By proclaiming you king," they answered.

"What about the reigning king?"

Faisal's question was answered by silence. Faisal stared intensely into the bearded faces of the senior princes before he continued. "In the House of Abdulaziz, we do not depose the king except after all attempts at persuasion have failed. Have you exhausted all means of persuasion?"

The group of princes sat in silence, stunned by the simple nobility of the crown prince. Suddenly, one of the princes cried out: "By God, Faisal, truly you are the king!" The others in the group repeated it almost as a whispered chant, and its muffled echoes ran through the dry wadi bed of the desert.

The delegation returned to Riyadh that night to report Faisal's reaction. According to an eyewitness, there were tears of pride on the face of Abdulaziz's brother, Abdullah ibn–Abdul Rahman, when he heard of his nephew's reluctance to depose the monarch. Once again a group of princes and members of the Ulema were sent to Saud's Nasseriah Palace. This time, however, King Saud was informed that he had only forty-eight hours in which to make up his mind to abdicate.

The following day Faisal returned to Riyadh for several hours. He drove himself to the Nasseriah Palace and spent an hour with Saud. The meeting was cordial, and abdication was not mentioned. At the conclusion of the meeting, Faisal drove south to Al-Kharj, where he stayed at Saud's huge weekend palace.

Saud ordered the guard on the palace tripled and left strict instructions that no one other than his own sons was to be admitted. Saud's sons met with their beleaguered father regularly. However, Saud's forty-plus sons were those with the most to lose should Saud abdicate, and their advice to their father was colored with self-interest. They urged their father to struggle to remain in power.

On Sunday, November 1, a group of princes arrived at the Nasseriah Palace and, after they had been made to wait almost two hours, were shown to Saud's huge *majlis* chamber. The princes informed Saud that the waiting time was over and asked if Saud would abdicate. Again Saud refused.

At this point the delegation of princes informed Saud that his legitimacy as king was based on the oath of loyalty that the Ulema and the House al-Saud had taken at the time of his ascension to the throne. They went on to explain that this oath of loyalty could and would be retracted if he did not abdicate voluntarily. It is reported that Saud responded to this threat by storming out of the *majlis* chamber.

That night, the princes and the Ulema met again at the Sahara Hotel. Just after evening prayers, the oath of loyalty to Saud was unanimously withdrawn and Faisal ibn-Abdulaziz al-Saud was proclaimed the new king of Saudi Arabia.

The next morning the Council of Ministers met in *pro forma* session and approved the decision to depose Saud and declare Faisal king. The meeting took less than five minutes. After this the entire Council of Ministers loaded themselves into motorcars and drove south to al-Kharj to inform Faisal of their action. Faisal met them in the *majlis* room of the weekend palace. He listened in silence to the events that had occurred in Riyadh. He appeared tired and worried, and his eyes reflected the new responsibility that had fallen on his shoulders. Finally, the Council of Ministers asked Faisal to return to Riyadh with them as the new king. Faisal nodded assent and thus became the third king of the modern state of Saudi Arabia.

On the evening of November 4, the same day Lyndon Johnson was elected president of the United States, King Faisal held a huge *majlis* at the Red Palace in Riyadh. Tribal chieftains and delegations from the major tribes of the Arabian peninsula arrived to kiss the shoulder of the new king. The National Guard, under the command of Prince Abdullah ibn-Abdulaziz, lined the streets in front of the Red Palace, visibly demonstrating their loyalty to King Faisal.

Saud was placed under house arrest in the Nasseriah Palace. He refused, even after he was deposed, to recognize either the authority of the Council of Ministers or Faisal as king. For the next several weeks Saud rather pathetically alternated between attempts to rally tribal support to his cause and negotiations with European countries for political asylum. Finally, seeing that he had completely lost his base of political support, Saud, a group of his sons, and several of his wives went into exile.

They never returned to Saudi Arabia. There is no way to avoid judging Saud a failure as king. However, he doesn't deserve the stigma of disgrace that the present regime has placed on him. He was neither an evil man nor a ruthless despot. He was simply a desert tribal leader, schooled in the traditional ways of maintaining authority and unable to adjust to the dramatic changes occurring both within and without his kingdom.

In many ways, Saud suffered from the same myopia as his father. Neither father nor son was able to recognize that Saudi Arabia had grown from an isolated desert sheikhdom to a wealthy international power. Saud insisted on ruling his kingdom as his father and his grandfather and his great-grandfather had before him. Joseph Alsop, the American columnist, wrote that Saud was a man "born in the old ways, attached to all that is customary and familiar, yet required by fate to carry his country through the baffling transition from the past into the present."[13]

---

[13]Butler, Grant C., *Kings and Camels*, Devin-Adair, New York, 1960.

13

From the Past into the Present

It was the age of insecurity. The kingdom was at the edge of bankruptcy. Egyptian troops were entrenched in Yemen. Petro-dollars were corrupting the House al-Saud. Like all insecure ages, this one went searching for a hero and forged one out of King Faisal.

If King Saud is a national disgrace, King Faisal is a national hero of whom no wrong can be said. He has been elevated in the popular mind into that mythic domain where founding fathers, saints, liberators, martyrs, and conquering generals dwell. It is commonplace to hear Saudi university students, many of them too young actually to remember the turbulence of Faisal's reign, bemoan the current state of Saudi leadership and look nostalgically to Faisal as the ideal of Arabian statesmanship.

King Saud was an easy act for Faisal to follow. Faisal was seen, and is still seen today, as the national savior who brought Saudi Arabia out of the mire of Saud's incompetence and into the limelight of international prominence.

To judge Faisal's accomplishments we should look at the influences which shaped him.

Faisal's mother was a member of the al-Sheikh family. It is this al-Sheikh clan which provides most of the religious hierarchy, the Ulema. Among Philby's recorded conversations with Abdulaziz, we find no reference to Tarfah al-Sheikh (Faisal's mother) as being among the monarch's favorites. Therefore, it is relatively safe to assume that the marriage between Abdulaziz and Tarfah al-Sheikh was arranged for political reasons. To consolidate his authority in the Nejd, Abdulaziz would have to have had the support of the al-Sheikh family.

Tarfah al-Sheikh died while Faisal was still a small boy. According to the traditions of Arabia, the child was taken to the home of his maternal grandparents, where he lived until he was ten or eleven. He then returned to live with his father. The predominant influence on the young Faisal was therefore his maternal grandparents.

The al-Sheikhs were known for their learning and scholarship. It is probable that Faisal came under this academic influence at an early age. Like the other sons of Abdulaziz, Faisal was made to memorize the Koran, which he apparently achieved with less difficulty than either Turki or Saud. Perhaps even more important to Faisal's education was the experience of living in a household of religious elders. In addition to teaching the boy how to argue and think on his feet, exposure to the inner religious courts also gave him firsthand knowledge of how the Ulema made decisions. This would become vitally important to Faisal later in life, when he was forced to argue with the Ulema over the implementation of controversial social reforms.

When Faisal came to live with his father he learned horsemanship, desert warfare, and political cunning. Faisal impressed Abdulaziz. Although he was smaller in stature than his brothers, Faisal had a quicker mind. The boy eagerly seized upon the problems that faced the House al-Saud, argued with men three and four times his age, and impressed the entire court of Abdulaziz with his sharp intellect.

In 1919 Abdulaziz chose Faisal, then fourteen, to represent him at a London conference. It was Faisal's first journey out of Arabia, and he was accompanied by an elder cousin, Ahmed al-Thunaiyan al-Saud, who would later become a close friend and confidant.

The Saudi delegation to the London conference started their journey in Riyadh and rode on horseback five hundred kilometers to Dammam, on the Arabian Gulf. They bought passage on a small dhow to Bahrain, an island some thirty kilometers off the Arabian coast. There the party boarded an aged paddle-steamer and sailed for Bombay, where Faisal and his entourage boarded a reconverted German naval vessel and sailed for Plymouth.

We have no record of Faisal's impressions of his journey to England. We do, however, have a fairly complete record of the prince's stay in England due to the fact that the prince's official guide in England was none other than Henry St. John Philby. Philby was at this point a relatively minor British civil servant who was yet to distinguish himself. Because he was one of the few Englishmen attached to Whitehall who spoke passable Arabic, Philby was chosen as guide-cum-host to the Arabian delegation.

Philby went by train to Plymouth to meet Faisal's entourage, but before doing so he asked where the Arabians would be staying. He was informed that arrangements had been made. Philby met the visitors in Plymouth and took them by train to London's Paddington Station. From Paddington, they drove to the Queen's Hotel in Upper Norwood.

The following morning, the manager of the Queen's Hotel told Philby that the rooms had been reserved for only one night and that the Arab guests would have to leave. Philby tried unsuccessfully to contact the Foreign Office. Apparently the entire British Foreign Office was out of town for the weekend. He then tried to obtain other rooms for Faisal's party. All the hotels he checked with were full. In desperation, Philby approached a friend in India House and asked if he would house the Arab delegation. Thus Faisal's first visit to England began on a less than gracious note. And it was destined to get worse.

On October 30, 1919, Faisal and his entourage made their way across London to Buckingham Palace. King George V received the Arabian delegation in the throne room of the palace. The queen and Princess Mary were also in attendance.

Prince Faisal presented the British king with two ornamental Arabian swords and a letter of greeting from his father. The British king, in return, gave Faisal an autographed photograph of himself and the queen. In retrospect, the king's gift seems artless at best. Faisal was a devoted Wahhabi Muslim, and believers consider any such representation of the human form a sacrilege. Nevertheless, Faisal accepted the gift graciously.

Both Faisal and his guardian-adviser Ahmed al-Thunaiyan were aware, probably through Philby's instructions, that no political discussions would take place with King George. The royal audience was purely ceremonial. The real business of politics would take place later in the gray offices of the Foreign Office.[1]

At this point in 1919, the British were still looking toward the sherif of Mecca as the strongman in the Arabian peninsula, and the sherif was receiving the vast majority of British aid to Arabia. Despite the reports from Englishmen in Dehli and Kuwait of Abdulaziz's growing strength in the Nejd, the Foreign Office in London still viewed the House al-Saud as a troublesome family. The fact that Abdulaziz's representative was invited to Britain at all must be considered a diplomatic triumph for the English diplomats in Kuwait and Dehli.

Unlike the reception they received at Buckingham Palace, their welcome at Whitehall was cool and condescending. Quite clearly, one of Faisal's diplomatic objectives during his visit to Britain was to convince the British to increase their support to his father and to turn away from the sherif of Mecca. The Foreign Office seemed amused by the suggestion.

Major N. N. E. Bray, who also served as Faisal's guide during the prince's stay in England, writes at length about the Arabian prince's reception at Whitehall. "Their reception at the Foreign Office was most unfortunate. The late Lord Curzon treated them ... so patronizingly that they left England enraged and swore that they would never visit the country again. ... I was sent to Paris to take charge of them during the temporary absence of Mr. Philby. I found them in a dangerous mood. 'If Captain Y. of the Foreign Office comes to the Nejd, we will cut his throat,' said Ahmed al-Thunaiyan and he glared. 'No, no,' I said. 'That would not accord with your own well-known hospitality.' He laughed heartily. 'Well perhaps not,' he said, 'still he had better not come.' "[2]

Despite the arrogance of the British Foreign Office, Faisal's visit to Britain wasn't a total failure. In the tactful hands of Bray

---

[1] For a detailed account of Faisal's trip to Britain in 1919, see Gerald De Gaury's *Faisal, King of Saudi Arabia*, Frederick A. Praeger, New York, 1967.

[2] N. E. Bray, *Shifting Sands*, London, 1934.

and Philby, Faisal toured England, Wales, and Ireland, attempted to climb Mt. Snowdon, was graciously entertained at London's most prestigious restaurants, and attended a performance of *The Mikado* at the Prince's Theatre. It is easy to lose sight of the fact that this was Faisal's first introduction to the Western world and that he was only fourteen years old, speaking at most a few dozen words of English.

Soon after Faisal returned to Arabia, Ahmed al-Thunaiyan left for Turkey. The al-Thunaiyan branch of the al-Saud family was descended from Thunaiyan, the great-grandson of Saud, the founder of the family, and from Abdullah ibn-Thunaiyan, who was the Emir of Riyadh from 1841 to 1842. Later in the nineteenth century, the al-Thunaiyan branch of the family settled in Turkey and intermarried with Turks and Albanians. Ahmed al-Thunaiyan, Faisal's adviser and friend, was brought up in Turkey and returned there soon after the visit to Britain in order to claim a Turkish bride. This marriage would, in years to come, have a fateful effect on Faisal's life and on the evolution of the desert kingdom.

A short while after Faisal returned to Arabia, his father appointed him to command the Ikhwan in the southern region of the Asir. There had been military trouble in the Asir for a number of years. The entire region was claimed by both the Hashemite sherif of Mecca and the Aidh family.

The Aidh brothers, Muhammed and Hassan, received military support from the Ikhwan in their struggle against the army of the sherif. By early 1924 the Aidh brothers and the Ikhwan had driven the sherif's army out of the Asir.

To the dismay of the Aidh family, the Ikhwan did not leave the Asir after the victory, nor did they seem to have any intention of leaving. For the Wahhabi Brotherhood, the victory over the sherif had been their own, and they considered the Asir part of the growing Saudi state.

The Aidh family promptly launched a rebellion against the Ikhwan. This rebellion may have been supported and financed by the sherif of Mecca.

Faisal's military career began here. He was nineteen years old when his father put him in command of the Ikhwan forces in the Asir. Despite his age and youthful appearance (Faisal was said to look no older than thirteen), he soon won the respect and admiration of the soldiers he commanded both for his personal bravery and for his skillful tactics in battle.

Faisal led five thousand Ikhwan warriors south into the Asir to put down the Aidh rebellion. The rebellion was crushed quickly, not so much because of brilliant strategy but through sheer numbers. Nevertheless, Faisal proved himself in battle and won the respect of the Ikhwan.

It was in February 1924 that the sherif of Mecca vaingloriously proclaimed himself the new caliph of the Islamic world. This proclamation received a negative response from Muslims everywhere. The British announced that they would no longer subsidize the sherif.

This was exactly the sort of circumstance Abdulaziz had been waiting for. With the withdrawal of British support to the sherif, Abdulaziz set the Ikhwan loose on the Hejaz. Initially, according to De Gaury, Abdulaziz had intended to place Faisal in full command of the Ikhwan. However, Prince Saud complained, and Abdulaziz, fearing sibling rivalry, appointed neither Saud nor Faisal to the position. De Gaury suggests that it was this hesitation on Abdulaziz's part that was indirectly responsible for the Ikhwan massacre at Taif.[3] It is probable that the massacre would not have occurred if Faisal had been in command, but the war against the Hashemites might have been much longer.

Fearing a repetition of the carnage that took place at Taif, Abdulaziz appointed Faisal to command the Ikhwan siege of Jeddah. Faisal handled the siege skillfully, and after a year's stalemate Ali, the son of the sherif of Mecca, boarded a boat to Basra in Iraq, abdicating all power and authority in the peninsula.

Faisal not only took Jeddah with a minimum of casualties but avoided disturbing the foreign diplomatic community in the port city. Some historians have criticized Faisal for the famine that existed in Jeddah during the year-long siege. However, the famine was a by-product of the siege, not its ultimate objective;

---

[3]Gerald De Gaury, *Faisal: King of Saudi Arabia*, p. 39.

and Faisal did guarantee the safety and well-being of the residents of Jeddah after its surrender.

Soon after the fall of Jeddah, Abdulaziz and Faisal went on the pilgrimage to Mecca together. During this hajj, a curious event occurred which illustrates well the personal bravery of Faisal and the degree of loyalty the Ikhwan felt toward him.

It had been traditional for a number of years for Egypt to supply a new woven covering for the Holy Kaaba each year. This *mahmal* was brought into Mecca with great pomp and ceremony, usually accompanied by a contingent of Egyptian soldiers and a full military brass band. Since such ceremonies and all music were anathema to the strict Wahhabi conquerers, the Egyptians were asked to avoid this display.

The Egyptians left their brass band in Cairo, but tensions remained high because of a rumor that some Egyptian soldiers had been seen smoking cigarettes outside the Holy Mosque. Real trouble occurred when an Egyptial officer, angered by the disorderly state of his soldiers, commanded his bugler to sound the rally. The Ikhwan, thinking that the Egyptians had brought their brass band, began to gather around the contingent of Egyptian soldiers and taunt them with insults. Soon, the Ikhwan were pelting the Egyptian troops with rocks.

The Egyptian commander fired several warning shots above the heads of the Ikhwan. Finally, realizing that his warning shots had only incited the Ikhwan even more, the Egyptian commander ordered his soldiers to open fire on the Wahhabis. Forty of the Ikhwan were killed instantly, and several hundred were wounded.

The Ikhwan, true believers one and all, immediately organized a counterattack. Hearing the shooting, Abdulaziz dispatched Faisal to see what was happening. Faisal leapt onto a horse and galloped bareback to where the battle was raging. The young prince then rode out into the fray, separating the combatants and beating them back with his camel-herding stick. It is said that one Ikhwan warrior, carried away with the frenzy of battle, attempted to topple Faisal from the saddle so that he could get at the Egyptian troops. However, his comrades, seeing what he intended to do to Faisal, shot him dead at point-blank range.

The Egyptian soldiers were expelled from Arabia, and Abdulaziz demanded that the Egyptian government pay the "blood money" for each of the Wahhabi warriors who had been killed. Egypt protested, saying that the Egyptian soldiers had been the victims of wanton and senseless violence. There is no record that Egypt did pay any reparations to Abdulaziz. In all likelihood, the incident, like so many in the Arab world, was simply forgotten.

It was not long after this that Abdulaziz appointed Faisal as viceroy of the Hejaz. This was a logical post for the young prince. Having traveled to Britain and France, Faisal was familiar with the customs and manners of the foreign diplomatic community in Jeddah and could act as a liaison between them and his father.

Faisal's prime concerns as viceroy were consolidating the authority of the al-Saud family in a region of Arabia that had previously been under the rather incompetent rule of the sherif of Mecca. In addition, during the final decade of Hashemite rule, the old sherif had ceased to pay the local Bedouin tribes bribes not to attack the pilgrims coming to Mecca. Since Faisal recognized that much of the legitimacy of the al-Saud family came from the support the family received from the rest of the Islamic world, he could not allow these local Bedouins to continue to raid pilgrim caravans.

Another difficulty facing Faisal in his administration of the Hejaz was that the western province had never really been subject to Muhammed ibn-Abdul Wahhab. The inhabitants of the Hejaz were hardly puritans. They took their religion in moderate doses and were genuinely frightened by the enthusiasts from the interior desert.

Faisal was himself a devoted Wahhabi but he was too perceptive to attempt to force Wahhabiism on the Hejaz overnight. He did, however, enforce the Wahhabi laws against public smoking, playing of musical instruments, and representations of the human form.

More fundamental, however, was Faisal's attempt to establish basic law in a region that had accepted graft, corruption, and banditry as a way of life under the misrule of the sherif. According to some sources, the decadence of the Hejaz had become so extreme in the final days of the sherif that prostitutes (virtually unknown elsewhere in Arabia) solicited openly in the streets of Mecca, Medina, and Jeddah, pickpockets were common, and the gates of the walled cities were locked at sundown to protect the citizens from the bands of marauding Bedouins.

Faisal reestablished Islamic law. He did this by making public displays of Islamic punishment as was the custom in the Nejd. He attended public executions and made a point to publicize the amputation of thieves' hands and the flogging of those found intoxicated. In a relatively short time, the caravan routes used by foreign pilgrims were secure again, and the local Bedouins had turned away from the pursuit of banditry. The prostitutes of the Western Province either changed vocations or unceremoniously met their ends beneath a hail of rocks in some local marketplace.

As efficient as Faisal was in reestablishing Islamic law in the Hejaz, he was even more successful in the deft handling of the foreign community in Jeddah. The diplomatic community in Jeddah had always been a source of worry and concern to Abdulaziz. The king desired friendly relations with other nations, but he was also anxious about the presence of foreigners in Arabia. Foreigners, in the eyes of the Wahhabi king, were the harbingers of decadence and the corrupters of Islamic morals.

In addition, the ever-zealous Ikhwan were murderously xenophobic toward anyone or anything that fell outside the extremely limited Wahhabi frame of reference. In fact, Abdulaziz was so concerned about the safety of the diplomatic community in Jeddah that he forbade them to travel more than five kilometers from the walls of the port city.

As viceroy of the Hejaz, Faisal maintained a modest palace in Mecca and a villa in Jeddah. He spent most of this time at the latter. It was during his time as viceroy that he learned most of his English. Publicly he continued to speak in Arabic and to employ a translator when he met with Western journalists; however, in private conversation his English was fluent and precise.

Faisal's travels in Europe had made him familiar with the ways and manners of foreigners in Arabia. He was tolerant of their social blunders, and on more than one occasion he interceded for foreigners facing harsh Islamic punishments for crimes involving Wahhabi traditions. Generally, the diplomatic community liked and respected Faisal. They found him an efficient administrator who could distinguish between the important and the trivial.

In 1925 Abdulaziz appointed Faisal to the position of secretary of state for foreign affairs. What the duties of this position were, no one knew. There had never been a Saudi Arabian foreign minister before. However, it was a good job for Faisal, since it assured him frequent trips abroad.

The following year Faisal made a state visit to Britain and Holland. In contrast to his visit to Britain in 1919, Faisal was accorded all the honors due a head of state. He was again met by the British king, presented with gifts, taken to various London theaters, and served smoked kippers for breakfast. He was taken to lunch at Claridges, out to the country to view a horse race, and for an airplane trip over London. All in all, he was entertained in what the British would consider a lavish fashion.

The visit was significant. Britain was, during the 1920s, carving up most of the Middle East into artificial national entities under the "mandate" system. Jordan (then called Transjordan) and Iraq were still British mandates, although they were nominally under the rule of the Hashemite brothers, Adbullah and Faisal. Palestine was under complete British control, as were the Gulf emirates (now the United Arab Emirates), Aden (now the People's Democratic Republic of Yemen), and Bahrain.

Faisal's concern was with a statement issued in 1917 by the British foreign secretary, Arthur James Balfour. The statement has been popularly known as the Balfour Declaration and is one of the most controversial documents of the twentieth century. The so-called declaration is as short as it is inane. It reads: "His Majesty's Government view with favour the establishment of a

National Home for the Jewish people, and will use their best en-
deavours to facilitate the achievements of this object, it being
clearly understood that nothing shall be done which may prejudice the civil and religious rights of the existing communities
in Palestine, or the rights and political status enjoyed by Jews in
any other country."

For several decades Jewish intellectuals had been discussing
the viability of a Jewish homeland called Zion (whence the label
"Zionist"). The founder of Zionism was a Hungarian journalist
by the name of Theodor Herzl. Herzl became enraged at the
overt anti-Jewish[4] prejudice in Europe that led to the conviction of Major Alfred Dreyfus for espionage in 1894. He perceived
accurately that the conviction of Dreyfus (who was later cleared
of all charges) heralded a new era of bigotry, intolerance, and
racism in Europe. In order to counter this insidious trend, Herzl
wrote and published a pamphlet titled *Der Judenstaat* which
proposed and discussed the creation of a Jewish national state.

It was not long before influential Jewish intellectuals, such as
Lord Rothschild and Chaim Weizmann, came under the spell of
Zionism. Herzl himself never suggested the creation of a Jewish
state in Palestine. He was not a very religious man; he was far
more interested in the political aspects of Zionism than he was
in the quasi-theological. Herzl, in all probability, would have
been just as pleased with a Jewish state in the heart of China as
with one in the middle of Arab Palestine.

It is at this point that Zionism as a political entity became
muddled with religiosity and emotionalism. Jews began to demand the creation of a Jewish state in Palestine, based on the
claim that Palestine was the "promised land" of Moses and the
home of their forefathers. Jerusalem (Zion) thus became a potent emotional and political symbol of this movement.

What Zionism ignored and continues to ignore to this day,
according to its critics, are the rights of the indigenous Arab

---

[4]It is incorrect and misleading to refer to hostility toward Jewish people as "anti-
Semitism." Anti-Semitism means an aversion to or prejudice against the Semitic peoples
(peoples of the eastern Mediterranean, Jews and Arabs alike). It is, therefore, not hard to
understand why President Anwar Sadat of Egypt burst into laughter at a press conference when an American journalist asked him if he were an "anti-Semite."

population of Palestine. While Balfour was not oblivious to the problem, his idealistic declaration did nothing to resolve the problem.

Viewed logically, the Balfour Declaration was a masterstroke of stupidity. How could a "national home" for the Jewish people be created without massive immigration of Jews into Palestine? More important, how could a massive immigration of European Jews into Palestine fail to prejudice the civil and religious rights of the Arab population?

The Arab world, at this time, was not anti-Jewish.[5] Jewish communities existed in most Arab states, including Saudi Arabia. Generally, relations between Arab Jews and Arab Muslims were good during this period. The tensions that developed in Palestine later were not so much a result of the immigrants' being Jewish as a result of their being non-Arab Europeans.

Faisal was, until his death, opposed to the creation of a Jewish state on Arab land. His opposition came not from the concept of a Jewish homeland (Faisal himself was a master of deliberately confusing religion and politics) but rather from the manner in which the Zionists set about acquiring the land for their homeland. Faisal, and the Arab world, saw it as bald-faced banditry.

In 1926 Faisal's objective was probably to explain the Arab position to the British government. In all likelihood, he would have embraced British assurances that Jewish immigration to Palestine would be limited. However, given the political prominence of Zionists in Britain at this point, the probability of his obtaining such assurances was remote at best. In fact, Faisal received no such promise from the British. He did, however, have an opportunity to argue the Arab position, and historical reports suggest that he was an able and articulate spokesman for the Arab perspective on Palestine.

Shortly after Faisal's return from his tour of Britain and Holland, he was married to a woman named Sultana bint-Ahmad al-Sudeiri. The marriage had been arranged in Faisal's absence.

---

[5]Many Saudis argue that even today the Arab world is not anti-Jewish *per se.* They separate the religion (Judaism) from the political movement (Zionism), and so oppose the policies of Israel while claiming no hostility towards Jews living elsewhere in the world.

Abdulaziz still perceived the key to al-Saud dominance of the peninsula in an alliance between certain powerful tribes and families. The al-Sudeiris were one of the most powerful families in all Arabia, and the marriage was seen as one additional bond between families. It is probable that Faisal did not see Sultana until the ritual unveiling of the bride at the wedding feast. It is also probable that Faisal had little in common with this illiterate, uneducated woman. Nevertheless, the marriage produced what Arabian marriages are supposed to produce—a son. Abdullah ibn-Faisal al-Saud survived the high infant mortality rate without becoming a statistic himself and is now a fabulously wealthy businessman and one of the most renowned poets in Saudi Arabia.

The years between 1926 and 1932 were essentially quiet ones for Faisal. He continued as viceroy of the Hejaz and as a liaison to the foreign community in Jeddah. He continued his study of English and made the annual hajj to Mecca.

Faisal constructed a villa on the Red Sea north of Jeddah where he and his family would vacation in the hot summer months. It is also during this period that he married Haya bint-Turki al-Jiluwi.

The al-Jiluwi family was powerful in the eastern province of El Hasa. It was Abdulaziz's cousin Abdullah ibn-Jiluwi who had saved the Saudi monarch's life during the siege of Riyadh in 1902. Abdullah ibn-Juluwi was subsequently made governor of El Hasa, and the position has stayed in the al-Jiluwi family ever since. El Hasa, oil-rich and strategically located on the Arabian Gulf, is the only province in Saudi Arabia that is governed by individuals who are not direct members of the al-Saud family.

Like his first marriage, this one was arranged for political purposes. With the al-Sudeiris, al-Jiluwis, and al-Sauds united by marriage and blood, there was no tribal force of opposition that could shake the authority of the ruling regime.

Haya bint-Turki al-Jiluwi (in Arabia women maintain their maiden names even after marriage) provided Faisal with two sons, Khalid and Saad. Khalid ibn-Faisal al-Saud is currently governor of the Asir, and Saad is active in the import-export business.

Much more important for both Faisal and Saudi Arabia than these two politically motivated marriages were the trips Faisal was making to Istanbul during this time.

In 1921 Faisal's friend and guardian during his first trip to London, Ahmed al-Thunaiyan al-Saud, died, leaving a widow in Turkey. Faisal visited Ahmed's widow on several occasions and helped to provide for her financially. Finally, in 1933, Faisal invited Ahmed's widow to Riyadh. She accepted the invitation as much to reclaim al-Thunaiyan land holdings in Arabia as to enjoy Faisal's hospitality.

Nevertheless, Ahmed's widow soon arrived in Riyadh with her niece and nephew in tow. Having grown up under the Western influence of Kemal Atatürk's reforms, neither aunt nor niece arrived in Arabia wearing a veil. Both women were not only literate but fluent in three languages. Both were also outspoken in favor of the emancipation of women in Islam.

Within weeks of their arrival Faisal married the niece. Her name was Iffat, and she was destined to become Faisal's favorite wife, a woman most of the rest of the world would view as Saudi Arabia's queen. Iffat was and remains the most powerful and influential woman in Saudi Arabia.

Unlike Sultana and Haya, whom he subsequently divorced, Faisal married Iffat out of love, and it was this love that kept them together as marriage partners and companions for more than forty years.

It was Iffat's influence that caused Faisal to send his sons to the United States for their education. All of Iffat's sons attended either the Hun School or Lawrenceville, and most then went on to Princeton University. Iffat's daughters were not sent to the United States for schooling, but their education was not ignored. Like their brothers, they memorized the Koran, learned to read and write Arabic, English, and French, and traveled throughout Europe. This, it should be remembered, was at a time when there was no public education for girls in Arabia and female illiteracy was almost one hundred percent.

Iffat had five sons, all but one of whom are currently involved in the government or the military. The eldest male, Muhammed, is currently in the water desalination business in Jeddah. He is the one who is working on towing icebergs from the South Pole to Saudi Arabia so to provide a source of inexpensive drinking water. The next eldest is Saud al-Faisal, the current foreign minister. Despite some early problems with Sheikh Ahmed Zaki Yamani, Saud al-Faisal has shown his intelligence and could be groomed to ascend the Saudi throne. The three younger sons, Abdul Rahman, Bandar, and Turki, are in the military service. Abdul Rahman heads an armed division in the army. Bandar is a major in the Saudi Royal Air Force, and secretive Turki is a military intelligence chief.

Iffat provided Faisal with the intelligent companionship that would help to make him a benevolent and successful ruler. It was, in part, the influence of this Turkish-born woman that would bring about the opening of a school for girls in Saudi Arabia in 1962, in spite of the rage and fury of the more conservative religious leaders. It was Iffat's influence that encouraged the University of Riyadh to open classes for women in 1976, and it was the influence of Sara, Iffat's daughter, that brought about the creation of Saudi Arabia's first women's organization, Al-Nahda Women's Club.

Faisal's marriage to Iffat had two more immediate effects in Riyadh. First, it is reported that Faisal's older brother Saud disliked Iffat's foreign manners. It is also said that he opposed the marriage and even went so far as to petition his father, Abdulaziz, to forbid it. This only increased the friction between the two brothers.

Second, and more important, Faisal's marriage to Iffat brought into their household Iffat's young half-brother, Kamal Adham. Kamal Adham was raised into manhood by Faisal and Iffat and soon became one of the most powerful men in the kingdom. Kamal Adham was one of the few men Faisal trusted completely. He advised Faisal on the kingdom's foreign policy, architected Faisal's reconciliation with Nasser, and developed one of the most remarkable and improbable espionage systems in the world. In the early 1970s it was said, not without some boastful exaggeration, that little happened in Mossad, Israeli Intelligence, without Kamal Adham's knowing about it within twenty-four hours.[6]

In 1932 Faisal's quiet years as viceroy of the Hejaz came to an end with his *de facto* appointment to the position of foreign minister. After the proclamation of the creation of the Kingdom of Saudi Arabia, Faisal was sent on a tour of European capitals. The tour was both a goodwill trip and an attempt on Faisal's part once again to win support for the Arab stance on Palestine.

As astute a diplomat as Faisal was, there were some aspects of his understanding of foreign affairs that were positively simple-minded. For instance, Faisal, like many Saudis, was conspiracy-conscious to the point of paranoia. He saw his country surrounded by the enemies of Islam. He assumed, quite illogically, that since the objectives of the kindgom's enemies were the same, these enemies were somehow allied in an enormous international conspiracy. In Faisal's mind, communism and Zionism became synonymous.

This leap of logic had little real effect on the kingdom's relations with either Israel or the Soviet Union, both of which were simply written off as enemies. The problem arose, and continues to arise, out of the relationship between Saudi Arabia and the United States. If Zionism and communism were the same, how could the United States be, at the same time, the world's foremost supporter of Zionism and the world's foremost opponent of communism?

Faisal never resolved this conflict, and thus his attitude toward the United States was always ambivalent. The conflicting feelings the Saudis have for the United States were summed up well by the Saudi foreign minister, Prince Saud al-Faisal, in an address to the annual Organization of Islamic Countries (OIC) Conference in Islamabad in the spring of 1980.

Saud al-Faisal soundly condemned both the United States and the Soviet Union for interfering in the internal affairs of

---

[6]For a more detailed account of Kamal Adham's achievements in espionage, see chapter fifteen.

countries of the Middle East—the Soviet Union in Afghanistan and the United States in Palestine. However, as soon as the Iranian-Iraqi war broke out in the fall of the same year, Prince Sultan, minister of defense and aviation, immediately requested that the United States provide Saudi Arabia with sophisticated AWAC aircraft to complement the Saudi Royal Air Force's early-warning system. The United States did provide such aircraft, as well as six hundred American military personnel to keep the four converted 707s in the air.

In early 1934 Abdulaziz ordered both Faisal and Saud to lead armies across the border into Yemen to subdue the raiding tribes. As previously mentioned, Saud's army became bogged down in the mountainous terrain of the interior, while Faisal's troops made swift progress toward the Yemeni capital city of Sanaa.

With Faisal's force of Ikhwan poised outside the capital, Imam Yahya contacted Abdulaziz and sued for peace. Abdulaziz agreed to a cease-fire and telegraphed Faisal to stop the attack. Faisal received the telegram but curiously, disregarded it. Whether the disappointment of not being allowed to capture the Yemeni capital had affected his judgment, we do not know. We do know that, contrary to his father's orders, Faisal continued the attack against Sanaa. Abdulaziz promptly dispatched a second telegram to Faisal. The second telegram brought Faisal's military adventure in Yemen to an immediate end.

Years later, author Vincent Sheean asked Faisal about the incident. Faisal's reply was curiously nostalgic: "I was young, very young. I did not understand. Military exploits, conquests, and all that kind of thing make an appeal to youth. My father was of course completely right, in that he drew the line at aggression. Provocation there was, but to take over a neighboring country is not right, it is an aggressive thing to do and I realize it now. I recall a Bedouin poem ... about the magic of youth. I thought the poem was not far off saying—in essence—something which used to be one of Bernard Shaw's famous remarks, that youth was much too good to be wasted on the young."[7]

---

[7]Vincent Sheean, *Faisal: The King and His Kingdom*, University Press of Arabia, Tavistock (England), 1975, p. 87.

Whether as a result of his disobedience or not, Faisal's campaign in Yemen was destined to be his last military command. The last half of the 1930s found Faisal again attempting to explain the Arab perspective on Palestine to European governments.

Events in Europe were overshadowing the situation in Palestine. Hitler's hostility to European Jewry invoked public sympathy in Britain, which still held the "mandate" for Palestine, for the Zionist movement.

To some degree, this sympathy was sanctimonious. The Zionists had not chosen to make their national homeland in Britain. Had Cornwall or Yorkshire been the destination of the tens of thousands of Jewish immigrants, there might have been an entirely different reaction on the part of the British public. In addition, some Arabs suggest that there existed a streak of racism in the British public, which chose to support the white-skinned Zionists over the dark-skinned Arabs.

In 1939 Britain called a conference on Palestine. Faisal was dispatched to London to head the Saudi Arabian delegation. Arab and Zionist delegates gathered in London in March. They refused to sit at the same table.

When there was no agreement between the Arab delegation and the Zionists, the British issued a "white paper" on Palestine. The "white paper" restricted Jewish immigration to seventy-five thousand over the following five years.

However sympathetic Faisal was to the plight of European Jewry, he was also aware that the extermination of the Jews in Europe was fanning the fires of Zionism in Palestine and that it was only a matter of time before Palestine became embroiled in a bloody and genocidal religious war.[8]

---

[8]Muslims are very sensitive to the charge that they are anti-Jewish. Following a bomb attack on a Paris synagogue in autumn 1980, the Israeli government charged that the PLO was supporting various neo-Nazi organizations in Europe. Nadil Ramlawi, the PLO's chief representative in London, responded, "I state categorically and unequivocally that the PLO has no links with any anti-Jewish organizations in Europe or elsewhere. We consider any act of discrimination against Jews to be a hostile act against the Palestinian People." On the same subject, Arabs often point out that the Prophet Muhammed himself had both Christian and Jewish wives.

Faisal looked to both Britain and the United States in his continuing search for a solution to the problem of Palestine. In 1943, in the midst of World War II, Faisal and his younger brother Khalid (now the king) departed on a state visit to the United States and Britain.

Faisal and Khalid landed in Miami in September and were flown to Washington. They were received by President Roosevelt and Secretary of State Cordell Hull. Faisal presented Roosevelt with a bejeweled Arabian sword, and Roosevelt gave a huge banquet in Faisal's honor which included among its guests the entire Cabinet and several score of important senators and congressmen.

Privately, Roosevelt and Faisal discussed Palestine. Roosevelt viewed Jewish immigration to Palestine as essentially a British problem which would be resolved after the conclusion of the war.

On November 17 Faisal and Khalid arrived in wartime London. It was a vastly different city from the one Faisal had known on previous visits. The blackout was in effect from twilight to dawn, sleep was regularly interrupted by the wail of air-raid sirens, and the menu of the Dorchester Hotel, where he stayed, was severely emaciated by food rationing.

Faisal experienced the bombings, visited military bases, was received by the king, and gave Winston Churchill a bejeweled Arabian sword, of which Faisal always seemed to have an abundant supply. He did manage a brief discussion with Churchill. However, in 1943 Jewish immigration into Palestine was hardly one of the pressing problems facing the British prime minister. Nevertheless, Churchill did reiterate Britain's resolve to protect the "civil and religious rights" of the non-Jewish population of Palestine.

Faisal and Khalid then returned to Saudi Arabia by way of North Africa, where they met briefly with the commander of the Free French, General Charles de Gaulle. While the tour accomplished little in terms of Palestine, it did serve to lessen the isolation of the Desert Kingdom and promote an atmosphere of cooperation between the governments of Saudi Arabia and Britain and the United States. However, Saudi Arabia did not truly enter the international community of nations until two years later, when Faisal was once again dispatched to the United States to represent the kingdom at the San Francisco Conference on the United Nations.

The years following the end of World War II saw the fulfillment of Faisal's grim prophecy. Palestine, dormant during the war years, erupted in violence. The violence was initially provoked by a British restriction limiting Jewish immigration to two thousand persons a month until one hundred thousand had been reached.

Jewish fanatics organized themselves into terrorist squads and attacked British military targets in Palestine. The Arab population of Palestine also became a target for the Irgun and the Stern Gang. Ironically, some of these Jewish terrorists, including Menachem Begin, have become high government officials who refuse to negotiate with Palestinian Arabs because they too have employed the tactics of terror.

Faisal struggled hard against the creation of the state of Israel. His plan, which shared almost universal support in the Arab world, called for the creation of a single state in Palestine in which the Jewish residents would have been a protected minority. This plan was vehemently opposed by the Zionists in Palestine and the growing Zionist population in the United States.

Faisal had genuine difficulty in comprehending the Zionist antagonism to the Arab proposal. As late as June 1, 1967, he expressed what he considered the complete senselessness of Zionism. *Al Safa*, the Beirut daily, reported Faisal at a press conference in Brussels as saying, "Perhaps there are those who would convey to the world that the Arabs oppose the Jews *as* Jews, but the fact is different. The Jews have lived with the Arabs in Arab countries and generally enjoyed a better life than the Arabs themselves. But when international Zionism came to us with its new policy calling for the creation of a state on the basis of a religious belief, we see what we have seen.[9] Since the creation of Israel, the Middle East has been continuously in unrest, because the fundamental idea of creating an Israeli state in the midst of the Arab body is an unnatural thing. The Jews were unjustly suppressed during the days of Hitler and the Nazi Party. While we do not agree with the oppression the Jews were subjected to by Hitler and the Nazis, we do not accept in any way that their revenge should be directed towards the Arabs as the Israeli Zionists have shown by usurping a part of the Arab world."[10]

The violence continued in Palestine during the years immediately following World War II. In 1947 the newly founded United Nations divided Palestine into a Jewish state, an Arab state, and a small international zone which included the religiously important city of Jerusalem. Count Folke Bernadotte, the nephew of the Swedish King Gustaf V, was appointed to be the United Nations mediator in Palestine. The United Nations' partition plan received little enthusiasm from either the Arabs or the Zionists. In fact, the radical Zionists promptly assassinated the U.N. mediator. While Israel was being formally proclaimed a nation in Tel Aviv on March 14, 1948, the Arab nations prepared for war.

The Arabs underestimated the determination of the small Zionist state, and they underestimated the support Israel would receive from the United States. The 1948 Arab-Israeli war ended with Israel almost twice its original size. Here also ended any hopes the Palestinian Arabs had for the immediate creation of a Palestinian state.

On November 4, 1964, the same day that Faisal became king, a rather daring reporter from Beirut's *Al Hayah* newspaper asked the new Saudi king how he could justify the existence of an absolute monarchy in the middle of the twentieth century.

---

[9]Faisal's rhetoric was often good. However, here he was speaking utter nonsense. There is nothing so old as creating a state on the basis of religious belief. In fact, Faisal could hardly have been ignorant of the fact that Saudi Arabia was just such a state whose "constitution" was the Holy Book of Islam, the Koran.
[10]*Al Safa*, June 1, 1967.

Faisal's reply included some of his best rhetoric: "The important thing about a regime is not what it is called but how it acts. There are corrupt republican regimes and sound monarchies and vice versa. The only true criterion of a regime—whether it be monarchical or republican—is the degree of reciprocity between the ruler and the ruled and the extent to which it symbolizes prosperity, progress, and healthy initiative. If a regime, be it of one kind or another, is unsound, it will generate hatred and antipathy among the people whatever the circumstances. So you see, the quality of a regime should be judged by its deeds and the integrity of its rulers, and not by its name....[11]"

Unlike many of his counterparts elsewhere in the world, Faisal genuinely did want to be judged by his actions. Even before officially being proclaimed king, he had statesmanlike deeds on his record by which he could be judged. Probably the most significant of these was his issuance, on November 6, 1962, of his now-famous ten-point program for social and political reform.

Earlier in that same year, Faisal had been in the United States where Kennedy, concerned that internal unrest in Saudi Arabia might interrupt the flow of Arabian oil to the West, urged Faisal to make some necessary reforms. Partly due to Kennedy's urging and partly out of his own sincere belief in the reforms themselves, Faisal drafted a statement designed to bring Saudi Arabia out of the past and into the present.

Significant among these reforms were the complete abolition of slavery, the establishment of a public education system for both boys and girls, the formation of a unified and consistent system of government with the Ulema as the official interpreters of the *sharia* law, and the establishment of a social security system which guaranteed employment to every Saudi male.

It should be remembered that until 1962 slavery had been the norm, education for females had been unthinkable, and the poor were left entirely on their own to suffer and die in their poverty. Faisal's reforms were revolutionary.

---

[11]*Al Hayah*, November 4, 1964.

Not everyone embraced them. Saudi Arabia had its share
of people who idealize the past. Many were willing to
give their lives to preserve the status quo. Two reforms
which caused King Faisal the greatest problems were the
introduction of female education and the introduction of television. On several occasions, Faitsal called out the army to
quell rioting religious fanatics who were attempting to
prevent girls from attending school.[12] On one occasion in Buraida, these frenzied Wahhabis actually succeeded in tearing down a newly constructed cinder-block
school with their bare hands.

Disturbances caused by the introduction of education for
girls were slight compared to the riots that followed the introduction of television. It should be remembered that the Koran
expressly forbids any representation of the human form. Nevertheless, Faisal used the same argument with the Ulema that his
father had when he first introduced the telephone. How
could an instrument, like a television or telephone, be
intrinsically evil if it could be used to promote the spread of
Islam? Correspondingly, the first television programs to be
seen in the kingdom were comprised solely of lessons from the
Koran.[13]

By 1966 the antitelevision riots had spread to Riyadh. During
a week of rioting, a policeman shot and killed a young prince. It
is not known whether the prince was part of the riot or whether
he was a bystander. His father claimed the latter, while the policeman claimed the former.

The prince's named was Khalid ibn-Mousaad al-Saud,
the eldest son of Prince Mousaad, who only a few years
earlier had scandalized the royal family by being arrested
for performing an Arabian sword dance naked in a Paris fountain. Prince Mousaad protested his son's death to the king,

---

[12]Although the University of Riyadh started correspondence courses for women in
1962, it did not actually open a women's college until 1976.
[13]Even today, the vast majority of television programs are lessons in or readings from
the Koran.

demanding that the policeman responsible be executed and that his family pay the required man-price.[14]

King Faisal studied the case and then ruled that the policeman had acted correctly. It has been alleged that, upon hearing the king's ruling, Prince Mousaad leapt to his feet in the royal *majlis* chamber and launched into a bitter and vindictive attack on Faisal personally.

Sources say that Mousaad went so far as to call Faisal a *khawarig* (infidel).[15] It is said that Mousaad provoked Faisal to the point where the king banished him from the kingdom on the spot.

Mousaad and his family, including his younger son, Faisal ibn-Mousaad, left Saudi Arabia and went into exile in Lebanon.

Not all the attacks on Faisal during this time were as private as Mousaad's supposed interruption of the *majlis*. Ex-King Saud, who, curiously enough, had taken up residence in Cairo as Nasser's personal guest, chose this time to make another comeback bid. Early in 1967 a handful of dissatisfied Saudis formed an underground organization called the Union of the Arab Peninsula. As the name suggests, this organization's objective was the unification of the peninsula under a socialist regime. The organization received financial support from the pro-Soviet regimes in the Middle East, including Egypt and the Yemen Arab Republic. Regardless, 1967 saw numerous bomb attacks on government ministries and oil installations in the Eastern Province of the kingdom.

On March 17 Prince Naif, Minister of the Interior, announced that seventeen Yemeni nationals had been found guilty of sabotage and terrorism after a secret trial in Riyadh. All were publicly executed in Dira Square.

---

[14]The payment of "blood money" no longer exists in Saudi Arabia in cases of criminal homicide. However, the payment of blood money is required by law in cases of fatal traffic accidents. The current amount set by the *sharia* courts is forty thousand riyals (approximately fourteen thousand dollars).

[15]The term *khawarig* can be used without negative connotation to describe any non-Muslim, but it is a mortal insult to a Muslim, suggesting that he has deviated from Islam. For example, the radicals who took over the Holy Mosque in Mecca in the fall of 1979 were declared *khawarig* by the Ulema before they were beheaded.

The government of Yemen immediately sent a letter of protest to the Arab League condemning the executions and calling for "urgent measures to save the lives of thousands of Yemenis who are suffering the worst tortures in Saudi prisons because of their refusal to join the ranks of the mercenaries who are fighting against their country."

Among the voices raised against the executions was that of ex-King Saud. On March 20 he went on Radio Cairo and denounced Faisal's brutal foreign policy of cooperating with imperialist nations. Saud publicly deplored the beheading of the seventeen Yemenis during the holy month of the pilgrimage.

Saud visited Yemen and was greeted by President Field Marshal Salleh as "the legal king of Saudi Arabia." Saud announced by way of reply that he extended full diplomatic recognition to the Yemeni Republic "on my own behalf and on behalf of my people."

Saud returned to Cairo and continued his public attacks on Faisal. On April 24 he told the Egyptian Press Agency, "I was forced to leave Saudi Arabia in order to avoid the spreading of violence and bloodshed, but the presence of foreign mercenaries in my country and the control of power by the Americans and the British oblige me to reexamine this question. I am convinced that a large number of tribes remain loyal to me and that the Saudi people condemn the present situation."

Saud got no further than this in his last grab for power. He died two years later in Athens. The intriguing question is what happened to Saud to turn him so completely against his brother and so fully behind Nasser and the socialists in Yemen.

Relations between Faisal and Nasser improved from 1967 onwards due to Israel's "pre-emptive" strike against her Arab neighbors. Once again, Egypt and Saudi Arabia had a common enemy. It was during the six-day war that Israel took control of the Golan Heights, the Sinai, and the religiously important city of Jerusalem. Israel's withdrawal from these territories became virtually an obsession with Faisal.

In 1972 President Nixon told Faisal that if he persuaded President Anwar Sadat of Egypt to reduce the Soviet military presence in Egypt, America would pressure the Israeli leadership to withdraw from the Arab territories conquered in the 1967 war.[16]

Faisal agreed and accordingly offered Sadat substantial Saudi financial aid if the Russians were expelled. Sadat accepted and threw out the Soviet military advisers. Nixon then ignored his part of the bargain. Israel continued to hold Arab land and continued to announce that the status of Jerusalem was non-negotiable.

Unquestionably, it was a sense of betrayal that encouraged Faisal and Sheikh Ahmed Zaki Yamani to plan the 1973 oil embargo against the United States.

Faisal's foreign policy after 1967 was predicated on impatience with continued Israeli occupation of Arab land, a fear of Saudi Arabia's growing too close or too dependent on the unreliable political forces in Washington, an aversion to communism, and a sincerely felt obligation to protect Islam from its enemies.

Faisal believed it was essential for the Saudi monarchy to forge close friendships with the other politically conservative Islamic monarchies in the area, notably Jordan, Kuwait, Bahrain, and the United Arab Emirates.

A special delegation of Kuwaitis was due to visit Faisal on the morning of March 25, 1975. March 25 was also the Prophet Muhammed's birthday, but such days are not celebrated by the austere Wahhabis. Faisal awaited the Kuwaitis in his private reception room in the Riasa Palace in Riyadh. The room was guarded by a special squad of palace guards, armed with Armalite submachine guns and silver-and-gold daggers. Ex-slaves scurried about, pouring Arabian coffee into tiny cups and refilling the bowls of dates and nuts that lay before the king.

At ten minutes to ten in the morning, the Kuwaiti delegation filed into the reception room past the armed guards. Just outside the room, unnoticed by the Kuwaitis, a Saudi man fell into step with the delegation and managed to get past the guards. The man was Prince Faisal ibn-Mousaad, the brother of the prince who had been killed during the riots provoked by the in-

---

[16]"House of Saud," *The New York Times Magazine*, July 6, 1975.

troduction of television into the kingdom and the son of Prince
Mousaad who was in exile in Beirut. As soon as the young
prince was inside the room, he approached the king, who in
turn bowed his head so that the young prince could bestow the
traditional kiss on the bridge of the nose. Instead of kissing the
king, Faisal ibn-Mousaad reached beneath his *thobe* and fired
three times into the king's face. According to eyewitnesses, the
assassin then shouted "Now my brother is avenged!"

One of the bullets struck King Faisal in the brain, blowing the
back of his head off and killing him instantly. King Faisal crum-
pled in a blood-stained heap on the floor of the reception room,
his golden *iqal* and white *ghutra* falling to the floor.

The palace guards wrestled with the young assassin until
they had torn the pistol from his grasp. There followed an argument among the guards as to whether they should arrest or kill
him. A member of the Kuwaiti delegation is said to have interceded and ordered the guards to arrest the young man.

Five days later, Prince Naif, Minister of the Interior, issued the
statement that the assassin had been found to have acted alone
and to be in complete control of his mental faculties when he
committed the crime. Naif's statement paved the way for a trial
on April 2, which found Faisal ibn-Mousaad guilty of murder
and sentenced him to death.

Faisal ibn-Mousaad had spent most of his adult life in the
United States, associating with militant Arab students. For several years he had attended San Francisco State College, and later
he had lived in a "radical commune" in Berkeley. In 1969 a
California court had placed him on probation for selling drugs.
As many conspiracy-conscious Saudis often point out, this was
the time in California when the CIA was carrying out experi-
ments by giving unwitting human subjects doses of various
hallucinogenic drugs. There is a quite popular belief in Saudi
Arabia, not shared by the government or the royal family, that
King Faisal was assassinated by the CIA in order to prevent another oil embargo of the United States.

Additional food for thought was given the conspiracy-
mongers when it was discovered that Faisal ibn-Mousaad's
passport contained a visa valid for travel to East Germany. Im-

mediately the Saudi gossip mill began to speculate that the assassination was supported and financed by the Soviets through their surrogates in Iraq or the People's Democratic Republic of Yemen.

More serious, however, is the charge that the Saudi royal family deliberately ignored the fact that Faisal ibn-Mousaad was a severely deranged young man and executed him to set a public example for other future Saudi dissidents. This is a difficult accusation either to prove or to deny, since most Western psychology is completely rejected by Islam and *sharia* law.

There is only one mental hospital in the kingdom, in Taif, which is managed by an Italian corporation. There are, however, repeated allegations that the hospital employs "reeducation" tactics which come very close to brainwashing. Fred Halliday, in *Arabia Without Sultans*, asserts that political prisoners are often forced to read aloud from the Koran for hours and hours at a time in order to restore their sanity.[17]

The execution attracted a crowd of thousands. Since Faisal ibn-Mousaad was a member of the royal family, he was accorded the dubious honor of having his head cut off with a golden sword.

Faisal's funeral took place in the huge Eid Mosque in Riyadh. Aside from the several thousand members of the al-Saud family who assembled, heads of state or their representatives were present to pay their last respects to the late king. The United States was represented by Vice President Nelson Rockefeller, who stood uncomfortably throughout the ten-minute prayer next to Uganda's portly Idi Amin.

As he left the Eid Mosque, Khalid ibn-Abdulaziz, Saudi Arabia's new king, wept openly and had to be supported on one arm by Anwar Sadat of Egypt and on the other by Yasser Arafat of the Palestine Liberation Organization. Faisal had led the kingdom out of the past and into the present, but in the process had become a part of the past, a mere memory himself.

---

[17]Fred Halliday, *Arabia Without Sultans*, Penguin, London, 1975.

14

Choice of a King

Only hours had elapsed between the assassination of King Faisal and the public proclamation of the new king, Khalid ibn-Abdulaziz al-Saud. The House al-Saud, ever concerned with its own survival, had made careful plans for the succession. Little is known about how a senior prince is elevated to the position of heir apparent. The process is one of the most closely guarded secrets in the kingdom.

In theory, the al-Saud line of succession works its way through all the sons of Abdulaziz in order of age and maternal tribal ties. Thus the eldest grandson of King Abdulaziz is a good forty to fifty steps removed from the throne.

In practice, however, the decision-making process is more complicated. It is a mixture of hereditary right, power politics, backroom bargaining, and just being in the right place at the right time. The senior members of the family and the Ulema first faced the problem of succession when they chose to revoke their oath of allegiance to King Saud and depose him. There was never a question about who would follow Saud. Faisal had been named crown prince by his father, and more important, he had already won the respect and loyalty of the majority of the royal family. The Ulema also supported Faisal because of his reputation for piety and the fact that his mother had been a member of the al-Sheikh family. The House al-Saud then turned its attention to whom should be chosen as King Faisal's crown prince. This was a difficult decision. It divided the royal family until Faisal himself intervened.

On purely hereditary grounds, the choice of the royal family should have been Prince Muhammed ibn-Abdulaziz, the son of King Abdulaziz and Al-Jauharh bint-Musaad al-Jiluwi. Muhammed was the senior son of Abdulaziz. He had commanded the Ikhwan forces during the surrender of Medina and had played a significant role in the ouster of King Saud. Significantly, too, he received some support from the powerful al-Jiluwi family. However, Muhammed, like other sons of Abdulaziz, had managed to acquire a reputation for himself as a drunkard and a degenerate. So low had his reputation sunk that he was popularly nicknamed "Muhammed of the Twin Evils" (presumably the "twin evils" of alcoholism and lechery).

A dispute soon arose between a faction of the royal family, who supported Muhammed's candidacy and declared the allegations against him to be false, and the majority of the House al-Saud, who saw too many similarities between Muhammed and his elder brother, the deposed King Saud.

The official Saudi version of this affair records that Prince Muhammed was offered the position of crown prince but refused it, claiming to be too busy with business affairs. While possible, this version ignores the fact that the royal family had just ousted one extravagant and degenerate monarch and would hardly turn around and offer the throne to a prince with a similar reputation.

Allegations of mental incompetence were directed at Prince Muhammed in 1978 when he shot his favorite granddaughter to death and then beheaded her boyfriend. Similar allegations were again made against him following the broadcast of the controversial British film on the subject of the killings, *Death of a Princess*. It is quite difficult to determine whether Prince Muhammed is sane or not. However, the cover-up of his execution of his granddaughter in 1978 is illustrative of the manner in which the royal family acts in times of internal crisis.

Prince Muhammed's granddaughter, Princess Mashayel, was born in the late 1950s to a slave woman serving in Muhammed's palace. Mashayel's father was Muhammed's son, and while he never married the slave woman, he did grant her freedom upon Mashayel's birth. Mashayel grew up during a very difficult period for a young woman in Saudi Arabia. While political reforms were underway, they were slow in coming. She had been born too early to benefit fully from King Faisal's introduction of female education but too late to be entirely content with the traditionally submissive and subservient role of the Saudi woman.

It appears that Mashayel was a bright child, vivacious and playful, with a quick wit and a well-developed sense of humor. A princess cousin and close friend recalls: "Mashayel was always making up stories. She loved to play at make-believe. She would build palaces in the sky, but none of us imagined that she would try to live in them."

As a Saudi princess, Mashayel lived a cloistered existence. She was bound to the house, prohibited from going out in public except for brief, closely supervised shopping forays. While surrounded with material affluence, Mashayel, like most Saudi women, was virtually under house arrest. Her entertainment consisted of visiting female relatives, listening to Western music, and watching American movies on the video machine.

Soon after her first menstrual period, Mashayel was married to a cousin. The marriage was arranged by her family, but Mashayel's permission was obtained before the ceremony was performed. The marriage was a bad one, and within a few years Mashayel and her husband were estranged and involved in divorce proceedings.

Her cousin the princess suggested that it was Mashayel's infatuation with American movies that caused problems in her marriage. "She saw herself as the romantic heroine. She wanted some handsome Italian count to seduce her in the same way she had seen in the movies. Even as a young woman, Mashayel was headstrong and impulsive."

It was at this time, while Mashayel was awaiting her divorce and living with her family in Jeddah, that she met Musleh al-Shaer. Musleh al-Shaer is reported to have been the nephew of the Saudi ambassador to Lebanon. We do not know how Mashayel and Musleh met. Some reports have them meeting in Beirut, others in Cairo, and still others say Musleh was a musician whom Mashayel had seen on Saudi television. Whatever the true story, they met and before long had fallen in love. Mashayel's make-believe world had become a very dangerous reality. According to her cousin, Mashayel and Musleh continued to meet in secret, using one of Mashayel's servants as a go-between.

When the servant perceived that the relationship might be developing into something serious, she went to Mashayel and pleaded with the princess to break it off. Apparently Mashayel refused, and at this point the servant, fearful now for her own safety, threatened to expose the affair to the rest of the family if Mashayel did not terminate it. This threat caused Mashayel and Musleh to make their fatal decision to run away together.

Like an actress in a grade B Hollywood romance, Mashayel went to a small beach on the Red Sea and scattered her clothes by the water's edge to give the impression that she had committed suicide. She also left a dramatic suicide note with her servant with instructions to give it to her family once she had left Jeddah.

Rather than attempting to escape directly out of the kingdom, the two lovers went secretly to Riyadh. Unable to anticipate the consequences of her actions, Mashayel probably thought that she could receive assistance from her cousins in Riyadh. The couple stayed at the Al-Yamamah Hotel on Shara Mathar. Mashayel telephoned a cousin in Riyadh to borrow her passport so that she could slip past immigration at the airport undetected. The cousin told Mashayel that her servant in Jeddah had told about her affair with Musleh. Mashayel also learned from her cousin that her grandfather had ordered the police to arrest her and Musleh on sight.

Acting out of panic, Mashayel disguised herself as a man, in *thobe, ghutra,* and *iqal,* and went to the airport in Riyadh with Musleh in the hope of slipping through exit-immigration procedures. The security police, alerted to watch for her, spotted her soon after she entered the airport. Dressing as a man was even more foolish than her pretended suicide, since Saudi women are expected to remain fully veiled in public, an immigration officer would never have asked her to remove her veil.[1]

---

[1]Since 1978 female agents have been added to the security at the kingdom's airports, but at the time Mashayel was trying to escape there were none.

Musleh witnessed her arrest and with futile gallantry attempted to come to her assistance. He too was arrested.

The couple was taken to Jeddah, where Mashayel was brought before her grandfather, Prince Muhammed. Mashayel's world came crumbling down around her. Suddenly she was confronted with the stark consequences of her action. She was a married woman who had run away with a man other than her husband. In Saudi Arabia the penalty for adultery is death.

As it was, Prince Muhammed probably felt he had no choice. His family had been publicly dishonored by the actions of Mashayel in Riyadh and had to be cleansed by her punishment. It is reliably reported that several senior princes, including King Khalid and Crown Prince Fahd, attempted to intercede with Prince Muhammed on behalf of Mashayel. At this point, the old man was beyond listening.

Two days later, Mashayel and Musleh were taken separately to a small vacant lot that served as a parking lot in Jeddah. Mashayel, still veiled, was made to kneel before a large mound of earth. Several hundred spectators were held back by a ring of policemen as Prince Muhammed strode forward to where his granddaughter was kneeling, shouted "In the Name of God," and fired a single shot into her head.

An eyewitness to the execution, an American teacher at Riyadh University, reports that at this point Musleh broke loose from the policemen who were holding him and tried to escape by beating his way through the crowd of onlookers. Musleh got no farther than twenty yards before the crowd had knocked him from his feet and dragged him back to the parking lot, where he was made to kneel. It is reported that it took Prince Muhammed four tries before he succeeded in completely severing the young man's head.

The question occurs: Does a sane man execute his own granddaughter?

Arab tradition makes the eldest male responsible for the family honor and gives him the right to pass judgment on his daughters or sisters and, in extreme cases to beat or even execute them. This tribal tradition is in no way sanctioned by Islamic law, which expressly requires a formal trial.

In a report presented to a United Nations human rights panel in August 1980, the London-based Minority Rights Group claimed that hundreds of women are killed every day in the Arab world. Jacqueline Thibault, who presented the report, said that women are condemned for having extramarital sex—willingly or by being raped—or "just because they were observed exchanging a few words with a young man and thus came under suspicion of having more intimate relations." The report went on to state that the victims had the "throats cut, were buried alive, poisoned and disemboweled by their father, their eldest brother, a cousin or a paid killer."

Ms. Thibault said that such practices remain a "horrifying reality" in Egypt, Iraq, Jordan, Israeli-occupied Arab land, and Saudi Arabia. However, according to the report, the practice is not rooted in religion but occurs in both Christian and Muslim families and dates back to ancient times.[2]

So Prince Muhammed's actions were in accordance with tribal tradition but contrary to Islamic and Saudi law. Islamic law expressly requires four witnesses to the actual act of sexual penetration before a *sharia* court will convict either a man or woman of adultery.

Convictions on the grounds of adultery are exceedingly rare. It should be noted here that neither Mashayel nor Musleh ever confessed. Neither was brought before a court. Neither was convicted of any crime. When Prince Muhammed was later asked about the executions in light of Islamic and Saudi law, he replied, "It was enough for me that they had been in the same room together."

Here is a classic example of tribal law in conflict with the laws of the nation. The senior princes, King Khalid and Crown

---

[2]Associated Press report, *Durham Morning Herald*, August 12, 1980. The situation that Ms. Thibault describes is unquestionably true, although I doubt the accuracy of the statement that "hundreds of women are killed every day ..." There is no way that Ms. Thibault or her researchers could have such statistics, since internal family matters are considered strictly private in the Arab world.

Prince Fahd included, treated the incident as though it never happened. No charges were brought against Prince Muhammed, nor was he ever censured for his actions. In fact, following the broadcast of *Death of a Princess*, government officials ignored the fact that Prince Muhammed had literally taken the law into his own hands and instead protested the film as "an attack on Islam."

Following the rejection of Muhammed to be the next crown prince, the senior princes considered various other candidates, including Prince Fahd ibn-Abdulaziz (the present crown prince). Prince Fahd actively sought the position but, like Muhammed, had a reputation for drunkenness and debauchery. Fahd's candidacy succeeded in dividing the royal family, until King Faisal intervened and announced that his choice would be Khalid ibn-Abdulaziz, the younger brother of Muhammed of the Twin Evils.

Very little was heard from Khalid during his years as crown prince. Western diplomats privately described him as a "desert Arab—a political nobody."

Various members of the royal household report that the only time King Khalid is truly alive is when he is in the desert with his horses and falcons. Falconry is still considered by the desert Bedouins as the noblest and most masculine of sports. However, it is rapidly becoming a sport only the very rich can pursue, because "manned" falcons fetch as much as twenty thousand dollars each. It should perhaps also be mentioned that falconry in Saudi Arabia differs greatly from its counterpart in Europe. Due to the scarcity of game in the desert, the quarry, usually a gazelle, is purchased by the hunter and then taken into the desert to be hunted.

The gazelle is held while several falcons peck out its eyes. It is then released and begins its blind and panicked flight across the desert with the falcons in hot pursuit. Just behind the falcons race the hunters in four-wheel-drive vehicles. The hunters must get to the blinded gazelle before the falcons have actually succeeded in killing it, since Muslims may not eat the flesh of an animal that has been killed improperly or without the obligatory prayer.[3] The actual hunt is usually quite short and is followed by a lengthy feast.

During the last ten years or so Khalid has been unable to participate as much as he would have liked in the sport. His health has deteriorated. In 1970 he suffered a massive heart attack and two years later underwent open-heart surgery. Khalid also suffers from diabetes and various circulatory ailments. In 1977 Khalid had his left hip surgically removed and replaced with a plastic prosthesis. Sources in Riyadh report that Khalid's private Boeing 747 is equipped with an in-flight operating theater and elaborate heart-monitoring devices that can relay information via satellite to Khalid's team of heart specialists in Cleveland, Ohio.[4]

This unlikely, undistinguished, and entirely disinterested man became the crown prince and, on March 25, 1975, only hours after Faisal had been declared dead, was proclaimed the new king.

Actually Khalid's presence was a godsend for the House al-Saud, since even before Faisal's assassination there had emerged two rival factions within the royal family, both eager to assume power once Faisal was no more. The first and most powerful faction was led by Prince Fahd, who was determined not to be bypassed by the royal family again. The second faction was led by Prince Abdullah, who had spent the previous ten years courting the loyalty and support of the Bedouin tribes. Had Khalid not been available to take over, the kingdom might have again been torn apart by yet another internal power struggle.

As it was, Prince Fahd was proclaimed the new crown prince, and Prince Abdullah was proclaimed second deputy prime minister and commander of the National Guard. Somewhere in this arrangement, we can find the dead hand of Faisal, who saw both Fahd and Abdullah as potential threats to the welfare of the kingdom. In all probability it was Faisal who, looking toward

---

[3]The sacrifice of sheep and goats at the feast of the Eid, during Ramadan and the hajj, is accomplished by the butcher's turning the animal's head in the direction of Mecca, uttering a short devotion to God, and then quickly cutting the beast's throat. The flesh is eaten immediately without being aged or hung.

[4]Also reported in *Newsweek*, April 7, 1975.

his own death, made the choice to put both men in power in the hope that they would counterbalance each other.

Nevertheless, Faisal's death brought life to one of the most dangerous internal disputes in modern Saudi history, one which has yet to be resolved and, with Khalid's health deteriorating daily, threatens the very stability of the richest oil-producing nation in the world.

15

Crown Prince Fahd and the Future

When Saudis discuss politics they rarely mention the name of the king. King Khalid holds very little real power in government. Throughout his reign, he has been a figurehead monarch, content to officiate at ceremonies, greet visiting heads of state, and oversee the preparations the kingdom makes for the annual influx of millions of Muslims making the pilgrimage to Mecca and Medina. Khalid, by personal choice, has almost completely removed himself from the day-to-day business of running the country.

The *de facto* head of state is Crown Prince Fahd, the strongman behind the throne. Fahd is the eldest of the seven sons of King Abdulaziz and Hussah al-Sudeiri, the so-called Sudeiri Seven. The Sudeiri Seven appear to have benefited from their father and mother both, inheriting at least some of their father's cunning and coming under the powerful influence of their mother.

Hussah al-Sudeiri was King Abdulaziz's most powerful and influential wife. She was never divorced and remained one of the closest women to the old monarch right up until his death. Hussah al-Sudeiri sought to actualize her power through her sons, training them to be fiercely loyal to each other. Until quite recently, Hussah al-Sudeiri held regularly weekly meetings with her seven sons to discuss the political status of the royal family.

Crown Prince Fahd's power and authority within the royal family come from this sense of loyalty instilled by his mother.

The Sudeiri Seven have succeeded in manipulating themselves into such positions of power that today they have absolute control of the government. In order of age, they are Prince Fahd, Prince Sultan, Prince Abdul Rahman, Prince Naif, Prince Turki, Prince Salman, and Prince Ahmed.

Crown Prince Fahd presides over the Council of Ministers and holds the power of veto over every branch of the government. Prince Sultan is the commander-in-chief of the army and the air force, the minister of defense, and the chairman of the board of directors of Saudia, the national airline. Prince Naif is the powerful Minister of the Interior, directly responsible for the regular police, the security police, the Frontier Guards, and the coast guard. Prince Salman is the governor of Riyadh, and Prince Ahmed holds the number two spot in the Ministry of the Interior. Prince Abdul Rahman and Prince Turki, the only two of the seven who do not hold government positions, have become fabulously wealthy businessmen and control the private purse strings of the family.

Crown Prince Fahd, who will ascend the throne upon the death of King Khalid, was born in a palace in Riyadh in 1922. He received a "court education," which is a euphemism used in the Saudi Ministry of Education to mean that a prince is literate in Arabic. Fahd was too young to be involved in any of his father's wars to unify Arabia, and, unlike King Saud and King Faisal, he has no military experience.

Fahd was first appointed to a government post in 1958, when Crown Prince Faisal announced the establishment of the kingdom's first Ministry of Education. Here he had the formidable task of bridging a system of public education, at all levels, to a portion of the world where none had previously existed. In addition, Fahd was the minister directly responsible for the implementation of female education. As the oil royalties grew larger, Fahd saw his primary task as the construction of schools. He officiated at the opening ceremonies of the University of Riyadh only months after he was appointed Minister of Education, and his interest in higher education has been a continuing one. In fact, Fahd has been one of the prime movers in the kingdom behind the dramatic expansion of the Saudi university system.[1]

In 1964, just after Faisal had ascended the throne, Fahd was appointed Minister of the Interior. This was a vastly more powerful position, and his appointment suggests that Faisal had already begun to recognize the potential political power of the seven sons of Hussah al-Sudeiri. It is a position that Faisal himself considered important enough to oversee personally and use as a stepping stone to the throne. In all likelihood, Fahd also viewed the appointment in this way.

As minister of the interior, Fahd soon earned himself a reputation for effectively and ruthlessly dealing with internal subversion. In 1967, after several terrorist attacks at oil installations and government ministries, Fahd ordered his security forces (different from the regular police) to round up everyone about whom there was the slightest suspicion. These mass arrests are reported to have numbered in the hundreds.

Fahd's speculation was that the terrorist attacks were originating in the People's Democratic Republic of Yemen. He therefore ordered the wholesale deportation of thousands and thousands of Yemeni manual laborers whose presence in the kingdom was seen as a potential threat to internal security.[2]

In 1969 it was reported widely in the Western press that thousands of young men, mostly army and air force officers, were involved in plotting a Nasser-backed coup that would oust King Faisal and the monarchy. It is repeatedly alleged that hundreds of young men were arrested and secretly executed. One individual interviewed in the British film *Death of a Princess* went so far as to state that three hundred of these young men were loaded onto American planes flown by American pilots and were thrown to their deaths over the Empty Quarter.

---

[1]In 1958, the University of Riyadh had twenty-one students. By 1980 the enrollment of both male and female students had passed fourteen thousand. As dramatic as the expansion has been, it is hardly an unqualified success story. The emphasis has remained on construction, while academic standards have been almost entirely ignored. The 1979 *Bulletin of the University of Riyadh* sets a 70 cumulative grade-point average as necessary for admission to the Colleges of Medicine and Dentistry, while most of the other colleges will accept any student with a secondary school certificate, regardless of his or her grades.

[2]Mordechai Abir, *Oil, Power, and Politics*, Frank Cass & Co., London, 1974, p. 53.

Linda Blandford, in her book *Super Wealth,* reports that Sheikh Abdulaziz Muammar, the ambassador to Switzerland under King Saud, was recalled to the kingdom following Saud's deposition and promptly arrested. Blandford does not tell us what Muammar was arrested for, but she does assert that he spent twelve years in the special security prison in Hofuf. At the time of his release, Abdulaziz Muammar claimed that there were seventy political prisoners in the Hofuf security prison.[3]

A small security prison exists in the Nasseriah area of Riyadh. It is housed in an unmarked villa surrounded by a high wall. Students of mine at the university said that political prisoners were taken to this villa for "reeducation," which included torture and brainwashing, the techniques of which were taught to the Saudis by American advisers, these students further allege.

Kamal Adham, King Faisal's brother-in-law and chief security adviser, was trained by the CIA in Langley, Virginia. Rather ironically, at the same time as the CIA was training Adham, they were also training General Zamir, head of Mossad, the crack Israeli secret service. While it is not known whether Adham and Zamir met in Langley, both used the CIA as a clearinghouse for information in their separate attempts to combat the spread of communism in the Middle East.

Despite his effectiveness in suppressing internal dissent, Fahd's relationship with King Faisal was a troubled one. Sources in Riyadh report that Faisal never really trusted Fahd's ambition. In addition, during the mid-1960s rumors spread about Fahd's gambling in Europe. At first these reports were discounted as Zionist propaganda. However, it was not long before the European and American press was publishing eyewitness accounts of Fahd's extravagant gambling sprees.

Time reported that three Saudi princes, including the Minister of the Interior, Prince Fahd ibn-Abdulaziz, had lost more than six million dollars in a single evening of gambling in Monte Carlo.[4] According to the *Time* report, Prince Fahd arrived at the Hôtel de Paris in Monte Carlo with "one thought

---

[3]Linda Blanford, *Super Wealth: The Secret Lives of the Oil Sheikhs,* William Morrow & Co., New York, 1977, p. 144.
[4]*Time,* October 21, 1974.

in mind: 'We have come to gamble...but on certain conditions. We're going to tell you when to close.'" Apparently, Prince Fahd's gambling system consisted of constantly raising the stakes in an attempt to recoup his previous losses. After doubling the normal limit on four-hundred-dollar chips, Fahd requested that the casino quadruple the limit. The casino agreed; at the standard roulette odds of thirty-five to one, a sixteen-hundred-dollar chip placed on the winning number would pay fifty-six thousand dollars.

A large crowd gathered to watch the Saudis try to break the bank. The crowd included journalists who provided the rest of the world with graphic descriptions of the action. While the crowd was disappointed that Fahd failed to break the bank, they may have been a little impressed when Fahd handed a four-hundred-dollar chip to a waiter as a tip for emptying his ashtray.

It was an expensive evening for Fahd. Not only did he lose more money than most people ever see in a lifetime, he also weakened his chances to become king. A cable arrived from King Faisal, ordering Fahd to return to Riyadh. Faisal was so furious with Fahd that he actively considered disinheriting him.

Recently, Crown Prince Fahd has again been a player in London casinos, along with the controversial Saudi billionaire Adnan Khashoggi. According to one report, the two of them dropped more than three quarters of a million dollars in one evening.[5]

As a puritan theocracy, Saudi Arabia bans all gambling, and having the crown prince openly violate this Islamic prohibition is equivalent to having the pope admit to accepting bribes. However, since the death of Faisal, there has been no one in the royal family powerful enough to take Fahd to task for his gambling.

As the architect of Saudi foreign policy for the past five years, Crown Prince Fahd has walked a tightrope between his inclination to be pro-American and his understanding that such pro-Americanism will fan the fires of resentment in the more radical Arab states. In addition, a substantial portion of the royal family

---

[5]*8 Days*, January 12, 1980; p. 52.

is vehemently anti-American, and Fahd cannot risk alienating himself from this group. Fahd is the spokesman who repeatedly denies that there is an American military presence in Saudi Arabia. True, there are thousands of American military personnel within the kingdom who have been assigned to train the various branches of the Saudi armed forces. One only has to have lunch at the Desert Inn, the restaurant of the American Military Mission in Riyadh, to appreciate how many American majors, captains, and colonels are actually working with the Saudi military.

Also, many of the private companies, such as Lockheed, provide ex-American air force pilots to fly for both the Royal Saudi Air Force and the National Guard. One American, working for Lockheed and flying C-130s for the National Guard, speculated that three out of every four of the planes in the Royal Saudi air force had American pilots and copilots. "About the only thing the Saudi air force understands well is money. And once they've spent millions on those American F-15s, they don't want some young Bedouin cowboy cracking them up."

The royal family has made several attempts to distance itself from the United States. On May 19, 1980, the Saudi foreign minister, Prince Saud al-Faisal, said that the United States supported the "gallant struggle of the Afghan people against Soviet invasion and occupation, but continued to ignore the legitimate rights of the Palestinian people under the yoke of Zionist occupation." He went on to denounce the Soviet Union, which "had always supported the struggle of the Palestinian and Arab people in Palestine against Israeli occupation and aggression, but then went on to invade and occupy the Islamic country of Afghanistan."[6]

More recently, Crown Prince Fahd's rhetorical call for a holy war against Israel over the annexation of Arab Jerusalem was designed to emphasize the kingdom's independence from the United States. Some observers have also speculated that Fahd's call for the *jihad* suggests that the Crown Prince sees himself as a potential leader of the Arab world. Under Islamic law, the only

---

[6]*The Arab News*, May 19, 1980.

person to have the power to call for the *jihad* is the caliph, the spiritual head of the Islamic world. However, there hasn't been a caliph since the end of World War I, when Kemal Atatürk abolished the caliphate.

Nevertheless, Crown Prince Fahd remains one of the most pro-American members of the royal family. One gets the impression that Fahd would like to be even closer to the United States, but due to immoderate American support for Israel, he must maintain a safe political distance from Washington.

Despite sanctimonious talk of Arab unity and the defense of Islam, the foreign policy of the kingdom is a combination of economic self-interest and the ever-pressing need to make the kingdom secure from the spread of Soviet influence in the Middle East.

All the major decisions made by Crown Prince Fahd and the senior princes are motivated by these two areas of concern. For example, Saudi Arabia's moderate stand on oil pricing can be traced directly to the fact that the kingdom does not want increased oil prices to have too inflationary an effect on the economy of the West. The vast majority of the kingdom's investments are in dollars and are housed in Europe or in the United States.

In a rare candid moment, Crown Prince Fahd himself explained why he had decided to continue accepting dollars as a means of paying oil bills. "We know that the kingdom's assets ... are in dollars so what is our interest in creating a crisis for the dollar for which we will have to pay? What other currencies can replace the dollar? The yen? The franc? The Mark? Gold? These are ... tied to the dollar.[7]

Economically, Saudi Arabia and its fabulously wealthy royal family are perched at the top of a precarious financial ladder. They perceive themselves as a group with everything to lose and nothing to gain by continued tensions in the Middle East. Dr. Ghazi al-Gosaibi put it concisely: "Development does not take place in a vacuum; it is allergic to wars and instability." The al-Saud clan is so conservative that even its radical members,

---

[7]*The Arab News*, January 12, 1980, p. 7.

such as prince Tallal, appear little more than liberal in Western eyes.

There is little agreement on how the kingdom should weather tension created by Israel's continued occupation of Arab Palestine, the proliferation of "friendship treaties" between Arab states and the Soviet Union, the continued discord between Iraq and Iran, and the isolation of Egypt due to the Camp David Accords.

Debate within the royal family is hardly a public affair, but it appears to follow the classic isolationist-interventionist lines. The older, more religiously conservative members of the royal family tend toward isolationism, while the younger, more pro-Western princes tend to advocate interventionism.

It should be understood that by interventionism, the Saudi princes do not mean military intervention. The kingdom's armed forces are barely sufficient to defend the kingdom, let alone become involved in military activity elsewhere in the Middle East. The tool, used by the more active interventionists such as Crown Prince Fahd and Prince Sultan, is financial pressure, and it has been remarkably successful in reshaping the politics of the area.

When in the early 1970s the Palestine Liberation Organization began to receive substantial financial assistance from the Soviet Union and appeared to be becoming an ideological puppet of Moscow, Saudi Arabia increased its own assistance to the PLO's more conservative factions.

It is not surprising that Yasser Arafat has purged the hard-line communists from the upper echelons of his organization and himself remains aloof from his benefactors in the Kremlin. When the al-Saud clan gives financial support, it makes sure the recipient knows what political strings are attached.

Elsewhere in the Middle East, Saudi Arabia has used its riches to thwart the spread of Soviet influence. For instance, in 1977 the senior al-Saud princes agreed to pay all expenses incurred by the Syrian-Arab peace-keeping force sent into Lebanon to monitor the cease-fire in the Lebanese civil war.

Saudi Arabia has also been sending large amounts of money into the Yemen Arab Republic to persuade Yemeni President Ali Abdullah Salleh to oust or at least limit the number of Soviet advisers in the country. President Salleh, in maneuvers reminiscent of those used by Nasser, has been playing the Soviets against the Americans and has accepted weaponry from both.

Jordan's King Hussein has also been the recipient of large amounts of Saudi money, first when his monarchy appeared to be threatened by a coalition of Jordanian leftists and Palestinian refugees in 1970 and again when Hussein felt threatened by Syrian President Assad's overtures to Moscow.

In many respects, the House al-Saud and, especially, Crown Prince Fahd have played a major role in reshaping the political ideologies of northwestern Africa. It was Saudi money, nearly a billion dollars of it, that convinced President Anwar Sadat to expel the thousands of Russian military advisers that Nasser had invited into Egypt. Similarly, millions and millions of Saudi riyals are funneled across the Red Sea into the strategically important Horn of Africa to support the Eritrean separatist movement, a guerrilla army struggling for the independence of Eritrea from the Soviety-backed Ethiopian government in Addis Ababa.

The Soviet military presence in Ethiopia has also spurred the Saudis to support Sudan's president, Jaffar Numeiri, who would have toppled from power many times had it not been for large transfusions of Saudi cash. Even more bizarre was a recent report out of Kampala, Uganda, broadcast by the World Service of the BBC, claiming that the forces loyal to deposed dictator Idi Amin, massing on the Ugandan border in a bid to return Amin to power, were financed by the Saudi Arabian royal family.

The Saudis were quick to deny this report, but they never denied reports that Idi Amin is living as a guest of the Saudi royal family in a luxurious hotel suite in Jeddah. Neither does the royal family deny that it provided Amin with financial support while he was in power.

General Zia ul-Haq financed his quasi-legal takeover of

Pakistan with Saudi funds. The major source of revenue for the Afghan rebels fighting the Soviet regime in Kabul is Saudi Arabia. Similarly, the Saudi royal family has financed the Muslim guerrillas in the southern Philippines in their struggle against Marcos's brutal dictatorship.

There have been allegations that Saudis have attempted to purchase influence in American politics. Mohammed Hassanein Heikal, editor of the semiofficial Egyptian newspaper *Al Ahram*, claims that ex-president Richard Nixon accepted more than twelve million dollars in illegal campaign contributions from the Arab world, much of it coming from Saudi Arabia. More recently, the so-called Abscam scandal, in which an FBI agent posed as an oil-rich Arab sheikh and attempted to bribe various politicians including several congressmen, suggests that there may well be more American politicians who are for sale than was imagined and that Arab mediation in Washington may be a much more common practice than was previously believed.

Columnist Jack Anderson has said that there exists a Saudi financial connection to ex-President Carter's peanut business in Georgia which may have influenced Carter's policy towards selling Saudi Arabia weaponry.[8]

Anderson's allegations are that following Bert Lance's forced resignation as Carter's budget director, Lance was in bad financial straits. In order to avoid bankruptcy, the former budget director and close friend of the president sold his controlling interest in the National Bank of Georgia to a Saudi businessman by the name of Ghaith R. Pharaon. Pharaon is the son of one of King Khalid's closest friends and advisers.

In the same year, 1978, the Carter peanut business, which was in serious financial trouble, received a sixty-thousand-dollar break on a loan held by the National Bank of Georgia, presumably as a result of some manipulations on the part of the new Saudi-controlled management.

Anderson speculates that there may have been a relationship between this favorable financial treatment and Carter's decision

---

[8]Jack Anderson, *The Washington Post*, July 11 & 12, 1980.

to sell Saudi Arabia the F-15s they had requested. Similar allega-tions were leveled against Carter during the summer of 1980 when the Saudis asked to purchase additional fuel tanks for these F-15s.[9]

In another controversial arrangement with the Saudis, Presi-dent Carter agreed on August 9, 1979, in a move kept secret from Congress until January 29, 1980, to pay the Saudi royal family in-terest on its prepayments for military equipment.[10]

Saudi Arabia, the largest military customer of the United States, with over 22.2 billion dollars' worth of orders still pend-ing, is required to pay in advance for the F-5 and F-15 fighters it wishes to purchase. The advance payment is then held in es-crow by the Department of Defense, which acts as a middleman in all foreign defense deals, and is distributed to the individual defense contractors (Lockheed, Raytheon, etc.) when the respec-tive bills fall due.

Critics of the arrangement have said that this was tanta-mount to having the American taxpayer subsidize the Saudi royal family—to the tune of two hundred million dollars a year—and that this was entirely unnecessary because there was nowhere else for Saudi Arabia to turn for its military equipment. Defenders of Carter's action, specifically Cyrus Vance and Harold Brown, claimed that two hundred million dollars a year was a small price to pay in return for continued Saudi modera-tion in OPEC oil pricing.

Although the royal family could hardly say so publicly be-cause of the numerous pro-Zionist remarks made during Ronald Reagan's presidential campaign, most of the senior princes were secretly pleased by Reagan's election because they believed he would take a hard line with the Soviets.

Without exception, the royal family views the presence of So-viet troops in Afghanistan as a prelude to Soviet intervention in the Arabian Gulf. The royal family acknowledges that militarily

---

[9]The sale of these additional fuel tanks created a great controversy in the American press. The additional tanks would increase the range of the F-15s to the extent that it are amused at this prospect and say privately that their primary concern is not Israel but Iran.

[10]Heretofore only Switzerland enjoyed this privilege.

Saudi Arabia cannot hope to take over the position Iran occupied under the shah as "the policeman of the Gulf." Since the Islamic revolution in Iran, a power vacuum has existed in the Gulf, which the Saudis believe the Soviets want to fill.

According to the Saudis, the most plausible scenario in the Gulf is that the ayatollahs will destroy Iran's economy and thus open the door for a left-wing regime, heavily backed by the Soviet Union, to take over the government. Although they cannot say so publicly for fear of being called puppets of the United States, many of the senior princes believe that a strong American naval presence in the Gulf is essential to the stability of the entire area. They also believe that President Reagan will provide such a military presence, which they hope will serve as a deterrent to further Soviet expansionism in the region.

In an article published during the summer of 1980, Wolf Blitzer analyzed the possibility of a Saudi-Reagan connection.[11] "Behind the Reagan camp's attempt to reassure the Saud is and other Arab interests are gold-plated corporate giants such as Bechtel and Fluor,[12] two California-based construction companies with huge investments in Saudi Arabia, whose corporate officers are among Reagan's staunchest backers.... For these companies, billions of dollars are at stake."

Blitzer goes on to point out the the vice chairman of Bechtel during Reagan's campaign was none other than George Schultz, former secretary of the treasury under President Nixon and long-time Reagan supporter.

Another of Bechtel's vice presidents was Caspar Weinberger, who served as director of finance for Reagan when he was governor of California before going on to become secretary of Health, Education, and Welfare under President Nixon. Caspar Weinberger is currently the secretary of defense and one of the most influential foreign policy advisers in Reagan's Cabinet. Ac-

---

[11]Wolf Blitzer, *The New Republic*, July 26, 1980, p. 10.
[12]L. J. Davis reported in the July 1980 issue of *Harper's* that the Bechtel Corporation stood to gross over fifty billion dollars over the next twenty years from its projects in Saudi Arabia. Davis also reported that Fluor Construction interests in Saudi Arabia will probably top twenty billion.

cording to *The New York Times*, Reagan frequently refers to Weinberger as "my Disraeli."

The fact that the higher executive positions at Bechtel were top-heavy with powerful Republicans can hardly be seen as an accident. Bechtel's board of directors obviously gambled that Reagan would be elected, and if that came to pass, they wanted a significant voice in the formulation of his Middle East policy. It should not be forgotten that the Saudi Arabian partner in Bechtel, the counterpart to George Schultz and Caspar Weinberger, is Prince Muhammed ibn-Fahd al-Saud the son of the crown prince.[13] It is very probable that both Schultz and Weinberger were involved in the questionable negotiations that resulted in Bechtel's being awarded the multibillion-dollar contract for the construction of the new international airport in Riyadh.

The numerous connections between Reagan's closest advisers during his campaign for the presidency and the Saudi Arabian government raise very serious questions as to foreign financial interference in the American electoral process.

As Terence Smith pointed out in a postelection article in the *International Herald Tribune*,[14] the presidential and congressional elections in 1980 cost approximately five hundred fifty million dollars, almost double what was spent in 1976, despite the enactment of a post-Watergate financing law that was designed to curb election spending.

Where did this money come from? A percentage of it certainly came from public funding and legitimate corporate and individual contributions. However, there is increasing evidence that a significant portion came from foreign governments like Saudi Arabia by way of political action committees. Terence Smith concludes his article by stating that "the possibility of abuse remains great, especially with the phenomenal growth of corporate and special interest political action committees, which gave an estimated $55 million to $60 million to House and Senate candidates."

---

[13]The other principal shareholder in Saudi Arabian Bechtel is Sulieman Saleh Olayan.
[14]Terence Smith, New York Times Service, *International Herald Tribune*, November 25, 1980.

One such political action committee is the California-based Americans for an Effective Presidency (AFEP). AFEP was founded by Bob Fluor, chairman of the board of Fluor Construction. AFEP is an organization of top corporate executives and former Republican officials that raised untold millions of dollars for Reagan during his presidential campaign. During this campaign, various Saudis alleged privately that Americans for an Effective Presidency was being used as a conduit for massive illegal foreign contributions. These allegations have never been investigated.

In addition, many of Reagan's closest campaign advisers had and still have close financial ties to Saudi Arabia, and at least two of Reagan's most senior advisers were actually in the pay of politically powerful Saudis. Aside from the Schultz–Weinberger–Muhammed ibn-Fahd link, other senior Reagan advisers with large business interests in Saudi Arabia include Walter Wriston, Donald Regan, and Donald Rumsfeld.

Walter Wriston, chairman of Citicorp, was being considered for the position of secretary of the treasury but his candidacy was apparently rejected on the grounds of conflict of interest. Both Wriston and Citicorp have a particularly close relationship with the Saudi royal family. In fact, Riyadh's branches of Citibank were for a number of years the only banks in the kingdom that were not government-owned. Even after the branches of Citibank in Saudi Arabia were nationalized (it is now called the Saudi-American Bank), Citibank held forty percent of the stock and a lucrative eight-year managerial contract.[15] Citicorp(formerly First National City Bank), the second largest bank in the world, has been for the past decade intricately involved with the management of Saudi surplus oil revenues.[16]

Citicorp, along with Morgan Guarantee Trust and Chase Manhattan, has been the principal recipient of billions and billions of Saudi petrodollar investments. There has existed over the years a close personal relationship between the Saudi royal

---

[15]*Saudi Business,* February 29, 1980, reports that "Citibank's Saudi operations are its most profitable outside the United States."

[16]Michael Field, *One Hundred Million Dollars a Day,* Praeger Publisher, New York, 1976, p. 116.

family and the senior executives at Citicorp. Even after national-ization, a Citicorp senior vice president, Michael Callen, headed the financial operations of the Saudi-American Bank. Further-more, along with IBM, Citibank is alleged to be one of the many U.S. companies with political connections that is receiving large, low-interest loans from the Saudi Arabian Monetary Agency (SAMA).

Donald Regan, now secretary of the treasury, was formerly president of Merrill Lynch Pierce Fenner &. Smith Inc., Wall Street's largest investment broker. Merrill Lynch, under the lead-ership of Regan, was one of the first investment houses to court Arab oil money, opening offices in Kuwait, Dubai, and Bahrain in the early 1970s.

While there are no investment brokers per se in Saudi Arabia (investment for the payment of interest is officially forbidden by Islamic law), wealthy Saudis including senior princes use Merrill Lynch to invest millions and millions of surplus petrodollars.

Donald Rumsfeld, former three-term congressman from Illi-nois, ambassador to NATO, and secretary of defense under Presi-dent Gerald Ford, is now president of the U.S. pharmaceutical firm G.D. Searle. Less widely known is that Donald Rumsfeld is also a director of the Bendix Corporation of Southfield, Michigan. For the public record, the Bendix Corporation is a worldwide manufacturer of automotive, aerospace, electronic, industrial, energy, and forest products. Like Bechtel and Fluor, Bendix has contracts with the Saudi government that run into the billions of dollars.

Regardless of how Bendix may officially describe itself, its contracts in Saudi Arabia are almost entirely of a military na-ture. In fact, Bendix is one of the largest defense contractors in Saudi Arabia. One can only speculate on whether Donald Rumsfeld was able to put Bendix's interests out of his mind while he was serving as a senior foreign policy adviser to the Reagan campaign.

Alan Greenspan, another of Reagan's closest campaign advis-ers, has had various connections with Sulieman Saleh Olayan, a Saudi billionaire with close political ties to the royal family.

Greenspan, former chairman of President Ford's Economic Council, is currently on the board of directors of the Mobil Oil Company, one of the four American oil companies that, along with the Saudi government, comprise ARAMCO.

It was Alan Greenspan who, while advising the Reagan campaign, also chaired the nominating committee of the board of directors of Mobil Oil and in November 1980, just before the election, personally nominated Sulieman Saleh Olayan to the board of Mobil. Olayan's appointment was approved, and he became an official member of the board of Mobil Oil on December 1, 1980. In addition to being a principal partner with Prince Muhammed ibn-Fahd in Saudi Arabian Bechtel, Olayan is a close friend and adviser to Prince Sultan, the Saudi minister of defense. Among their other business ventures, Prince Sultan and Olayan both sit on the board of directors of Saudia, the Saudi Arabian national airline. While Mobil Oil's connection to Saudi Arabia is long-established, it is curious that in 1980 Mobil formed a partnership with Prince Muhammed ibn-Fahd, the son of the crown prince, in the Saudi Arabian Maritime Company. Three directors of Mobil Oil sit on the board of this company.

Why would a senior Reagan adviser nominate a Saudi with close political ties to the royal family to the board of Mobil Oil immediately before the presidential election? Was Olayan's nomination purely a business matter or was it a reward for some financial service Olayan or the Saudi government rendered to the Reagan campaign? Has Olayan been acting as a private businessman or has he, in his dealings with Greenspan, been acting as an agent for the Saudi Arabian government?

The Olayan connection to the Reagan campaign is even more fascinating when one looks at William Simon, secretary of the treasury from 1974 to 1977. Simon has had a long history of close ties to Saudi Arabia. He was one of the senior members of the Joint U.S.–Saudi Arabian Commission on Economic Cooperation (JECOR). Simon was also a staunch opponent, during the Ford administration, of anti-Arab boycott legislation.

During Reagan's 1980 campaign Simon served as chairman of an executive board of about sixty people who oversaw the entire campaign. At the same time as Simon was senior adviser to Reagan, he was also chairman of Crescent Diversified, Inc., and deputy chairman of the Olayan Investment Company. Both Crescent Diversified and Olayan Investment are owned by Sulieman Saleh Olayan. Crescent Diversified is an investment company that helps recycle billions of petrodollars.

It was Olayan's investment companies that caused controversy recently by purchasing eighteen million dollars' worth of shares in the First Chicago Corporation, the ninth largest bank holding company in the United States.

Following Reagan's election, Simon was being considered for a Cabinet-level position in the new administration. However, Simon (speaking from Riyadh, where he was "on business") stated that he did not want to be considered for any position in government. This was a 180-degree reversal from earlier press reports that claimed that Simon was actively campaigning for a Cabinet post.

Simon gave "family reasons" as the basis of his decision. However, it is widely believed in Riyadh that Simon removed himself as a candidate at the request of the Saudi royal family, who were said to believe that his confirmation hearing might expose financial connections between Saudi Arabia and Reagan's campaign for the presidency.

Curiously enough, *Who's Who* in 1980 listed William Simon as a member of the board of directors of Citicorp. On December 8, 1980, *The New York Times* stated that William Simon was a company director of United Technologies, the third largest American defense contractor, which has large business interests in Saudi Arabia. Alexander Haig was president of United Technologies until he took over as secretary of state. In addition, it has been widely reported that William Simon is a director of Bechtel.[17]

By far the most interesting Saudi connection to the Reagan campaign was William Middendorf, former secretary of the navy and U.S. ambassador to the Netherlands. Middendorf served as President-elect Reagan's chairman of the Advisory Committee on Economic Policy. At the same time, Middendorf

---

[17]Bechtel's official list of board members does not include William Simon.

was (and still is) president, chief executive officer, and a director of Financial General Bankshares of Washington, D.C.

Financial General Bankshares is a 2.2-billion-dollar bank holding company which controls banks in Washington, New York, Tennessee, and Virginia. In late 1977 and early 1978 four Arab investors and Mrs. Bert Lance, wife of the former director of the budget under President Carter, bought almost twenty percent of the outstanding stock in Financial General Bankshares.

The leader of the Arab investors was none other than Kamal Adham, brother-in-law of the late King Faisal and CIA-trained chief of the Saudi Arabian secret service. The semiofficial *Dictionary of National Biography of Saudi Arabia* (*Who's Who in Saudi Arabia*, published by Tihama, Jeddah, 1978) describes Kamal Adham as currently serving as "an advisor to the Royal Cabinet of His Majesty King Khalid and His Majesty's Special Envoy to Arab and foreign countries in many political tasks and consultations with other heads of state."

Following the Saudi takeover of Financial General Bankshares, Kamal Adham instructed Middendorf to place prominent American political figures on the payroll of Financial General. These appointments included ex-senator Stuart Symington and Clark Clifford, former U.S. secretary of defense.

Thus, one is confronted with the situation of having the senior economic adviser to the newly elected president of the United States on the payroll of a company owned and controlled by a foreign intelligence service. To further compound an already strange situation, it was William Middendorf who, during the transition period (November 4, 1980, to January 20, 1981), headed Reagan's advisory panel on the reorganization of the CIA.

Soon after Kamal Adham's takeover of Financial General Bankshares there were charges in the Egyptian press that Crown Prince Fahd had been trying to undermine President Carter's reelection campaign.

Crown Prince Fahd took these charges seriously enough to warrant a public denial on his part. On Octover 10, 1979, both *The Arab News* and the *Saudi Gazette* carried front-page denials by Fahd of any interference in the American electoral system.

Given the fact that Fahd is a regular target in the radical Arab world, it is interesting that the crown prince should choose to respond to these particular accusations. *The Arab News* quoted Fahd as saying, "How could anyone believe such nonsense? Everyone knows the American electoral system. It is hermetically sealed against interference, however strong. In addition, it must be repeated once again, the Kingdom of Saudi Arabia does not meddle in other countries' internal affairs, nor will it act through faction or pact."

On November 27, 1980, three weeks after Ronald Reagan's election, his foreign policy transition team announced the new president's five foreign policy priorities, in order of their importance. U.S. relations with Saudi Arabia ranked number two on the list. It was second only to U.S. relations with the Soviet Union.[18] For all Reagan's pro-Zionist campaign rhetoric, U.S. relationswith Israel was nowhere among his top foreign policy priorities.

Even more powerful than the vast Saudi financial reserves is the ever-present threat that the royal family will order the oil to stop flowing to the West. Since the oil embargo of 1973–74, Crown Prince Fahd and Sheikh Ahmed Zaki Yamani have reiterated on numerous occasions that oil and politics do not mix. Over and over again, Yamani has replied to the questions of European and American journalists by saying that Saudi Arabia does not see its oil reserves as a potential weapon.

When Yamani and senior princes deny that Saudi Arabia has any intention of using oil as a weapon, they are unquestionably responding to the realization that the United States might not tolerate an oil embargo and could be forced by economic consequences to respond militarily and seize the oil fields. Thus, when these men say that oil is not a weapon, they are using the word "weapon" in the sense of an oil embargo similar to the one attempted in 1973.

Most Middle East observers see the use of the oil weapon by Saudi Arabia as ultimately self-defeating. Professor Ramon Knauerhase, writing in a recent issue of *Current History*, sug-

---

[18]*Arab News, Nov. 28, 1980.*

gests that an oil embargo of the United States would spell economic ruin for the Arab world as well as for the West. Saudi Arabia, Knauerhase writes, "is integrated into the world economy and, except for very short-run advantages, her use of the oil weapon would be self-defeating. The Saudis need Western technology to develop their economy, Western markets for their exports and Western financial markets to invest their excess oil revenues."[19]

It is a mistake to view Saudi Arabia purely in economic terms. Remember that the Saudi royal family views itself as the defender of Islam and Islamic holy places. The problem of the Israeli occupation of Jerusalem is seen by many senior princes not as a political but as a religious problem. The royal family's obsession with Jerusalem cannot be exaggerated, and their statements about the Third Sanctuary cannot be interpreted as merely empty rhetoric.[20]

In the eyes of the Saudis, to compromise on Muslims' having free access to pray at the Al-Aqsa Mosque in Jerusalem would be a betrayal of Islam and a sacrilege in the eyes of God.

Sheikh Yamani has warned the United States on numerous occasions that it is not in the best interest of Saudi Arabia to keep oil production at its current high levels. The kingdom increased oil production by approximately a million barrels a day at the request of the United States following the Islamic revolution in Iran. Saudi Arabia again raised oil production in October 1980 to compensate for the oil that was not flowing from Iraq and Iran because of the Gulf war.

Saudi Arabia doesn't need the revenue from such high production levels and finds it impossible to spend it all. It does not have the "absorptive capacity" to handle billions and billions of surplus petrodollars. Thus vast amounts of Saudi surplus revenue must be funneled into the financial investment markets of Western Europe and the United States. Most often these investments are in short-term, relatively low-interest notes. In many

---

[19]Ramon Knauerhase, "Saudi Arabia: Our Conservative Muslim Ally," *Current History*, January 1980, p. 17.
[20]After Mecca and Medina, the first two Sanctuaries of Islam, Jerusalem is considered the most holy city, the Third Sanctuary.

cases the percentage of interest paid is lower than the annual rate of inflation, so that in terms of buying power the Saudis are losing money.

Saudi Arabia could cut oil production by from one to three million barrels a day without having to modify its huge development projects. The high oil-production rate reflects the demands of the industrialized world rather than the needs of the kingdom.

A significant portion of the royal family strongly favor oil production cutbacks. This group includes the more conservative and religious princes led by Prince Abdullah, second deputy prime minister and commander of the National Guard, and Prince Muhammed ("of the Twin Evils"). For Abdullah and Muhammed, oil production cutbacks represent a means to convince the United States to pressure Israel to withdraw from occupied Arab territories and to slow internal development in Saudi Arabia.

Advocates of production cutbacks are quick to point out that oil appreciates in value more rapidly in the ground than financial investments do in New York or London. In addition, both Prince Abdullah and Prince Muhammed see the kingdom traveling too fast along the road of modernization.

In October 1979 Saudi Oil Minister Yamani was reported by the Associated press as saying that the leadership of the Saudi royal family was split over the question of oil production and prices. Yamani was reported to have said that "a group of young Saudis were demanding that oil production be cut in half and that Saudi Arabia follow the lead of other OPEC nations in adopting substantial price increases."[21]

Dr. Mohammed Abdu Yamani, Saudi Arabia's minister of information, went on Radio Riyadh on October 21 and vehemently denied that Sheikh Ahmed Zaki Yamani ever made the remarks attributed to him by the Associated Press. The minister of information also denied that there was a split in the royal family over oil policy.

---

[21]*Arab Oil and Economic Review,* November 1979, p. 9.

The royal family is extremely sensitive to allegations in the foreign press of dissension in its ranks. The *Los Angeles Times* reported in May 1979 that the CIA chief in Riyadh was expelled from the kingdom for asking too many questions about the royal family. "Saudi displeasure focused on the CIA station chief because he was well known to have been making inquiries about the extent of dissension among the four brothers who dominate the royal family."[22] The four brothers are King Khalid, Crown Prince Fahd, Prince Sultan, and Prince Abdullah.

The conflict between Prince Abdullah and Crown Prince Fahd reaches its most dangerous peak when it comes to the question of succession. While Saudis almost universally expect Fahd to take over the monarchy after King Khalid's death, there is no consensus as to who will be his crown prince. As second deputy prime minister, Prince Abdullah is the logical choice. However, Saudis will point out privately that Fahd himself favors his full brother, Sultan.

With King Khalid's health a matter of daily concern, the problem of ascendency has become acute. While the royal family itself officially denies the existence of such a problem, Saudis privately speculate that Abdullah will be rejected by Fahd. Others guess that Fahd will have to appoint Abdullah as crown prince in order to get the conservative Ulema to support him as king. Still others foresee the emergence of a compromise candidate such as Prince Abdul Mohsen (currently governor of Medina) or Prince Majed (currently governor of Mecca) or even King Faisal's son, Prince Saud al-Faisal, the present foreign minister.

A few Saudis anticipate more severe problems on the death of King Khalid. A student at the University of Riyadh explained, "Underneath the glass and steel buildings, Saudi Arabia is still very much a tribal society. Our system of government is based on the structure of the Bedouin tribe. We have no machinery for the transfer of power as they do in England or the United States. Each time a king dies, the Kingdom of Saudi Arabia faces the possibility of internal disruption and civil war. There are many

---

[22]*Los Angeles Times*, May 9, 1979.

Saudis who secretly pray to God that King Khalid will outlive both Fahd and Abdullah."

This sentiment may well be shared by American and European political leaders, since the welfare and even the survival of virtually all the economies of the West depend on this extremely delicate tribal balance of power.

IV

An Arabian
Tinderbox

Here [in Saudi Arabia] we are blessed with the freedom of belief and are free to uphold and advocate it without running the risk of persecution.

—Abu Abdul Rehman ibn-Aqeel, Al Medina,
December 2, 1979

The regular Saudi army has been ripe for revolution for some time .... Members of the Saudi upper crust ... regard the kingdom primarily as a kind of money factory.... The monetary greed of the country's leading businessmen and middlemen—names like Khashoggi and Pharaon are among the most prominent—has become almost pathologically insatiable.

—Arnold Hottinger, "Does Saudi Arabia Face
Revolution?" Neue Zürcher Zeitung

16

November 1979

November 20, 1979, was the first day of Moharram in the year A.H. 1400, the beginning of the fifteenth century in the Hejira calendar. In the predawn darkness, forty-thousand Muslims responded to the muezzin's call to prayer and gathered in the enormous square surrounding the Holy Kaaba in the Great Mosque of Mecca to perform their morning devotions and herald the advent of a new Islamic century. Scattered throughout the Mosque were scores of coffins, over which the families and friends of the deceased were preparing to say the traditional and obligatory prayers for the dead.

Suddenly, groups of bearded young men, mostly in their twenties, began throwing open the coffins. Concealed within were caches of weapons and food, automatic and semiautomatic American- and Russian-made rifles, submachine guns, grenades, and enough bread and rice for the rebels to withstand a siege for at least a week.

The weapons were quickly distributed into the hands of hundreds of young men and women, who immediately sealed all forty-eight doors of the Holy Mosque, posted snipers on the roof and in the strategically located minarets, and then seized the mosque's public address system and announced to the stunned worshipers that a revolution had taken place in Saudi Arabia.

Thus began the so-called "siege of Mecca."

On the morning of November 20 I was teaching at the University of Riyadh. The first inkling I had that anything was wrong was when I was told by a student that the Special Security Forces had closed the international airport. When a colleague attempted to place an overseas telephone call to his sister in the States, the overseas operator informed him that all overseas calls were prohibited indefinitely.

My students were excitedly exchanging rumors on what was happening. Some believed that the disturbance was caused by Libyan or South Yemeni radicals. Others thought the trouble in Mecca was being caused by Iranian Shiites in the pay of Khomeini.

By afternoon my students appeared shocked that fighting was taking place within the Holy Haram in Mecca. One student, who drove me home, explained that he had just spoken to his uncle in Mecca. "There has been shooting all morning and afternoon. My uncle says there is trouble in Medina as well. You remember Abdullah Abdulatef?"—a student of mine in the same class. "He is in Mecca in the mosque."

Later that afternoon my wife brought home the news that the large American corporations in Riyadh had ordered their American employees to "keep a low profile"—exactly the same phraseology they used in the final days of the Islamic revolution in Iran. That evening our Saudi next-door neighbor dropped by to explain that the disruption in Mecca was larger than anyone was yet willing to admit. "The Holy Mosque is huge. To hold it for one hour, let alone a whole day, would take hundreds if not thousands of well-trained soldiers. If a foreign country has supplied the weapons, it will mean war."

He went on to explain, "There is a tradition in Islam—not part of the Koran, just a popular legend—that at the beginning of the fifteenth Hejira century a great Muslim leader will emerge. The rebels in Mecca are taking advantage of that prophecy." He also told us that one of the rebels had been captured in possession of an American-made rifle. "That is bad. Many old men, who don't know any better, will think the CIA is behind the attack. Don't go into the *suq*. It's not safe for Americans now."

The following day overseas phone communication was restored, although for the following two months it was closely monitored by the Special Security Forces, and on more than one occasion colleagues of mine had their conversations terminated when the subject of Mecca was brought up.

The international airport was also reopened, albeit with tripled security.

Lockheed, Bechtel, and Western Electric issued special instructions to their American staff members, and we heard on the BBC that the American embassy in Pakistan was under attack by mobs of furious Muslims who had believed the Ayatollah Khomeini's accusation that the United States was behind the seizure of the Holy Mosque in Mecca.

That evening I telephoned Tony, a British ex-RAF officer who currently works as a communications adviser to the Royal Saudi Arabian Air Force. "Jesus Christ, Bill, you probably know more than I do about what's happening in Mecca. It's big, that's for sure. The Saudis are trying to handle the whole thing themselves. All I know is that we dispatched a paratroop division to Mecca this afternoon. It looks like the royal family will try to take the mosque by force."

Don P., an American expatriate who works for Lockheed flying the big C-130 troop transport planes for the National Guard, had more information. "We can't fly into Mecca. That's what's prolonging this whole thing. Most of the pilots are American or British. Only Muslims are allowed inside Mecca. We've had to fly the National Guard to Jeddah. I've flown a thousand men there myself. From Jeddah, the troops are loaded into pilgrimage buses and taken to Mecca." I asked Don if he had heard anything about a paratroop division being sent to Mecca. "Not a word. The Saudis are playing the whole thing close to the chest. Not even consulting the American advisers."

The "siege of Mecca" was still in full swing a week later. The university had let it be known that foreign teachers should not discuss the events in Mecca with their students, which limited my sources of information to just a few trusted students. Meanwhile, the foreign press was having a heyday speculating on who the rebels might really be, what foreign support they might have received, and how stable the Saudi monarchy really was. These reports infuriated the senior princes and resulted in wholesale censorship of mail leaving the kingdom.

About a week after the beginning of the takeover, Tony called and asked if I had heard about the paratroopers. "The day after the whole thing started, the Ulema issued some kind of religious order saying that the National Guard couldn't carry weapons into the mosque.[1] So the airborne National Guard dropped a hundred unarmed paratroopers into the mosque. The snipers in the minarets picked them off like flies. Not a single one hit the ground alive. The National Guard's taking one hell of a beating."

Soon after I got off the phone with Tony, I called Don at Lockheed. He wasn't in, but I spoke with another American pilot who shares his villa. "God only knows when Don will be back. We're all on twenty-four-hour alert. I haven't seen Don in forty-eight hours. We've been flying the wounded out of Jeddah. The hospitals in Mecca, Medina, and Jeddah are overflowing."

Two days later I met Mike S. at the Riyadh Intercontinental Hotel, and we had lunch together. Mike is a senior administrator at Riyadh's largest hospital, King Faisal. He confirmed that planeloads of wounded were being flown into Riyadh. "King Faisal Hospital has been on full alert for the past five days. All leave has been canceled and the doctors are on twenty-four-hour call. We've been getting three to four planeloads a night. They only fly the wounded in at night so that the Saudis won't see how many are really being brought in. Each of the C-130s holds about a hundred litters. We must be getting between two and three hundred wounded a night. We've got stretchers in the corridors, in the lobbies, even in the johns. But the strangest thing of all is that most of the wounded, nine out of ten of them, have leg wounds."

That evening we had invited guests to dinner. Among the guests was Louise D., senior matron at the British Military Hospital in Riyadh. "Don't talk to me about leg wounds," she replied to my question. "We've had to open two additional orthopedic wards just to handle the soldiers coming in from Mecca. One of the soldiers told me that they had been ordered to retake the mosque armed only with knives."

---

[1]After the fact, we discovered that this order had never been issued. The decision to send in the troops unarmed had been made by the senior princes.

During the next few days, the conversation in Riyadh's expatriate community focused almost entirely on the attack on the American embassy in Tripoli, Libya, the ongoing battle in Mecca, and a BBC report that there was widespread rioting in the eastern oil fields of Saudi Arabia. Several of my students, whose homes were in the Eastern Province, confirmed that rioting was taking place and that the city of Qatif was surrounded with tanks and armored personnel carriers.

On the afternoon of December 8 I called the American embassy liaison office in Riyadh to see if they had any further information on either Mecca or the rioting in the oil fields. A very polite but very proper woman at the liaison office explained that they had only the information that was printed in the newspaper or broadcast on Radio Riyadh. However, she went on, the company I worked for had coordinated all necessary evacuation plans with the embassy.

"But I work for the Saudi government. For the Ministry of Education," I replied, shaken by the fact that evacuation plans had already been drawn up.

"In that case . . ." She paused. "Actually, I'm not sure what you should do. Maybe you should get out now. That's unofficial, of course."

Such were the truths, half-truths, and rumors that were eagerly passed around the expatriate communities in Saudi Arabia. In the two years that have followed the attempted seizure of the mosque in Mecca, various accounts and theories have been offered, some reasonable, others ridiculous. Perhaps the most ludicrous of these accounts is the official Saudi version.

According to the Ministry of Information, there were only three hundred "renegades," who were simply demented religious fanatics analagous to those in Jonestown, Guyana. The reason the National Guard took so long (two weeks) to dislodge the rebels was that the troops were ordered not to damage the mosque. Again, according to the official version, there was nothing political in the motives of the "renegades," and the actions of the National Guard and the Ministry of the Interior cast no doubts on the ability of the kingdom to maintain internal stability.

No one, Saudi or foreigner alike, whom I have spoken with believes this obviously fabricated account. First of all, the leadership of the insurgent forces was far from demented; fanatical, perhaps, but certainly not in the same category as Jim Jones of the People's Temple. Second, it would be a military impossibility for fewer than five hundred to one thousand relatively well rehearsed commandos to hold a structure the size of the Great Mosque. It should be remembered here that the central area surrounding the Holy Kaaba is larger than three football fields and can contain as many as three million people. In addition, the interior of the mosque has more than two thousand rooms, forty-eight separate entrances, and hundreds of windows. Third, it was obvious from the tape-recorded speeches[2] of the insurgents during the occupation of the Holy Mosque that their motives were inextricably *both* religious and political. In short, the insurgent forces did not see themselves as attacking the Holy Mosque. Instead, they saw themselves as rescuing the First Sanctuary of Islam from the sinful and degenerate hands of the royal family. In addition, there can be absolutely no doubt that the National Guard and the Ministry of the Interior thoroughly disgraced themselves. They showed themselves to be unquestionably courageous, hopelessly disorganized, and, in the final analysis, models of ineptitude and incompetence.

Due in large part to strict Saudi censorship, the reports in most foreign magazines, journals, and newspapers were equally inaccurate. Reports appeared in otherwise credible newspapers claiming that the insurgents were variously Iranian agents, communist-backed revolutionaries from South Yemen, religious madmen backed by the CIA, terrorists belonging to the radical Popular Front for the Liberation of Palestine, and, on one occasion, Syrian commandos armed and trained by the Soviet KGB. All such theories have proved to be without foundation.

The insurgents probably did not receive assistance from foreign governments. However, although the vast majority of Saudis were genuinely shocked and appalled that bloodshed

---

[2]These tapes have never been available in Saudi Arabia, for obvious reasons. However, pirate copies have been available in Kuwait and the United Arab Emirates.

had taken place within the Holy Mosque, a significant portion of the population sympathized with the ends, if not the means, of the insurgents.

The events seem to have their origin in 1973, when a young man, then twenty-nine years old, named Juhayman ibn-Seif al-Oteibi dropped out of the Islamic University in Medina. It has been reported, although the Saudi government denies that Juhayman was ever a student in Medina, that he repeatedly argued with his professors over the interpretation of *sharia* law. The following year found Juhayman involved in studying the conditions of Islam in Saudi Arabia. As a strict fundamentalist, he found the current state of Islam wanting. It was at this same time that Juhayman became associated with another young man, Muhammed ibn-Abdullah al-Qahtani. The names are important, for the al-Oteibi and al-Qahtani tribes are among the largest and most powerful in Arabia.[3] In addition, Juhayman ibn-Seif al-Oteibi was a full blood-cousin to Emir Sabah al-Sabah, the ruler of Kuwait.

The two young men apparently rented a house in Medina and began to gather a following of other fundamentalist Islamic students. In 1974 Juhayman was arrested several times. Specific charges against him were never cited, and he was never brought to trial. Juhayman came to the attention of the Security Forces in the Ministry of the Interior, and he was picked up for routine questioning. After the siege of Mecca, the Ministry of the Interior announced that in 1974 Juhayman had been arrested for trafficking in alcohol and drugs. This is unlikely, since conservative members of the Ulema, hardly men who would have sympathy for a smuggler of alcohol or drugs, intervened on Juhayman's behalf and obtained his release. Juhayman was arrested on several other occasions that year, and his supporters finally succeeded in persuading him to go into hiding.

From 1975 on, both Juhayman and Muhammed ibn-Abdullah al-Qahtani were fugitives. Their large and sympathetic families provided them with numerous "safe houses," and the pair

---

[3]The al-Qahtani family holds several important positions in the Saudi government, as do the al-Oteibis. The oil minister of the United Arab Emirates is a member of the al-Oteibi tribe.

crossed easily into Kuwait and Qatar, where their followers grew in number. In a post-mortem investigation of the seizure of the Holy Mosque, Western diplomatic sources report that Juhayman and Muhammed drew most of their political support from the Harb, Shammer, Qahtani, and Oteibi tribes, all of which had opposed the unification of Saudi Arabia under King Abdulaziz.

In addition to recruiting members for his religious-political movement between 1975 and 1979 Juhayman also wrote manifestoes and delivered harangues in local mosques.

It was during this time that he wrote "Rule, Allegiance, and Obedience," a short analysis of political rule in an Islamic country. According to this unpublished work, the Koran calls upon Muslims to choose their political leaders as those individuals best capable of defending and upholding the Islamic faith. Addressing himself to the political situation in Saudi Arabia, Juhayman wrote, "We are living today under an imposed royalty where it is not the Muslims who choose the *khalifat* (ruler) but the rulers who have imposed themselves on the ruled, and where the disapproval of the Muslim does not result in removing the monarchy."[4]

It appears that by 1979 Juhayman and his followers had completely despaired of reforming Saudi Arabia by peaceful means and had come to see revolution as their only alternative. Correspondingly, Juhayman's followers were ordered to secure weapons and participate in commando training at remote desert locations. It was at this same time that Juhayman was actively recruiting members of the National Guard,[5] and it was through his contacts in the National Guard that he received much of the American-made weaponry that was used in the Mecca takeover. The Russian-made weapons were reported to have been smuggled into the country from Iraq in egg crates. Following the seizure of the Holy Mosque, the security forces

---

[4]Juhayman ibn-Seif al-Oteibi, "Rule, Allegiance, and Obedience," as quoted in *The New York Times,* February 25, 1980, p. A10.

[5]*Fortune,* March 10, 1980, reported that Juhayman was himself a corporal in the National Guard. Official Saudi reports refute this.

became suspicious of incoming shipments of eggs, resulting in a nationwide egg shortage.

When Juhayman and his followers seized the Holy Mosque, another group of Juhayman's followers entered the Prophet's Mosque in Medina with the intention of seizing it also. There are several reports as to why the second group failed in its attempt. The most widely accepted in Saudi Arabia is that the second group, lacking the leadership of Juhayman and Muhammed al-Qahtani, lost heart before they ever entered the Prophet's Mosque. Another report, published in *The Washington Star*, claimed that the insurgents actually entered the Prophet's Mosque in Medina but found there a unit of National Guardsmen who had paused from early morning maneuvers to say their prayers. According to the same report, a few shots were exchanged (this assumes that the National Guardsmen entered the mosque armed, in violation of Islamic law), and the insurgents withdrew after perceiving that they were outnumbered.

Meanwhile, in the Great Mosque in Mecca, Juhayman ibn-Seif al-Oteibi had broadcast via the public address system one of the most misunderstood messages in Saudi history. The Saudi Arabian government claims that he announced the coming of the *mahdi* ("the expected or awaited one," a name often given to firstborn males). According to the official version, the *mahdi* was claimed by Juhayman to be a quasi-divine, vaguely messianic personage who had been sent by God to lead the Arabian people. Naturally, the strict Wahhabi Ulema could not tolerate such messianic trends and immediately branded Juhayman and his followers as *khawarig* (infidels).

In actuality, Juhayman ibn-Seif al-Oteibi did not proclaim the coming of a messiah at all. He announced that his friend and follower, Muhammed ibn-Abdullah al-Qahtani, was the new political and spiritual leader of the Arabian peninsula. According to sources who were inside the mosque at the time of the takeover, including a student in one of my classes, Juhayman defined the *mahdi* as the long-awaited one who would restore Islam from the sinful hands of the royal family. At no time did

Juhayman, himself a devoted Wahhabi Muslim, credit his friend with divine or supernatural power or authority.

Again according to the Saudi government, Juhayman held thirty-five thousand Muslims hostage, ordering them at gunpoint to pray to the *mahdi*. However, according to sources present in the Great Mosque at the time, Juhayman ordered the huge crowd of Muslims *either* to declare their loyalty to the new Islamic leadership (that is, Muhammed ibn-Abdullah al-Qahtani) or to leave the mosque in peace. At no time did Juhayman or his followers take or hold hostages, nor did they force anyone to pray at gunpoint. Most of the thirty-five thousand Muslims present left the mosque without being harmed. The twenty or so innocent bystanders who were wounded or killed in the mosque happened to be standing by a doorway which the National Guard blasted with plastic explosives in a vain attempt to retake the Mosque.

Rumors abound about the possibility that King Khalid had made plans to say his early morning prayers in the Great Mosque on the morning of the seizure and that it was he that the insurgents were after. This is possible. It is traditional for the king or his deputies to say their devotions in the Great Mosque on holy days or special occasions (such as the beginning of a new century).

A *Washington Star* report, written by Walter Taylor, states that King Khalid was expected to attend the early morning prayers but had to cancel at the last minute due to ill health and the coldness of the morning. The report speculates that had King Khalid been present, he would have been held hostage until the demands of the insurgents had been met.[6]

After the first wave of guardsmen entered the mosque and were repulsed by the insurgents, the leadership of the government troops dissolved into anarchy. It appears that no one commanded the situation. The governor of Mecca, Prince Fawaz; the director of public security, General Fayez al-Awfi; the commander of the Royal Saudi Air Force, General Assad Abdulaziz al-Zuhair; and the commander of the Special Security Forces,

---

[6]Walter Taylor, *The Washington Star*.

General Muhammed ibn-Hilal were all issuing orders to their respective men in absolute ignorance of what the others were doing.

Saud al-Faisal took command. The daily casualty rate in the government forces fell dramatically. The foreign minister must have been aware that the only way to dislodge the insurgents without destroying the mosque itself, was to starve them out. This was essentially what he did. He waited until the insurgents were weak from hunger and lack of sleep and then had his men attack.

It took three days of round-the-clock fighting to get the insurgents who had fled to the basement of the mosque to surrender; and then it was only after the government forces used tear gas and flooded the basement with water to drown the remaining rebels.

Of the insurgents, less than seventy-five were taken alive. Muhammed ibn-Abdullah al-Qahtani was killed by the government forces. Juhayman ibn-Seif al-Oteibi was captured, and despite Saudi government claims that he gave a full confession, sources close to the royal family state that he refused to answer any questions and that his only response to interrogation was prayer. Of the seventy-five insurgents captured, twelve were women and children who were taken to undisclosed locations for what the Ministry of Information referred to as "reeducation." The remaining sixty-three men, including Juhayman, were given swift trials and sentenced to death. The group was divided up and sent to various cities throughout the kingdom. On January 9, 1980, at 4:45 a.m., just after the dawn prayer, all sixty-three men were publicly beheaded.

The motivation behind the seizure of the mosque is found in Juhayman ibn-Seif al-Oteibi's writings and the tapes made of his speeches during the occupation. His writings indicate that he received no aid from other governments. He was vehemently anticommunist, anti-Jewish and anti-Christian. In addition, his writings contain passages which refer to the Shiites as "outlaws" of Islam, so it is hardly likely that he sought or received assistance from Khomeini. From the tape recordings made of his speeches inside the Holy Mosque, we learn that Juhayman believed that the royal family had betrayed Islamic ideals, were mired in financial corruption, and had entirely abused the trust of the Arabian people. In addition, Juhayman accused the Ulema of having "sold out" to the West. Curiously, this is almost exactly the same charge that Libya's Colonel Qaddafi made during the 1980 hajj. In fact, it was Qaddafi's accusations against Saudi Arabia and his incitement of the pilgrims in Mecca to violence that caused the Saudi government to sever diplomatic relations with Libya. The accusations against the Saudi royal family made by Juhayman and Qaddafi were almost identical.

17

Everything to Lose

There is a saying that when a person deliberately puts all his eggs in one basket, he had better watch that basket carefully. In Saudi Arabia, Allah put all the eggs in one basket, and the royal family is desperately trying to watch it.

Petroleum is, of course, what the royal family is guarding. Although Saudi Arabia is attempting to exploit its other mineral deposits, petroleum will be the lifeblood of the kingdom for the foreseeable future. It is no longer possible for Saudi Arabia to retreat into the past, to return to the days before television, automobiles, and frozen food. The Saudis are entirely dependent on the continued flow of oil to the West. They are also dependent on political stability within the kingdom allowing the oil to flow. Political stability is, without a doubt, the most important ingredient in the lifestyle of the average Saudi.

Does the present regime in Saudi Arabia enjoy popular support? From my observations, it does not. The royal family is not hated or despised, as was the late shah of Iran. But at the moment, the average Saudi is too busy chasing after what he sees as his share of the oil boom to be concerned with politics.

This apparent apathy is not indifference. The Saudi, by training and nature, is a political animal. Any foreigner who has ever negotiated a contract with Saudis will tell you that centuries of Bedouin cunning are employed at every step of the bargaining. The apathy is simply a result of official intimidation. Saudi Arabians are forbidden to criticize their rulers. Those who do are arrested and jailed.

Regardless of what question I put to my students at the University of Riyadh, their response was almost always, "We like the royal family." It was only after knowing some of them for months that they dared to confide in me their unhappiness with their rulers. The House al-Saud is tolerated by the vast majority of the population because no alternative government is available.

One of my students summed up the status of the royal family by way of a rhetorical question: "What truly popular regime needs to imprison those who criticize its leadership?"

The senior princes of the House al-Saud seem to perceive themselves as unpopular. The fact that no freedom of political expression is tolerated suggests that the senior princes imagine themselves to be potential targets. Everything published in the kingdom, written for publication within the kingdom, or published elsewhere and imported into Saudi Arabia must be approved and censored by the Ministry of Information. The kingdom's newspapers, magazines, and television and radio stations serve little purpose other than as publicity agents for the senior princes.

A vastly more significant indication that the Royal Family perceives itself as an unpopular regime is the ever-increasing technical and manpower strength of the Saudi Arabian National Guard (SANG). The sole function of SANG is to protect the House al-Saud from being overthrown. Exact figures on the strength of SANG are classified, and are therefore very hard to come by. However, responsible estimates place the troop strength of SANG at somewhere between 50,000 and 100,000 men. It is hard to imagine a family developing a bodyguard army of this size if it didn't feel profoundly threatened.

More enlightening still are the enormous amounts of money being funneled into this enormous bodyguard army. Billions of dollars are being spent annually for equipment, training, and construction of barracks. SANG is trained exclusively by Americans, under an odd Pentagon–C.I.A. umbrella arrangement. In 1972, the Pentagon, in an attempt to cut costs, initiated a policy whereby it would act as a general contractor and subcontract out the training of foreign armies in the Middle East to private mercenary companies. In the summer of 1973, a 19-man U.S. military team of advisors went to Saudi Arabia to assess the needs of SANG. After lengthy negotiations with the Saudis, the Pentagon invited bids from American companies.

In the mid-1970s, the U.S. Army Corps of Engineers was awarded a sixty-two-million dollar job constructing barracks for the Saudi Arabian National Guard (SANG), and the Vinnell Corporation of Alhambra, California, was given a 76.9-million-dollar contract for troop training.[1] According to one report, one thousand ex-Special Forces officers under the command of one-eyed Colonel James D. Holland were dispatched to Saudi Arabia.[2] However, the Pentagon, in a very strange arrangement, remains the general contractor and maintains high-ranking officers in Saudi Arabia to oversee Vinnell's training. At present the highest ranking Pentagon officer permanently assigned to SANG is Brigadier General Gerald T. Bartlett, who is project manager of SANG modernization.

There have been allegations of corruption and conflict of interest involving Vinnell's presence in Saudi Arabia. Many reports suggest that Vinnell may in fact be a CIA cover—a way for the United States to keep a military presence in Saudi Arabia without attracting attention.

In *Super Wealth: The Secret Lives of the Oil Sheikhs*,[3] Linda Blandford states that Ghassam Shaker negotiated the Vinnell deal for the Saudis and received a four-and-a-half-million-dollar "commission" for his trouble. Blandford does not tell us who supposedly paid this alleged "kickback," but as the primary contractor, it would have been the Pentagon's direct responsibility.

Despite the Pentagon and Vinnell, SANG remains essentially a Bedouin army, ill-organized and unable to protect either the royal family or the oil fields in the east. The level of technical expertise is low, as is the general morale within the ranks. Fred Halliday reports that the absent-without-leave rate in SANG is

[1]*Time*, February 24, 1975.
[2]*Newsweek*, February 24, 1975.
[3]William Morrow & Co., New York, 1977.

so high that only seventeen of the National Guard's forty units are functioning.[4]

The AWOL rates in SANG reflect the bitterness on the part of the average soldier over both length of service and salary. The salary received by a National Guardsman is a fraction of what he could earn as a civilian. A private first class in the National Guard is paid approximately a thousand dollars a month. An illiterate taxi driver in Riyadh, on the other hand, can earn three times that. A new recruit joins the National Guard for life; there is no reenlistment, and no resignation is permitted.

A former American employee of Vinnell reports that the essential character of the Bedouin is antithetical to the regimentation demanded by a modern military force. "Time was the worst problem we encountered. We would order a training maneuver at 0800 hours, and the Bedouins would wander along at noon. They couldn't understand why we were in a hurry. Punishments didn't solve the problem either. You just can't rip out a thousand-year-old heritage in one generation."

The same ex-Vinnell officer described a desert training exercise. "We were going to do four days of desert training south of Riyadh. When the SANG trucks arrived at the site in the desert, we found that fifty Yemenis were already there. The Yemenis had pitched the tents, set up the cot beds, and dug the latrines. A senior officer in SANG then informed us that the desert exercise was being catered by a leading hotel in Riyadh. Four hours later, six trucks rolled in, carrying hot meals for the men."

A Syrian lieutenant colonel, acting as an adviser to the National Guard, also experienced the same kind of training problems. For several years he commanded small-arms training at the National Guard Academy in Riyadh. In order for a cadet to graduate from the academy, he had to be able to hit the target twenty times in twenty-five tries. After the Syrian lieutenant colonel had witnessed a particularly poor round of firing, he informed the group of cadets that their accuracy would have to

---

[4]Fred Halliday, "The Shifting Sands Beneath the House of Saud," *The Progressive*, March 1980, p. 40.

improve. "Why?" one of the cadets replied. "Do we get a bonus if we hit the target more often?"

With the National Guard unable to assure the continuation of the present regime in power, the question is often asked, Will Saudi Arabia go the way of Iran? Probably not. Saudi Arabia and Iran are quite different.

Saudi Arabia is a nation of five to six million people with oil revenues of more than ninety billion dollars a year. Iran under the shah had a population of thirty-five million and oil revenues which ran about twenty billion dollars annually. While, like Iran, the distribution of wealth in Saudi Arabia is unequal, it is impossible for even the poorest person to escape the benefits of modernization. Some of the oil wealth does filter down even to the bottom rungs of the Saudi economic ladder.

Saudi Arabia is overwhelmingly a Sunni Muslim country (ninety percent of the population is Sunni). Iran, on the other hand, is predominantly Shiite. In the tradition and practice of Sunni Islam, the religious leadership does not play the kind of political role that the ayatollahs and mullahs have adopted in Iran. In fact, the senior princes, with the possible exceptions of Muhammed ibn-Abdulaziz and Abdullah ibn-Abdulaziz, recognize the Ulema as a force of extreme political conservatism and have attempted to keep the Ulema as far removed from politics as possible.

Like Iran under the shah, the House al-Saud has a large secret police force which gathers information on dissidents. Torture is also employed in Saudi Arabia as an interrogation technique. However, in Saudi Arabia there is no overt evidence of the kind of widespread terrorizing of the population that was practiced under SAVAK, the gestapo of the late shah.

There now exists in Saudi Arabia an educated middle class that has become separated from the Bedouin heritage of the desert, is growing in numbers, and is rapidly becoming dissatisfied with the paternalism and corruption which have been the trademarks of the House al-Saud in recent years.

Ibrahim is a classic example of this cultural phenomenon. He spent three years living in California attending U.C.L.A. as an undergraduate student in sociology before returning to the University of Riyadh to finish his degree.

Soon after his return, he suffered a severe depression which lasted several months. His academic work became haphazard, and his relationships with others disintegrated.

Later, when he and I became friends, Ibrahim described to me what he had felt. "From the moment I landed at the Riyadh airport, I knew I couldn't fit in. This country is artificially backward. The royal family has replaced Bedouin tents with steel and glass, but the backwardness is the same. Islam is not a straitjacket, it is a glorious, freedom-giving religion. But Islam is not a religion in Saudi Arabia. It is the weapon used by the royal family to keep itself in power."

Culturally disoriented university students are only one of the potentially disruptive forces at work in the kingdom. Saudi Arabia has so many profound internal sources of dissent that a secret CIA report warned that the al-Saud regime's survival could not be guaranteed beyond 1982.[5] It is crucial for the oil-dependent West to examine some of the possible sources of internal subversion.

Foreign Workers

Estimates vary, but between one quarter and one third of the population of Saudi Arabia is comprised of foreign workers. These foreign workers range from unskilled Yemeni ditch diggers to highly trained Western computer analysts. Their languages, cultures, values, standards of living, and appearances vary. However, all foreign workers in Saudi Arabia share the fact that they have been brought to the kingdom to do jobs that native Saudis either will not or cannot perform for themselves.

While exact figures are not available, various estimates place the number of foreigners working in Saudi Arabia at 350,000 Egyptians, 500,000 to 700,000 Yemenis, 120,000 Indians and Pakistanis, and at least 600,000 Palestinians.[6] In addition, there are at least 100,000 South Koreans; 75,000 Indonesians, Thais,

---

[5]*Newsweek*, March 3, 1980.
[6]*The Washington Star*, August 21, 1980.

and Filipinos; 50,000 Lebanese, Jordanians, Iraqis, Syrians, and Iranians; and 30,000 Europeans, Canadians, and Americans. There are also significant numbers of Sudanese, Eritreans, and Tunisians.

The fact of the matter is that the entire Saudi development program for the foreseeable future is dependent on foreign labor. This is because of three interrelated and serious problems. Primary among them is the small population of the kingdom in comparison with its grandiose development plans. Even if the entire population of the kingdom were ready and willing to work, Saudi Arabia would still have to import a large number of foreigners.

However, most Saudis are not ready or willing to work. Women are forbidden by law from working except as teachers or nurses. Saudi males consider manual labor beneath them.

There is almost no incentive for young Saudi males to become skilled technologists. Fearing an embittered and unemployed intelligentsia, the Saudi government has guaranteed employment to all university graduates. With lucrative, undemanding employment assured them, few students are motivated to acquire technological skills. Thus the military, social services, telephone network, schools, universities, and industries are managed and operated almost exclusively by skilled expatriate labor.

In addition, the sudden prosperity of the average Saudi has eroded his interest in work. The vast majority of secondary school and university graduates see their future as business agents. A Saudi business agent is nothing more than the individual who secures the necessary visas for a foreign company to do business in the kingdom and then sits back and collects his percentage of the profits. The economic problem the kingdom faces is that the money generated from business commissions is essentially unearned and unproductive income. It does not produce other employment, nor does it serve to stabilize the kingdom's economy.

The Saudi technocrats who head the nation's development program are aware of the problem. They know that the younger generation has embraced wealth as the "gateway to Utopia."

Dr. Ghazi al-Gosaibi, Minister of Industry and Electricity, is quite justifiably frightened by what he sees as the decline of the work initiative in Saudi Arabia. In a recent speech, he announced, "Past civilizations did not wither away for lack of material resources but because their morals had decayed from within. They collapsed regardless of their stockpiled heaps of gold."[7]

As serious as the lack of work initiative among Saudis is the disruptive effect that the foreign workers have on this once homogeneous society. Though the vast majority of foreign workers are Muslim, their practice of Islam is quite different from the strict Wahhabi doctrine of the Arabian desert. Lebanese women appear in public only partially veiled, Palestinian teachers debate the merits of socialism, and Egyptians scorn the Saudi puritanism. Even more disruptive are the European and American expatriate workers, whose dress, manners, and values are now on constant display in all Saudi urban centers.

The government attempts to limit the impact of the foreign worker by mandating "enclave development." It tries to keep foreign workers, particularly the Western non-Muslims, separate from the native Saudis. Western expatriates, for the most part, are compelled to live in specially constructed compounds which are off-limits to Saudi nationals. This enclave development has been notably unsuccessful in insulating the Saudi from the influence of the foreign worker.

The foreign worker is also a potential source of political subversion in and of himself. Most of the non-Western foreign workers in Saudi Arabia live in truly appalling conditions, are grossly exploited by their Saudi employers, and are ripe for revolt.

It is not uncommon for teams of Indian and Pakistani manual laborers to be housed in the cellar of the building they are constructing. Nor is it uncommon for foreign laborers to be brought into the kingdom on the basis of indentured servitude. In others words, the Saudi employer, who is the only person capable of securing entrance and exit visas for the foreign worker,

---

[7]Dr. Ghazi al-Gosaibi, "The Illusions of the Road to Development," unpublished speech.

can and often does make it impossible for an expatriate to terminate his contract.[8]

By law, no labor organizations or unions are permitted in Saudi Arabia. There is a Saudi labor board which is supposed to regulate the working conditions of foreign workers. However, this board has no power of enforcement and is often ignored.

There have been several extralegal attempts within the kingdom to set up labor organizations to represent foreign workers. ARAMCO has witnessed several attempts on the part of its foreign employees to organize. Each attempt has been brutally suppressed by the Special Security Forces. Reports say that the leaders of the labor organization in ARAMCO were summarily executed and hundreds of their followers deported.

In 1980 rioting broke out in Jubail, the industrial city north of Dhahran. According to sources in Jubail, the twenty thousand or so Korean workers located there made an attempt to express grievances over the quality of food served in their mess hall. The leaders of the unrest were deported, so the rest of the workers rioted.

More recently, the Saudi Arabian Public Transportation Company (SAPTCO) has experienced wide-ranging labor problems. SAPTCO is a semiprivate company that has the monopoly on the kingdom's bus routes. It employs large numbers of Southeast Asians as conductors and drivers.

In 1979 a Thai bus driver hit and killed a young Saudi child who had run into the street in front of the bus. The child turned out to be the son of a prince. The Thai driver was arrested and taken to prison to face homicide charges. Two days later, the driver's body was returned to SAPTCO with the explanation that, fearing decapitation, the bus driver had committed suicide in prison. However, it soon became evident to his coworkers that no suicide had taken place: the driver's corpse was bruised and swollen virtually beyond recognition.

---

[8]Situations like this are not uncommon. An American teacher at the University of Riyadh requested that his resignation be accepted in February 1980. The University administration refused to secure him an exit visa unless he paid the equivalent of $4,500. It is not known who was to receive this money, but he did not pay it. Thus, because of economic pressure, the American teacher was kept against his will in Saudi Arabia.

The Southeast Asian employees at SAPTCO immediately stopped work in protest. The next day seventy-seven Southeast Asians were arrested for the work stoppage, taken to prison, flogged, and then deported.

The senior princes of the royal family do not underestimate the threat presented by the large number of foreign workers in the kingdom. In January 1980 Prince Naif, minister of the interior, signed a 730-million-riyal (221-million-dollar) contract with William Hoover, chairman of Computer Science Corporation, to buy and install a comprehensive information-gathering system at four locations in the kingdom. The computers, programmed and operated by American experts, will be used by the Saudi Special Security Forces to gather information on foreign workers.

Despite official denials to the contrary, a secret agreement was signed between the Republic of South Korea and senior al-Saud princes on the status of Korean workers in Saudi Arabia. The senior princes agreed to award several enormous construction projects to Korean companies in return for assurances that the Korean workers would serve, in times of emergency, as a mercenary army in defense of the royal family. The Korean construction companies coordinate their "civil defense" responsibilities through the offices of Vinnell, the American company responsible for the training of the Saudi National Guard.

While there is little doubt that the numbers and working conditions of foreigners in Saudi Arabia will continue to threaten the internal security of the kingdom, it is very doubtful that these foreign workers will bring down the monarchy.

The Shiite Minority

Unlike the transient foreign workers, who can always be deported, the native Shiite population in Saudi Arabia poses a constant and continuing threat to the al-Saud regime. The Shiites (or Shiah) are a group of Muslims who split from the rest of Islam by holding that Ali (son-in-law of the Prophet Muhammed) and his successors are divinely ordained caliphs. Shiites, unlike the Sunnis, also accept the notion of sainthood in Islam. Chief among the Shiite saints is Husayn, the second son of Ali and Fatima, whom they venerate as a martyr.

There are at least three hundred thousand Shiites in Saudi Arabia. Some estimates put the figure as high as a million. They live almost exclusively in enclaves in the eastern province of El Hasa.

On the surface, little separates the Shiite minority from the Sunni majority. They share the same holy book (the Koran), they celebrate the same religious holidays, and, at least in Saudi Arabia, they speak the same language. However, in practice, the gulf between the Sunni and Shiite is enormous.

Since King Abdulaziz seized El Hasa in 1913, strict Wahhabi (Sunni) Islam has been the law of the land in the east. Shiite literature is considered heretical and is banned by law. Schools refuse to teach Shiite history, and the government refuses to allocate money for the repair, maintenance, or construction of Shiite mosques.

The Shiite population is openly scorned by the Sunni majority. The Shiites in the east are distinctly less socially mobile than their Sunni counterparts. Oil revenue finds its way slowly, if at all, into the prominent Shiite cities. While the rest of the kingdom is witnessing a boom in the construction of schools, universities, hospitals, and roads, the Shiite settlements (most notably Qatif and Seihat) remain dusty, undeveloped poverty centers.

In addition to the profound difference in per capita income between the Sunni majority and the Shiite minority, there also exist numerous government regulations which infuriate the Shiite communities in the east. Shiites are barred from working in the government other than at the lowest clerical levels. Shiite women are barred from teaching. The Saudi military, particularly the National Guard, excludes all Shiites from service.

There also exists a less official form of discrimination against the Shiites. *The New York Times*, in an article on the Shiite minority in Saudi Arabia, quotes a young man from Qatif as saying, "In Sunni eyes, there are Sunnis; below them are the Christians, and below the Christians are the Jews. We (Shiites) are below the

Jews."[9] There is virtually no intermarriage between the Sunni and Shiite populations, and inter-sect business ventures are the exception rather than the rule.

The official and unofficial discrimination against the Shiite population in Saudi Arabia has led to violence. This violence is of great concern to the royal family due to the close proximity of the Shiite settlements to the oil fields and the large number of Shiites employed by ARAMCO.

An official visit to the eastern oil fields by King Saud in 1953 prompted an estimated thirteen thousand oil field workers—the majority Shiite—to demonstrate against their second-class treatment. The demonstration led to a strike of oil field workers, and for about three weeks the production of oil was brought to a complete halt. According to Fred Halliday,[10] Saudi troops were sent into the oil fields, and hundreds of Shiites may have been killed. While the strike did prompt ARAMCO to make some reforms in salaries and working conditions, the royal family remained rigidly opposed to the creation of trade unions.

In 1970, there were further disturbances in the oil fields. These disturbances continued and increased during the following two years, and finally came to a head in 1972. Again large numbers of National Guardsmen were sent in, and the city of Oatif was sealed off for more than six weeks. Some reports claim that thousands of Shiites were arrested, and hundreds killed.

In 1978, there was another outbreak of violence in the predominantly Shiite oil fields of Al-Hasa. During a demonstration protesting working conditions, two American ARAMCO employees were burned alive in the car they were riding in. This action in Saudi Arabia set off demonstrations and riots in the Shiite community of Bahrain, an island only twenty miles off the Saudi Arabian coast.

While the traditional frustration of the Shiite minority in Saudi Arabia has been generated from religious and economic persecution, the attempts on the part of Iran's militant religious

[9]John S. Rossant, "Saudi Shiites Say They Receive Second-Class Treatment," *The New York Times*, January 3, 1980, p. A2.
[10]Fred Halliday, *Arabia Without Sultans*, Penguin, London, 1975, pp. 72–78.

leaders to export their revolution has given the Shiite problem in Al-Hasa a distinctly political aspect. In the eyes of the majority of Sunnis, not only are the Shiites heretics, but also a potential fifth column for Iranian expansionism.

The tension between the Sunni and Shiite communities in Saudi Arabia seems destined to intensify especially in light of the conflict between Iraq and Iran. Undoubtedly there will be more outbreaks of violence, and further religious and political repression. While it is unlikely that the Shiite population by itself could manage to overthrow the Royal Family, they could quite easily sabotage the oil fields and cause politically significant disruptions in the flow of vital crude oil.

Tribal Discord

Despite rhetoric to the contrary, the primary loyalty of the average Saudi is first to his family and then to his tribe. Tribal loyalty is the product of thousands of years of Bedouin heritage and cannot be wiped out by a mere two generations of Western gadgetry.

The entire structure of Saudi society is formed around time-honored tribal lines. A man's name is an immediate indication not only of his tribe and his economic and social class but also his relationship to other tribe members and his rank within the tribe. In essence, the social stratification of Saudi Arabia follows historic tribal prejudices.

The so-called "noble" tribes, the Bedouin warriors of the central Nejd, have risen economically and socially to a level just below the aristocracy (the al-Sauds, the al-Sudeiris, and the al-Jiluwis). In this economic class are the families of the "merchant princes" such as al-Rajhi and al-Kaki (bankers and financiers) and al-Gosaibi, Khashoggi, Alireza, and Pharaon (investment entrepreneurs).

Beneath the upper crust of the superwealthy is a middle class composed primarily of the so-called "ignoble" tribes, those Arabs who, prior to the oil boom, were village dwellers. The oil prosperity has made social mobility a reality for this almost exclusively urban-centered group. It is within this emerging middle class that one sees the influence of Western materialism and consumerism.

However, a substantial portion of the Saudi population is still nomadic. Somewhere between ten and thirty percent of the population of Saudi Arabia still lives today as it did a thousand years ago. This is the invisible poverty behind the development façade. The nomadic Bedouins have resisted every offer by the government to resettle in urban centers. They have resisted public education, modern health facilities, low-income housing projects, and welfare payments, choosing instead to herd and graze their livestock in the desert as their ancestors did.

The nomadic Bedouins in Saudi Arabia still live exclusively by tribal law and traditions. While they are unquestionably aware that a modern state exists, they perceive it as existing solely in the urban centers. For them, the desert is as it has always been—untouched by governmental bureaucracy or complicated legal systems. It is common knowledge that the desert Bedouins of the Arabian peninsula have no nationality in the legal sense of the word. They carry no passports, recognize no national borders, and bow to no authority higher than God and and the sheikh of their tribe.

The nomadic Bedouins are also a constant source of annoyance to the government. Many of the tribes continue to feud among themselves as they have done for hundreds of years. If this intertribal warfare took place solely in the remote desert regions, the House al-Saud might be able to ignore it. But tribal disputes spill out of the desert and into urban centers. The major traffic arteries in the northwest of the kingdom, including the all-important Tabuk-Amman highway, had to be closed for several weeks in 1979 because of tribal warfare.

King Abdulaziz attempted to settle the Bedouins in Ikhwan encampments. The present royal family has continued the idea by creating military cities such as Tabuk, King Khalid City, and Khamis-Mushayt.[11]. These fortified cities serve the dual pur-

---

[11]All three military cities are strategically located. Tabuk is near the Jordanian border, King Khalid City is near the Iraqi border, and Khamis-Mushayt is close to the border of the Yemen Arab Republic.

poses of protecting the borders of the kingdom and preventing intertribal warefare from disrupting commerce.

Although most Bedouin hostility is directed at other Bedouin tribes and not at the royal family, there is always the possibility that a charismatic leader might unite the Bedouin tribes against the monarchy, just as King Abdulaziz did against the sherif of Mecca. It has also been widely reported that King Saud, in an unsuccessful attempt to prevent his own deposition as monarch, tried to rally the military support of the Bedouins against Crown Prince Faisal.

The royal family has attempted to win the loyalty of, or ator at least neutralize, the nomadic Bedouin tribes through the National Guard. SANG is composed exclusively of men hand-picked from the "noble" tribes. It is a Bedouin army in whose ranks one finds representatives of the largest and most powerful tribal families on the peninsula. While the ranks of SANG owe their allegiance to the person of its commander, Prince Abdullah, its tribal composition hardly insures the loyalty of the nomadic tribes to the House al-Saud.

In fact, exactly the opposite could be the case. It is one thing for the National Guard to open fire on a demonstration of Shiites in the Eastern Province, but it is quite another for them to be ordered to attack members of their own tribes. In such a situation, it would be difficult to predict how the National Guard would act. Thus, given a conflict between family and monarch, the National Guard itself might become a serious threat to the royal family.

Radical Students

University students in Saudi Arabia appear at first glance to be apolitical. Their interests seem to be soccer, fast cars, and the ever-pressing quest for the accumulation of material wealth. However, like many things in Arabia, appearances are deceptive.

Students are reluctant to criticize the ruling regime. When they do, they do so only among trusted friends. Those who have traveled abroad seem slightly less reluctant to express political opinions, but every student knows that the universities are closely monitored by the Special Security Forces. The grievances expressed by students fall into three distinct categories: ideological, generational, and informational. The ideological grievances are related to the inequality in the distribution of wealth. The poverty factor in a country as wealthy as Saudi Arabia is incongruous to the students. They perceive the poverty to be a product of the corrupt business dealings of the royal family. While this is obviously oversimplistic, a significant number of students are outraged by the disparity between the superrich and the very poor.

This sense of social justice is ideological, but it does not have roots in either socialism or Marxism. For the most part, students are ignorant of and hostile to communist ideology, which they believe is the enemy of Islam. The foundation beneath their outrage is Islam itself, which lauds egalitarianism and social justice and scorns avarice and materialism.

Women students who have traveled or studied outside the kingdom frequently express generational grievances. In their minds, the kingdom has been too slow to adopt modern values and manners. Often the word "modern" is used synonymously with "Western." These students also blame the royal family for keeping the kingdom artificially backward. They see the traditional *majlis* system as hopelessly inadequate for the complex administrative needs of a modern state.

A significant portion of the Saudi university population resents the government's control of the flow of information. Few would like to see the kingdom importing Western pornography or other material deeply offensive to Islam, but many would welcome an easing of censorship.

The students are frustrated by libraries that refuse to loan certain books, refuse to stock certain magazines and periodicals, and act as though their job was to prevent rather than purvey information. Students are aware that pages have been cut out of their university texts and that all film and tape destined for classroom use must undergo a screening procedure.

Censorship in Saudi Arabia is not simply an attempt on the part of the ruling regime to stifle critics. As it is practiced in the kingdom, its justification is rooted in Islamic theology. It has been said that everything that is not forbidden in Saudi Arabia is obligatory. While an exaggeration, this comment does contain a kernel of truth. There does seem to exist a gulf between what is *haram* (taboo) and what is obligatory.

The notion that the individual can face a moral choice and express his or her freedom to choose "the good" is nonexistent in Wahhabi Islam. The decisions have all been made. The moral challenge for the Wahhabi Muslim is to obey the complicated behavioral regulations that are imposed upon the individual. In other words, the Wahhabi Muslim is not asked to make moral decisions per se. The moral structure has already been defined, and the duty of the Saudi citizen is simply to adhere to it.

The denial of the individual moral decision-making process results in the development of a "conscience" quite different from its Judeo-Christian counterpart. Since moral restraint in Wahhabiism is almost entirely external to the individual, the concept of the conscience as an internal battleground between the forces of good and evil is virtually unknown. Conscience in Wahhabi Islam becomes synonymous with public reputation, the record not of moral decision making but of how successfully external, social forces have been in restraining the individual.

Among the younger generation of Saudi university students, the austere dialectic between taboo and obligation is in the process of breaking down. These students are not demanding the right to question the veracity of Islam. They are, however, questioning the social and political regulations that the royal family has imposed upon them in the name of Islam. Many students understand that the enforced intellectual isolation of the kingdom hinders this questioning process. In some respects it is ironic that the Koran itself is permitted in Saudi Arabia, since it is for the most part the students of the Koran who are, for one reason or another, most dissatisfied with the present political regime.

One of my students summed it up concisely: "We are told by the government that we are not developed enough as a people to participate in governing the kingdom. We are told that we are backward people. We have been kept backward by the royal family. But what the princes do not understand is that we don't need foreign newspapers and magazines to tell us how oppressed we really are. The only thing we really need is the Koran."

During my second semester teaching at the University of Riyadh, I had an older student who attended classes for about a month and did quite well on the examinations. After one month, he stopped coming to class and failed to appear for the mid-term exam. When I asked the other students if they knew why he had stopped coming to class, they all claimed not to know him. However, privately two students came to me and explained that the student in question was an undercover security policeman from the Ministry of the Interior. Why, I asked, had he stopped coming to class? The students replied that the class began too early in the morning. Apparently, the security policeman received his salary whether he passed the course or not.

An indication that the senior princes look upon the students as a potential source of unrest is that after the seizure of the Holy Mosque in Mecca, construction on the University of Riyadh campus at Diriyah was halted.

An official at the Ministry of Planning explained that originally the campus was going to house twenty thousand students, both Saudi and foreign. However, following the rebellion in Mecca, gathering so many students in one place seemed too great a security risk.

Of the potentially disruptive forces, the one most likely to draw popular support from the student population is a movement to return to a stricter, more puritanical interpretation of Islam.

Religious Fanaticism

It has become common to read that a fundamentalist Islamic revolution such as the one spearheaded by Khomeini in Iran could not possibly take place in Saudi Arabia. This optimistic conclusion, put forth by various American news analysts, is predicated on the fact that Saudi Arabia already practices the strictest and most puritanical form of Islam of any country in the world, including postrevolution Iran. The arguments follow that either reactionary Muslims in Saudi Arabia already have what they desire and therefore have no grounds to complain or that the vast majority of the Saudi population would not tolerate any further religious repression.

Unfortunately, these arguments are fallacious.

One can only perceive that Saudi Arabia practices the strictest form of Islam by way of a comparison with other Islamic countries. This may be an interesting exercise for the news analysts, but is certainly not something that most Saudis can do. The majority of the population of this closed society have not traveled outside its borders. The majority are also still illiterate.

Many Saudis see the country drifting away from the true Islamic path. They see the proliferation of luxury shops, expensive automobiles, and video machines as clear evidence that Islam has degenerated and is in desperate need of fundamentalist reform.

Ironically, the only enthusiasm that is officially tolerated in the kingdom is religious, and it is this religious fanaticism that presents one of the most serious threats to the ruling regime.

The most profound charge leveled against the House al-Saud by religious radicals is that the House al-Saud has no religious legitimacy as a ruling body. In Islam, hereditary power is explicitly forbidden. In fact, some Islamic scholars interpret the Koran as calling for democratically held elections.

Hammudah Abdalati writes that "after the people make their choice through election or selection of their ruler, every citizen is enjoined to supervise, with his means, the conduct of the administration and question its handling of public affairs, whenever he sees anything wrong with it. If the administration betrays the trust of God and the public, it has no right to continue in office. It must be ousted and replaced by another, and it is the responsibility of every citizen to see that this is done in the public interest. The question of hereditary power or lifetime government is therefore inapplicable to an Islamic State."[12]

---

[12]Hammudah Abdalati, *Islam in Focus*, The Holy Koran Publishing House, Damascus, 1977, p. 133.

This interpretation of the Koran is at substantial variance with the political reality of modern Saudi Arabia. Not only are there no elections, but the individual is not permitted to question or criticize the royal family's administration of the affairs of state. It was exactly this charge that Juhayman al-Oteibi, the leader of the insurgents during the seizure of the Holy Mosque in Mecca, leveled at the royal family.

According to the tapes of his speeches during the occupation of the mosque, he is quoted as calling the House al-Saud a "corruption of Islam." He went on to argue that the *shura* principle in the Koran dictates consultation with the people in the affairs of state. In addition to this basic charge, Juhayman spoke for many Saudis when he announced that the royal family had forfeited its right to rule through its corruption and decadence.

It is exactly these charges that most worry the senior princes. These are accusations that the majority of Saudis can understand, if not accept. Thus, we have the royal family furious over a film like *Death of a Princess* not so much because the film attacks Islam (which it doesn't) or that it presents a poor image of Saudi Arabia (which it does) but because the film graphically presents a senior member of the royal family ignoring *sharia* justice and taking the law into his own hands.

The senior members of the royal family take the charges of corruption quite seriously and have attempted to halt the payment of questionable "commissions." In addition, the Sudeiri Seven have become concerned about the reputation the House al-Saud has acquired for raucous behavior in Las Vegas, Dubai, and Monte Carlo. Some forty princes and princesses have had their passports confiscated and are now forbidden to leave the kingdom, due to their past antics abroad.

Ironically, the general population is not required to apply for exit permits to leave the kingdom, whereas every member of the royal family (excluding, of course, the senior princes) must have the written permission of the king.

The real danger to the royal family's regime would come if the religious zealots in the kingdom could ever coalesce around a single charismatic leader. This was exactly what Juhayman al-Oteibi hoped would happen during the siege of Mecca, and, in retrospect, he had very good reasons to suspect that the actions of his group of followers would meet with relatively wide popular support. Prior to the seizure of the Holy Mosque, it was widely rumored in Saudi Arabia that there was a rift between the royal family and the Ulema. The Ulema was furious with the senior princes because of the obvious corruption in government and the diminishing power of the religious leadership. Juhayman mistakenly thought that the seizure of the Holy Mosque would further polarize the Ulema and the royal family. We know now that the Ulema did not support Juhayman. In fact, they condemned the seizure and threw their entire support behind the senior princes.

Nevertheless, the possibility still exists for a schism between the religious and political leadership, especially if the senior princes are unsuccessful in controlling graft and corruption in government. In such a case, the Saudi people would follow the Ulema and turn against the royal family. However, it is unlikely that the Ulema would act without at least the tacit support of one of the major branches of the military.

A Military-Backed Coup

The most serious threat to the present regime would appear to come from the military. The richer the royal family grows, the greater the risk of a takeover attempt. Recent Saudi Arabian history is littered with the corpses of just such attempted coups.

In 1962 a group of princes formed an underground organization called the Committee for the Liberation of Saudi Arabia (CLSA). The group was widely rumored to have supporters in the Saudi military. Although nothing was heard from this group after about 1965, another military-backed organization emerged in 1969, possibly containing many of the organizers of the CLSA. During the summer of 1969 the Special Security Forces managed to infiltrate this clandestine organization, and there were unsubstantiated reports of mass arrests. The majority of arrests were said to have been young air force officers. In fact, according to Fred Halliday, some officers were recalled from training in England on the pretext of "illness in the family" and, upon their arrival in Saudi Arabia, were executed. Among those who were said to have been arrested were the military attachés in London and Karachi and the former military commander in Mecca.[13]

While every prince and princess in the House al-Saud receives a relatively generous allowance from the government (approximately sixty thousand dollars per year), the allowance is nothing compared to the billions of dollars that flow into the personal coffers of the senior princes annually. This disparity of wealth within the royal family is a source of jealousy and resentment.

Many of the minor princes find themselves faced with no prospect of advancement in government service, so they turn increasingly to the military. Most of the higher-ranking officers in the Royal Saudi Air Force are princes who, because of their rank in the family, have no hope of either ascending the throne or having any influence in the ruling circle.

Traditionally, the Saudi military has been divided into the regular army, the air force, and the National Guard. The logic behind this was to prevent any one branch from becoming too powerful and posing a threat to the monarchy. However, in recent years the major portion of the defense budget has gone to the regular army and the air force, which are both under the control of Prince Sultan, Crown Prince Fahd's full brother.

The National Guard has been seen increasingly as a potential source of unrest. This was, in part, confirmed by the reports that National Guard officers were involved in the seizure of the mosque in Mecca. While the National Guard is seen as the most likely source of trouble, the air force and the regular army also have their share of discontented officers who would like nothing more than to see the present regime deposed.

Conclusion

Rarely in the history of the world has a society undergone as many profound changes as Saudi Arabia has in such an incredibly short period of time. It is natural, given the magnitude of the

---

[13]Fred Halliday, *Arabia Without Sultans*, p. 80.

economic, social, and cultural upheaval that continues to take place, that both radical and reactionary political forces will emerge and attempt to impose their own particular ideology and/or theology on the peninsula. How successful they are will depend on several important factors.

The House al-Saud has endeavored to keep close touch with the population. They have not been aloof rulers, as was the late shah of Iran. However, the traditional *majlis* system, whereby any citizen can bring his grievance directly to the monarch, is completely antithetical to the bureaucratic maze demanded by the administration of a modern nation. The *majlis* system, which once provided the Bedouin tribes of Arabia with a form of "democracy," is now obsolete. What remains is simple and unadulterated autocracy. There can be no doubt that the senior princes are growing farther and farther removed from the people they rule. If this continues, the monarchy will not survive the next decade.

The senior princes, and particularly Crown Prince Fahd, recognize this problem. Fahd's proposed reforms of government, including the creation of a "Consultative Assembly," suggest that at least some of the senior princes recognize the absolute necessity of providing the citizens with more opportunities for participation in government. None of the proposed reform plans has been implemented as of this writing.

The stability of the monarchy will be further undermined if the disparity in wealth continues to grow. Despite developing systems of social welfare, grotesque poverty is still very much in evidence in the kingdom.

The security of the House al-Saud also rests on its reputation as a sterling example of Islamic virtue. There are literally thousands of reactionary and fundamentalist theology students in the kingdom who, like Juhayman al-Oteibi, watch the royal family with critical eyes. An alliance between the radical theology students, the Ulema, and a branch of the military, such as the National Guard, would spell the end of the monarchy.

Appendixes

Appendix A

THE HOUSE AL-SAUD

Emir Abdul Rahman al-Saud — Sara bint-Ahmed al-Kabir al-Sudeiri

KING ABDULAZIZ IBN-ABDUL RAHMAN AL-SAUD

His Important Wives*

- **Wadha bint-Hazami**
  - Turki (died aged 20 years)
  - KING SAUD (1953–1964)

- **Tarfah al-Sheikh**
  - KING FAISAL (1964–1975)

- **Al-Jawharh bint-Musaad al-Jiluwi**
  - Muhammed ("of the Twin Evils")
  - KING KHALID (1975–)

- **Hussah al-Sudeiri**
  - Fahd (Crown Prince)
  - Sultan (Defense Minister)
  - Abdul Rahman (Businessman)
  - Naif (Interior Minister)
  - Turki (Businessman)
  - Salman (Governor of Riyadh)
  - Ahmed (Deputy Minister of the Interior)

- **Bint-Asi al-Shureimi**
  - Abdullah (Commander of SANG)

- **Al-Johara al-Sudeiri**
  - Saad (Refused crown)
  - Mousaad (Father of assassin of Faisal)
  - Abdul Mohsen (Governor of Medina)

- **Haya al-Sudeiri**
  - Badr (Deputy Commander of SANG)
  - Abdul Illah (Governor of Qassim)
  - Abdul Majed (Governor of Tabuk)

According to King Abdulaziz's own calculations, there were over 275 additional wives, over twenty-seven other sons, and uncounted daughters.

GENEALOGY, HOUSE AL-SAUD, 1720–1982

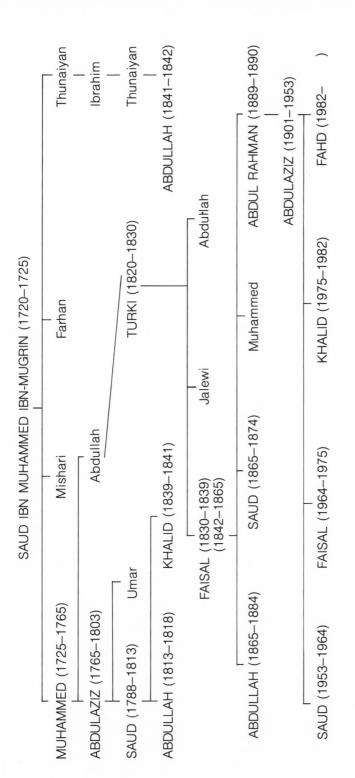

Appendix B

KING ABDULAZIZ AL SAUD — TARFAH AL-SHEIKH

KING FAISAL AL-SAUD

His wives and children

Haya bint-Turki al-Jiluwi
- Khalid (Governor of the Asir)
- Saad (Businessman)

Iffat
- Muhammed (Businessman)
- Saud (Foreign Minister)
- Abdul Rahman (Armored Corps Chief)
- Bandar (Air Force Major)
- Turki (Intelligence Chief)

Sultana bint-Ahmed al-Sudeiri
- Abdullah (Businessman and Poet)

Appendix C

CHRONOLOGY OF THE RULERS
OF THE SAUDI STATE SINCE 1727

1. Saud ibn-Muhammed ibn-Mugrin, 1720–1725
2. Muhammed ibn-Saud, 1725–1765
3. Abdulaziz ibn-Muhammed, 1765–1803
4. Saud ibn-Abdulaziz, 1788–1813
5. Abdullah ibn-Saud, 1813–1818
6. Mishari ibn-Saud and Muhammed ibn-Mishari ibn-Mu'amar (fought for leadership for 18 months during Egyptian occupation), 1818–1820
7. Turki ibn-Abdullah ibn-Muhammed ibn-Saud, 1820–1830
8. Mishari ibn-Abdullah ibn-Hassan ibn-Mishari ibn-Saud, 1830
9. Faisal ibn-Turki (first rule), 1830–1839
10. Khalid ibn-Saud ibn Abdulaziz, 1839–1841
11. Abdullah ibn-Thunaiyan ibn-Saud, 1841–1842
12. Faisal ibn-Turki (second rule), 1842–1865
13. Abdullah ibn-Faisal and Saud ibn-Faisal (fought for leadership for 9 years), 1865–1874
14. Abdullah ibn-Faisal, 1874–1884
15. Occupation and rule by al-Rashid family, 1884–1889
16. Abdul Rahman ibn-Faisal, 1889–1890
17. Occupation and rule by al-Rashid family, 1891–1901
18. Abdulaziz ibn–Abdul Rahman, 1901–1953
19. Saud ibn-Abdulaziz, 1953–1964
20. Faisal ibn-Abdulaziz, 1964–1975
21. Khalid ibn-Abdulaziz, 1975–

Appendix D

THE MOST POWERFUL SENIOR PRINCES, 1981

1. H.M. King Khalid ibn-Abdulaziz al-Saud
2. H.R.H. Crown Prince Fahd ibn-Abdulaziz al-Saud (Deputy Prime Minister)
3. H.R.H. Prince Abdullah (Second Deputy Prime Minister and Commander of the National Guard)
4. H.R.H. Prince Sultan (Minister of Defense and Aviation)
5. H.R.H. Prince Naif (Minister of the Interior)
6. H.R.H. Prince Saud al-Faisal (Foreign Minister)
7. H.R.H. Prince Salman (Governor of Riyadh)
8. H.R.H. Prince Saud ibn-Abdul Mohsen (State Security)
9. H.R.H. Prince Abdul Mohsen ibn-Jiluwi (Governor of the Eastern Province)
10. H.R.H. Prince Sattam (Deputy Governor of Riyadh)
11. H.R.H. Prince Saud ibn-Fahd (Owner of Tihama Public Relations Company)
12. H.R.H. Prince Muhammed ibn-Fahd ibn-Jiluwi (Governor of Hofuf)
13. H.R.H. Prince Abdul Mohsen (Governor of Medina)
14. H.R.H. Prince Bandar ibn-Faisal (Air Force Major)
15. H.R.H. Prince Muhammed ibn-Faisal (Water Desalination Chief, Jeddah)
16. H.R.H. Prince Majed (Governor of Mecca)
17. H.R.H. Prince Tallal (Special Envoy to UNICEF)
18. H.R.H. Prince Abdul Illah (Governor of Qassim)
19. H.R.H. Prince Faisal ibn-Fahd (Minister of Sports and Recreation)
20. H.R.H. Prince Fahd ibn-Sultan (Undersecretary for Social Welfare)
21. H.R.H. Prince Abdullah ibn-Faisal (Businessman, Poet)
22. H.R.H. Prince Badr (Deputy Commander of the National Guard)
23. H.R.H. Prince Ahmed (Deputy Commander of the National Guard)
24. H.R.H. Prince Abdul Majed (Governor of Tabuk)
25. H.R.H. Prince Khalid ibn-Faisal (Governor of the Asir)
26. H.R.H. Prince Muhammed ibn-Abdulaziz (Businessman)
27. H.R.H. Prince Muhammed ibn-Fahd (Businessman)

THE MOST POWERFUL MEMBERS OF THE ULEMA

1. Sheikh Muhammed ibn-Sobil, Imam of the Holy Haram, Mecca
2. Sheikh Ahmed Shu Ali, Minister of State for Religious Affairs
3. Sheikh Abdul Wahab Abdul Wasei, Minister of the Pilgrimage
4. Sheikh Saleh al-Luhaidan, Supreme Counsel of the Judicature
5. Sheikh Abdulaziz ibn-Saleh, Imam of the Prophet's Mosque, Medina
6. Sheikh Abdulaziz ibn-Abdullah al-Sheikh, Imam of the Grand Mosque
7. Sheikh Ibrahim ibn-Muhammed al-Sheikh, Minister of Justice
8. Sheikh Abdulaziz ibn-Ibrahim al-Sheikh, Head of the Religious Police (*mutawa*)
9. Sheikh Abdullah ibn-Hamid, Head of the Religious Courts
10. Sheikh Abdulaziz ibn-Abdullah ibn-Baz, Head of the Council of Islamic Research (Ulema)
11. Dr. Abdullah Abdulmohsen al-Turki, Influential Islamic Theologian

THE MOST POWERFUL TECHNOCRATS AND ADVISERS

1. Sheikh Ahmed Zaki Yamani, Minister of Petroleum and Minerals
2. Sheikh Hisham Nazir, Minister of Planning
3. Sheikh Ghazi al-Gosaibi, Minister of Industry and Electricity
4. Sheikh Muhammed Aba al-Khail, Minister of Finance
5. Dr. Mohammed Abdu Yamani, Minister of Information
6. Dr. Rashid Pharaon, Adviser to the Royal Cabinet
7. Kamal Adham, Adviser to the Royal Cabinet

THE MOST POWERFUL MILITARY OFFICERS

1. General Muhammed Saleh al-Hammad, Chief of General Staff
2. Lt. General Abdul Mohsen Ali al-Omran, Commander of the Army
3. Lt. General Muhammad Sabri, Commander of the Royal Saudi Air Force
4. General Abdullah al-Sheikh, Director of Public Security
5. Lt. General Muhammed al-Balagh, Director of Special Security Forces
6. General Muhammed Hilal, Commander of Frontier Forces

Appendix E

ANNUAL BUDGETS FOR SAUDI ARABIA, 1978–1981[1]

Total budget 1979–80 $50,000,000,000
Total budget 1980–81 $66,000,000,000

Breakdown of annual budgets in millions of U.S. dollars

	1978–79[2]	1979–80	1980–81
1. Development of Human Resources		5,180.0	6,850.0
2. Transportation and Communication		7,193.0	9,725.0
3. Development of Economic Resources		3,910.0	5,870.0
4. Health and Social Services		2,784.0	3,700.0
5. Infrastructure Development		5,604.0	3,565.0
6. Defense[3]		14,485.0	20,892.0
7. Municipal Services			6,030.0
8. Public Administration		3,137.0	4,747.0
9. Local Subsidies		1,600.0	1,500.0
10. Internal Government Loans		3,920.0	5,900.0
Nonministerial Funds 1. Municipalities and Rural Settlement	2,574.0	2,200.7	3,061.8
2. Pensions	501.1	631.0	753.0
3. Riyadh University	574.0	647.4	948.0
4. King Abdulaziz University	373.33	282.5	384.7
5. University of Petroleum and Minerals	185.6	240.7	281.8

6. King Faisal University	53.6	106.3	163.8
7. Imam Muhammed ibn-Saud Islamic University	50.1	54.61	75.0
8. Public Administration Institute	27.17	33.05	40.54
9. Standard Organization	3.917	4.127	14.66
10. General Organization for Flour Mills and Grain Silos	96.0	124.33	230.48
11. Saline Water Conversion	1,209.33	1,088.28	2,102.47
12. General Electricity	308.4	417.87	915.38
13. Ports Authority	1,854.63	1,810.604	1,402.54
14. Saudia Airlines	886.38	1,030.909	1,526.233
15. Saudi Railway Authority	92.16	128.23	214.69
16. Petromin	78.478	112.01	117.36
17. Saudi Red Crescent Society	16.14	18.01	34.648

[1]*The Arab News*, May 15, 1980.

[2]Ministerial budgets not available for 1978–79.

[3]Defense spending includes all branches of the military including the National Guard. The breakdown among the branches of the military is a closely guarded secret.

Appendix F

TRANSLATION OF A LETTER SENT OUT
BY THE ORGANIZATION FOR THE ENCOURAGEMENT OF VIRTUE
AND THE ELIMINATION OF VICE
GIVING ADVICE TO FOREIGN WORKERS
AND THEIR FAMILIES LIVING IN SAUDI ARABIA

No. 1039.
A. H. 9/1/1399
A. D. 7/25/1979

Guidelines to Our Brothers in Humanity
About Proper Dress and Behavior in Saudi Arabia

We thank Allah and ask his blessing on his last Prophet.

It is an internationally accepted principle that a visitor from a foreign country should observe the rules and regulations of the country he is visiting. This country—Saudi Arabia—tries to apply Islamic *sharia* in all its aspects, whether in belief, legislature or personal behavior, so we request our brothers in humanity, who are residing in this country, or visiting it, to observe the following very strictly:

1. Ladies should not expose their legs or arms or bosom or hair and should refrain from wearing too thin or tight clothes. This should be observed at all times and especially during the month of Ramadan.
2. Men should not wear small shorts that cover only about one third of the thigh leaving the rest exposed. For men to walk publicly in such attire is considered indecent.
3. Both men and women should refrain from any public display of affection. For instance, to put one's arm around the shoulders of one's wife in public is considered indecent.
4. Both men and women should avoid mixed crowding in marketplaces.

We hope and expect that all visitors and expatriates will kindly observe the above strictly so that they will not be subject to penalty.

Saad B.H. Mutrafi
Director
Haiat al-Amr bil Maroof[1]
Jeddah, Saudi Arabia

---

[1]Organization for the Encouragement of Virtue and Elimination of Vice, also known as *mutawa*, the religious or morals police.

Appendix G

TEXT OF PRINCE TALLAL'S PRESS CONFERENCE, AUGUST 15, 1962, BEIRUT, LEBANON, AS REPORTED IN *AL SAFA*

I believe that public opinion, both in the Arab world and abroad, was astonished to learn about the seizure of my property in Saudi Arabia. The Koran forbids homes being entered, let alone occupied, without their owner's permission, as do the laws of all nations. But in our country, there is no law that upholds the freedom and rights of the citizen. For a long time now we have been demanding the introduction of a system of government which would protect the rights of the individual and define the responsibilities of the rulers within a democratic and constitutional framework. If a person like myself, who is considered to have some influence, is treated with such harshness, what must be the position of the ordinary man?

The fact is that I know of no reason why this vindictive measure should have been taken, apart from those suggested by certain papers and radio stations: namely, my visit to Egypt and my cable to President Nasser (congratulating him on the successful launching of Egyptian-made rockets). But to visit an Arab state is not forbidden, nor have I ever heard before of anyone calling on the Arab people to boycott each other. Moreover, to offer congratulations on the rocket launching is only to express the pride felt by every Arab in a scientific and military achievement of such high order.

As regards reports published by some newspapers concerning the freeing of my slaves and concubines, they are quite unfounded because I don't have any slaves or concubines to free. But I will say that I am opposed to slavery. Nor is there any truth in the report that I sold some jewelry.

I wish to take this opportunity to rebuke those who continue to attack my father, Abdulaziz. I have already protested to heads of certain Arab governments' information services, but unfortunately these attacks are renewed from time to time. I am not defending Abdulaziz simply because he is dead or because he is my father, but because he is a national hero who succeeded in unifying a large part of the Arabian peninsula into one state. I do hope that in the future the gentlemen of the press and others will weigh carefully what they have to say. At the moment, exaggerations and misinformation tend to shadow the element of fact which reports also contain.

I also wish it to be fully understood that I belong to no group but only to my people, and it is in their interest alone that I work. If in the course of doing my duty, I am faced with trials and tribulations, this will only strengthen me and make me more patient and confident in the course which I have espoused. All my property means nothing to me now that I have dedicated myself to my country's welfare. Peace be with all who are just, who uphold right and renounce falsehood.

Appendix H

TEXT OF PRINCE ABDULLAH IBN-ABDULAZIZ'S REPLY
TO PRINCE TALLAL'S PRESS CONFERENCE, AUGUST 18, 1962
AS REPORTED IN *AL SAFA*

I and my brothers have generally refrained from replying to Tallal, but after the publications of his latest statements to the press with all their distortions and fabrications, I had no choice but to make the truth known to the Arab public.

Tallal alleges that there is no constitution in Saudi Arabia which safeguards democratic freedoms. But Tallal knows full well that Saudi Arabia has a constitution inspired by God and not drawn up by man. I do not believe there is any Arab who believes that the Koran contains a single loophole which would permit an injustice to be done. All laws and regulations in Saudi Arabia are inspired by the Koran, and Saudi Arabia is proud to have such a constitution.

Before Tallal was Minister of Finance, he told the press that he had prepared a draft constitution for the country and a sweeping program of reform. But no sooner had he been appointed a Cabinet Minister than he declared the Koran to be the only constitution of the Kingdom. It is curious that he should now revert to his old theme. Does he think that in so doing he will regain his post? A man of principle, would he change his principles to suit circumstances? Tallal has made glowing promises about reform but has produced no concrete proposals for the reform of a single village, let alone a state.

As for his statement about socialism, there is no such thing as rightist or leftist socialism; true socialism is the Arab socialism laid down by the Koran.

Tallal talked at length about democracy. He knows that if there is any truly democratic system in the world it is the one now existing in Saudi Arabia. Our understanding of democracy is that it permits direct contact between the people and the ruler and removes all obstacles between the head of state and the humblest person in the land. Anyone can secure an audience with the King and argue with him about the *sharia*. In denying the existence of a democratic system in Saudi Arabia, Tallal betrays a lack of understanding of the Arab individual. The Arab is democratic by temperament, so much so that his democracy permits him to address the head of state by his first name.

Tallal can return to Saudi Arabia whenever he wishes. Saudi Arabia will always welcome any Arab who believes that life should be lived constructively rather than destructively. I wish Tallal had never left and now I wish he would return. He who desires to serve his country should not take the struggle outside its borders, especially if he claims a large following, as Tallal does.[1]

[1]It should be noted that Prince Abdullah at no point in his reply addresses himself to the question of the seizure of Tallal's property in Saudi Arabia.

Bibliography

Abdalati, Hammudah. *Islam in Focus.* International Islamic Federation of Student Organizations, The Holy Koran Publishing House, Damascus, 1977.

Abir, Mordechai. *Oil, Power, and Politics.* Frank Cass & Co., London, 1974.

Akins, James. "Middle East Wars in the Wake of a Reagan Victory," *The Arab News,* November 18, 1980.

_____. The Oil Crisis: This Time the Wolf is Here," *Foreign Affairs* 51, July 1973, pp. 676–689.

Aldington, Richard. *Lawrence of Arabia.* Henry Regnery, Chicago, 1955.

Ali, Maulana Muhammed. "Penal Laws in Islam," *Islamic Review* XXXVII, June 1949.

Alireza, Marianne. *At the Drop of a Veil.* Houghton Mifflin Co., Boston, 1971.

Antonius, George. *The Arab Awakening.* Hamish Hamilton, London, 1938.

Arab Information Guide, ed. *The Status of Women in the Arab World.* The League of Arab States, Arab Information Guide, 1974.

ARAMCO. *The ARAMCO Handbook.* Arabian-American Oil Company, Dhahran, Saudi Arabia, 1960.

Arberry, A. J., transl. *The Koran Interpreted.* Macmillan, New York, 1973.

Archer, Jules. *Legacy of the Desert.* Little, Brown & Company, Boston, 1976.

Armstrong, H. C. *Lord of Arabia.* Arthur Baker Publishers, London, 1934.

Arnold J. *Golden Swords and Pots and Pans.* London, 1962.

Badeau, John S. *The American Approach to the Arab World.* Council of Foreign Relations, 1968.

Beling, Willard, ed. *King Faisal and the Modernization of Saudi Arabia.* Cromm Helm/Westview, London, 1979.

Bell, Gertrude. *The Arab War.* Golden Cockerel Press, London.

Benoist-Mechin, J. *Le Roi Saud.* Paris, 1960.

Blandford, Linda. *Super Wealth: The Secret Lives of the Oil Sheikhs.* William Morrow & Co., New York, 1977.

Bray, N. E. *Shifting Sands.* London, 1934.

Bremond, E. *Yemen et Saoudia: L'Arabie actuelle.* Paris, 1937.

Brouke, J. *L'Empire arabe de Ibn el-Seoud.* Brussels, 1929.

Brunson, Erika. "The Saudis," *Town and Country,* October 1979.

Bryson, Thomas A. *American Diplomatic Relations with the Middle East, 1784–1975: A Survey.* The Scarecrow Press, Metuchen, N. J., 1977.

Bullard, Sir Reader. *The Camels Must Go.* Faber and Faber, London, 1961.

Burkhardt, J. I. *Travels in Arabia.* Colburn, London, 1829.

Burton, Sir Richard. *Pilgrimage to Al-Medinah and Meccah.* Longmann, London, 1955.

Bustani, Emile. *Doubts and Dynamite: The Middle East Today.* Allan Wingate, London, 1958.

Butler, Grant C. *Kings and Camels.* The Devin-Adair Company, New York, 1960.

Carruthers, D. "Captain Shakespear's Last Journey," *The Geographic Journal*, London, 1961.

Cherif, Ahmed. *Le pelerinage à la Mecque*. Beirut, 1930.

Chessman, R. E. *In Unknown Arabia*. Macmillan, London, 1926.

Clifford, Mary Louise. *The Land and People of the Arabian Peninsula*. Lippincott, New York, 1977.

Cobbold, Lady Evelyn. *Pilgrimage to Mecca*. London, 1934.

DeGaury, Gerald. *Arabian Journey*. London, 1950.

_____. *Arabia Phoenix*. London, 1946.

_____. *Faisal: King of Saudi Arabia*. Frederick A. Praeger, New York, 1967.

_____. *Rulers of Mecca*. London, 1951.

Dickson, H. R. P. *Arabs of the Desert*. George Allen & Unwin Ltd., London, 1949.

Dorsey, James. "Saudi Women Gain Status—Slowly," *Christian Science Monitor*, February 26, 1980.

Doughty, Charles, M. *Travels in Arabia Deserts*. C. H. P., 1888.

Ellis, Harry B. *Hermitage of the Desert*. Ronald Press Co., New York, 1956.

Engler, Robert. *The Politics of Oil*. University of Chicago Press, Chicago, 1967.

Field, Michael. *One Hundred Million Dollars a Day: Inside the World of Middle Eastern Money*. Frederick A. Praeger, New York, 1975.

Gendzier, Irene. *A Middle East Reader*. Penguin, London, 1969.

Ghaith, Abdelhakin. *The Marching Caravan: The Story of Modern Saudi Arabia*. Almadina Almonawarra Printing and Publications Co., Jeddah.

Goodwin, June. "Arab Women Lift the Veil from Western Eyes," *Christian Science Monitor*, August 5, 1980.

Halliday, Fred. *Arabia Without Sultans*. Penguin, London, 1975.

_____. "The Shifting Sands Beneath the House of Saud," *The Progressive*, March 1980.

Harrison, Charles. "The Saudi Council of Ministers," *Middle East Journal*, No. 1, 1958.

Hitti, Philip, K. *History of the Arabs*. Macmillan, New York, 1952.

Hobday, Peter. *Saudi Arabia Today*. Macmillan, New York, 1978.

Holden, David. *Farewell to Arabia*. Faber & Faber, London, 1966.

Hopwood, Derek. *The Arabian Peninsula: Society and Politics*. George Allen & Unwin Ltd., London, 1972.

"House of Saud," *The New York Times Magazine*, July 6, 1975.

Howarth, David. *The Desert King*. McGraw-Hill, New York, 1964.

Ibrahim, Youssef M. "New Data Link Mecca Takeover to Political Rift," *The New York Times*, February 26, 1980.

_____. "A Prince and the People: How Saudis and Royalty Interact," *The New York Times*, March 17, 1980.

Insight Team of *The Sunday Times*. *The Yom Kippur War*. Andre Deutsche, London, 1975.

International Labor Organization. "Labour Migration in the Arab World," I. L. O. Publication, July 1980.

Iseman, Peter A. "The Arabian Ethos," *Harper's*, February 1978.

Izzeddin, Nejla. *Arab World: Past, Present, and Future.* Henry Regnery Co., Chicago, 1953.

Knauerhase, Ramon. "Saudi Arabia: Our Conservative Muslim Ally," *Current History*, January 1980.

Lawrence, T. E. *Seven Pillars of Wisdom.* London, 1926.

Lebkircher, and Rentz, G. *Arabia of ibn-Saud.* New York, 1952.

Lenczowski, George. "Tradition and Reform in Saudi Arabia," *Current History* 52, February 1967.

Lewis, Flora. "Basis of New Moslem Fervor Seen as Rejection of Alien Values," *The New York Times*, December 28, 1979.

London Institute for Strategic Studies. *Military Balance 1976–1977.* London, 1976.

Lubin, Peter. "The Second Pillar of Ignorance," *The New Republic*, December 22, 1978.

Maududi, Abul A'la. *Towards Understanding Islam.* Holy Koran Publishing House, Damascus, 1977.

Miesell, Raymond F. *Arabian Oil: American Stake in the Middle East.* University of North Carolina Press, Chapel Hill, 1949.

Mikdashi, Zuhayr. *The Community of Oil Exporting Nations.* George Allen & Unwin Ltd., London.

O'Connor, Harvey. *World Oil in Crisis.* London, 1962.

Philby, Henry St. John. *Arabia.* Ernest Benn Ltd., London, 1930.

———. *Arabia of the Wahhabis.* Constable, London, 1928.

———. *Arabian Days.* Hale, London, 1948.

———. *Arabian Jubilee.* Hale, London, 1952.

———. *Forty Years in the Wilderness.* Hale, London, 1957.

———. *The Heart of Arabia.* Constable, London, 1922.

———. *A Pilgrim in Arabia.* Hale, London, 1946.

———. *Saudi Arabia.* Ernest Benn Ltd., London, 1955.

Rahman, Fazlur. *Islam.* Doubleday, New York, 1968.

Rihani, A. *Arabian Peak and Desert.* London, 1934.

———. *Around the Coasts of Arabia.* London, 1930.

———. *Ibn Sa'oud of Arabia.* London, 1928.

———. *The Nejd and Its Dependencies.* London.

Roosevelt, Kermit. *Arabs, Oil, and History.* Harper & Row, New York, 1949.

Rossant, John S. "Saudi Shiites Say They Receive Second-Class Treatment," *The New York Times*, January 3, 1980.

Rouham, Fuad. *A History of OPEC.* Frederick A. Praeger, New York.

Sampson, Anthony. *The Seven Sisters: The Great Oil Companies and the World They Made.* Viking, New York, 1975.

Sayeh, Fayez A. *Arab Unity: Hope and Fulfillment.* The Devin-Adair Co., New York, 1958.

Schechtman, Joseph. *Arab Refugee Problem.* Philosophical Library, New York, 1952.

Sheean, Vincent. *Faisal: The King and His Kingdom.* University Press of Arabia, Tavistock, England, 1975.

Smith, Adam. "Superinflation," *Atlantic,* December 1978.

Stookey, Robert W. *America and the Arab States: An Uneasy Encounter.* John Wiley & Sons, New York, 1975.

Thesiger, Wilfred. *Arabian Sands.* Longmanns Green, London, 1959.

Tingay, Michael. "The House of Saud Is Shamed," *The New York Times,* May 14, 1980.

Tinnin, David B. "Saudis Recognize Their Vulnerability, *Fortune,* March 10, 1980.

Tuohy, William. "Will Saudi Arabia Keep the Oil Flowing?" *Newsday,* May 1, 1980.

Twitchell, K. S. *Saudi Arabia.* Princeton University Press, Princeton, N.J., 1958.

Voll, John O. "The Islamic Past and the Present Resurgence," *Current History,* No. 456, April 1980.

Walt, Joseph W. "Saudi Arabia and the Americans 1928–1951," unpublished dissertation, Northwestern University.

Who's Who in Saudi Arabia, Tihama Publications, Jeddah, 1979.

Williams, John Alden. *Islam.* George Braziller, New York, 1962.

Williams, Kenneth. *Ibn Sa'ud.* Khan and Sparrow Press, London, 1933.

Index

All members of the House al-Saud will be listed alphabetically under their first names.
In Arabic names *abu* (father), *umm* (mother), *ibn, bin* (son), and *ahu* (brother) are considered to begin the surname and therefore determine the alphabetical position.
Articles—*al-, ad-, ar-, as-, at-, az-*—are disregarded in determining the alphabetical position but are not inverted.